Visualizing Data

Ben Fry

Beijing · Cambridge · Farnham · Köln · Sebastopol · Taipei · Tokyo

Visualizing Data
by Ben Fry

Published by O'Reilly Media, Inc., 1005 Gravenstein Highway North, Sebastopol, CA 95472.

O'Reilly books may be purchased for educational, business, or sales promotional use. Online editions are also available for most titles (*safari.oreilly.com*). For more information, contact our corporate/institutional sales department: (800) 998-9938 or *corporate@oreilly.com*.

Editor: Andy Oram
Production Editor: Loranah Dimant
Copyeditor: Genevieve d'Entremont
Proofreader: Loranah Dimant

Indexer: Ellen Troutman Zaig
Cover Designer: Karen Montgomery
Interior Designer: David Futato
Illustrator: Jessamyn Read

Printing History:

December 2007:   First Edition.

 This book uses RepKover™, a durable and flexible lay-flat binding.

ISBN: 978-0-596-51455-6
[C].

Table of Contents

Preface

When I show visualization projects to an audience, one of the most common questions is, "How do you do this?" Other books about data visualization do exist, but the most prominent ones are often collections of academic papers; in any case, few explain how to actually *build* representations. Books from the field of design that offer advice for creating visualizations see the field only in terms of static displays, ignoring the possibility of dynamic, software-based visualizations. A number spend most of their time dissecting what's wrong with given representations—sometimes providing solutions, but more often not.

In this book, I wanted to offer something for people who want to get started building their own visualizations, something to use as a jumping-off point for more complicated work. I don't cover everything, but I've tried to provide enough background so that you'll know where to go next.

I wrote this book because I wanted to have a way to make the ideas from *Computational Information Design*, my Ph.D. dissertation, more accessible to a wider audience. More specifically, I wanted to see these ideas actually applied, rather than limited to an academic document on a shelf. My dissertation covered the process of getting from data to understanding; in other words, from considering a pile of information to presenting it usefully, in a way that can be easily understood and interacted with. This process is covered in Chapter 1, and used throughout the book as a framework for working through visualizations.

Most of the examples in this book are written from scratch. Rather than relying on toolkits or libraries that produce charts or graphs, instead you learn how to create them using a little math, some lines and rectangles, and bits of text. Many readers may have tried some toolkits and found them lacking, particularly because they want to customize the display of their information. A tool that has generic uses will produce only generic displays, which can be disappointing if the displays do not suit your data set. Data can take many interesting forms that require unique types of display and interaction; this book aims to open up your imagination in ways that collections of bar and pie charts cannot.

This book uses Processing (*http://processing.org*), a simple programming environment and API that I co-developed with Casey Reas of UCLA. Processing's programming environment makes it easy to sit down and "sketch" code to produce visual images quickly. Once you outgrow the environment, it's possible to use a regular Java IDE to write Processing code because the API is based on Java. Processing is free to download and open source. It has been in development since 2001, and we've had about 100,000 people try it out in the last 12 months. Today Processing is used by tens of thousands of people for all manners of work. When I began writing this book, I debated which language and API to use. It could have been based on Java, but I realized I would have found myself re-implementing the Processing API to make things simple. It could have been based on Actionscript and Flash, but Flash is expensive to buy and tends to break down when dealing with larger data sets. Other scripting languages such as Python and Ruby are useful, but their execution speeds don't keep up with Java. In the end, Processing was the right combination of cost, ease of use, and execution speed.

The Audience for This Book

In the spring of 2007, I co-taught an Information Visualization course at Carnegie Mellon. Our 30 students ranged from a freshman in the art school to a Ph.D. candidate in computer science. In between were graduate students from the School of Design and various other undergrads. Their skill levels were enormously varied, but that was less important than their level of curiosity, and students who were curious and willing to put in some work managed to overcome the technical difficulties (for the art and design students) or the visual demands (for those with an engineering background).

This book is targeted at a similar range of backgrounds, if less academic. I'm trying to address people who want to ask questions, play with data, and gain an understanding of how to communicate information to others. For instance, the book is for web designers who want to build more complex visualizations than their tools will allow. It's also for software engineers who want to become adept at writing software that represents data—that calls on them to try out new skills, even if they have some background in building UIs. None of this is rocket science, but it isn't always obvious how to get started.

Fundamentally, this book is for people who have a data set, a curiosity to explore it, and an idea of what they want to communicate about it. The set of people who visualize data is growing extremely quickly as we deal with more and more information. Even more important, the audience has moved far beyond those who are experts in visualization. By making these ideas accessible to a wide range of people, we should see some truly amazing things in the next decade.

Background Information

Because the audience for this book includes both programmers and non-programmers, the material varies in complexity. Beginners should be able to pick it up and get through the first few chapters, but they may find themselves lost as we get into more complicated programming topics. If you're looking for a gentler introduction to programming with Processing, other books are available (including one written by Casey Reas and me) that are more suited to learning the concepts from scratch, though they don't cover the specifics of visualizing data. Chapters 1–4 can be understood by someone without any programming background, but the later chapters quickly become more difficult.

You'll be most successful with this book if you have some familiarity with writing code—whether it's Java, C++, or Actionscript. This is not an advanced text by any means, but a little background in writing code will go a long way toward understanding the concepts.

Overview of the Book

Chapter 1, *The Seven Stages of Visualizing Data*, covers the process for developing a useful visualization, from acquiring data to interacting with it. This is the framework we'll use as we attack problems in later chapters.

Chapter 2, *Getting Started with Processing*, is a basic introduction to the Processing environment and syntax. It provides a bit of background on the structure of the API and the philosophy behind the project's development.

Chapters 3 through 8 cover example projects that get progressively more complicated.

Chapter 3, *Mapping*, plots data points on a map, our first introduction to reading data from the disk and representing it on the screen.

Chapter 4, *Time Series*, covers several methods of plotting charts that represent how data changes over time.

Chapter 5, *Connections and Correlations*, is the first chapter that really delves into how we acquire and parse a data set. The example in this chapter reads data from the MLB.com web site and produces an image correlating player salaries and team performance over the course of a baseball season. It's an in-depth example illustrating how to scrape data from a web site that lacks an official API. These techniques can be applied to many other projects, even if you're not interested in baseball.

Chapter 6, *Scatterplot Maps*, answers the question, "How do zip codes relate to geography?" by developing a project that allows users to progressively refine a U.S. map as they type a zip code.

Chapter 7, *Trees, Hierarchies, and Recursion*, discusses trees and hierarchies. It covers recursion, an important topic when dealing with tree structures, and treemaps, a useful representation for certain kinds of tree data.

Chapter 8, *Networks and Graphs*, is about networks of information, also called graphs. The first half discusses ways to produce a representation of connections between many nodes in a network, and the second half shows an example of doing the same with web site traffic data to see how a site is used over time. The latter project also covers how to integrate Processing with Eclipse, a Java IDE.

The last three chapters contain reference material, including more background and techniques for acquiring and parsing data.

Chapter 9, *Acquiring Data*, is a kind of cookbook that covers all sorts of practical techniques, from reading data from files, to spoofing a web browser, to storing data in databases.

Chapter 10, *Parsing Data*, is also written in cookbook-style, with examples that illustrate the detective work involved in parsing data. Examples include parsing HTML tables, XML, compressed data, and SVG shapes. It even includes a basic example of watching a network connection to understand how an undocumented data protocol works.

Chapter 11, *Integrating Processing with Java*, covers the specifics of how the Processing API integrates with Java. It's more of an appendix aimed at advanced Java programmers who want to use the API with their own projects.

Safari® Books Online

When you see a Safari® Books Online icon on the cover of your favorite technology book, that means the book is available online through the O'Reilly Network Safari Bookshelf.

Safari offers a solution that's better than e-books. It's a virtual library that lets you easily search thousands of top tech books, cut and paste code samples, download chapters, and find quick answers when you need the most accurate, current information. Try it for free at *http://safari.oreilly.com*.

Acknowledgments

I'd first like to thank O'Reilly Media for taking on this book. I was initially put in touch with Steve Weiss, who met with me to discuss the book in the spring of 2006. Steve later put me in touch with the Cambridge office, where Mike Hendrickson became a champion for the book and worked to make sure that the contract happened. Tim O'Reilly's enthusiasm along the way helped seal it.

I owe a great deal to my editor, Andy Oram, and assistant editor, Isabel Kunkle. Without Andy's hard work and helpful suggestions, or Isabel's focus on our schedule, I might still be working on the outline for Chapter 4. Thanks also to those who reviewed the draft manuscript: Brian DeLacey, Aidan Delaney, and Harry Hochheiser.

This book is based on ideas first developed as part of my doctoral work at the MIT Media Laboratory. For that I owe my advisor of six years, John Maeda, and my committee members, David Altshuler and Chris Pullman. Chris also pushed to have the ideas published properly, which was a great encouragement.

I'd also like to thank Casey Reas, my friend, inspiration, and collaborator on Processing, who has ensured that the project continues several years after its inception.

The content of the examples has been influenced by many courses I've taught as workshops or in classrooms over the last few years—in particular, my visualization courses at Harvard University and Carnegie Mellon (co-taught with Golan Levin), and workshops at Anderson Ranch in Colorado and at Hangar in Barcelona. I owe a lot to these student guinea pigs who taught me how to best explain this work.

Finally, thanks to my family, and immeasurable thanks to Shannon Hunt for editing, input, and moral support. Hers will be a tough act to follow while I return in kind as she writes *her* book in the coming months.

Conventions Used in This Book

The following typographical conventions are used in this book:

Plain text
>   Indicates menu titles, menu options, menu buttons, and keyboard accelerators (such as Alt and Ctrl).

Italic
>   Indicates new terms, URLs, email addresses, filenames, file extensions, pathnames, directories, and Unix utilities.

`Constant width`
>   Indicates commands, options, variables, functions, types, classes, methods, HTML and XML tags, the contents of files, and the output from commands.

`Constant width bold`
>   Shows commands or other text that should be typed literally by the user.

`Constant width italic`
>   Shows text that should be replaced with user-supplied values.

This icon signifies a tip, suggestion, or general note.

 This icon indicates a warning or caution.

Using Code Examples

This book is here to help you get your job done. In general, you may use the code in this book in your programs and documentation. You do not need to contact us for permission unless you're reproducing a significant portion of the code. For example, writing a program that uses several chunks of code from this book does not require permission. Selling or distributing a CD-ROM of examples from O'Reilly books *does* require permission. Answering a question by citing this book and quoting example code does not require permission. Incorporating a significant amount of example code from this book into your product's documentation *does* require permission.

We appreciate, but do not require, attribution. An attribution usually includes the title, author, publisher, and ISBN. For example: "*Visualizing Data* by Ben Fry. Copyright 2008 Ben Fry, 978-0-596-51455-6."

If you think your use of code examples falls outside fair use or the permission given here, feel free to contact us at *permissions@oreilly.com*.

We'd Like to Hear from You

Please address comments and questions concerning this book to the publisher:

O'Reilly Media, Inc.
1005 Gravenstein Highway North
Sebastopol, CA 95472
800-998-9938 (in the United States or Canada)
707-829-0515 (international or local)
707-829-0104 (fax)

We have a web page for this book, where we list errata, examples, and any additional information. You can access this page at:

http://www.oreilly.com/catalog/9780596514556

The author also has a site for the book at:

http://benfry.com/writing

To comment or ask technical questions about this book, send email to:

bookquestions@oreilly.com

For more information about our books, conferences, Resource Centers, and the O'Reilly Network, see our web site at:

http://www.oreilly.com

## CHAPTER 1

The Seven Stages of Visualizing Data

The greatest value of a picture is when it forces us to
notice what we never expected to see.
—John Tukey

What do the paths that millions of visitors take through a web site look like? How do the 3.1 billion A, C, G, and T letters of the human genome compare to those of the chimp or the mouse? Out of a few hundred thousand files on your computer's hard disk, which ones are taking up the most space, and how often do you use them? By applying methods from the fields of computer science, statistics, data mining, graphic design, and visualization, we can begin to answer these questions in a meaningful way that also makes the answers accessible to others.

All of the previous questions involve a large quantity of data, which makes it extremely difficult to gain a "big picture" understanding of its meaning. The problem is further compounded by the data's continually changing nature, which can result from new information being added or older information continuously being refined. This deluge of data necessitates new software-based tools, and its complexity requires extra consideration. Whenever we analyze data, our goal is to highlight its features in order of their importance, reveal patterns, and simultaneously show features that exist across multiple dimensions.

This book shows you how to make use of data as a resource that you might otherwise never tap. You'll learn basic visualization principles, how to choose the right kind of display for your purposes, and how to provide interactive features that will bring users to your site over and over again. You'll also learn to program in Processing, a simple but powerful environment that lets you quickly carry out the techniques in this book. You'll find Processing a good basis for designing interfaces around large data sets, but even if you move to other visualization tools, the ways of thinking presented here will serve you as long as human beings continue to process information the same way they've always done.

Why Data Display Requires Planning

Each set of data has particular display needs, and the *purpose* for which you're using the data set has just as much of an effect on those needs as the data itself. There are dozens of quick tools for developing graphics in a cookie-cutter fashion in office programs, on the Web, and elsewhere, but complex data sets used for specialized applications require unique treatment. Throughout this book, we'll discuss how the characteristics of a data set help determine what kind of visualization you'll use.

Too Much Information

When you hear the term "information overload," you probably know exactly what it means because it's something you deal with daily. In Richard Saul Wurman's book *Information Anxiety* (Doubleday), he describes how the *New York Times* on an average Sunday contains more information than a Renaissance-era person had access to in his entire lifetime.

But this is an exciting time. For $300, you can purchase a commodity PC that has thousands of times more computing power than the first computers used to tabulate the U.S. Census. The capability of modern machines is astounding. Performing sophisticated data analysis no longer requires a research laboratory, just a cheap machine and some code. Complex data sets can be accessed, explored, and analyzed by the public in a way that simply was not possible in the past.

The past 10 years have also brought about significant changes in the graphic capabilities of average machines. Driven by the gaming industry, high-end 2D and 3D graphics hardware no longer requires dedicated machines from specific vendors, but can instead be purchased as a $100 add-on card and is standard equipment for any machine costing $700 or more. When not used for gaming, these cards can render extremely sophisticated models with thousands of shapes, and can do so quickly enough to provide smooth, interactive animation. And these prices will only decrease—within a few years' time, accelerated graphics will be standard equipment on the aforementioned commodity PC.

Data Collection

We're getting better and better at collecting data, but we lag in what we can do with it. Most of the examples in this book come from freely available data sources on the Internet. Lots of data is out there, but it's not being used to its greatest potential because it's not being visualized as well as it could be. (More about this can be found in Chapter 9, which covers places to find data and how to retrieve it.)

With all the data we've collected, we still don't have many satisfactory answers to the sort of questions that we started with. This is the greatest challenge of our information-rich era: how can these questions be answered quickly, if not instantaneously? We're getting so good at measuring and recording things, why haven't we kept up with the methods to understand and communicate this information?

Thinking About Data

We also do very little sophisticated thinking about information itself. When AOL released a data set containing the search queries of millions of users that had been "randomized" to protect the innocent, articles soon appeared about how people could be identified by—and embarrassed by—information regarding their search habits. Even though we can collect this kind of information, we often don't know quite what it means. Was this a major issue or did it simply embarrass a few AOL users? Similarly, when millions of records of personal data are lost or accessed illegally, what does that mean? With so few people addressing data, our understanding remains quite narrow, boiling down to things like, "My credit card number might be stolen" or "Do I care if anyone sees what I search?"

Data Never Stays the Same

We might be accustomed to thinking about data as fixed values to be analyzed, but data is a moving target. How do we build representations of data that adjust to new values every second, hour, or week? This is a necessity because most data comes from the real world, where there are no absolutes. The temperature changes, the train runs late, or a product launch causes the traffic pattern on a web site to change drastically.

What happens when things start moving? How do we interact with "live" data? How do we unravel data as it changes over time? We might use animation to play back the evolution of a data set, or interaction to control what time span we're looking at. How can we write code for these situations?

What Is the Question?

As machines have enormously increased the capacity with which we can create (through measurements and sampling) and store data, it becomes easier to disassociate the data from the original reason for collecting it. This leads to an all-too frequent situation: approaching visualization problems with the question, "How can we possibly understand so much data?"

As a contrast, think about subway maps, which are abstracted from the complex shape of the city and are focused on the rider's goal: to get from one place to the next. Limiting the detail of each shape, turn, and geographical formation reduces this complex data set to answering the rider's question: "How do I get from point A to point B?"

Harry Beck invented the format now commonly used for subway maps in the 1930s, when he redesigned the map of the London Underground. Inspired by the layout of circuit boards, the map simplified the complicated Tube system to a series of vertical, horizontal, and 45°diagonal lines. While attempting to preserve as much of the relative physical layout as possible, the map shows only the connections between stations, as that is the only information that riders use to decide their paths.

When beginning a visualization project, it's common to focus on all the data that has been collected so far. The amounts of information might be enormous—people like to brag about how many gigabytes of data they've collected and how difficult their visualization problem is. But great information visualization never starts from the standpoint of the data set; it starts with questions. Why was the data collected, what's interesting about it, and what stories can it tell?

The most important part of understanding data is identifying the question that you want to answer. Rather than thinking about the data that was collected, think about how it will be used and work backward to what was collected. You collect data because you want to know something about it. If you don't really know why you're collecting it, you're just hoarding it. It's easy to say things like, "I want to know what's in it," or "I want to know what it means." Sure, but what's meaningful?

The more specific you can make your question, the more specific and clear the visual result will be. When questions have a broad scope, as in "exploratory data analysis" tasks, the answers themselves will be broad and often geared toward those who are themselves versed in the data. John Tukey, who coined the term Exploratory Data Analysis, said "…pictures based on exploration of data should force their messages upon us."* Too many data problems are labeled "exploratory" because the data collected is overwhelming, even though the original purpose was to answer a specific question or achieve specific results.

One of the most important (and least technical) skills in understanding data is asking good questions. An appropriate question shares an interest you have in the data, tries to convey it to others, and is curiosity-oriented rather than math-oriented. Visualizing data is just like any other type of communication: success is defined by your audience's ability to pick up on, and be excited about, your insight.

Admittedly, you may have a rich set of data to which you want to provide flexible access by not defining your question too narrowly. Even then, your goal should be to highlight key findings. There is a tendency in the visualization field to borrow from the statistics field and separate problems into *exploratory* and *expository*, but for the purposes of this book, this distinction is not useful. The same methods and process are used for both.

In short, a proper visualization is a kind of narrative, providing a clear answer to a question without extraneous details. By focusing on the original intent of the question, you can eliminate such details because the question provides a benchmark for what is and is not necessary.

* Tukey, John Wilder. *Exploratory Data Analysis*. Reading, MA: Addison-Wesley, 1977.

A Combination of Many Disciplines

Given the complexity of data, using it to provide a meaningful solution requires insights from diverse fields: statistics, data mining, graphic design, and information visualization. However, each field has evolved in isolation from the others.

Thus, visual design—-the field of mapping data to a visual form—typically does not address how to handle thousands or tens of thousands of items of data. Data mining techniques have such capabilities, but they are disconnected from the means to interact with the data. Software-based information visualization adds building blocks for interacting with and representing various kinds of abstract data, but typically these methods undervalue the aesthetic principles of visual design rather than embrace their strength as a necessary aid to effective communication. Someone approaching a data representation problem (such as a scientist trying to visualize the results of a study involving a few thousand pieces of genetic data) often finds it difficult to choose a representation and wouldn't even know what tools to use or books to read to begin.

Process

We must reconcile these fields as parts of a single process. Graphic designers can learn the computer science necessary for visualization, and statisticians can communicate their data more effectively by understanding the visual design principles behind data representation. The methods themselves are not new, but their isolation within individual fields has prevented them from being used together. In this book, we use a process that bridges the individual disciplines, placing the focus and consideration on how data is understood rather than on the viewpoint and tools of each individual field.

The process of understanding data begins with a set of numbers and a question. The following steps form a path to the answer:

Acquire
> Obtain the data, whether from a file on a disk or a source over a network.

Parse
> Provide some structure for the data's meaning, and order it into categories.

Filter
> Remove all but the data of interest.

Mine
> Apply methods from statistics or data mining as a way to discern patterns or place the data in mathematical context.

Represent
> Choose a basic visual model, such as a bar graph, list, or tree.

Refine
> Improve the basic representation to make it clearer and more visually engaging.

Interact
> Add methods for manipulating the data or controlling what features are visible.

Of course, these steps can't be followed slavishly. You can expect that they'll be involved at one time or another in projects you develop, but sometimes it will be four of the seven, and at other times all of them.

Part of the problem with the individual approaches to dealing with data is that the separation of fields leads to different people each solving an isolated part of the problem. When this occurs, something is lost at each transition—like a "telephone game" in which each step of the process diminishes aspects of the initial question under consideration. The initial format of the data (determined by how it is acquired and parsed) will often drive how it is considered for filtering or mining. The statistical method used to glean useful information from the data might drive the initial presentation. In other words, the final representation reflects the results of the statistical method rather than a response to the initial question.

Similarly, a graphic designer brought in at the next stage will most often respond to specific problems with the representation provided by the previous steps, rather than focus on the initial question. The visualization step might add a compelling and interactive means to look at the data filtered from the earlier steps, but the display is inflexible because the earlier stages of the process are hidden. Furthermore, practitioners of each of the fields that commonly deal with data problems are often unclear about how to traverse the wider set of methods and arrive at an answer.

This book covers the whole path from data to understanding: the transformation of a jumble of raw numbers into something coherent and useful. The data under consideration might be numbers, lists, or relationships between multiple entities.

It should be kept in mind that the term *visualization* is often used to describe the art of conveying a physical relationship, such as the subway map mentioned near the start of this chapter. That's a different kind of analysis and skill from *information visualization*, where the data is primarily numeric or symbolic (e.g., A, C, G, and T— the letters of genetic code—and additional annotations about them). The primary focus of this book is information visualization: for instance, a series of numbers that describes temperatures in a weather forecast rather than the shape of the cloud cover contributing to them.

An Example

To illustrate the seven steps listed in the previous section, and how they contribute to effective information visualization, let's look at how the process can be applied to understanding a simple data set. In this case, we'll take the zip code numbering system that the U.S. Postal Service uses. The application is not particularly advanced, but it provides a skeleton for how the process works. (Chapter 6 contains a full implementation of the project.)

What Is the Question?

All data problems begin with a question and end with a narrative construct that provides a clear answer. The Zipdecode project (described further in Chapter 6) was developed out of a personal interest in the relationship of the zip code numbering system to geographic areas. Living in Boston, I knew that numbers starting with a zero denoted places on the East Coast. Having spent time in San Francisco, I knew the initial numbers for the West Coast were all nines. I grew up in Michigan, where all our codes were four-prefixed. But what sort of area does the second digit specify? Or the third?

The finished application was initially constructed in a few hours as a quick way to take what might be considered a boring data set (a long list of zip codes, towns, and their latitudes and longitudes) and create something engaging for a web audience that explained how the codes related to their geography.

Acquire

The acquisition step involves obtaining the data. Like many of the other steps, this can be either extremely complicated (i.e., trying to glean useful data from a large system) or very simple (reading a readily available text file).

A copy of the zip code listing can be found on the U.S. Census Bureau web site, as it is frequently used for geographic coding of statistical data. The listing is a freely available file with approximately 42,000 lines, one for each of the codes, a tiny portion of which is shown in Figure 1-1.

```
00210    +43.005895    -071.013202    U    PORTSMOUTH    33    015
00211    +43.005895    -071.013202    U    PORTSMOUTH    33    015
00212    +43.005895    -071.013202    U    PORTSMOUTH    33    015
00213    +43.005895    -071.013202    U    PORTSMOUTH    33    015
00214    +43.005895    -071.013202    U    PORTSMOUTH    33    015
00215    +43.005895    -071.013202    U    PORTSMOUTH    33    015
00501    +40.922326    -072.637078    U    HOLTSVILLE    36    103
00544    +40.922326    -072.637078    U    HOLTSVILLE    36    103
00601    +18.165273    -066.722583         ADJUNTAS      72    001
00602    +18.393103    -067.180953         AGUADA        72    003
00603    +18.455913    -067.145780         AGUADILLA     72    005
00604    +18.493520    -067.135883         AGUADILLA     72    005
00605    +18.465162    -067.141486    P    AGUADILLA     72    005
00606    +18.172947    -066.944111         MARICAO       72    093
00610    +18.288685    -067.139696         ANASCO        72    011
00611    +18.279531    -066.802170    P    ANGELES       72    141
00612    +18.450674    -066.698262         ARECIBO       72    013
00613    +18.458093    -066.732732    P    ARECIBO       72    013
00614    +18.429675    -066.674506    P    ARECIBO       72    013
00616    +18.444792    -066.640678         BAJADERO      72    013
```

Figure 1-1. Zip codes in the format provided by the U.S. Census Bureau

Acquisition concerns how the user downloads your data as well as how you obtained the data in the first place. If the final project will be distributed over the Internet, as you design the application, you have to take into account the time required to download data into the browser. And because data downloaded to the browser is probably part of an even larger data set stored on the server, you may have to structure the data on the server to facilitate retrieval of common subsets.

Parse

After you acquire the data, it needs to be parsed—changed into a format that tags each part of the data with its intended use. Each line of the file must be broken along its individual parts; in this case, it must be delimited at each tab character. Then, each piece of data needs to be converted to a useful format. Figure 1-2 shows the layout of each line in the census listing, which we have to understand to parse it and get out of it what we want.

Figure 1-2. Structure of acquired data

Each field is formatted as a data type that we'll handle in a conversion program:

String
    A set of characters that forms a word or a sentence. Here, the city or town name is designated as a string. Because the zip codes themselves are not so much numbers as a series of digits (if they were numbers, the code 02139 would be stored as 2139, which is not the same thing), they also might be considered strings.

Float
    A number with decimal points (used for the latitudes and longitudes of each location). The name is short for *floating point*, from programming nomenclature that describes how the numbers are stored in the computer's memory.

Character
> A single letter or other symbol. In this data set, a character sometimes desig-
> nates special post offices.

Integer
> A number without a fractional portion, and hence no decimal points (e.g., –14,
> 0, or 237).

Index
> Data (commonly an integer or string) that maps to a location in another table of
> data. In this case, the index maps numbered codes to the names and two-digit
> abbreviations of states. This is common in databases, where such an index is
> used as a pointer into another table, sometimes as a way to compact the data
> further (e.g., a two-digit code requires less storage than the full name of the state
> or territory).

With the completion of this step, the data is successfully tagged and consequently
more useful to a program that will manipulate or represent it in some way.

Filter

The next step involves filtering the data to remove portions not relevant to our use.
In this example, for the sake of keeping it simple, we'll be focusing on the contiguous 48 states, so the records for cities and towns that are not part of those states—
Alaska, Hawaii, and territories such as Puerto Rico—are removed. Another project
could require significant mathematical work to place the data into a mathematical
model or normalize it (convert it to an acceptable range of numbers).

Mine

This step involves math, statistics, and data mining. The data in this case receives
only a simple treatment: the program must figure out the minimum and maximum
values for latitude and longitude by running through the data (as shown in
Figure 1-3) so that it can be presented on a screen at a proper scale. Most of the time,
this step will be far more complicated than a pair of simple math operations.

Represent

This step determines the basic form that a set of data will take. Some data sets are
shown as lists, others are structured like trees, and so forth. In this case, each zip
code has a latitude and longitude, so the codes can be mapped as a two-dimensional
plot, with the minimum and maximum values for the latitude and longitude used for
the start and end of the scale in each dimension. This is illustrated in Figure 1-4.

The Represent stage is a linchpin that informs the single most important decision in
a visualization project and can make you rethink earlier stages. How you choose to
represent the data can influence the very first step (what data you acquire) and the
third step (what particular pieces you extract).

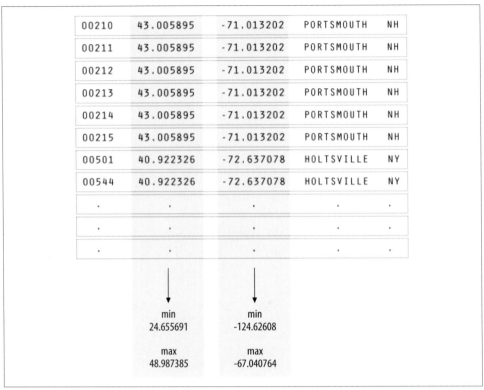

00210	43.005895	-71.013202	PORTSMOUTH	NH
00211	43.005895	-71.013202	PORTSMOUTH	NH
00212	43.005895	-71.013202	PORTSMOUTH	NH
00213	43.005895	-71.013202	PORTSMOUTH	NH
00214	43.005895	-71.013202	PORTSMOUTH	NH
00215	43.005895	-71.013202	PORTSMOUTH	NH
00501	40.922326	-72.637078	HOLTSVILLE	NY
00544	40.922326	-72.637078	HOLTSVILLE	NY
.	.	.	.	.
.	.	.	.	.
.	.	.	.	.

min
24.655691

max
48.987385

min
-124.62608

max
-67.040764

Figure 1-3. Mining the data: just compare values to find the minimum and maximum

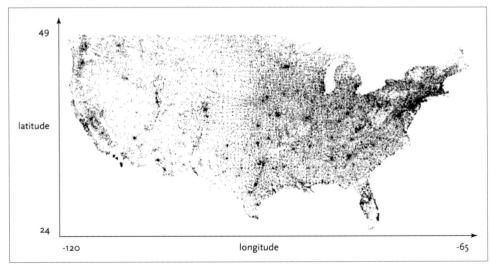

Figure 1-4. Basic visual representation of zip code data

Refine

In this step, graphic design methods are used to further clarify the representation by calling more attention to particular data (establishing hierarchy) or by changing attributes (such as color) that contribute to readability.

Hierarchy is established in Figure 1-5, for instance, by coloring the background deep gray and displaying the selected points (all codes beginning with four) in white and the deselected points in medium yellow.

Figure 1-5. Using color to refine the representation

Interact

The next stage of the process adds interaction, letting the user control or explore the data. Interaction might cover things like selecting a subset of the data or changing the viewpoint. As another example of a stage affecting an earlier part of the process, this stage can also affect the refinement step, as a change in viewpoint might require the data to be designed differently.

In the Zipdecode project, typing a number selects all zip codes that begin with that number. Figures 1-6 and 1-7 show all the zip codes beginning with zero and nine, respectively.

Another enhancement to user interaction (not shown here) enables the users to traverse the display laterally and run through several of the prefixes. After typing part or all of a zip code, holding down the Shift key allows users to replace the last number typed without having to hit the Delete key to back up.

Figure 1-6. The user can alter the display through choices (zip codes starting with 0)

Figure 1-7. The user can alter the display through choices (zip codes starting with 9)

Typing is a very simple form of interaction, but it allows the user to rapidly gain an understanding of the zip code system's layout. Just contrast this sample application with the difficulty of deducing the same information from a table of zip codes and city names.

The viewer can continue to type digits to see the area covered by each subsequent set of prefixes. Figure 1-8 shows the region highlighted by the two digits 02, Figure 1-9 shows the three digits 021, and Figure 1-10 shows the four digits 0213. Finally, Figure 1-11 shows what you get by entering a full zip code, 02139—a city name pops up on the display.

Figure 1-8. Honing in with two digits (02)

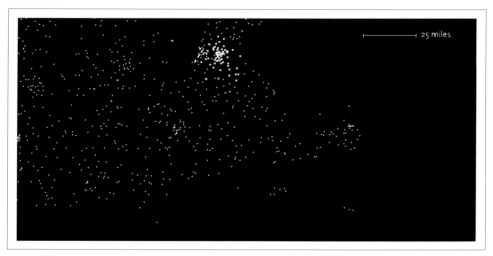

Figure 1-9. Honing in with three digits (021)

In addition, users can enable a "zoom" feature that draws them closer to each subsequent digit, revealing more detail around the area and showing a constant rate of detail at each level. Because we've chosen a map as a representation, we could add more details of state and county boundaries or other geographic features to help viewers associate the "data" space of zip code points with what they know about the local environment.

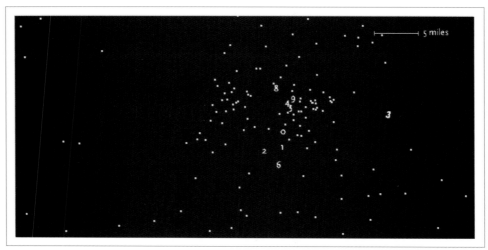

Figure 1-10. Honing in further with four digits (0213)

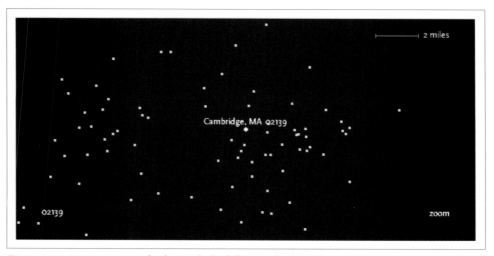

Figure 1-11. Honing in even further with the full zip code (02139)

Iteration and Combination

Figure 1-12 shows the stages in order and demonstrates how later decisions commonly reflect on earlier stages. Each step of the process is inextricably linked because of how the steps affect one another. In the Zipdecode application, for instance:

- The need for a compact representation on the screen led me to refilter the data to include only the contiguous 48 states.

- The representation step affected acquisition because after I developed the application I modified it so it could show data that was downloaded over a slow

Internet connection to the browser. My change to the structure of the data allows the points to appear slowly, as they are first read from the data file, employing the data itself as a "progress bar."

• Interaction by typing successive numbers meant that the colors had to be modified in the visual refinement step to show a slow transition as points in the display are added or removed. This helps the user maintain context by preventing the updates on-screen from being too jarring.

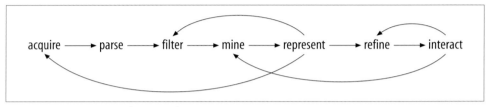

Figure 1-12. Interactions between the seven stages

The connections between the steps in the process illustrate the importance of the individual or team in addressing the project as a whole. This runs counter to the common fondness for assembly-line style projects, where programmers handle the technical portions, such as acquiring and parsing data, and visual designers are left to choose colors and typefaces. At the intersection of these fields is a more interesting set of properties that demonstrates their strength in combination.

When acquiring data, consider how it can change, whether sporadically (such as once a month) or continuously. This expands the notion of graphic design that's traditionally focused on solving a specific problem for a specific data set, and instead considers the meta-problem of how to handle a certain *kind* of data that might be updated in the future.

In the filtering step, data can be filtered in real time, as in the Zipdecode application. During visual refinement, changes to the design can be applied across the entire system. For instance, a color change can be automatically applied to the thousands of elements that require it, rather having to make such a tedious modification by hand. This is the strength of a computational approach, where tedious processes are minimized through automation.

Principles

I'll finish this general introduction to visualization by laying out some ways of thinking about data and its representation that have served me well over many years and many diverse projects. They may seem abstract at first, or of minor importance to the job you're facing, but I urge you to return and reread them as you practice visualization; they just may help you in later tasks.

Each Project Has Unique Requirements

A visualization should convey the unique properties of the data set it represents. This book is not concerned with providing a handful of ready-made "visualizations" that can be plugged into any data set. Ready-made visualizations can help produce a quick view of your data set, but they're inflexible commodity items that can be implemented in packaged software. Any bar chart or scatter plot made with Excel will look like a bar chart or scatter plot made with Excel. Packaged solutions can provide only packaged answers, like a pull-string toy that is limited to a handful of canned phrases, such as "Sales show a slight increase in each of the last five years!" Every problem is unique, so capitalize on that uniqueness to solve the problem.

Chapters in this book are divided by types of data, rather than types of display. In other words, we're not saying, "Here's how to make a bar graph," but "Here are several ways to show a correlation." This gives you a more powerful way to think about maximizing what can be said about the data set in question.

I'm often asked for a library of tools that will automatically make attractive representations of any given data set. But if each data set is different, the point of visualization is to expose that fascinating aspect of the data and make it self-evident. Although readily available representation toolkits are useful starting points, they must be customized during an in-depth study of the task.

Data is often stored in a generic format. For instance, databases used for annotation of genomic data might consist of enormous lists of start and stop positions, but those lists vary in importance depending on the situation in which they're being used. We don't view books as long abstract sequences of words, yet when it comes to information, we're often so taken with the enormity of the information and the low-level abstractions used to store it that the narrative is lost. Unless you stop thinking about databases, everything looks like a table—millions of rows and columns to be stored, queried, and viewed.

In this book, we use a small collection of simple helper classes as starting points. Often, we'll be targeting the Web as a delivery platform, so the classes are designed to take up minimal time for download and display. But I will also discuss more robust versions of similar tools that can be used for more in-depth work.

This book aims to help you learn to understand data as a tool for human decision-making—how it varies, how it can be used, and how to find what's unique about your data set. We'll cover many standard methods of visualization and give you the background necessary for making a decision about what sort of representation is suitable for your data. For each representation, we consider its positive and negative points and focus on customizing it so that it's best suited to what you're trying to convey about your data set.

Avoid the All-You-Can-Eat Buffet

Often, less detail will actually convey more information because the inclusion of overly specific details causes the viewer to miss what's most important or disregard the image entirely because it's too complex. Use as little data as possible, no matter how precious it seems.

Consider a weather map, with curved bands of temperatures across the country. The designers avoid giving each band a detailed edge (particularly because the data is often fuzzy). Instead, they convey a broader pattern in the data.

Subway maps leave out the details of surface roads because the additional detail adds more complexity to the map than necessary. Before maps were created in Beck's style, it seemed that knowing street locations was essential to navigating the subway. Instead, individual stations are used as waypoints for direction finding. The important detail is that your target destination is near a particular station. Directions can be given in terms of the last few turns to be taken after you exit the station, or you can consult a map posted at the station that describes the immediate area aboveground.

It's easy to collect data, and some people become preoccupied with simply accumulating more complex data or data in mass quantities. But more data is not implicitly better, and often serves to confuse the situation. Just because it can be measured doesn't mean it should. Perhaps making things simple is worth bragging about, but making complex messes is not. Find the smallest amount of data that can still convey something meaningful about the contents of the data set. As with Beck's underground map, focusing on the question helps define those minimum requirements.

The same holds for the many "dimensions" that are found in data sets. Web site traffic statistics have many dimensions: IP address, date, time of day, page visited, previous page visited, result code, browser, machine type, and so on. While each of these might be examined in turn, they relate to distinct questions. Only a few of the variables are required to answer a typical question, such as "How many people visited page x over the last three months, and how has that figure changed each month?" Avoid trying to show a burdensome multidimensional space that maps too many points of information.

Know Your Audience

Finally, who is your audience? What are their goals when approaching a visualization? What do they stand to learn? Unless it's accessible to your audience, why are you doing it? Making things simple and clear doesn't mean assuming that your users are idiots and "dumbing down" the interface for them.

In what way will your audience use the piece? A mapping application used on a mobile device has to be designed with a completely different set of criteria than one used on a desktop computer. Although both applications use maps, they have little to do with each other. The focus of the desktop application may be finding locations and print maps, whereas the focus of the mobile version is actively following the directions to a particular location.

Onward

In this chapter, we covered the process for attacking the common modern problems of having too much data and having data that changes. In the next chapter, we'll discuss Processing, the software tool used to handle data sets in this book.

## CHAPTER 2

Getting Started with Processing

The Processing project began in the spring of 2001 and was first used at a workshop in Japan that August. Originally built as a domain-specific extension to Java targeted at artists and designers, Processing has evolved into a full-blown design and prototyping tool used for large-scale installation work, motion graphics, and complex data visualization. Processing is a simple programming environment that was created to make it easier to develop visually oriented applications with an emphasis on animation and provide users with instant feedback through interaction. As its capabilities have expanded over the past six years, Processing has come to be used for more advanced production-level work in addition to its sketching role.

Processing is based on Java, but because program elements in Processing are fairly simple, you can learn to use it from this book even if you don't know any Java. If you're familiar with Java, it's best to forget that Processing has anything to do with it for a while, at least until you get the hang of how the API works. We'll cover how to integrate Java and Processing toward the end of the book.

The latest version of Processing can be downloaded at:

http://processing.org/download

An important goal for the project was to make this type of programming accessible to a wider audience. For this reason, Processing is free to download, free to use, and open source. But projects developed using the Processing environment and core libraries can be used for any purpose. This model is identical to GCC, the GNU Compiler Collection. GCC and its associated libraries (e.g., libc) are open source under the GNU Public License (GPL), which stipulates that changes to the code must be made available. However, programs created with GCC (examples too numerous to mention) are not themselves required to be open source.

Processing consists of:

- The Processing Development Environment (PDE). This is the software that runs when you double-click the Processing icon. The PDE is an Integrated Development Environment with a minimalist set of features designed as a simple introduction to programming or for testing one-off ideas.
- A collection of commands (also referred to as functions or methods) that make up the "core" programming interface, or API, as well as several libraries that support more advanced features, such as drawing with OpenGL, reading XML files, and saving complex imagery in PDF format.
- A language syntax, identical to Java but with a few modifications. The changes are laid out in detail toward the end of the book.
- An active online community, hosted at *http://processing.org*.

For this reason, references to "Processing" can be somewhat ambiguous. Are we talking about the API, the development environment, or the web site? I'll be careful to differentiate them when referring to each.

Sketching with Processing

A Processing program is called a *sketch*. The idea is to make Java-style programming feel more like scripting, and adopt the process of scripting to quickly write code. Sketches are stored in the *sketchbook*, a folder that's used as the default location for saving all of your projects. When you run Processing, the sketch last used will automatically open. If this is the first time Processing is used (or if the sketch is no longer available), a new sketch will open.

Sketches that are stored in the sketchbook can be accessed from File → Sketchbook. Alternatively, File → Open… can be used to open a sketch from elsewhere on the system.

Advanced programmers need not use the PDE and may instead use its libraries with the Java environment of choice. (This is covered toward the end of the book.) However, if you're just getting started, it's recommended that you use the PDE for your first few projects to gain familiarity with the way things are done. Although Processing is based on Java, it was never meant to be a Java IDE with training wheels. To better address our target audience, its conceptual model (how programs work, how interfaces are built, and how files are handled) is somewhat different from Java's.

Hello World

Programming languages are often introduced with a simple program that prints "Hello World" to the console. The Processing equivalent is simply to draw a line:

```
line(15, 25, 70, 90);
```

Enter this example and press the Run button, which is an icon that looks like the Play button on any audio or video device. The result will appear in a new window, with a gray background and a black line from coordinate (15, 25) to (70, 90). The (0, 0) coordinate is the upper-lefthand corner of the display window. Building on this program to change the size of the display window and set the background color, type in the code from Example 2-1.

Example 2-1. Simple sketch

```
size(400, 400);
background(192, 64, 0);
stroke(255);
line(150, 25, 270, 350);
```

This version sets the window size to 400×400 pixels, sets the background to an orange-red, and draws the line in white, by setting the stroke color to 255. By default, colors are specified in the range 0 to 255. Other variations of the parameters to the stroke( ) function provide alternate results:

```
stroke(255);             // sets the stroke color to white
stroke(255, 255, 255);   // identical to stroke(255)
stroke(255, 128, 0);     // bright orange (red 255, green 128, blue 0)
stroke(#FF8000);         // bright orange as a web color
stroke(255, 128, 0, 128); // bright orange with 50% transparency
```

The same alternatives work for the fill( ) command, which sets the fill color, and the background( ) command, which clears the display window. Like all Processing methods that affect drawing properties, the fill and stroke colors affect all geometry drawn to the screen until the next fill and stroke commands are executed.

 It's also possible to use the editor of your choice instead of the built-in editor. Simply select "Use External Editor" in the Preferences window (Processing → Preferences on Mac OS X, or File → Preferences on Windows and Linux). When using an external editor, editing will be disabled in the PDE, but the text will reload whenever you press Run.

Hello Mouse

A program written as a list of statements (like the previous examples) is called a *basic* mode sketch. In basic mode, a series of commands are used to perform tasks or create a single image without any animation or interaction. Interactive programs are drawn as a series of frames, which you can create by adding functions titled setup( ) and draw( ), as shown in the *continuous* mode sketch in Example 2-2. They are built-in functions that are called automatically.

Example 2-2. Simple continuous mode sketch

```
void setup( ) {
  size(400, 400);
  stroke(255);
  background(192, 64, 0);
}

void draw( ) {
  line(150, 25, mouseX, mouseY);
}
```

Example 2-2 is identical in function to Example 2-1, except that now the line follows the mouse. The setup( ) block runs once, and the draw( ) block runs repeatedly. As such, setup( ) can be used for any initialization; in this case, it's used for setting the screen size, making the background orange, and setting the stroke color to white. The draw( ) block is used to handle animation. The size( ) command must always be the first line inside setup( ).

Because the background( ) command is used only once, the screen will fill with lines as the mouse is moved. To draw just a single line that follows the mouse, move the background( ) command to the draw( ) function, which will clear the display window (filling it with orange) each time draw( ) runs:

```
void setup( ) {
  size(400, 400);
  stroke(255);
}

void draw( ) {
  background(192, 64, 0);
  line(150, 25, mouseX, mouseY);
}
```

Basic mode programs are most commonly used for extremely simple examples, or for scripts that run in a linear fashion and then exit. For instance, a basic mode program might start, draw a page to a PDF file, and then exit.

Most programs employ continuous mode, which uses the setup( ) and draw( ) blocks. More advanced mouse handling can also be introduced; for instance, the mousePressed( ) method will be called whenever the mouse is pressed. So, in the following example, when the mouse is pressed, the screen is cleared via the background( ) command:

```
void setup( ) {
  size(400, 400);
  stroke(255);
}

void draw( ) {
  line(150, 25, mouseX, mouseY);
}
```

```
void mousePressed( ) {
  background(192, 64, 0);
}
```

More about basic versus continuous mode programs can be found in the Programming Modes section of the Processing reference, which can be viewed from Help → Getting Started or online at *http://processing.org/reference/environment*.

Exporting and Distributing Your Work

One of the most significant features of the Processing environment is its ability to bundle your sketch into an applet or application with just one click. Select File → Export to package your current sketch as an applet. This will create a folder named *applet* inside your sketch folder. Opening the *index.html* file inside that folder will open your sketch in a browser. The applet folder can be copied to a web site intact and will be viewable by users who have Java installed on their systems. Similarly, you can use File → Export Application to bundle your sketch as an application for Windows, Mac OS X, and Linux.

The applet and application folders are overwritten whenever you export—make a copy or remove them from the sketch folder before making changes to the *index.html* file or the contents of the folder.

More about the export features can be found in the reference; see *http://processing. org/reference/environment/export.html*.

Saving Your Work

If you don't want to distribute the actual project, you might want to create images of its output instead. Images are saved with the saveFrame( ) function. Adding saveFrame( ) at the end of draw( ) will produce a numbered sequence of TIFF-format images of the program's output, named *screen-0001.tif*, *screen-0002.tif*, and so on. A new file will be saved each time draw( ) runs. Watch out because this can quickly fill your sketch folder with hundreds of files. You can also specify your own name and file type for the file to be saved with a command like:

```
saveFrame("output.png")
```

To do the same for a numbered sequence, use #s (hash marks) where the numbers should be placed:

```
saveFrame("output-####.png");
```

For high-quality output, you can write geometry to PDF files instead of the screen, as described in the section "More About the size( ) Method," later in this chapter.

Examples and Reference

While many programmers learn to code in school, others teach themselves. Learning on your own involves looking at lots of other code: running, altering, breaking, and enhancing it until you can reshape it into something new. With this learning model in mind, the Processing software download includes dozens of examples that demonstrate different features of the environment and API.

The examples can be accessed from the File → Examples menu. They're grouped into categories based on their functions (such as Motion, Typography, and Image) or the libraries they use (such as PDF, Network, and Video).

Find an interesting topic in the list and try an example. You'll see commands that are familiar, such as stroke( ), line( ), and background( ), as well as others that have not yet been covered. To see how a function works, select its name, and then right-click and choose Find in Reference from the pop-up menu (Find in Reference can also be found beneath the Help menu). That will open the reference for that function in your default web browser.

In addition to a description of the function's syntax, each reference page includes an example that uses the function. The reference examples are much shorter (usually four or five lines apiece) and easier to follow than the longer code examples.

More About the size( ) Method

The size( ) command also sets the global variables width and height. For objects whose size is dependent on the screen, always use the width and height variables instead of a number (this prevents problems when the size( ) line is altered):

```
size(400, 400);

// The wrong way to specify the middle of the screen
ellipse(200, 200, 50, 50);

// Always the middle, no matter how the size( ) line changes
ellipse(width/2, height/2, 50, 50);
```

In the earlier examples, the size( ) command specified only a width and height for the new window. An optional parameter to the size( ) method specifies how graphics are rendered. A *renderer* handles how the Processing API is implemented for a particular output method (whether the screen, or a screen driven by a high-end graphics card, or a PDF file). Several renderers are included with Processing, and each has a unique function. At the risk of getting too far into the specifics, here are examples of how to specify them with the size( ) command along with descriptions of their capabilities.

```
size(400, 400, JAVA2D);
```
The Java2D renderer is used by default, so this statement is identical to `size(400, 400)`. The Java2D renderer does an excellent job with high-quality 2D vector graphics, but at the expense of speed. In particular, working with pixels is slower compared to the P2D and P3D renderers.

```
size(400, 400, P2D);
```
The Processing 2D renderer is intended for simpler graphics and fast pixel operations. It lacks niceties such as stroke caps and joins on thick lines, but makes up for it when you need to draw thousands of simple shapes or directly manipulate the pixels of an image or video.

```
size(400, 400, P3D);
```
Similar to P2D, the Processing 3D renderer is intended for speed and pixel operations. It also produces 3D graphics inside a web browser, even without the use of a library like Java3D. Image quality is poorer (the `smooth()` command is disabled, and image accuracy is low), but you can draw thousands of triangles very quickly.

```
size(400, 400, OPENGL);
```
The OpenGL renderer uses Sun's Java for OpenGL (JOGL) library for faster rendering, while retaining Processing's simpler graphics APIs and the PDE's easy applet and application export. To use OpenGL graphics, you must select Sketch → Import Library → OpenGL in addition to altering your `size()` command. OpenGL applets also run within a web browser without additional modification, but a dialog box will appear asking users whether they trust "Sun Microsystems, Inc." to run Java for OpenGL on their computers. If this poses a problem, the P3D renderer is a simpler, if less full-featured, solution.

```
size(400, 400, PDF, "output.pdf");
```
The PDF renderer draws all geometry to a file instead of the screen. Like the OpenGL library, you must import the PDF library before using this renderer. This is a cousin of the Java2D renderer, but instead writes directly to PDF files.

Each renderer has a specific role. P2D and P3D are great for pixel-based work, while the JAVA2D and PDF settings will give you the highest quality 2D graphics. When the Processing project first began, the P2D and P3D renderers were a single choice (and, in fact, the only available renderer). This was an attempt to offer a unified mode of thinking about drawing, whether in two or three dimensions. However, this became too burdensome because of the number of tradeoffs that must be made between 2D and 3D. A very different expectation of quality exists for 2D and 3D, for instance, and trying to cover both sides in one renderer meant doing both poorly.

Loading and Displaying Data

One of the unique aspects of the Processing API is the way files are handled. The `loadImage( )` and `loadStrings( )` functions each expect to find a file inside a folder named *data*, which is a subdirectory of the *sketch* folder.

The data Folder

The *data* folder addresses a common frustration when dealing with code that is tested locally but deployed over the Web. Like Java, software written with Processing is subject to security restrictions that determine how a program can access resources such as the local hard disk or other servers via the Internet. This prevents malicious developers from writing code that could harm your computer or compromise your data.

The security restrictions can be tricky to work with during development. When running a program locally, data can be read directly from the disk, though it must be placed relative to the user's "working directory," generally the location of the application. When running online, data must come from a location on the same server. It might be bundled with the code itself (in a JAR archive, discussed later, or from another URL on the same server). For a local file, Java's `FileInputStream` class can be used. If the file is bundled in a JAR archive, the `getResource( )` function is used. For a file on the server, `URL.openStream( )` might be employed. During the journey from development to deployment, it may be necessary to use all three of these methods.

With Processing, these scenarios (and some others) are handled transparently by the file API methods. By placing resources in the *data* folder, Processing packages the files as necessary for online and offline use.

File handling functions include `loadStrings( )`, which reads a text file into an array of `String` objects, and `loadImage( )`, which reads an image into a `PImage` object, the container for image data in Processing.

```
// Examples of loading a text file and a JPEG image
// from the data folder of a sketch.
String[] lines = loadStrings("something.txt");
PImage image = loadImage("picture.jpg");
```

These examples may be a bit easier to read if you know the programming concepts of data types and classes. Each variable has to have a data type, such as `String` or `PImage`.

The `String[]` syntax means "an array of data of the class `String`." This array is created by the `loadStrings` command and is given the name `lines`; it will presumably be used later in the program under that name. The reason `loadStrings` creates an array is that it splits the *something.txt* file into its individual lines. The second command creates a single variable of class `PImage`, with the name `image`.

To add a file to a Processing sketch, use the Sketch → Add File command, or drag the file into the editor window of the PDE. The *data* folder will be created if it does not exist already.

To view the contents of the *sketch* folder, use the Sketch → Show Sketch Folder command. This opens the sketch window in your operating system's file browser.

In the file commands, it's also possible to use full path names to local files, or URLs to other locations if the *data* folder is not suitable:

```
// Load a text file and an image from the specified URLs
String[] lines = loadStrings("http://benfry.com/writing/map/locations.tsv");
PImage image = loadImage("http://benfry.com/writing/map/map.png");
```

Functions

The steps of the process outlined in the first chapter are commonly associated with specific functions in the Processing API. For instance:

Acquire
    loadStrings( ), loadBytes( )

Parse
    split( )

Filter
    for( ), if (item[*i*].startsWith( ))

Mine
    min( ), max( ), abs( )

Represent
    map( ), beginShape( ), endShape( )

Refine
    fill( ), strokeWeight( ), smooth( )

Interact
    mouseMoved( ), mouseDragged( ), keyPressed( )

This is not an exhaustive list, but simply another way to frame the stages of visualization for those more familiar with code.

Libraries Add New Features

A *library* is a collection of code in a specified format that makes it easy to use within Processing. Libraries have been important to the growth of the project because they let developers make new features accessible to users without making them part of the core Processing API.

Several core libraries come with Processing. These can be seen in the Libraries section of the online reference (also available from the Help menu from within the PDE); see *http://processing.org/reference/libraries*.

One example is the XML import library. This is an extremely minimal XML parser (based on the open source project NanoXML) with a small download footprint (approximately 30KB) that makes it ideal for online use.

To use the XML library in a project, choose Sketch → Import Library → xml. This will add the following line to the top of the sketch:

```
import processing.xml.*;
```

Java programmers will recognize the import command. In Processing, this line also determines what code is packaged with a sketch when it is exported as an applet or application.

Now that the XML library is imported, you can issue commands from it. For instance, the following line loads an XML file named *sites.xml* into a variable named xml:

```
XMLElement xml = new XMLElement(this, "sites.xml");
```

The xml variable can now be manipulated as necessary to read the contents. The full example can be seen in the reference for its class, XMLElement, at *http://processing.org/reference/libraries/xml/XMLElement.html*.

The this variable is used frequently with library objects because it lets the library make use of the core API functions to draw to the screen or load files. The latter case applies to the XML library, allowing XML files to be read from the *data* folder or other locations supported by the file API methods.

Other libraries provide features such as writing QuickTime movie files, sending and receiving MIDI commands, sophisticated 3D camera control, and access to MySQL databases.

Sketching and Scripting

Processing sketches are made up of one or more tabs, with each tab representing a piece of code. The environment is designed around projects that are a few pages of code, and often three to five tabs in total. This covers a significant number of projects developed to test and prototype ideas, often before embedding them into a larger project or building a more robust application for broader deployment.

This small-scale development style is useful for data visualization in two primary scenarios. The most common scenario is when you have a data set in mind, or a question that you're trying to answer, and you need a quick way to load the data, represent it, and see what's there. This is important because it lets you take an inventory of the data in question. How many elements are there? What are the largest and smallest values? How many dimensions are we looking at? We'll return to this notion of exploring data in future chapters.

In the second scenario, the desired outcome is known, but the correct means of representing the data and interacting with it have not yet been determined.

The idea of sketching is identical to that of scripting, except that you're not working in an interpreted scripting language, but rather gaining the performance benefit of compiling to Java class files. Of course, strictly speaking, Java itself is an interpreted language, but its bytecode compilation brings it much closer to the "metal" than languages such as JavaScript, ActionScript, Python, or Ruby.

Processing was never intended as the ultimate language for visual programming; instead, we set out to make something that was:

- A sketchbook for our own work, simplifying the majority of tasks that we undertake
- A programming environment suitable for teaching programming to a nontraditional audience
- A stepping stone from scripting languages to more complicated or difficult languages such as full-blown Java or C++

At the intersection of these points is a tradeoff between speed and simplicity of use. If we didn't care about speed, it might make sense to use Python, Ruby, or many other scripting languages. That is especially true for the education side. If we didn't care about making a transition to more advanced languages, we'd probably avoid a C++ or Java-style syntax. But Java is a nice starting point for a sketching language because it's far more forgiving than C/C++ and also allows users to export sketches for distribution via the Web.

Processing assembles our experience in building software of this kind (sketches of interactive works or data-driven visualization) and simplifies the parts that we felt should be easier, such as getting started quickly, and insulates new users from issues like those associated with setting up Java.

Don't Start by Trying to Build a Cathedral

If you're already familiar with programming, it's important to understand how Processing differs from other development environments and languages. The Processing project encourages a style of work that builds code quickly, understanding that either the code will be used as a quick sketch or that ideas are being tested before developing a final project. This could be misconstrued as software engineering heresy. Perhaps we're not far from "hacking," but this is more appropriate for the roles in which Processing is used. Why force students or casual programmers to learn about graphics contexts, threading, and event handling methods before they can show something on the screen that interacts with the mouse? The same goes for advanced developers; why should they always need to start with the same two pages of code whenever they begin a project?

In another scenario, if you're doing scientific visualization, the ability to try things out quickly is a far higher priority than sophisticated code structure. Usually you don't know what the outcome will be, so you might build something one week to try an initial hypothesis and build something new the next based on what was learned in the first week. To this end, remember the following considerations as you begin visualizing data with Processing:

- Be careful about creating unnecessary structures in your code. As you learn about encapsulating your code into classes, it's tempting to make ever-smaller classes because data can always be distilled further. Do you need classes at the level of molecules, atoms, or quarks? Just because atoms go smaller doesn't mean that we need to work at a lower level of abstraction. If a class is half a page long, does it make sense to have six additional subclasses that are each half a page long? Could the same thing be accomplished with a single class that is a page and a half in total?

- Consider the scale of the project. It's not always necessary to build enterprise-level software on the first day. We're asking questions about data, so figure out the minimum code necessary to help answer that question.

- Do you really need to use a database? If you're manipulating half a gigabyte of data and have a gigabyte of RAM, can you shove the data into memory and play with it directly? If so, use that option; it lets you avoid developing a schema for the database before you actually know what you're doing (or want to do) with the data.

- Do you need to start with *all* the data? Having collected precious terabytes of potentially useful information, do you need all of it to answer your first round of questions? A small percentage, which will require less infrastructure, is usually enough to indicate whether a larger project is even worth pursuing.

The point is to delay engineering work until it's appropriate. The threshold for where to begin engineering a piece of visualization software is much later than for traditional programming projects because there is a kind of "art" to the early process of quick iteration.

Of course, once things are working, avoid the urge to rewrite for its own sake. A rewrite should be used when addressing a completely different problem. If you've managed to hit the nail on the head, you should refactor to clean up method names and class interactions. But a full rewrite of already finished code is almost always a bad idea, no matter how "ugly" it seems.

Ready?

In this chapter, we covered the basics of the Processing environment, as well as a bit of the philosophy behind the environment itself and the type of software built with the language. In the next chapter, we'll get started representing our first data set.

## CHAPTER 3

Mapping

This chapter covers the basics of reading, displaying, and interacting with a data set. As an example, we'll use a map of the United States, and a set of data values for all 50 states. Drawing such a map is a simple enough task that could be done without programming—either with mapping software or by hand—but it gives us an example upon which to build. The process of designing with data involves a great deal of iteration: small changes that help your project evolve in usefulness and clarity. And as this project evolves through the course of the chapter, it will become clear how software can be used to create representations that automatically update themselves, or how interaction can be used to provide additional layers of information.

Drawing a Map

Some development environments separate work into projects; the equivalent term for Processing is a *sketch*. Start a new Processing sketch by selecting File → New.

For this example, we'll use a map of the United States to use as a background image. The map can be downloaded from *http://benfry.com/writing/map/map.png*.

Drag and drop the *map.png* file into the Processing editor window. A message at the bottom will appear confirming that the file has been added to the sketch. You can also add files by selecting Sketch → Add File. A sketch is organized as a folder, and all data files are placed in a subfolder named *data*. (The *data* folder is covered in Chapter 2.)

Then, enter the following code:

```
PImage mapImage;

void setup() {
  size(640, 400);
  mapImage = loadImage("map.png");
}
```

```
void draw( ) {
  background(255);
  image(mapImage, 0, 0);
}
```

Finally, click the Run button. Assuming everything was entered correctly, a map of the United States will appear in a new window.

Explanation of the Processing Code

Processing API functions are named to make their uses as obvious as possible. Method names, such as loadImage( ), convey the purpose of the calls in simple language. What you may need to get used to is dividing your code into functions such as setup( ) and draw( ), which determine how the code is handled. After clicking the Run button, the setup( ) method executes once. After setup( ) has completed, the draw( ) method runs repeatedly. Use the setup( ) method to load images, fonts, and set initial values for variables. The draw( ) method runs at 60 frames per second (or slower if it takes longer than 1/60th of a second to run the code inside the draw( ) method); it can be used to update the screen to show animation or respond to mouse movement and other types of input.

Our first function calls are very basic. The loadImage( ) function reads an image from the data folder (URLs or absolute paths also work). The PImage class is a container for image data, and the image( ) command draws it to the screen at a specific location.

Locations on a Map

The next step is to specify some points on the map. To simplify this, a file containing the coordinates for the center of each state can be found at *http://benfry.com/ writing/map/locations.tsv*.

In future chapters, we'll explore how this data is read. In the meantime, some code to read the location data file can be found at *http://benfry.com/writing/map/Table.pde*.

Add both of these files to your sketch the same way that you added the *map.png* file earlier.

The Table class is just two pages of code, and we'll get into its function later. In the meantime, suffice it to say that it reads a file as a grid of rows and columns. The class has methods to get an int, float, or String for a specific row and column. To get float values, for instance, use the following format:

```
table.getFloat(row, column)
```

Rows and columns are numbered starting at zero, so the column titles (if any) will be row 0, and the row titles will be column 0.

In the previous section, we saw how displaying a map in Processing is a two-step process:

1. Load the data.
2. Display the data in the desired format.

Displaying the centers of states follows the same pattern, although a little more code is involved:

1. Create locationTable and use the locationTable.getFloat( ) function to read each location's coordinates (x and y values).
2. Draw a circle using those values. Because a circle, geometrically speaking, is just an ellipse whose width and height are the same, graphics libraries provide an ellipse-drawing function that covers circle drawing as well.

A new version of the code follows, with modifications highlighted:

```
PImage mapImage;
Table locationTable;
int rowCount;

void setup( ) {
  size(640, 400);
  mapImage = loadImage("map.png");
  // Make a data table from a file that contains
  // the coordinates of each state.
  locationTable = new Table("locations.tsv");
  // The row count will be used a lot, so store it globally.
  rowCount = locationTable.getRowCount( );
}

void draw( ) {
  background(255);
  image(mapImage, 0, 0);

  // Drawing attributes for the ellipses.
  smooth( );
  fill(192, 0, 0);
  noStroke( );

  // Loop through the rows of the locations file and draw the points.
  for (int row = 0; row < rowCount; row++) {
    float x = locationTable.getFloat(row, 1);  // column 1
    float y = locationTable.getFloat(row, 2);  // column 2
    ellipse(x, y, 9, 9);
  }
}
```

The smooth( ), fill( ), and noStroke( ) functions apply to any drawing we subsequently do in the draw( ) function. Later, we'll look at the aspects of drawing you can control; here I'll just mention that the fill( ) function assigns red, green, and blue elements to the color. I've chosen to show all of the circles in red.

Figure 3-1 shows the map and points for each location.

Figure 3-1. U.S. map and centers of states

Data on a Map

Next we want to load a set of values that will appear on the map itself. For this, we add another Table object and load the data from a file called *random.tsv*, available at *http://benfry.com/writing/map/random.tsv*.

It's always important to find the minimum and maximum values for the data, because that range will need to be mapped to other features (such as size or color) for display. To do this, use a for loop to walk through each line of the data table and check to see whether each value is bigger than the maximum found so far, or smaller than the minimum. To begin, the dataMin variable is set to MAX_FLOAT, a built-in value for the maximum possible float value. This ensures that dataMin will be replaced with the first value found in the table. The same is done for dataMax, by setting it to MIN_FLOAT. Using 0 instead of MIN_FLOAT and MAX_FLOAT will not work in cases where the minimum value in the data set is a positive number (e.g., 2.4) or the maximum is a negative number (e.g., –3.75).

The data table is loaded in the same fashion as the location data, and the code to find the minimum and maximum immediately follows:

```
PImage mapImage;
Table locationTable;
int rowCount;
```

```
Table dataTable;
float dataMin = MAX_FLOAT;
float dataMax = MIN_FLOAT;

void setup( ) {
  size(640, 400);
  mapImage = loadImage("map.png");
  locationTable = new Table("locations.tsv");
  rowCount = locationTable.getRowCount( );

  // Read the data table.
  dataTable = new Table("random.tsv");

  // Find the minimum and maximum values.
  for (int row = 0; row < rowCount; row++) {
    float value = dataTable.getFloat(row, 1);
    if (value > dataMax) {
      dataMax = value;
    }
    if (value < dataMin) {
      dataMin = value;
    }
  }
}
```

The other half of the program (shown later) draws a data point for each location. A drawData( ) function is introduced, which takes x and y coordinates as parameters, along with an abbreviation for a state. The drawData( ) function grabs the float value from column 1 based on a state abbreviation (which can be found in column 0).

The getRowName( ) function gets the name of a particular row. This is just a convenience function because the row name is usually in column 0, so it's identical to getString(row, 0). The row titles for this data set are the two-letter state abbreviations. In the modified example, getRowName( ) is used to get the state abbreviation for each row of the data file.

The getFloat( ) function can also use a row name instead of a row number, which simply matches the String supplied against the abbreviation found in column 0 of the *random.tsv* data file. The results are shown in Figure 3-2.

The rest of the program follows:

```
void draw( ) {
  background(255);
  image(mapImage, 0, 0);

  smooth( );
  fill(192, 0, 0);
  noStroke( );
```

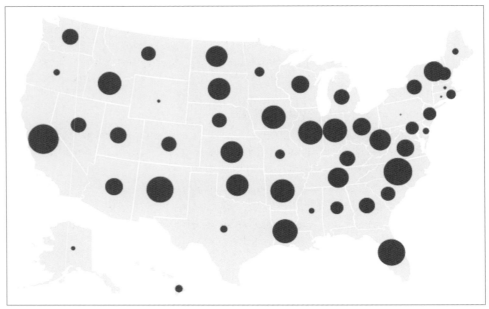

Figure 3-2. Varying data by size

```
for (int row = 0; row < rowCount; row++) {
  String abbrev = dataTable.getRowName(row);
  float x = locationTable.getFloat(abbrev, 1);
  float y = locationTable.getFloat(abbrev, 2);
  drawData(x, y, abbrev);
}
}

// Map the size of the ellipse to the data value
void drawData(float x, float y, String abbrev) {
  // Get data value for state
  float value = dataTable.getFloat(abbrev, 1);
  // Re-map the value to a number between 2 and 40
  float mapped = map(value, dataMin, dataMax, 2, 40);
  // Draw an ellipse for this item
  ellipse(x, y, mapped, mapped);
}
```

The map( ) function converts numbers from one range to another. In this case, value is expected to be somewhere between dataMin and dataMax. Using map( ) reproportions value to be a number between 2 and 40. The map( ) function is useful for hiding the math involved in the conversion, which makes code quicker to write and easier to read. A lot of visualization problems revolve around mapping data from one range to another (e.g., from the min and max of the input data to the width or height of a plot), so the map( ) method is used frequently in this book.

Another refinement option is to keep the ellipse the same size but interpolate between two different colors for high and low values. The norm( ) function maps values from a user-specified range to a *normalized* range between 0.0 and 1.0. The percent value is a percentage of where value lies in the range from dataMin to dataMax. For instance, a percent value of 0.5 represents 50%, or halfway between dataMin and dataMax:

```
float percent = norm(value, dataMin, dataMax);
```

The lerp( ) function converts a normalized value to another range (norm( ) and lerp( ) together make up the map( ) function), and the lerpColor( ) function does the same, except it interpolates between two colors. The syntax:

```
color between = lerpColor(color1, color2, percent)
```

returns a between value based on the percentage (a number between 0.0 and 0.1) specified. To make the colors interpolate between red and blue for low and high values, replace the drawData( ) function with the following:

```
void drawData(float x, float y, String abbrev) {
  float value = dataTable.getFloat(abbrev, 1);
  float percent = norm(value, dataMin, dataMax);
  color between = lerpColor(#FF4422, #4422CC, percent);  // red to blue
  fill(between);
  ellipse(x, y, 15, 15);
}
```

Results are shown in Figure 3-3.

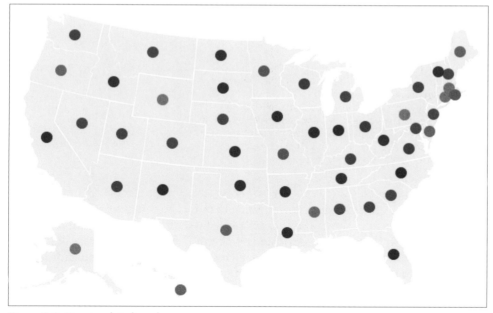

Figure 3-3. Varying data by color

This illustrates the problem with interpolating between two unrelated colors. Two separate colors make sense for positive and negative values (see the next section "Two-Sided Data Ranges" and Figure 3-6), but the idea of purple as an in-between value is confusing to read because it's difficult to say just how red or blue the values are—everything becomes a muddy purple. If using two different colors, a better option is to provide a neutral value in between the two colors, such as white or black.

On the other hand, to make color interpolation work, it's better to employ a pair of similar colors. For instance, blue and green provide an alternative gradation of values that is easier to read than the red-to-purple-to-blue range. Replace the lerpColor line with the following:

```
color between = lerpColor(#296F34, #61E2F0, percent);
```

and take a look at the result in Figure 3-4.

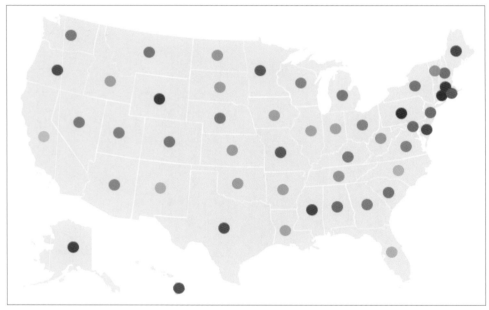

Figure 3-4. Varying data by color: better color choices

The interpolated values tend to be "muddy" because the interpolation is calculated in RGB color space. To preserve the saturation and brightness of colors, a better option is the HSB color space, particularly when dealing with colors that are similar in hue. A fourth parameter to lerpColor( ) allows you to change the color space used for interpolation:

```
color between = lerpColor(#296F34, #61E2F0, percent, HSB);
```

Changing to the HSB color model improves brightness and contrast; see Figure 3-5.

RGB and HSB Color Spaces

The HSB color space defines colors based on hue, saturation, and brightness instead of the red, green, and blue values used in RGB. The RGB color space has more to do with how color is represented by computer screens than how we actually perceive color. Intermediate steps in each of the hue, saturation, and brightness components of a color provide better interpolation because each of the perceptual aspects of the color are broken apart—the shift in the hue component is separated from the shift in saturation and the shift in brightness.

In the RGB color space, a gray value occurs whenever the R, G, and B components are identical (or at least similar). In RGB space, the color halfway between orange (255, 128, 0) and light blue (0, 128, 255) is gray (128, 128, 128). So using lerpColor( ) in RGB mode would cause the orange to become more gray at each step, until it reaches gray; then, it would slowly move from gray to blue. Not too pleasing to look at.

On the other hand, RGB mode is preferred when there are significant changes in hue. For instance, if you begin at red and interpolate to green in HSB space, you'll iterate through all the spectrum colors in between: from red, to orange, then to yellow, and finally to green.

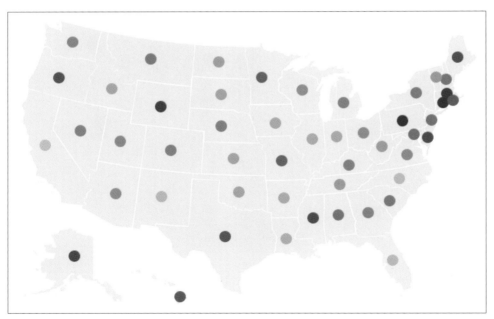

Figure 3-5. Varying data by color: better color space

But the color mix is still lacking, so next let's look at other options.

Two-Sided Data Ranges

Because the values in the data set are positive and negative, a better option would be to use separate colors for positive or negative while changing the size of each ellipse to reflect the range. The following replacement for drawData( ) separates positive and negative values as well as indicating the magnitude (absolute value) of each value.

In this case, positive values are remapped from 0 through the maximum data value into a value between 3 and 30 for the diameter of the ellipse. Negative values are mapped in a similar fashion, where the most negative (dataMin) will be mapped to size 30, and the least negative (0) will be mapped to size 3. Positive values are drawn with blue ellipses and negative values with red; see Figure 3-6.

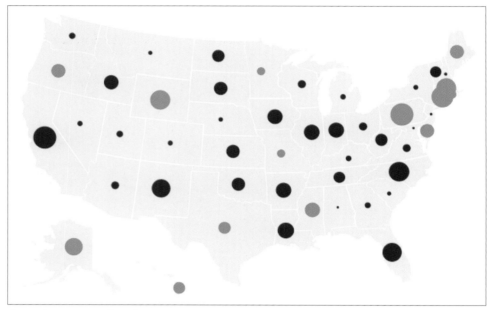

Figure 3-6. Magnitude and positive/negative

```
void drawData(float x, float y, String abbrev) {
  float value = dataTable.getFloat(abbrev, 1);
  float diameter = 0;
  if (value >= 0) {
    diameter = map(value, 0, dataMax, 3, 30);
    fill(#333366);  // blue
  } else {
    diameter = map(value, 0, dataMin, 3, 30);
    fill(#EC5166);  // red
  }
  ellipse(x, y, diameter, diameter);
}
```

Figure 3-6 is much easier to read and interpret than the previous representations; however, we've used up two visual features (size and color) on a single dimension of the data. For a simple data set such as this one, it's not a problem, but if we look at a pair of data values, we would want to use color for one dimension of the data and size for the other. In some cases, showing one variable two ways can be helpful for reinforcing the meaning of the values, but it's often done without consideration. The approach used in Figure 3-6 would be an appropriate solution if the difference between positive and negative values was our primary or secondary interest.

To preserve size for another aspect of the data, another option would be to map the *transparency* of the ellipses to their relative values. Transparency is also referred to as *alpha transparency* or usually just *alpha*. It's controlled by an optional second parameter to the fill( ) function; 0 means that the entire background shows though the object, whereas 255 means the object is totally opaque.

Yet another revision of the drawData( ) function shows how transparency is controlled; see Figure 3-7.

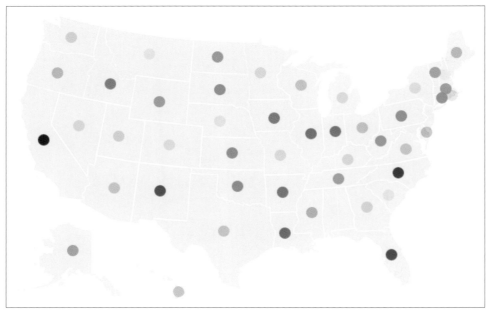

Figure 3-7. Magnitude and positive/negative using transparency

```
void drawData(float x, float y, String abbrev) {
  float value = dataTable.getFloat(abbrev, 1);
  if (value >= 0) {
    float a = map(value, 0, dataMax, 0, 255);
    fill(#333366, a);
  } else {
    float a = map(value, 0, dataMin, 0, 255);
```

```
    fill(#EC5166, a);
  }
  ellipse(x, y, 15, 15);
}
```

Transparency can be useful for features at a glance, but it doesn't provide a lot of differentiation between the values (as can be seen here). For this particular data set, Figures 3-2 and 3-6 provide the best solutions in terms of visual design. The others are included to show alternatives and demonstrate the thinking process behind visual refinements.

Provide More Information with a Mouse Rollover (Interact)

Adding a small amount of interaction can help make a display more useful, and this feature shows how Processing makes mouse information readily available. As the mouse hovers above a particular state, additional information about that location can be revealed.

To show the extra information as text, a font is required. Use the Create Font option under the Tools menu. For this example, a typeface named Univers Bold was chosen from the list, and the size was set to 12. (Univers may not be available on your machine, so choose any font you'd like.)

Clicking OK adds a file named *Univers-Bold-12.vlw* to the *data* folder. Now when the sketch is exported as an applet or application, the font can be used on other machines, even if Univers is not installed on them.

Adding these lines to setup( ) sets the font:

```
PFont font = loadFont("Univers-Bold-12.vlw");
textFont(font);
```

Because fonts are loaded from files, loadFont( ) should be used only inside setup( ) (and not from the draw( ) method); otherwise, the font will be loaded repeatedly and slow down the program.

The location of the loadFont( ) call reiterates a valuable principle that may guide you when placing other function calls. The setup( ) method runs only once, when a browser or other program loads a sketch. The draw( ) method runs repeatedly (several times a second) so that sketches can be updated over time and animated.

The textFont( ) command sets the current font.

The rollover itself is handled by checking the distance between the mouse and the data point. If the mouse is within a certain range of the point, the text appears. The distance is calculated with the dist( ) function, and because this will calculate the radius between the location and the mouse, we issue ellipseMode(RADIUS) to draw the data points before dist( ). Using the radius also helps because it can be used to place the text above the data point: the distance to the bottom of the text will be the radius plus a few pixels of space. As the default `ellipseMode` is `DIAMETER` (and a radius is half a diameter), we'll adjust the preceding `map( )` function to use the values 1.5 and 15 instead of 3 and 30:

```
void drawData(float x, float y, String abbrev) {
  float value = dataTable.getFloat(abbrev, 1);
  float radius = 0;
  if (value >= 0) {
    radius = map(value, 0, dataMax, 1.5, 15);
    fill(#4422CC);  // blue
  } else {
    radius = map(value, 0, dataMin, 1.5, 15);
    fill(#FF4422);  // red
  }
  ellipseMode(RADIUS);
  ellipse(x, y, radius, radius);

  if (dist(x, y, mouseX, mouseY) < radius+2) {
    fill(0);
    textAlign(CENTER);
    // Show the data value and the state abbreviation in parentheses.
    text(value + " (" + abbrev + ")", x, y-radius-4);
  }
}
```

The parameters to text( ) are a bit complex. The first argument—which is the text to display—combines the data itself (value) with the state abbreviation (abbrev), enclosing the abbreviation in parentheses. The second and third parameters specify the x and y position of the text. The vertical location is y-radius-4, which is the y-coordinate at the center of the circle, minus the radius to get to the edge of the circle, minus four more pixels.

Because the mouse cursor extends to the right and downward, we've placed the text above the circle to prevent the arrow from covering up the data itself. This is a general problem with rollovers that we'll return to later: rollover text or the means for selecting it can obscure the data underneath.

With the rollover, you might want to bring in additional types of data as well. An additional data file that maps abbreviations to the full state name can be found at *http://benfry.com/writing/map/names.tsv*.

The table in this data file will be used in conjunction with the others to look up names for the individual states. More commonly, this particular data would be found in the same data file as the others, but it's useful to introduce the idea of joining multiple sets of data. Joining data frequently is necessary, and the opportunity to combine data sets from different sources is a powerful aspect of data visualization.

First, add a `nameTable` declaration after the `locationTable` declaration at the beginning of the code:

```
Table nameTable;
```

Handling Mouse Interaction

In more sophisticated programs, it's common to package how elements are drawn into an individual *class*—a set of code that groups together related functions and variables. For instance, each state could be an instance of a class that contains the name, data value, and location on screen for each state. Mouse interaction would be handled by a function inside the class that checks whether the mouse location is near the location value for the state. We'll see this method used in later chapters.

The Processing API provides few high-level elements—there is currently no Shape class that handles such things automatically. Instead, the API is designed so that such classes are either unnecessary or simple for others to build into their own projects.

Next, load the nameTable along with the others inside the setup( ) function:

```
nameTable = new Table("names.tsv");
```

Finally, when drawing the text for the rollover, grab the full name from the table and display it:

```
String name = nameTable.getString(abbrev, 1);
text(name + " " + value, x, y-radius-4);
```

With the longer text showing, sometimes the parts of the text will appear behind other points because the states are all drawn in order. Because Massachusetts is drawn after Connecticut, the dot for Massachusetts will cover the rollover text for Connecticut. To change this behavior, first draw the data points for all the states, and then draw the rollover text for the current selection. When drawing each state, we'll check to see whether the mouse is in the vicinity, and if so, that state is a candidate for having its name drawn.

You might also notice that when using the mouse in the area of smaller states (such as those in the Northeast), several names will show up. To handle this, we'll keep track of the state that is closest to the mouse and show only the information for that state. As each state is drawn, we'll check whether the distance from the state's location to the mouse is the smallest found so far, and if so, store its X and Y position along with the text to show at that position. These three variables will be updated as each data point within range of the mouse is drawn. After the data points have finished drawing, the text can be drawn at that particular X and Y point.

The mouseX and mouseY variables are updated on each trip through draw( ). Because the draw( ) method runs repeatedly (at around 60 frames per second), updates for the rollover happen almost instantaneously.

The top of the program remains unchanged, but the draw( ) and drawData( ) functions are replaced with the following:

```
// Global variables set in drawData( ) and read in draw( )
float closestDist;
String closestText;
float closestTextX;
float closestTextY;

void draw( ) {
  background(255);
  image(mapImage, 0, 0);

  closestDist = MAX_FLOAT;

  for (int row = 0; row < rowCount; row++) {
    String abbrev = dataTable.getRowName(row);
    float x = locationTable.getFloat(abbrev, 1);
    float y = locationTable.getFloat(abbrev, 2);
    drawData(x, y, abbrev);
  }

  // Use global variables set in drawData( )
  // to draw text related to closest circle.
  if (closestDist != MAX_FLOAT) {
    fill(0);
    textAlign(CENTER);
    text(closestText, closestTextX, closestTextY);
  }
}

void drawData(float x, float y, String abbrev) {
  float value = dataTable.getFloat(abbrev, 1);
  float radius = 0;
  if (value >= 0) {
    radius = map(value, 0, dataMax, 1.5, 15);
    fill(#4422CC);  // blue
  } else {
    radius = map(value, 0, dataMin, 1.5, 15);
    fill(#FF4422);  // red
  }
  ellipseMode(RADIUS);
  ellipse(x, y, radius, radius);

  float d = dist(x, y, mouseX, mouseY);
  // Because the following check is done each time a new
  // circle is drawn, we end up with the values of the
  // circle closest to the mouse.
  if ((d < radius + 2) && (d < closestDist)) {
    closestDist = d;
    String name = nameTable.getString(abbrev, 1);
    closestText = name + " " + value;
    closestTextX = x;
    closestTextY = y-radius-4;
  }
}
```

Updating Values over Time (Acquire, Mine)

A static map isn't particularly interesting, especially when there's the possibility of an interactive environment. In addition, data values are often dynamic. They might change every second, every hour, or every year, but in each case, we'll want to depict the change over time. For example, we can replace the data with random values each time a key is pressed. Again, because draw( ) is called repeatedly, the values shown on screen will update immediately.

The code in this section provides an initial illustration of how to handle user interaction, a theme I'll expand in the book.

One problem with changing data is that the minimum and maximum values need to stay fixed. You'll need to figure out the absolute values for each because recalculating dataMin and dataMax each time new data is found will make the data points appear out of proportion to the previous set of values. For this example, we'll set the minimum and maximum values to −10 and 10, when the variables are first declared at the beginning of the program:

```
Table dataTable;
float dataMin = -10;
float dataMax = 10;
```

This change means that the code to find the minimum and maximum values can be removed from the setup( ) method.

The following code builds on the previous step and adds a function to randomize the data values each time the Space bar is pressed:

```
void keyPressed() {
  if (key == ' ') {
    updateTable();
  }
}

void updateTable() {
  for (int row = 0; row < rowCount; row++) {
    float newValue = random(dataMin, dataMax);
    dataTable.setFloat(row, 1, newValue);
  }
}
```

The random( ) function takes a minimum and maximum value, and returns a value starting with the minimum, up to but not including the maximum. The setFloat( ) function overwrites the old value from the data table with the new random value.

When running this code, press the Space bar once to see a new set of data appear. You might also notice that the rollovers now look a bit silly because the randomized values might have six or seven digits of precision. This can be changed with the nf( ) function, which is used to format numbers for printing.

The basic form of nf( ) specifies the number of digits to the left and right of the decimal point. Specifying 0 for either position means "any" number of digits. So, to allow any number of digits to the left of the decimal point and two digits to the right, the line that sets closestText changes from:

```
closestText = name + " " + value;
```

to the following:

```
closestText = name + " " + nf(value, 0, 2);
```

The name for nf( ) is intentionally terse (if a bit cryptic) because it's almost always used in situations when it's being concatenated to another part of a String. Two related functions are:

nfp( )
> Requires each number to be shown with a + or – sign.

nfs( )
> Pads values with spaces to fill out the number of digits specified. This is useful in some situations for lining up values in vertical columns.

Because we care about positive and negative, nfp( ) is probably best suited for our purpose. This turns "North Dakota 6.15234534" into "North Dakota +6.15", which is far more readable.

Instead of randomizing the data, updateTable( ) could be used to load a new set of values from another data source, whether another file or a location online. For instance, the following URL can be used to read a new set of data from the Web:

http://benfry.com/writing/map/random.cgi

At this location is a simple Perl script that generates a new set of values and sends them over a CGI connection. The code follows, with comments for those not familiar with Perl syntax:

```perl
#!/usr/bin/perl

# An array of the 50 state abbreviations
@states = ('AL', 'AK', 'AZ', 'AR', 'CA', 'CO', 'CT', 'DE', 'FL', 'GA',
           'HI', 'ID', 'IL', 'IN', 'IA', 'KS', 'KY', 'LA', 'ME', 'MD',
           'MA', 'MI', 'MN', 'MS', 'MO', 'MT', 'NE', 'NV', 'NH', 'NJ',
           'NM', 'NY', 'NC', 'ND', 'OH', 'OK', 'OR', 'PA', 'RI', 'SC',
           'SD', 'TN', 'TX', 'UT', 'VT', 'VA', 'WA', 'WV', 'WI', 'WY');

# A CGI script must identify the type of data it's sending;
# this line specifies that plain text data will follow.
print "Content-type: text/plain\n\n";

# Loop through each of the state abbreviations in the array.
foreach $state (@states) {
```

```
    # Pick a random number between -10 and 10. (rand( ) returns a
    # number between 0 and 1; multiply that by 20 and subtract 10.)
    $r = (rand( ) * 20) - 10;

    # Print the state name, followed by a tab,
    # then the random value, followed by a new line.
    print "$state\t$r\n";
}
```

To use this URL, the code for the updateTable( ) function changes to the following:

```
void updateTable( ) {
  dataTable = new Table("http://benfry.com/writing/map/random.cgi");
}
```

Even though this script just produces randomized data, the same model could be used in actual practice, where a data set is generated online—perhaps from a database or something else that is accessible only through a network connection.

Smooth Interpolation of Values over Time (Refine)

When updating data, it's important to show users the transition over time. Interpolating between values helps users track where the changes occur and provides context for the change as it happens. The way to think about interpolation is that your data values are never "equal" to some number; rather, they're always "becoming" or "transitioning to" another value.

For this, we use another class called an Integrator. The contents of the code will be explained shortly, but for the time being, it can be downloaded from *http://benfry. com/writing/map/Integrator.pde*.

This code implements a simple physics-based interpolator. A force is exerted by which a value can "target" another, in the manner of a spring (more about this later). The important thing to understand is that an Integrator object represents a single data value. When the Integrator is constructed, an initial value is set:

```
Integrator changingNumber = new Integrator(4);
```

To make the value transition from 4 (its initial value) to −2, use the target( ) method:

```
changingNumber.target(-2);
```

This has no effect yet on the display. For the value to update, you must call the update( ) method of the Integrator:

```
changingNumber.update( );
```

Usually this is done at the beginning of draw( ). The target( ) method is called whenever a state changes, and the constructor is used inside setup( ). The Integrator has a value field that always holds its current value. To set the diameter of an ellipse based on the changing value, a line like this would be used inside draw( ):

```
ellipse(x, y, changingNumber.value, changingNumber.value);
```

Because our state example uses 50 values, we need to create an array of Integrator objects inside setup( ), update each of them at the beginning of setup( ), and target( ) them to new values each time the display changes, effectively producing an animation. Instead of using getFloat( ) to read values from the dataTable object, the dataTable object will be used to target( ) the Integrator list.

The modified code looks like this:

```
PImage mapImage;
Table locationTable;
Table nameTable;
int rowCount;

Table dataTable;
float dataMin = -10;
float dataMax = 10;

Integrator[] interpolators;

void setup( ) {
  size(640, 400);
  mapImage = loadImage("map.png");
  locationTable = new Table("locations.tsv");
  nameTable = new Table("names.tsv");
  rowCount = locationTable.getRowCount( );

  dataTable = new Table("random.tsv");

  // Setup: load initial values into the Integrator.
  interpolators = new Integrator[rowCount];
  for (int row = 0; row < rowCount; row++) {
    float initialValue = dataTable.getFloat(row, 1);
    interpolators[row] = new Integrator(initialValue);
  }

  PFont font = loadFont("Univers-Bold-12.vlw");
  textFont(font);

  smooth( );
  noStroke( );
}

float closestDist;
String closestText;
float closestTextX;
float closestTextY;


void draw( ) {
  background(255);
  image(mapImage, 0, 0);
```

```
  // Draw: update the Integrator with the current values,
  // which are either those from the setup() function
  // or those loaded by the target() function issued in
  // updateTable().
  for (int row = 0; row < rowCount; row++) {
    interpolators[row].update();
  }

  closestDist = MAX_FLOAT;

  for (int row = 0; row < rowCount; row++) {
    String abbrev = dataTable.getRowName(row);
    float x = locationTable.getFloat(abbrev, 1);
    float y = locationTable.getFloat(abbrev, 2);
    drawData(x, y, abbrev);
  }

  if (closestDist != MAX_FLOAT) {
    fill(0);
    textAlign(CENTER);
    text(closestText, closestTextX, closestTextY);
  }
}

void drawData(float x, float y, String abbrev) {
  // Figure out what row this is.
  int row = dataTable.getRowIndex(abbrev);
  // Get the current value.
  float value = interpolators[row].value;

  float radius = 0;
  if (value >= 0) {
    radius = map(value, 0, dataMax, 1.5, 15);
    fill(#4422CC);  // blue
  } else {
    radius = map(value, 0, dataMin, 1.5, 15);
    fill(#FF4422);  // red
  }
  ellipseMode(RADIUS);
  ellipse(x, y, radius, radius);

  float d = dist(x, y, mouseX, mouseY);
  if ((d < radius + 2) && (d < closestDist)) {
    closestDist = d;
    String name = nameTable.getString(abbrev, 1);
    // Use target (not current) value for showing the data point.
    String val = nfp(interpolators[row].target, 0, 2);
    closestText = name + " " + val;
    closestTextX = x;
    closestTextY = y-radius-4;
  }
}
```

```
void keyPressed( ) {
  if (key == ' ') {
    updateTable( );
  }
}

void updateTable( ) {
  for (int row = 0; row < rowCount; row++) {
    float newValue = random(-10, 10);
    interpolators[row].target(newValue);
  }
}
```

The changes will transition very quickly, and there are two ways to handle this. The first is to adjust the frame rate of your application, which may be very high. By default, the frame rate is capped to 60 frames per second (fps). When building animated graphics, it's important to keep an eye on the frame rate to avoid situations in which a faster computer runs your code too quickly. Simply setting the maximum frame rate lower results in a more visually pleasing presentation. This line, added to the end of setup( ), sets the maximum to 30 fps:

```
frameRate(30);
```

Another option is to use the Integrator class's own parameters. We mentioned that the Integrator class uses math for simple physics that simulate a spring. The target value is the resting length of the spring. The other parameters are defined in terms of physical properties, which include the damping (how much friction exists to prevent the changes from being too wobbly) and the degree of attraction (how quickly the value will become another). You can set the damping and attraction in the constructor. The default damping is 0.5 and the attraction is 0.2. Even without modifying the frameRate( ) setting, changing the constructor can make things move much more slowly:

```
interpolators[row] = new Integrator(initialValue, 0.5, 0.01);
```

Cutting down the damping makes things bouncy:

```
interpolators[row] = new Integrator(initialValue, 0.9, 0.1);
```

Using Your Own Data

The file format presented in this chapter is straightforward, so try replacing the *random.tsv* file with your own data based on the 50 states. It's remarkably easy to plot your own values to individual locations. You'll probably still use the map( ) function, but you don't have to use ellipses or colors to plot your data points. You could draw an image at each location, varying its size based on the data. Or some points could be hidden or reorganize themselves in various ways. The points might refer to anything from chain coffee shops per capita to poverty levels in each state.

Taking Data from the User

Not everyone wants to employ data relating to the United States, but the same technique is sound for any type of data mapped to particular points. In later chapters, we'll get into mapping latitude and longitude coordinates, as well as using shape data for locations, but even the simple example presented in this chapter can be used in many other ways.

The following code reads from the *names.tsv* file and asks the user to indicate a location for each in turn, by clicking the mouse where the user wants the data to be placed. Start this example as a separate sketch. It requires a *map.png* file, a *names.tsv* file, and the *Table.pde* file used throughout this chapter. The map image and names file can be replaced with data of your choice, and this code produces a *locations.tsv* file that can be added to the *data* folder of the new sketch:

```
PImage mapImage;
Table nameTable;

int currentRow = -1;
PrintWriter writer;

void setup() {
  size(640, 400);
  mapImage = loadImage("map.png");
  nameTable = new Table("names.tsv");
  writer = createWriter("locations.tsv");
  cursor(CROSS);  // make easier to pinpoint a location
  println("Click the mouse to begin.");
}

void draw() {
  image(mapImage, 0, 0);
}

void mousePressed() {
  if (currentRow != -1) {
    String abbrev = nameTable.getRowName(currentRow);
    writer.println(abbrev + "\t" + mouseX + "\t" + mouseY);
  }

  currentRow++;
  if (currentRow == nameTable.getRowCount()) {
    // Close the file and finish.
    writer.flush();
    writer.close();
    exit();
  } else {
    // Ask for the next coordinate.
    String name = nameTable.getString(currentRow, 1);
    println("Choose location for " + name + ".");
  }
}
```

Next Steps

In this chapter, we learned the basics of reading, displaying, and interacting with a data set. The chapters that follow delve into far more sophisticated aspects of each, but all of them build on the basic skills you've picked up here.

CHAPTER 4

Time Series

The time series is a ubiquitous type of data set. It describes how some measurable feature (for instance, population, snowfall, or items sold) has changed over a period of time. Edward Tufte credits Johann Heinrich Lambert with the formal introduction of the time series to scientific literature in the 1700s.[*]

Because of its ubiquity, the time series is a good place to start when learning about visualization. With it we can cover:

- Acquiring a table of data from a text file
- Parsing the contents of the file into a usable data structure
- Calculating the boundaries of the data to facilitate representation
- Finding a suitable representation and considering alternatives
- Refining the representation with consideration for placement, type, line weight, and color
- Providing a means of interacting with the data so that we can compare variables against one another or against the average of the whole data set

For a straightforward data set, let's turn to the U.S. Department of Agriculture (USDA) for statistics on beverage consumption. Government sites are a terrific resource for data; see Chapter 9 for more information about them and other sources of data.

Most methods will be implemented "by hand" in this section. Further down the line, we'll make generalized code to handle different scenarios, such as reading a table from a file or placing labels and grid lines on a plot.

---

[*] Tufte, Edward R. *The Visual Display of Quantitative Information*. Cheshire, Conn.: Graphics Press, 1983.

Milk, Tea, and Coffee (Acquire and Parse)

The data set we use was originally downloaded from *http://www.ers.usda.gov/Data/FoodConsumption/FoodAvailQueriable.aspx*.

The page lets you define a query to download a data set of interest. The site claims that the data is in Excel format, but a glance at the contents of the resulting file shows that it's only an HTML file with an *.xls* extension that fools Excel into opening it. Rather than getting into the specifics of how to download and clean the data, I offer an already processed version here:

> *http://benfry.com/writing/series/milk-tea-coffee.tsv*

This data set contains three columns: the first for milk, the second for coffee, and the third for tea consumption in the United States from 1910 to 2004.

To read this file, use this modified version of the `Table` class from the previous chapter:

> *http://benfry.com/writing/series/FloatTable.pde*

The modified version handles data stored as `float` values, making it more efficient than the previous version, which simply converted the data whenever `getString()`, `getFloat()`, or `getInt()` were used.

Open Processing and start a new sketch. Add both files to the sketch by either dragging each into the editor window or using Sketch → Add File.

Cleaning the Table (Filter and Mine)

It's necessary to determine the minimum and maximum of each of the columns in the pre-filtered data set. These values are used to properly scale plotted points to locations on the screen.

The `FloatTable` class has methods for calculating the min and max for the rows and columns. These methods are worth discussing because they are important in later code. The following example calculates the minimum value for a column (comments denote important portions of the code):

```
float getColumnMax(int col) {
  // Set the value of m arbitrarily high, so the first value
  // found will be set as the maximum.
  float m = MIN_FLOAT;

  // Loop through each row.
  for (int row = 0; row < rowCount; row++) {

    // Only consider valid data elements (see later text).
    if (isValid(row, col)) {
```

```
      // Finally, check to see if the value
      // is greater than the maximum found so far.
      if (data[row][col] > m) {
        m = data[row][col];
      }
    }
  }
  return m;
}
```

The isValid( ) method is important because most data sets have incomplete data. In the *milk-tea-coffee.tsv* file, all of the data is valid, but in most data sets (including others used in this chapter), missing values require extra consideration.

Because the values for milk, coffee, and tea will be compared against one another, it's necessary to calculate the maximum value across all of the columns. The following bit of code does this after loading the *milk-tea-coffee.tsv* file:

```
FloatTable data;
float dataMin, dataMax;

void setup() {
  data = new FloatTable("milk-tea-coffee.tsv");

  dataMin = 0;
  dataMax = data.getTableMax();
}
```

Sometimes, it's also useful to calculate the minimum value, but setting the minimum to zero provides a more accurate comparison between the three data sets. The minimum for this data set is 5.1, and the values for the tea column hover around 6, so using 5.1 as the dataMin value would produce a chart that looked as though the beverage history included periods of no (or nearly no) tea consumption in the U.S. In addition, if the value is 6, it's important that the relative difference seen by the viewer is not just 0.9, but that it shows the full range from 0 up to 5.1 and how it compares to a value of 6.

Each row name specifies a year, which will be used later to draw labels on the plot. To make them useful in code, it's also necessary to get the minimum and maximum year after converting the entire group to an int array. The getRowNames( ) method inside FloatTable returns a String array that can be converted with the int( ) casting function:

```
FloatTable data;
float dataMin, dataMax;

int yearMin, yearMax;
int[] years;

void setup() {
  data = new FloatTable("milk-tea-coffee.tsv");
```

```
    years = int(data.getRowNames());
    yearMin = years[0];
    yearMax = years[years.length - 1];

    dataMin = 0;
    dataMax = data.getTableMax();
  }
```

A Simple Plot (Represent and Refine)

To begin the representation, it's first necessary to set the boundaries for the plot location. The plotX1, plotY1, plotX2, and plotY2 variables define the corners of the plot. To provide a nice margin on the left, set plotX1 to 50, and then set the plotX2 coordinate by subtracting this value from width. This keeps the two sides even, and requires only a single change to adjust the position of both. The same technique is used for the vertical location of the plot:

```
FloatTable data;
float dataMin, dataMax;

float plotX1, plotY1;
float plotX2, plotY2;

int yearMin, yearMax;
int[] years;


void setup() {
  size(720, 405);

  data = new FloatTable("milk-tea-coffee.tsv");

  years = int(data.getRowNames());
  yearMin = years[0];
  yearMax = years[years.length - 1];

  dataMin = 0;
  dataMax = data.getTableMax();

  // Corners of the plotted time series
  plotX1 = 50;
  plotX2 = width - plotX1;
  plotY1 = 60;
  plotY2 = height - plotY1;

  smooth();
}
```

Next, add a draw() method that sets the background to a light gray and draws a filled white rectangle for the plotting area. That will make the plot stand out against the background, rather than a color behind the plot itself—which can muddy its appearance.

The `rect()` function normally takes the form `rect(x, y, width, height)`, but `rectMode(CORNERS)` changes the parameters to `rect(left, top, right, bottom)`, which is useful because our plot's shape is defined by the corners. Like other methods that affect drawing properties, such as `fill()` and `stroke()`, `rectMode()` affects all geometry that is drawn after it until the next time `rectMode()` is called:

```
void draw() {
  background(224);

  // Show the plot area as a white box.
  fill(255);
  rectMode(CORNERS);
  noStroke();
  rect(plotX1, plotY1, plotX2, plotY2);

  strokeWeight(5);
  // Draw the data for the first column.
  stroke(#5679C1);
  drawDataPoints(0);
}


// Draw the data as a series of points.
void drawDataPoints(int col) {
  int rowCount = data.getRowCount();
  for (int row = 0; row < rowCount; row++) {
    if (data.isValid(row, col)) {
      float value = data.getFloat(row, col);
      float x = map(years[row], yearMin, yearMax, plotX1, plotX2);
      float y = map(value, dataMin, dataMax, plotY2, plotY1);
      point(x, y);
    }
  }
}
```

Because the data is drawn as points using the `drawDataPoints()` method, a stroke color and weight are set. This method also takes a column index to draw as a parameter. The results are in Figure 4-1. For the first step, I've shown only the first column of data (the values for milk consumption).

The `map()` function does most of the work. The x coordinate is calculated by mapping the year for each row from `yearMin` and `yearMax` to `plotX1` and `plotX2`. Another option would be to use the `row` variable, instead of the year:

```
float x = map(row, 0, rowCount-1, plotX1, plotX2);
```

But a value for `row` would be less accurate because a year or two might be missing from the data set, which would skew the representation. Again, this data set is complete, but often that is not the case.

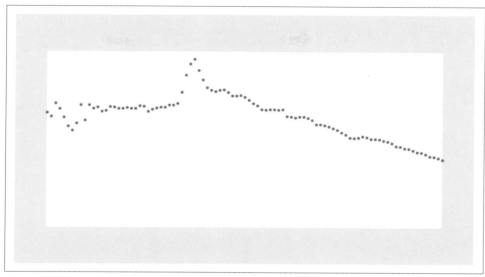

Figure 4-1. One set of points over time

Labeling the Current Data Set (Refine and Interact)

Missing from the previous code is an indicator of the currently visible column of data (whether milk, tea, or coffee) and a means to swap between each of the three. For this, we add a variable to keep track of the current column, and another for the font used for the title. And few lines of code are added to the draw( ) method to write the name of the column with the text( ) method:

```
FloatTable data;
float dataMin, dataMax;

float plotX1, plotY1;
float plotX2, plotY2;

int currentColumn = 0;
int columnCount;

int yearMin, yearMax;
int[] years;

PFont plotFont;


void setup( ) {
  size(720, 405);
```

```
data = new FloatTable("milk-tea-coffee.tsv");
columnCount = data.getColumnCount( );

years = int(data.getRowNames( ));
yearMin = years[0];
yearMax = years[years.length - 1];

dataMin = 0;
dataMax = data.getTableMax( );

// Corners of the plotted time series
plotX1 = 50;
plotX2 = width - plotX1;
plotY1 = 60;
plotY2 = height - plotY1;

plotFont = createFont("SansSerif", 20);
textFont(plotFont);

smooth( );
}


void draw( ) {
  background(224);

  // Show the plot area as a white box.
  fill(255);
  rectMode(CORNERS);
  noStroke( );
  rect(plotX1, plotY1, plotX2, plotY2);

  // Draw the title of the current plot.
  fill(0);
  textSize(20);
  String title = data.getColumnName(currentColumn);
  text(title, plotX1, plotY1 - 10);

  stroke(#5679C1);
  strokeWeight(5);
  drawDataPoints(currentColumn);
}
```

The text( ) line draws the text 10 pixels above plotY1, which represents the top of
the plot, and the drawDataPoints( ) line uses currentColumn instead of just 0. Results
are shown in Figure 4-2.

The createFont( ) function is used to create a font from one of the built-in typefaces.
The built-in typefaces are Serif, SansSerif, Monospaced, Dialog, and DialogInput;
they map to the default fonts on each operating system. On Mac OS X, for instance,
SansSerif maps to Lucida Sans, whereas on Windows it maps to Arial. The default
fonts are useful when you don't want to deal with the Create Font tool, but the font

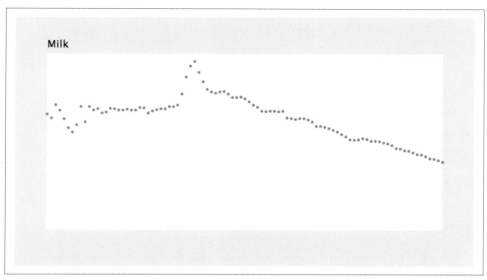

Milk

Figure 4-2. Time series with data set labeled

choices are not particularly inspiring, and they don't guarantee consistent output across different operating systems. For instance, making pixel-level decisions with a built-in font is a bad idea because the shaping and spacing of the characters can be significantly different on other operating systems.

One advantage of using `createFont()` is that the text will look smooth at any size, unlike a font used with `loadFont()`, which may be distorted as it is resized.

It is possible to use `createFont()` to specify something besides a built-in font, but there's no guarantee that the font will be installed on another user's system. This can be useful for testing, after which you can use the Create Font tool before deployment. The name of a font used by `createFont()` should be identical to how it is listed in the Create Font tool. You can also get a list of the available fonts with the `PFont.list()` method, which returns a `String` array. The following will print the list of all available fonts to the console:

```
println(PFont.list());
```

 If you have a lot of fonts installed on your system, there might be a long delay before they are listed.

The `createFont()` method can also be used with a TrueType (*.ttf*) or OpenType (*.otf*) file added to the *data* folder. Most TrueType fonts will work, but OpenType support varies by platform. Be mindful of copyrighted fonts when using this method in a sketch for public distribution.

A simple means of swapping between columns of data is to add a keyPressed( ) method, which will automatically run any time a key is pressed:

```
void keyPressed( ) {
  if (key == '[') {
    currentColumn--;
    if (currentColumn < 0) {
      currentColumn = columnCount - 1;
    }
  } else if (key == ']') {
    currentColumn++;
    if (currentColumn == columnCount) {
      currentColumn = 0;
    }
  }
}
```

This method will rotate through the columns as the user presses the [and] (bracket) keys. When the number gets too big or too small, it wraps around to the beginning or end of the list. Because columnCount is 3, the possible currentColumn values are 0, 1, and 2. So, when currentColumn reaches a value less than zero, it wraps around to 2 (columnCount - 1).

Drawing Axis Labels (Refine)

An unlabeled plot has minimal utility. It clearly displays relative up or down swings, but without a sense of the time period or amounts to indicate the degree of swing, it's impossible to know whether values have changed by, say, 5% or 50%. And some indication is required to explain that the horizontal axis represents the year and the vertical axis represents actual volumes: the amount consumed of a particular beverage, measured in gallons per capita per year.

There are clever (and complicated) means of selecting intervals, but for this project, we will pick the interval by hand. Choosing a proper interval and deciding whether to include major and minor tick marks depends on the data, but a general rule of thumb is that five intervals is at the low end, and more than ten is likely a problem. Too many labels make the diagram look like graph paper, and too few suggests that only the minimum and maximum values need to be shown.

The most important consideration is the way the data is used. Are minute, year-by-year comparisons needed? Always use the fewest intervals you can get away with, as long as the plot shows the level of detail the reader needs. Sometimes no labels are necessary—if values are only meant to be compared against one another. For instance, you might dispense with labels if you want to show only upward and downward trends. Other factors, such as the width of the plot, also play a role, so determining the correct level of detail usually requires a little trial and error.

Year Labels

Creating the year axis is straightforward. The data ranges from 1910 to 2004, so an interval of 10 years means marking 10 individual years: 1910, 1920, 1930, and so on, up to 2000. Add the yearInterval variable to the beginning of the code before setup( ):

```
int yearInterval = 10;
```

Next, add the following function to draw the year labels:

```
void drawYearLabels( ) {
  fill(0);
  textSize(10);
  textAlign(CENTER, TOP);
  for (int row = 0; row < rowCount; row++) {
    if (years[row] % yearInterval == 0) {
      float x = map(years[row], yearMin, yearMax, plotX1, plotX2);
      text(years[row], x, plotY2 + 10);
    }
  }
}
```

The fill color is set to black, the text size to 10, and the alignment to the middle so that the year number centers on the position of the data point for that year.

Two lines in this code deserve further consideration. The first is the line that makes use of the %, or *modulo*, operator. A modulo operation returns the remainder from a division. So, for example, 7 % 2 is equal to 1, and 8 % 5 equals 3. It's useful for drawing labels because it provides a way to easily identify a year ending in 0. Dividing 1910 by 10 returns 0, so a label is drawn, whereas dividing 1911 by 10 produces 1, and so it continues until the loop reaches 1920, which also returns 0 when divided by 10.

A second parameter to textAlign( ) sets the vertical alignment of the text. The options are TOP, BOTTOM, CENTER, and BASELINE (the default). The TOP and CENTER parameters are straightforward. The BOTTOM parameter is the same as BASELINE when only one line of text is used, but for multiple lines, the final line will be aligned to the baseline, with the previous lines appearing above it. When only one parameter is used, the vertical alignment resets to BASELINE.

The resulting image is shown in Figure 4-3.

 To draw text that does not bump into the elements above it, you need to know the height of the tallest character in the font. Typographers refer to this as the *ascent*. Traditionally, the ascent of a font is the height to the top of a capital H character. Characters such as the capital O or a capital B are in fact slightly taller than the letter H and dip slightly below the *baseline*—the bottom line from which text is drawn. The ascent value essentially refers to the *optical* height of the font, which is the height perceived by our eyes.

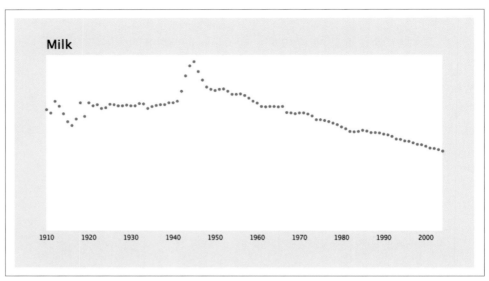

Figure 4-3. Time series with labeled x-axis

Simple grid lines can also help the presentation by identifying each interval. The following modifications add a grid to the drawYearLabels( ) function:

```
void drawYearLabels( ) {
  fill(0);
  textSize(10);
  textAlign(CENTER, TOP);

  // Use thin, gray lines to draw the grid.
  stroke(224);
  strokeWeight(1);

  for (int row = 0; row < rowCount; row++) {
    if (years[row] % yearInterval == 0) {
      float x = map(years[row], yearMin, yearMax, plotX1, plotX2);
      text(years[row], x, plotY2 + 10);
      line(x, plotY1, x, plotY2);
    }
  }
}
```

Figure 4-4 shows the result.

Notice that because the fill color does not affect lines, and a stroke color does not affect text, it is not necessary to use noFill( ) or noStroke( ) in this method.

With a separate method to draw the year labels, it makes sense to put the code that draws the title into its own method. The drawTitle( ) method takes this code from the draw( ) function. Just replace the title drawing code inside draw( ) with:

```
drawTitle( );
```

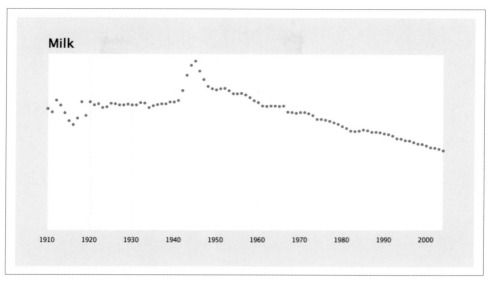

Figure 4-4. Time series with vertical grid

and then add the following method to the code:

```
void drawTitle() {
  fill(0);
  textSize(20);
  textAlign(LEFT);
  String title = data.getColumnName(currentColumn);
  text(title, plotX1, plotY1 - 10);
}
```

Because the drawYearLabels() function changes the text alignment, a line is added to reset to textAlign(LEFT) before drawing the title. Otherwise, the title would appear centered at plotX1 on the next trip through the draw() method, inheriting the text alignment settings from the previous draw().

Labeling Volume on the Vertical Axis

The vertical axis can be handled the same way as the horizontal, but it is a bit trickier. A quick println(dataMax) added to setup() tells us that the maximum value is 46.4. Intervals of 10 will again suffice, this time producing only 5 divisions (as opposed to 10 in the horizontal):

```
int volumeInterval = 10;
```

With a dataMax value of 46.4 and intervals of 10, rounding up dataMax to the nearest interval will make the maximum value on the plot 50, making it a little easier to read changes in vertical values. To do so automatically, divide dataMax by volumeInterval.

The result is 4.64. Next, use ceil( ), which rounds a float up to the next int value (in this case, 5), called the *ceiling* of a float. Then, set dataMax to the rounded value multiplied by volumeInterval. That calculation took a few sentences to explain, but the code consists of a one-line change to setup( ):

```
dataMax = ceil(data.getTableMax( ) / volumeInterval) * volumeInterval;
```

To draw the labels, create a loop that iterates from the minimum to maximum data values. Use an increment of volumeInterval to draw a label at each interval:

```
void drawVolumeLabels( ) {
  fill(0);
  textSize(10);
  textAlign(RIGHT, CENTER);

  for (float v = dataMin; v <= dataMax; v += volumeInterval) {
    float y = map(v, dataMin, dataMax, plotY2, plotY1);
    text(floor(v), plotX1 - 10, y);
  }
}
```

When you're drawing the text label, the floor( ) function removes decimals from the number value because there's no need to write 10.0, 20.0, 30.0, etc. when 10, 20, and 30 will suffice. If dataInterval included decimal points, the nf( ) method could be used instead to format the value to a specific number of decimal places.

 The text( ) method can draw int or float values instead of just String objects. For float values, it is best to use the nf( ) method to first convert the float to a specific number of decimal places. By default, text( ) will format a float to three decimal places. That is different from Java, which can have many digits in the decimal place for a float, because using just a few digits is usually more useful for a graphical display. To get the full 4-, 8-, or 15-digit version of the float value, use the str( ) function to convert the float to a String. For Java programmers, using str( ) is equivalent to String.valueOf( ).

The x-coordinate of the label text is the lefthand edge of the plot minus a few pixels. Also note the use of textAlign( ) to vertically center the text.

With the vertical centering, the label drawn at 0 is visually a little too close to the year markers below. In its current state, this example is not detailed enough to be used for real analysis and is better at showing upward and downward trends. In that context, it's clear from a glance that the bottom of the plot is 0, so the bottom label could be left out completely. The same goes for the top value, which gets close to the title. To leave these out, alter the first value drawn by adding a volumeInterval to dataMin, and end the loop at v < dataMax instead of v <= dataMax so that the 50 won't be drawn:

```
void drawVolumeLabels( ) {
  fill(0);
  textSize(10);
  textAlign(RIGHT, CENTER);
```

```
    float dataFirst = dataMin + volumeInterval;
    for (float v = dataFirst; v < dataMax; v += volumeInterval) {
      float y = map(v, dataMin, dataMax, plotY2, plotY1);
      text(floor(v), plotX1 - 10, y);
    }
  }
```

In other cases, it might not be appropriate to remove upper and lower values. If dataMin were something other than 0, or the intervals more awkward than simple intervals of 10, viewers might be confused without the minimum and maximum values. In such cases, the maximum value (50) can be vertically aligned to the top of the plot, and the minimum value (0) to the bottom, rather than centered vertically like the rest of the labels:

```
void drawVolumeLabels() {
  fill(0);
  textSize(10);

  for (float v = dataMin; v <= dataMax; v += volumeInterval) {
    float y = map(v, dataMin, dataMax, plotY2, plotY1);
    if (v == dataMin) {
      textAlign(RIGHT); // Align by the bottom
    } else if (v == dataMax) {
      textAlign(RIGHT, TOP); // Align by the top
    } else {
      textAlign(RIGHT, CENTER); // Center vertically
    }
    text(floor(v), plotX1 - 10, y);
  }
}
```

Horizontal lines can be fashioned in the same manner as those for the year. Choosing whether to use a horizontal or vertical grid depends on the axis with data that is most important to be measured. If this plot is being used to analyze exact changes in milk consumption, the horizontal gridlines will better help with identifying changes. But if the purpose is to compare upward and downward trends across different years (for instance, to understand how milk consumption changed during and after World War II), the vertical gridlines are more valuable. For this data set, it's most interesting to compare changes over the years, so we'll stick with vertical lines.

Instead of gridlines, small tick marks near the labels on the vertical axis can be produced with the same technique, by drawing a short line just outside the edge of the plot. Minor gridlines or tick marks can be drawn by including a variable for a second interval that's a multiple of the first and incrementing by that interval in the loop. The following modification to drawVolumeLabels() adds major and minor tick marks to the volume axis:

```
int volumeIntervalMinor = 5; // Add this above setup()

void drawVolumeLabels() {
  fill(0);
  textSize(10);
```

```
stroke(128);
strokeWeight(1);

for (float v = dataMin; v <= dataMax; v += volumeIntervalMinor) {
  float y = map(v, dataMin, dataMax, plotY2, plotY1);
  if (v % volumeInterval == 0) { // If a major tick mark
    if (v == dataMin) {
      textAlign(RIGHT); // Align by the bottom
    } else if (v == dataMax) {
      textAlign(RIGHT, TOP); // Align by the top
    } else {
      textAlign(RIGHT, CENTER); // Center vertically
    }
    text(floor(v), plotX1 - 10, y);
    line(plotX1 - 4, y, plotX1, y); // Draw major tick
  } else {
    line(plotX1 - 2, y, plotX1, y); // Draw minor tick
  }
}
}
```

The result with the tick marks and vertical labels is shown in Figure 4-5.

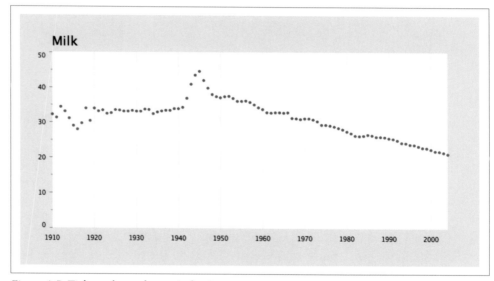

Figure 4-5. Tick marks on the vertical axis

Strictly speaking, the minor tickmarks in this example are not very informative. They can be removed to avoid visual clutter; simply comment out the line that draws the minor ticks.

Bringing It All Together and Titling Both Axes

So far, anyone looking at this diagram should be able to guess that it has something to do with milk from 1910 to sometime after 2000. To further explain the plot, the next step is to provide titles for the year and volume axes. Informative axis titles are important for the people viewing your data.

The year axis title is simple: just a piece of text centered between plotX1 and plotX2. After centering the text in both directions with textAlign(CENTER, CENTER), the text is drawn centered between plotY1 and plotY2. To fit both, the values for plotX1 and friends must be changed to make room for the labels. In this case, eyeballing the placement is sufficient, though textWidth( ) could be used to accurately size the left-hand margin, and textAscent( ) could do the same for the label below.

For the vertical axis, it might be tempting to rotate the title on its side, but more often than not it is more effective at giving your viewer eyestrain than it is at communicating. I've kept the text horizontal and broken the label into three lines by inserting newline characters (\n) into the string.

Figure 4-6 shows our progress.

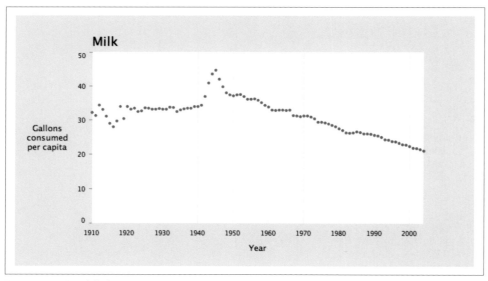

Figure 4-6. Axis labels

Here's the code listing for the program thus far, with the lines highlighted that were altered to display the titles:

```
FloatTable data;
float dataMin, dataMax;
```

```
float plotX1, plotY1;
float plotX2, plotY2;
float labelX, labelY;

int rowCount;
int columnCount;
int currentColumn = 0;

int yearMin, yearMax;
int[] years;

int yearInterval = 10;
int volumeInterval = 10;
int volumeIntervalMinor = 5;

PFont plotFont;


void setup() {
  size(720, 405);

  data = new FloatTable("milk-tea-coffee.tsv");
  rowCount = data.getRowCount();
  columnCount = data.getColumnCount();

  years = int(data.getRowNames());
  yearMin = years[0];
  yearMax = years[years.length - 1];

  dataMin = 0;
  dataMax = ceil(data.getTableMax() / volumeInterval) * volumeInterval;

  // Corners of the plotted time series
  plotX1 = 120;
  plotX2 = width - 80;
  labelX = 50;
  plotY1 = 60;
  plotY2 = height - 70;
  labelY = height - 25;

  plotFont = createFont("SansSerif", 20);
  textFont(plotFont);

  smooth();
}


void draw() {
  background(224);

  // Show the plot area as a white box
  fill(255);
  rectMode(CORNERS);
  noStroke();
  rect(plotX1, plotY1, plotX2, plotY2);
```

```
  drawTitle();
  drawAxisLabels();

  drawYearLabels();
  drawVolumeLabels();

  stroke(#5679C1);
  strokeWeight(5);
  drawDataPoints(currentColumn);
}


void drawTitle() {
  fill(0);
  textSize(20);
  textAlign(LEFT);
  String title = data.getColumnName(currentColumn);
  text(title, plotX1, plotY1 - 10);
}


void drawAxisLabels() {
  fill(0);
  textSize(13);
  textLeading(15);

  textAlign(CENTER, CENTER);
  // Use \n (aka enter or linefeed) to break the text into separate lines.
  text("Gallons\nconsumed\nper capita", labelX, (plotY1+plotY2)/2);
  textAlign(CENTER);
  text("Year", (plotX1+plotX2)/2, labelY);
}


void drawYearLabels() {
  fill(0);
  textSize(10);
  textAlign(CENTER, TOP);

  // Use thin, gray lines to draw the grid.
  stroke(224);
  strokeWeight(1);

  for (int row = 0; row < rowCount; row++) {
    if (years[row] % yearInterval == 0) {
      float x = map(years[row], yearMin, yearMax, plotX1, plotX2);
      text(years[row], x, plotY2 + 10);
      line(x, plotY1, x, plotY2);
    }
  }
}

void drawVolumeLabels() {
  fill(0);
  textSize(10);
```

```
    stroke(128);
    strokeWeight(1);

    for (float v = dataMin; v <= dataMax; v += volumeIntervalMinor) {
      float y = map(v, dataMin, dataMax, plotY2, plotY1);
      if (v % volumeInterval == 0) { // If a major tick mark
        if (v == dataMin) {
          textAlign(RIGHT); // Align by the bottom
        } else if (v == dataMax) {
          textAlign(RIGHT, TOP); // Align by the top
        } else {
          textAlign(RIGHT, CENTER); // Center vertically
        }
        text(floor(v), plotX1 - 10, y);
        line(plotX1 - 4, y, plotX1, y); // Draw major tick
      } else {
        // Commented out; too distracting visually
        //line(plotX1 - 2, y, plotX1, y); // Draw minor tick
      }
    }
  }

  void drawDataPoints(int col) {
    for (int row = 0; row < rowCount; row++) {
      if (data.isValid(row, col)) {
        float value = data.getFloat(row, col);
        float x = map(years[row], yearMin, yearMax, plotX1, plotX2);
        float y = map(value, dataMin, dataMax, plotY2, plotY1);
        point(x, y);
      }
    }
  }

  void keyPressed() {
    if (key == '[') {
      currentColumn--;
      if (currentColumn < 0) {
        currentColumn = columnCount - 1;
      }
    } else if (key == ']') {
      currentColumn++;
      if (currentColumn == columnCount) {
        currentColumn = 0;
      }
    }
  }
```

Choosing a Proper Representation (Represent and Refine)

A series of points can be difficult to follow if they're not connected. It's not as easy to compare milk and coffee in these images, for instance, because the predominant difference between the two plots is that the coffee values are far more erratic than those for milk. Instead of a specific shape, the points make an indeterminate cloud that is difficult to make sense of at a quick glance.

When values are truly a series and there is no missing data, it's possible to use a line graph and simply connect the points. The beginShape() and endShape() methods provide a means for drawing irregular shapes. The vertex() method adds a single point to the shape. To connect the dots in a line, replace the point() method with vertex().

Three examples follow that show the basic drawing modes of beginShape() and endShape(). See Figure 4-7. Using noFill() will produce the image at left, and the default fill and stroke settings will produce the image in the center. The CLOSE parameter in the endShape() method handles the connection of the final point to the first, so that the stroke completely outlines the shape. Always use endShape(CLOSE) when closing a shape because the alternative—repeating the first point—may cause unexpected visual defects.

Figure 4-7. Examples using beginShape() and endShape()

```
// Leftmost image: fill disabled and the default stroke
noFill();
beginShape();
vertex(10, 10);
vertex(90, 30);
vertex(40, 90);
vertex(50, 40);
endShape();

// Center image: default fill (white) and stroke (black)
beginShape();
vertex(10, 10);
vertex(90, 30);
vertex(40, 90);
vertex(50, 40);
endShape();
```

```
// Rightmost image: default fill and stroke, closed shape
beginShape();
vertex(10, 10);
vertex(90, 30);
vertex(40, 90);
vertex(50, 40);
endShape(CLOSE);
```

To represent a time series, we want a simple line with no fill, so we'll use the nofill()
form of the shape. The following method is a variation of drawPoints() that draws the
data with beginShape() and endShape(), with the alterations highlighted:

```
void drawDataLine(int col) {
  beginShape();
  int rowCount = data.getRowCount();
  for (int row = 0; row < rowCount; row++) {
    if (data.isValid(row, col)) {
      float value = data.getFloat(row, col);
      float x = map(years[row], yearMin, yearMax, plotX1, plotX2);
      float y = map(value, dataMin, dataMax, plotY2, plotY1);
      vertex(x, y);
    }
  }
  endShape();
}
```

Inside draw(), comment out the line that reads:

```
drawDataPoints(currentColumn);
```

by placing a pair of slashes (//) in front of it. On the line that follows, add:

```
noFill();
drawDataLine(currentColumn);
```

The noFill() command is important; without it, the shape would have a strange black
background because the fill was last set to black in the prior lines that draw the text
label for the plot. This version of the code produces the image shown in Figure 4-8.

It could also be used to draw all three series (milk, tea, and coffee) on a single plot.
To do this, call drawDataLine() once for each of the three columns, and set a different stroke color for each.

It's also easy to mix lines and points in the representation to create a background line
that highlights the individual data points. To do so, set the stroke weight to
something smaller while drawing the lines and keep the thicker weight for the points.
Modify the end of draw() to read as follows:

```
stroke(#5679C1);
strokeWeight(5);
drawDataPoints(currentColumn);
noFill();
strokeWeight(0.5);
drawDataLine(currentColumn);
```

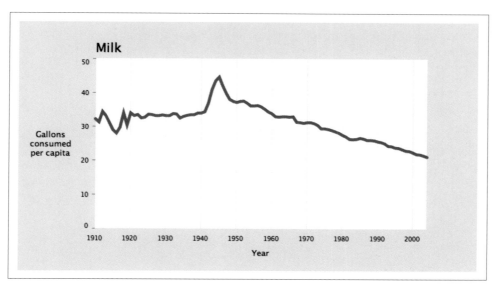

Figure 4-8. Continuously drawn time series using vertices

The result appears in Figure 4-9.

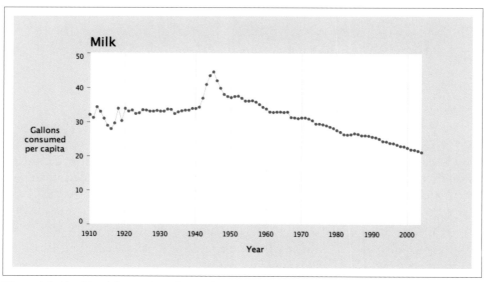

Figure 4-9. Combined dots and continuous line

Note that the functions themselves should not be merged, as other shape commands (such as point( )) are not permitted inside a beginShape( ) and endShape( ) block.

Depending on how you use this code, it may be important to draw the points after the lines. For example, if you set the stroke of the line to a light gray, it would be best to draw the blue points on top of the line so that the points are not bisected by an odd gray line (which has poor contrast with blue).

Using Rollovers to Highlight Points (Interact)

The lines and points combination is overkill for this data set: there are so many data points horizontally that the individual dots (at a size of five pixels) are nearly the size of the space allotted for each data point (around seven pixels), leaving only two pixels between them. Another option is to highlight individual points when the mouse is nearby. This is technique is nearly identical to the one used at the end of the previous chapter, and the function looks like the following:

```
void drawDataHighlight(int col) {
  for (int row = 0; row < rowCount; row++) {
    if (data.isValid(row, col)) {
      float value = data.getFloat(row, col);
      float x = map(years[row], yearMin, yearMax, plotX1, plotX2);
      float y = map(value, dataMin, dataMax, plotY2, plotY1);
      if (dist(mouseX, mouseY, x, y) < 3) {
        strokeWeight(10);
        point(x, y);
        fill(0);
        textSize(10);
        textAlign(CENTER);
        text(nf(value, 0, 2) + " (" + years[row] + ")", x, y-8);
      }
    }
  }
}
```

The stroke weight for the point is set to 10 because the weight used in the drawDataPoints() method (5) would not contrast enough with the rest of the image. Similarly, the stroke weight for the lines is set to 2, rather than the 0.5 stroke used when combining drawDataLines() and drawDataPoints(), because it should stand out more. But strokeWeight(2) is still thinner than the strokeWeight(5) used when the drawDataLines() method is run by itself because if the line itself is too thick, the rollover won't be prominent enough.

The modified draw() method to draw the highlight follows:

```
void draw() {
  background(224);

  // Show the plot area as a white box.
  fill(255);
  rectMode(CORNERS);
  noStroke();
  rect(plotX1, plotY1, plotX2, plotY2);
```

```
    drawTitle();
    drawAxisLabels();

    drawYearLabels();
    drawVolumeLabels();

    stroke(#5679C1);
    noFill();
    strokeWeight(2);
    drawDataLine(currentColumn);
    drawDataHighlight(currentColumn);
}
```

An image of the result is shown in Figure 4-10.

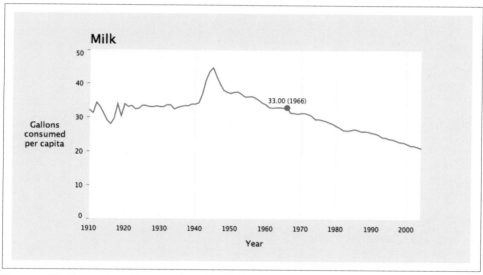

Figure 4-10. Time series with user-selected highlight

Ways to Connect Points (Refine)

Connecting the points with a curve is often a better option because it prevents the spikiness of the plot from overwhelming the data itself. The curveVertex( ) function is similar to the vertex( ) function, except that it connects successive points by fitting them to a curve.

The drawDataCurve( ) method, a modification of drawDataLine( ), follows:

```
void drawDataCurve(int col) {
  beginShape();
  for (int row = 0; row < rowCount; row++) {
    if (data.isValid(row, col)) {
      float value = data.getFloat(row, col);
```

```
      float x = map(years[row], yearMin, yearMax, plotX1, plotX2);
      float y = map(value, dataMin, dataMax, plotY2, plotY1);

      curveVertex(x, y);
      // Double the curve points for the start and stop
      if ((row == 0) || (row == rowCount-1)) {
        curveVertex(x, y);
      }
    }
  }
  endShape();
}
```

To draw a curve with curveVertex( ), at least four points are necessary because the first and last coordinates in curveVertex( ) are used to guide the angle at which the curve begins and ends. In this particular example, doubling start and stop points will work fine. In other cases, additional points can be used to maintain continuity between two connected curves.

The results of using a smooth curve can be seen most clearly when comparing the coffee data drawn with vertex( ) and curveVertex( ) in Figure 4-11.

Showing Data As an Area

Another variation of drawDataLine( ) draws the values as a filled area. Before calling endShape( ), add the lower-right corner and then the lower-left corner to complete the outline of the shape to be filled. And instead of endShape( ) with no parameters, use endShape(CLOSE) to close it, reconnecting it to the first vertex.

The new drawDataArea( ) function is:

```
void drawDataArea(int col) {
  beginShape();
  for (int row = 0; row < rowCount; row++) {
    if (data.isValid(row, col)) {
      float value = data.getFloat(row, col);
      float x = map(years[row], yearMin, yearMax, plotX1, plotX2);
      float y = map(value, dataMin, dataMax, plotY2, plotY1);
      vertex(x, y);
    }
  }
  // Draw the lower-right and lower-left corners.
  vertex(plotX2, plotY2);
  vertex(plotX1, plotY2);
  endShape(CLOSE);
}
```

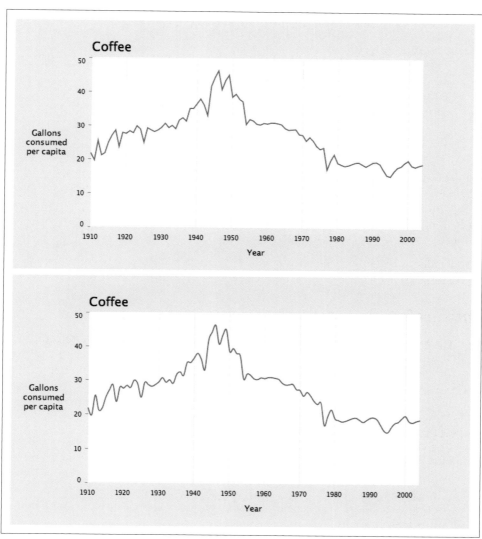

Figure 4-11. Comparison of the use of vertices (top) and curve vertices (bottom)

Next, modify the end of the draw( ) method to replace the stroke(#5679C1) line with fill(#5679C1), and change noFill( ) to noStroke( ); drawing an outline around an already filled shape is unnecessary:

```
noStroke();
fill(#5679C1);
drawDataArea(currentColumn);
```

The new plot is shown in Figure 4-12.

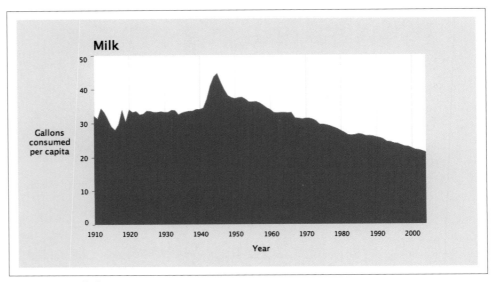

Figure 4-12. Filled time series

This makes a more attractive plot, and because the data set considers the actual volume of consumption—that is, the vertical axis starts at 0—it makes sense to fill the area beneath the data points. Whenever filling a plot, consider whether the data being shown refers to some kind of actual area or volume. For instance, it would not be appropriate to fill the area beneath a plot of temperature because the lower bound is arbitrary (unless you're measuring temperatures above absolute zero). A graph of rainfall, however, refers to the actual volume or amount that can be measured upward from "none," making it a candidate for a filled plot.

Further Refinements and Erasing Elements

The highest priority of any information graphic is to place the data it represents first and foremost. A filled area can seem too much like the background, so sometimes it's best to remove the background. Without the gray background, the grid lines become awkward without some kind of box around them to contain the plot. A box adds no additional usefulness, just clutters the composition, so a better option is to remove the background and make the gridlines part of the graphic itself by setting their color to white. To draw the gridlines on top of the data, move the drawYearLabels() method after drawDataArea() inside draw() so that the grid lines will be drawn after the filled shape. The new draw() method is very sparse:

```
void draw() {
  background(255);

  drawTitle();
  drawAxisLabels();
  drawVolumeLabels();

  noStroke();
  fill(#5679C1);
  drawDataArea(currentColumn);

  drawYearLabels();
}
```

Inside drawYearLabels(), use stroke(255) instead of stroke(224) to make the gridlines white. The results are shown in Figure 4-13.

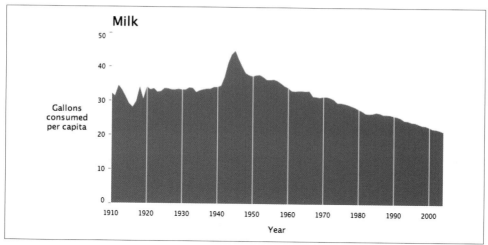

Figure 4-13. Unboxed plot with reverse-color gridlines

Such minimization of graphic elements has long been the province of those who champion a "less is more" approach to design. Edward Tufte later popularized this approach in his series of books on information graphics.

Discrete Values with a Bar Chart (Represent)

When values are discrete and cannot be shown in a series, a bar chart might be more suitable. A common example is when data is missing and therefore does not represent a complete series. Drawing a bar chart is a matter of using rectangles instead of individual points, and then drawing the data centered at each horizontal location.

The following replacement for drawDataArea( ) creates a bar chart:

```
float barWidth = 4; // Add to the top of the page, before end of setup( )

void drawDataBars(int col) {
  noStroke( );
  rectMode(CORNERS);

  for (int row = 0; row < rowCount; row++) {
    if (data.isValid(row, col)) {
      float value = data.getFloat(row, col);
      float x = map(years[row], yearMin, yearMax, plotX1, plotX2);
      float y = map(value, dataMin, dataMax, plotY2, plotY1);
      rect(x-barWidth/2, y, x+barWidth/2, plotY2);
    }
  }
}
```

Here, the barWidth variable makes the bars four pixels wide. Calculating widths for a bar chart can be done with algebra (by dividing the distance between plotX2 and plotX1 by the number of rows of data) or by trial and error.

It's also necessary to disable the lines drawn in drawYearLabels( ) because vertical grid lines will conflict with the bars.

Unfortunately, this is too much data to show at this width, resulting in the vibrating texture shown in Figure 4-14, which looks more like a swatch of patterned fabric.

This example highlights an important consideration: when deciding on a representation, use a bar chart only when there's enough room to leave clear gaps between bars.

Once a bar chart is laid out properly, the method of using white grid lines in Figure 4-13 could be better utilized to highlight the divisions on the left axis by erasing thin horizontal lines across the plot. Like the version that sliced the area plot into individual decades, this would provide another cue to help the viewer quickly read data values.

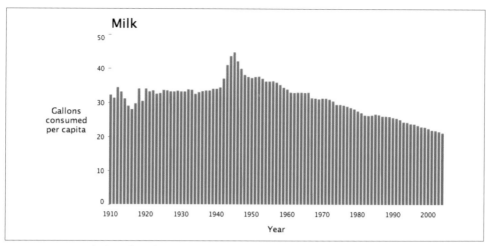

Figure 4-14. Overly busy bar chart

Text Labels As Tabbed Panes (Interact)

Using keys to navigate an interface should be used only during testing. A more sophisticated method is to use on-screen buttons, as users expect from a modern interface. This section describes how to replace the drawTitle( ) function with drawTitleTabs( ) to introduce a series of tabbed panel—one for each data series.

Adding the Necessary Variables

The tabTop and tabBottom variables specify the upper and lower edge of the tabs. The tabLeft and tabRight variables store the coordinates for the left and right edges of each tab so that we can detect mouse clicks inside the tabs. The tabPad variable specifies the amount of padding on the left and right of the tab text:

```
float[] tabLeft, tabRight; // Add above setup( )
float tabTop, tabBottom;
float tabPad = 10;
```

Drawing Tabs Instead of a Single Title

The important part of this method keeps track of a value named runningX to calculate the positions of each tab. The width of each tab is calculated using textWidth( ), and the tabPad value is added to provide padding on the sides:

```
void drawTitleTabs() {
  rectMode(CORNERS);
  noStroke();
  textSize(20);
  textAlign(LEFT);

  // On first use of this method, allocate space for an array
  // to store the values for the left and right edges of the tabs.
  if (tabLeft == null) {
    tabLeft = new float[columnCount];
    tabRight = new float[columnCount];
  }

  float runningX = plotX1;
  tabTop = plotY1 - textAscent() - 15;
  tabBottom = plotY1;

  for (int col = 0; col < columnCount; col++) {
    String title = data.getColumnName(col);
    tabLeft[col] = runningX;
    float titleWidth = textWidth(title);
    tabRight[col] = tabLeft[col] + tabPad + titleWidth + tabPad;

    // If the current tab, set its background white; otherwise use pale gray.
    fill(col == currentColumn ? 255 : 224);
    rect(tabLeft[col], tabTop, tabRight[col], tabBottom);

    // If the current tab, use black for the text; otherwise use dark gray.
    fill(col == currentColumn ? 0 : 64);
    text(title, runningX + tabPad, plotY1 - 10);

    runningX = tabRight[col];
  }
}
```

This piece of code also introduces the conditional operator, identified by the ?. The conditional statement:

```
fill(col == currentColumn ? 0 : 64);
```

is equivalent to writing:

```
if (col == currentColumn) {
  fill(0);
} else {
  fill(64);
}
```

The benefit of the former is compact code: a single line instead of five. The conditional operator is most useful in situations such as this one, where a simple if test is used to control something straightforward like the fill color. In this case, it can be argued that the shorter code is more readable than all five lines. However, use the conditional operator sparingly because overuse can result in code that is difficult to read.

Handling Mouse Input

Next, we'll add the mousePressed( ) method, which tests whether the mouse is inside one tab or another. This method is a simple matter of iterating through each tab and checking the mouseX and mouseY coordinates against the variables that contain the boundaries of each tab rectangle. If the mouseY value is in the correct range, mouseX is tested against each tabLeft and tabRight value. If inside, the value of currentColumn is updated with the setColumn( ) method:

```
void mousePressed() {
  if (mouseY > tabTop && mouseY < tabBottom) {
    for (int col = 0; col < columnCount; col++) {
      if (mouseX > tabLeft[col] && mouseX < tabRight[col]) {
        setColumn(col);
      }
    }
  }
}

void setColumn(int col) {
  if (col != currentColumn) {
    currentColumn = col;
  }
}
```

The setColumn( ) method is expressed in a separate piece of code because it will be modified in the next section, and the keyPressed( ) method should simply be removed.

Finally, the result is shown in Figure 4-15.

Better Tab Images (Refine)

The tabs in Figure 4-15 look pretty boring, but some tweaking of the text, the colors, and a line here and there could improve them. Another option is to load the tabs from a series of image files. Three separate image files would be used for the non-selected state of the tabs, and three others would be used for the selected state. Then, instead of setting the fill differently for the rectangle and the text title, one of the six images would be used in its place. A modified version of the code looks like this:

```
float[] tabLeft, tabRight; // Add above setup()
float tabTop, tabBottom;
float tabPad = 10;
PImage[] tabImageNormal;
```

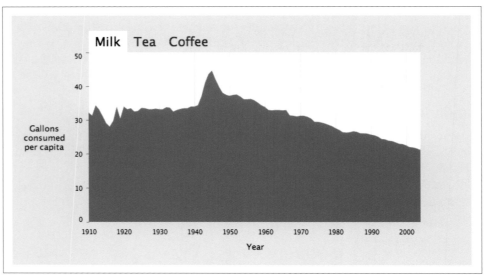

Figure 4-15. Clickable tabs

```
PImage[] tabImageHighlight;

void drawTitleTabs() {
  rectMode(CORNERS);
  noStroke();
  textSize(20);
  textAlign(LEFT);

  // Allocate the tab position array, and load the tab images.
  if (tabLeft == null) {
    tabLeft = new float[columnCount];
    tabRight = new float[columnCount];

    tabImageNormal = new PImage[columnCount];
    tabImageHighlight = new PImage[columnCount];
    for (int col = 0; col < columnCount; col++) {
      String title = data.getColumnName(col);
      tabImageNormal[col] = loadImage(title + "-unselected.png");
      tabImageHighlight[col] = loadImage(title + "-selected.png");
    }
  }

  float runningX = plotX1;
  tabBottom = plotY1;
  // Size based on the height of the tabs by checking the
  // height of the first (all images are the same height)
  tabTop = plotY1 - tabImageNormal[0].height;

  for (int col = 0; col < columnCount; col++) {
    String title = data.getColumnName(col);
    tabLeft[col] = runningX;
    float titleWidth = tabImageNormal[col].width;
```

```
    tabRight[col] = tabLeft[col] + tabPad + titleWidth + tabPad;

    PImage tabImage = (col == currentColumn) ?
      tabImageHighlight[col] : tabImageNormal[col];
    image(tabImage, tabLeft[col], tabTop);

    runningX = tabRight[col];
  }
}
```

When preparing the images, be sure to keep their heights the same. As with the text version, the widths of the titles can vary, but the width of the selected versus non-selected version should always be the same. The images should be named based on the title of each column, so, in this case, the following six files are used:

- *Milk-selected.png*
- *Tea-selected.png*
- *Coffee-selected.png*
- *Milk-unselected.png*
- *Tea-unselected.png*
- *Coffee-unselected.png*

For those who want to use standard interface components instead of making their own, later chapters cover integrating Processing with Java code. Custom components are useful when a unique interface is preferred, but they are less helpful if a standard interface is more appropriate for your audience.

Interpolation Between Data Sets (Interact)

Chapter 3 showed how to interpolate between values in a data set with the use of the Integrator class. Download itfrom *http://benfry.com/writing/series/Integrator.pde*.

The changes are identical to those in the previous chapter. First, declare the array of Integrator objects before setup( ):

```
Integrator[] interpolators;
```

Inside setup( ), create each Integrator and set its initial value:

```
interpolators = new Integrator[rowCount];
for (int row = 0; row < rowCount; row++) {
  float initialValue = data.getFloat(row, 0);
  interpolators[row] = new Integrator(initialValue);
  interpolators[row].attraction = 0.1; // Set lower than the default
}
```

The attraction value is set to 0.1 (instead of the default, 0.2) so that the interpolation occurs at a less frantic pace.

In draw( ), each Integrator is updated:

```
for (int row = 0; row < rowCount; row++) {
  interpolators[row].update( );
}
```

Next, for whatever variation of the drawData( ) function you would like to use, replace its data.getFloat( ) line. The original looks like this:

```
float value = data.getFloat(row, col);
```

Change the line to the following to use the interpolated values:

```
float value = interpolators[row].value;
```

Finally, modify setColumn( ) to set each Integrator to target the value for the current column:

```
void setColumn(int col) {
  currentColumn = col;

  for (int row = 0; row < rowCount; row++) {
    interpolators[row].target(data.getFloat(row, col));
  }
}
```

The final code, with modifications highlighted, follows:

```
FloatTable data;
float dataMin, dataMax;

float plotX1, plotY1;
float plotX2, plotY2;
float labelX, labelY;

int rowCount;
int columnCount;
int currentColumn = 0;

int yearMin, yearMax;
int[] years;

int yearInterval = 10;
int volumeInterval = 10;
int volumeIntervalMinor = 5;

float[] tabLeft, tabRight;
float tabTop, tabBottom;
float tabPad = 10;

Integrator[] interpolators;

PFont plotFont;


void setup( ) {
  size(720, 405);
```

```
  data = new FloatTable("milk-tea-coffee.tsv");
  rowCount = data.getRowCount( );
  columnCount = data.getColumnCount( );

  years = int(data.getRowNames( ));
  yearMin = years[0];
  yearMax = years[years.length - 1];

  dataMin = 0;
  dataMax = ceil(data.getTableMax( ) / volumeInterval) * volumeInterval;

  interpolators = new Integrator[rowCount];
  for (int row = 0; row < rowCount; row++) {
    float initialValue = data.getFloat(row, 0);
    interpolators[row] = new Integrator(initialValue);
    interpolators[row].attraction = 0.1; // Set lower than the default
  }

  plotX1 = 120;
  plotX2 = width - 80;
  labelX = 50;
  plotY1 = 60;
  plotY2 = height - 70;
  labelY = height - 25;

  plotFont = createFont("SansSerif", 20);
  textFont(plotFont);

  smooth( );
}


void draw( ) {
  background(224);

  // Show the plot area as a white box
  fill(255);
  rectMode(CORNERS);
  noStroke( );
  rect(plotX1, plotY1, plotX2, plotY2);

  drawTitleTabs( );
  drawAxisLabels( );

  for (int row = 0; row < rowCount; row++) {
    interpolators[row].update( );
  }

  drawYearLabels( );
  drawVolumeLabels( );

  noStroke( );
  fill(#5679C1);
  drawDataArea(currentColumn);
}
```

```
void drawTitleTabs( ) {
  rectMode(CORNERS);
  noStroke( );
  textSize(20);
  textAlign(LEFT);

  // On first use of this method, allocate space for an array
  // to store the values for the left and right edges of the tabs.
  if (tabLeft == null) {
    tabLeft = new float[columnCount];
    tabRight = new float[columnCount];
  }

  float runningX = plotX1;
  tabTop = plotY1 - textAscent( ) - 15;
  tabBottom = plotY1;

  for (int col = 0; col < columnCount; col++) {
    String title = data.getColumnName(col);
    tabLeft[col] = runningX;
    float titleWidth = textWidth(title);
    tabRight[col] = tabLeft[col] + tabPad + titleWidth + tabPad;

    // If the current tab, set its background white; otherwise use pale gray.
    fill(col == currentColumn ? 255 : 224);
    rect(tabLeft[col], tabTop, tabRight[col], tabBottom);

    // If the current tab, use black for the text; otherwise use dark gray.
    fill(col == currentColumn ? 0 : 64);
    text(title, runningX + tabPad, plotY1 - 10);

    runningX = tabRight[col];
  }
}


void mousePressed( ) {
  if (mouseY > tabTop && mouseY < tabBottom) {
    for (int col = 0; col < columnCount; col++) {
      if (mouseX > tabLeft[col] && mouseX < tabRight[col]) {
        setColumn(col);
      }
    }
  }
}


void setCurrent(int col) {
  currentColumn = col;

  for (int row = 0; row < rowCount; row++) {
    interpolators[row].target(data.getFloat(row, col));
  }
}
```

```
void drawAxisLabels() {
  fill(0);
  textSize(13);
  textLeading(15);

  textAlign(CENTER, CENTER);
  text("Gallons\nconsumed\nper capita", labelX, (plotY1+plotY2)/2);
  textAlign(CENTER);
  text("Year", (plotX1+plotX2)/2, labelY);
}


void drawYearLabels() {
  fill(0);
  textSize(10);
  textAlign(CENTER);

  // Use thin, gray lines to draw the grid
  stroke(224);
  strokeWeight(1);

  for (int row = 0; row < rowCount; row++) {
    if (years[row] % yearInterval == 0) {
      float x = map(years[row], yearMin, yearMax, plotX1, plotX2);
      text(years[row], x, plotY2 + textAscent() + 10);
      line(x, plotY1, x, plotY2);
    }
  }
}


void drawVolumeLabels() {
  fill(0);
  textSize(10);
  textAlign(RIGHT);

  stroke(128);
  strokeWeight(1);

  for (float v = dataMin; v <= dataMax; v += volumeIntervalMinor) {
    if (v % volumeIntervalMinor == 0) { // If a tick mark
      float y = map(v, dataMin, dataMax, plotY2, plotY1);
      if (v % volumeInterval == 0) { // If a major tick mark
        float textOffset = textAscent()/2; // Center vertically
        if (v == dataMin) {
          textOffset = 0; // Align by the bottom
        } else if (v == dataMax) {
          textOffset = textAscent(); // Align by the top
        }
        text(floor(v), plotX1 - 10, y + textOffset);
        line(plotX1 - 4, y, plotX1, y); // Draw major tick
      } else {
        //line(plotX1 - 2, y, plotX1, y); // Draw minor tick
```

```
        }
      }
    }
  }

  void drawDataArea(int col) {
    beginShape();
    for (int row = 0; row < rowCount; row++) {
      if (data.isValid(row, col)) {
        float value = interpolators[row].value;
        float x = map(years[row], yearMin, yearMax, plotX1, plotX2);
        float y = map(value, dataMin, dataMax, plotY2, plotY1);
        vertex(x, y);
      }
    }
    vertex(plotX2, plotY2);
    vertex(plotX1, plotY2);
    endShape(CLOSE);
  }
```

End of the Series

In this chapter, we looked at the most common form of data plot: the time series. The point was to get comfortable with functions such as map( ), pick up some principles on how to choose a representation, and see how a few lines of code can help produce an alternate representation or a more refined appearance. The techniques implemented here are useful for nearly any type of plot, as the algebra for placement and considerations for use will be identical across all other data sets that we examine.

Developers familiar with Processing or Java might want to make this code into a class. Classes are a useful means for encapsulating data sets. For instance, this code could be made into a class named TimeSeries to handle arbitrary data stored in a table. This might be a useful abstraction, but keep in mind how you customize the code once it's in a class. The final version of the program listing in this chapter is just over 200 lines (a little more than three printed pages). Once you've moved this code into a 200-line class, how do you keep it flexible? Do you modify it directly or subclass it? Is it necessary to create a new subclass for each new type of representation, when each new representation is between 5 and 20 lines apiece? Always weigh such decisions in terms of how the code will be used. If only one representation is required for your particular project, why bother maintaining multiple subclasses? Just do the representation right the first time. And when reusing the code in your next project, you'll probably change at least 10% of the base code anyway, so there's no need to maintain several subclasses. As our projects become more complicated, we'll do more to encapsulate code into modular units, while doing our best to avoid needless levels of abstraction.

Of course, there are libraries that allow you to plot data in a number of ways, particularly for simple things such as time series or bar charts. For Java coders, JFreeChart is a widely used example (see *http://www.jfree.org/jfreechart*). JFreeChart is a nice tool for basic charting and graphing, but it doesn't allow the kind of flexible customization taught here—which you are hopefully coming to appreciate. This book intends to teach you the starting point for drawing basic representations, such as a plot or chart, and then goes on to show how they can be manipulated in a more sophisticated manner than can be done with standard tools.

CHAPTER 5

Connections and Correlations

Data that varies across multiple dimensions is common, and it can be difficult to represent in traditional charts that exploit only the two dimensions of the screen or printed page. In particular, you often have an independent variable and a dependent variable that change over time. Many techniques for representing change exist, but one of the most engaging ways is animation.

In this chapter, we'll create a display of baseball results to explore how relationships can be instantly and powerfully conveyed through the spatial arrangement of data, visual elements such as icons and lines, and most significantly, the use of animation. You don't have to understand baseball to understand this chapter; it's less about the game than it is about the numbers and depicting those numbers.

The display used in this chapter is uniquely suited to the baseball data provided and the relationships within that data. You might choose to use a different sort of display for your data, but you can learn a lot by following the use of font, color, stroke weight, and other parameters shown here. The example demonstrates how to keep the basic goal of a display in mind and how to choose each element to meet that goal. Along the way, we'll see how to parse text data and convert it from simple plain-text files to internal formats that are easy for our program to mine. We'll also study how to mix text data (including numeric data) with lines and other visual elements and how to correlate parameters, such as dates, with physical screen positions that allow the user to control the display using the mouse.

Changing Data Sources

Data collection is significantly more involved here than in the other chapters, and we'll spend a lot more time learning about parsing HTML pages to acquire data, as well as exploring tools for parsing text data.

At times, the methods we're using will seem very specific to the data set we're looking at, which leaves us open to the danger of URLs changing or pages going out of date. But therein lies the point of the chapter: when the data source does change, you'll use similar methods to parse the updated information, and you need to understand how this process works so that you can effectively handle the new data. Chapters 9 and 10 also cover data acquisition and parsing in greater detail and provide a helpful guide for common practices. The same methods can be applied to all manner of information sources—even those that have nothing to do with baseball.

Problem Statement

In 2004, the Boston Red Sox won the World Series after an 86-year championship drought. As a Red Sox fan, this was a bittersweet victory in the sense that the Sox were the second-highest-paid team in baseball and had just now managed to win a championship. With a total salary budget of around $133 million dollars, they weren't exactly young upstarts. That made me curious about the relationships between raw salaries and the general performance of the individual teams across the league.

For instance, George Steinbrenner, the owner of the New York Yankees, had in recent years been accused of trying to "buy" the World Series trophy by assembling a collection of highly paid all-stars. On the other hand, the performance of the Oakland Athletics (the A's) had in prior years far exceeded their overall salary. In the book *Moneyball* (W.W. Norton & Company), Michael Lewis tells the story of how Billy Beane, the general manager (GM) of the A's, made use of statistics to pursue players who had promising numbers but were below the radar because they weren't always standouts in the traditional sense.

Bill James was one of pioneers of statistics-oriented thinking in regards to baseball, first with his analytical sports columns and later with *The Bill James Baseball Abstract*, first published in 1977. Similar ideas led to the founding of the Society for American Baseball Research (SABR), from which came the term for this numbers-driven approach to the game, *sabermetrics*. The extent to which statistics can be applied to sports remains a controversial topic, pitting the appreciation of the intangible, underlying traits of highly talented people against a perceived reduction of noble games to mere mathematics.

As with any narrative, *Moneyball* presents an over-simplification of the system, as does the simple relationship of total salaries in a given year to performance-to-date. More complex factors come into play, including how contracts work over multiple years, the health of a team's farm system (their minor-league teams), and scoring methods for individual players. The original version of this project was thrown together while watching a game on television and should not be ranked alongside the many professional analyses of sports statistics.

However, a win is a win, and as a gross measure, showing the simple correlation between team salaries and standings can be quite revealing, particularly to observe shifts over the course of a season. Non-baseball fans also seem to enjoy this demonstration because wins and losses can be understood without intimate knowledge of the game, and because it fuels a popular discussion topic: that of the seemingly limitless salaries paid to professional athletes.

Preprocessing

In the examples so far, the data has been reasonably clean. That is rare; most data sets you find will need some amount of preprocessing before they're even usable. Returning to the seven-step process outlined in Chapter 1, it's not uncommon to first take a data set through the acquire, parse, filter, and mine steps, only to return to the beginning of the process and go through each step again with the resulting clean set of data (acquiring the clean data, parsing it, filtering and mining, etc.). For this chapter, we'll be preprocessing the data, and then starting all over again to represent the results.

Retrieving Win/Loss Data (Acquire)

Increasingly, many organizations make data available through *web services*, APIs, and acquisition methods (known by acronyms such as REST and SOAP) that distribute data in a neatly packaged format (usually XML-formatted text). When available, such services can be extremely useful, and they are a good starting point when dealing with a provider's data.

But most data still appears in the form of HTML-formatted tables, which may be attractive to human readers but is difficult for programs to understand. Although the sites may look relatively structured from our perspective, they are quite unstructured from the point of view of a program trying to organize and perform calculations on the data. Extracting the data from the HTML with a program is often called *screen-scraping*.

To get such data, you have to look at the HTML and write code to parse it. Luckily, most HTML is machine-generated and therefore is in a pretty regular format. You just have to locate the table you want among the JavaScript and other HTML tags used to display the web page.

The main hurdle you face is that the web site designers can change the format on a whim and with a click of a button in some web page layout tools. Upon complaints from users of your program that it no longer works, you'll have to rush back to the site where you got your data to see what change they introduced. REST and SOAP eliminate this problem; they represent an implicit commitment by the data's providers that they won't change their means of publishing data, even if they decide to change how the data is displayed.

Data source for baseball statistics

To find win/loss records for each team, we turn to MLB.com, the web site of Major League Baseball. The standings page, found at *http://mlb.mlb.com/mlb/standings/index.jsp and* illustrated in Figure 5-1, is a suitable place to get the information.

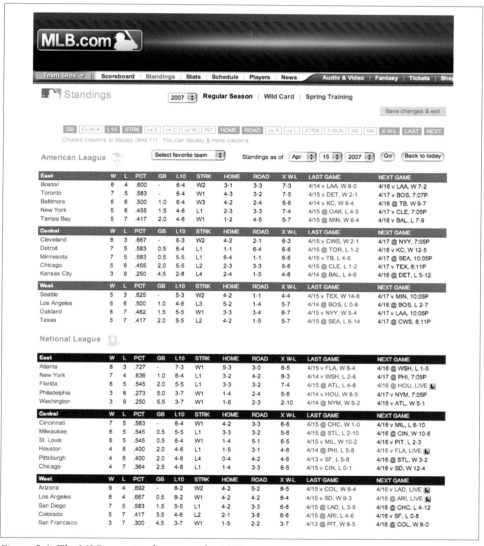

Figure 5-1. The MLB.com standings page for 2007

We'll use this page to explore the general problem of extracting data from web sites that are not deliberately designed to facilitate such extraction.

Screen-scraping requires the following general process:

1. Navigate to the page that contains the data. Because there will be lots of header and footer material, make a note of unique text or HTML tags that will reliably identify, even as the page is updated, the starting point of the data you want. In this case, our program can assume the table starts after the text American League, specifically beneath the table heading East.

   It's important to choose unique and stable identifiers. For instance, although it might be tempting to use the first data element in the table, Boston, as a starting point, it won't work because the "Select favorite team" pop-up menu already contains a "Boston" entry that will throw off your search.

2. Choose View Source from the browser's menu and take a look at the code. Use the Find command to look for your identifiers (e.g., "American League" or "East") to see where the data begins. In most cases, the data will begin near the identifier you've chosen. In our data (and in most other web pages with interesting data, because they're arranged in tabular form), the identifying portions will be part of an HTML <TABLE> tag, with the data stored inside a <TD> and </TD> pair.

   To make things trickier, in this example, the relevant HTML is actually built using JavaScript. The location near American League, where we might normally find the data, instead contains lines that use a pair of functions named buildTitleRows( ) and buildRows( ):

```
            <div style="padding-top:15px;">
                <h1>American League</h1>
                <img src="/mlb/images/al_symbol.gif" width="38" height="31"
    alt="American League" border="0" align="absmiddle" />
            </div>
        </td>
    </tr>

    <script>dataExists();</script>

    <script>buildTitleRows("ale"); </script>
    <tbody id="ale"><script>buildRows (standings_rs_ale); <script><tbody>

    <script>buildTitleRows("alc"); </script>
    <tbody id="alc"><script>buildRows (standings_rs_alc); <script><tbody>

    <script>buildTitleRows("alw"); </script>
    <tbody id="alw"><script>buildRows (standings_rs_alw); <script><tbody>

    <tr>
        <td colspan="16" style="padding-top:15px;">
            <h1>National Leaguew<h1>
            <img src="/mlb/images/nl_symbol.gif" width="38" height="31"
    t="National League" border="0" align="absmiddle" />
        </td>
    </tr>
```

```
<script>buildTitleRows("nle");</script>
<tbody id="nle"><script>buildRows(standings_rs_nle);</script><t/body>

<script>buildTitleRows("nlc");</script>
<tbody id="nlc"><script>buildRows(standings_rs_nlc);</script><t/body>

<script>buildTitleRows("nlw");</script>
<tbody id="nlw"><script>buildRows(standings_rs_nlw);</script><t/body>
```

An educated guess will tell you that ale is an abbreviation for the American League East division, alc stands for American League Central, and so on. (A less-educated guess could ascertain the same by noting that this is the American League [AL] table, with subheadings East, Central, and West, abbreviated E, C, and W.)

3. If the web page we were interested in contained our data directly in its HTML, we could write a program that read lines from the page and parsed them to remove the data. But in this case, we need to derive our data from JavaScript output, so we have to look at the JavaScript code to find how that program stores the data.

Another use of the Find command reveals lines that load each array from individual *.js* (JavaScript) files:

```
<script
src="/components/game/year_2007/month_04/day_15/standings_rs_ale.js"
type="text/javascript">/* " */</script>
<script
src="/components/game/year_2007/month_04/day_15/standings_rs_alc.js"
type="text/javascript">/* " */</script>
<script
src="/components/game/year_2007/month_04/day_15/standings_rs_alw.js"
type="text/javascript">/* " */</script>
<script
src="/components/game/year_2007/month_04/day_15/standings_rs_nle.js"
type="text/javascript">/* " */</script>
<script
src="/components/game/year_2007/month_04/day_15/standings_rs_nlc.js"
type="text/javascript">/* " */</script>
<script
src="/components/game/year_2007/month_04/day_15/standings_rs_nlw.js"
type="text/javascript">/* " */</script>

<script src="/components/game/year_2007/month_04/day_15/
<script src="/components/game/year_2007/month_04/day_15/
<script src="/components/game/year_2007/month_04/day_15/
<script src="/components/game/year_2007/month_04/day_15/
<script src="/components/game/year_2007/month_04/day_15/
```

The URL for the first item reads:

```
/components/game/year_2007/month_04/day_15/standings_rs_ale.js
```

Because a forward slash is found at the beginning, the reference points to the root of the site, *http://mlb.mlb.com*, meaning that the full URL is *http://mlb.mlb. com/components/game/year_2007/month_04/day_15/standings_rs_ale.js*.

If the text did not begin with a slash, the URL would instead be *relative* to the original page number, meaning that you would have to append it to the directory of the page that referred to it (*http://mlb.mlb.com/mlb/standings/index.jsp*), which would make the new URL *http://mlb.mlb.com/mlb/standings/components/ game/year_2007/month_04/day_15/standings_rs_ale.js*.

So, our data will come from three JavaScript files representing results for the three American League divisions:

> *http://mlb.mlb.com/components/game/year_2007/month_04/day_15/standings_rs_ ale.js*
> *http://mlb.mlb.com/components/game/year_2007/month_04/day_15/standings_rs_ alc.js*
> *http://mlb.mlb.com/components/game/year_2007/month_04/day_15/standings_rs_ alw.js*

and three more files for the National League (NL) teams:

> *http://mlb.mlb.com/components/game/year_2007/month_04/day_15/standings_rs_ nle.js*
> *http://mlb.mlb.com/components/game/year_2007/month_04/day_15/standings_rs_ nlc.js*
> *http://mlb.mlb.com/components/game/year_2007/month_04/day_15/standings_rs_ nlw.js*

Unpacking the Win/Loss files (Mine and Filter)

Entering the first URL for *standings_rs_ale.js* into a browser will display the JavaScript source file. To parse the data, we are particularly interested in the structure that the JavaScript program gives to that data. This structure is defined by a standings_rs_ale array:

```
var standings_rs_ale = [{
w: '6',
elim: '-',
rs: '51',
div: 'ale',
gameid: '2007_04_16_anamlb_bosmlb_1',
status: 'F',
pre: null,
last10: '6-4',
onerun: '1-0',
xtr: '0-0',
nextg: '4/16 v LAA, W 7-2',
vsW: '4-3',
ra: '28',
gb: '-',
```

```
  wrap:
  '/NASApp/mlb/news/wrap.jsp?ymd=20070414&content_id=1898390&vkey=wrapup2005&fext=.
  jsp&c_id=mlb',
  home: '3-1',
  code: 'bos',
  pct: '.600',
  league_sensitive_team_name: 'Boston',
  vsC: '2-1',
  vsE: '0-0',
  vsR: '5-4',
  vsL: '1-0',
  xwl: '7-3',
  strk: 'W2',
  l: '4',
  lastg: '4/14 v LAA, W 8-0',
  interleague: '0-0',
  team: 'Boston',
  road: '3-3'
}, {
```

Web developers might recognize this as JavaScript Object Notation (JSON) syntax. We won't get into the specifics of JSON here; see Chapter 10 for more information.

The previously shown code encompasses the content for the first team, and four additional blocks in the same format follow. We need only a few fields from the information. The field we'll use the most is the two- or three-digit code that identifies the team, which we'll use to index other kinds of data:

```
code: 'bos',
```

Next, we need the line for wins:

```
w: '6',
```

and the line for losses:

```
l: '4',
```

We also want a team name to show in the interface, and luckily there is a variable named team that looks like it might do the trick. However, it lists New York as the value for the New York Yankees, which won't be useful when trying to differentiate the Yankees from the Mets, who also hail from New York. Instead, the league_sensitive_ team_name value will be more useful. For instance, the entry for the Mets reads:

```
league_sensitive_team_name: 'NY Mets',
```

As in the previous section, where we looked for some salient string or character that we could use to find the start of our data, we now want to find something that differentiates one team from another. In the JSON format of the standings_rs_ale array, a { character begins each block of data for a new team. Each time that character is found, our program can retrieve information for a new team. Similarly, when the program finds the corresponding closing } character, it can add the new team's information to its own list. Grabbing the data for all of the teams is simply a matter of parsing the information properly. The code in the next section reads one of the files and parses the data into attribute and value pairs.

There are several publicly available JSON parsers we could use to read the data. But because the data shown here is so simple, using a formal parser would be overkill, making the program run more slowly and increasing its download size.

Introducing regular expressions

The following function will read from one of the *.js* files discussed in the previous sections and print each team code that it finds, followed by the win-loss record for that team. The code introduces *regular expressions*, which are extremely useful when parsing data:

```
void parseWinLoss(String[] lines) {
  Pattern p = Pattern.compile("\\s+([\\w\\d]+):\\s'(.*)',?");

  String teamCode = "";
  int wins = 0;
  int losses = 0;

  for (int i = 0; i < lines.length; i++) {
    Matcher m = p.matcher(lines[i]);

    if (m.matches()) {
      String attr = m.group(1);
      String value = m.group(2);

      if (attr.equals("code")) {
        teamCode = value;
      } else if (attr.equals("w")) {
        wins = int(value);
      } else if (attr.equals("l")) {
        losses = int(value);
      }

    } else {
      if (lines[i].startsWith("}")) {
        // This is the end of a group; print the values.
        println(teamCode + " " + wins + "-" + losses);
      }
    }
  }
}
```

If you're not already familiar with them, regular expressions can take a long time to get used to, but their usefulness makes it worth the initial difficulty. To understand what the code is doing, let's start by looking at the format of the original data. Because the code takes advantage of the presence of blank spaces, I'm including them in the format's representation here:

```
[space] [attribute name] : [space] ' [value] ' ,
```

This sort of template is common when parsing data, and it can be handled with a regular expression (or *regexp*). A regexp is defined by a *pattern*, such as the one just shown, and a *matcher*, which checks the pattern against some input data.

A pattern is made up of a series of symbols that identify whitespace, characters, numbers, and how many of each are expected. Although the way I represented the pattern with words and square brackets makes it easier for humans to read, the regexp APIs of programming languages use a more precise format. The symbols used in regexps initially appear as a confusing mess, but after some time, you'll become familiar with them (in other words, they'll be less confusing, even if they still look like a mess). The pattern \\s+([\\w\\d]+):\\s'(.*)',? in the code that started this section has the following meaning:

\\s+

> This part matches the space at the beginning of the line. It's made up of two different tokens that are meaningful in regexps:
>
> \s
>
>> This means "any whitespace character." But why is the backslash doubled? In Java and other C-like languages, a backslash is used to identify special characters in a String (e.g., \t for Tab or \n for newline). Similarly, an actual slash is specified by a double slash: \\.
>
> +
>
>> This means to look for one or more characters. This makes our regexp more robust because the programmer who wrote the JSON we're parsing might put an arbitrary number of space characters at the start of the line.

([\\w\\d]+)

> This portion matches the attribute name (such as w or team). The most powerful part of this string is the enclosing parentheses, which mark that set of characters as a *group*. This means the program can later point to and extract the matching characters.
>
> Inside the grouping parentheses are a set of square brackets, which denote a *character class*. This is a way to match a variety of different characters that can appear at this point in the input text. Our particular character class matches two types of characters:
>
> \w
>
>> Any word character (i.e., a letter)
>
> \d
>
>> Any digit (0–9)
>
> So [\\w\\d] means "any word or digit character." The + at the end specifies "one or more," just as it did previously in our string \\s+.

:

> This is literally just the colon character, which is found after the variable name.

`\\s`

Matches a single whitespace character (the space after the colon).

`'`

Matches the single quote at the beginning of the variable's value.

`(.*)`

This part matches the value found inside the single quotes. We've already seen what the grouping parentheses mean. Inside these parentheses are:

`.` *(period)*

Matches anything. Any character is possible in the input.

`*`

Specifies zero or more of the character that precedes it (similar to how the + operator matches one or more of that character).

`'`

Matches the closing single quote after the variable's value.

`,?`

Matches the optional comma at the end of the line. Similar to + and *, the ? modifier specifies "zero or one" matches.

To use a regexp in Java, we first create a `Pattern` object, as seen in the first line of the method. Next, we iterate through each line of the input data and attempt to match it to the `Pattern`. Inside the loop, the `Matcher` object holds the result of our attempt to match input. The `matches()` method returns true if the specified `lines[i]` value fits the pattern. Next, we use the `group()` method to retrieve each group that was captured by the parentheses in our regexp. The first group is the attribute (or variable name), and the second group is the value (the variable contents).

If the line does not match, the final part of the method checks whether the line begins with a }, which specifies a break between data from two teams, at which point the values collected so far are printed to the console with `println`.

A complete program to acquire and parse the data for all six divisions from MLB. com follows. It creates two text files—one for the standings and one for the team codes and team names:

```java
import java.util.regex.*;

PrintWriter standings;
PrintWriter teams;

void setup() {
  String base = "http://mlb.mlb.com/components/game" +
    "/year_2007/month_04/day_15/";

  standings = createWriter("standings.tsv");
  teams = createWriter("teams.tsv");
```

```
    parseWinLoss(loadStrings(base + "standings_rs_ale.js"));
    parseWinLoss(loadStrings(base + "standings_rs_alw.js"));
    parseWinLoss(loadStrings(base + "standings_rs_alc.js"));

    parseWinLoss(loadStrings(base + "standings_rs_nle.js"));
    parseWinLoss(loadStrings(base + "standings_rs_nlw.js"));
    parseWinLoss(loadStrings(base + "standings_rs_nlc.js"));

    // Finish writing and close each file.
    standings.flush();
    standings.close();
    teams.flush();
    teams.close();

    println("Done.");
  }


void parseWinLoss(String[] lines) {
  Pattern p = Pattern.compile("\\s+([\\w\\d]+):\\s'(.*)',?");

  String teamCode = "";
  int wins = 0;
  int losses = 0;
  String teamName = "";

  for (int i = 0; i < lines.length; i++) {
    Matcher m = p.matcher(lines[i]);

    if (m.matches()) {
      String attr = m.group(1);
      String value = m.group(2);

      if (attr.equals("code")) {
        teamCode = value;
      } else if (attr.equals("w")) {
        wins = int(value);
      } else if (attr.equals("l")) {
        losses = int(value);
      } else if (attr.equals("league_sensitive_team_name")) {
        teamName = value;
      }

    } else {
      if (lines[i].startsWith("}")) {
        // This is the end of a group; print the values.
        standings.println(teamCode + TAB + wins + TAB + losses);
        teams.println(teamCode + TAB + teamName);
      }
    }
  }
}
```

The resulting *standings.tsv* file reads:

```
bos     6       4
tor     7       5
bal     6       6
nyy     5       6
tb      5       7
sea     5       3
ana     6       6
oak     6       7
tex     5       7
cle     6       3
det     7       5
min     7       5
cws     5       6
kc      3       9
atl     8       3
nym     7       4
fla     6       5
phi     3       8
was     3       9
ari     9       4
la      8       4
sd      7       5
col     5       7
sf      3       7
cin     7       5
mil     6       5
stl     6       5
hou     4       6
pit     4       6
chc     4       7
```

And the *teams.tsv* file contains:

```
bos     Boston
tor     Toronto
bal     Baltimore
nyy     NY Yankees
tb      Tampa Bay
sea     Seattle
ana     LA Angels
oak     Oakland
tex     Texas
cle     Cleveland
det     Detroit
min     Minnesota
cws     Chi White Sox
kc      Kansas City
atl     Atlanta
nym     NY Mets
fla     Florida
phi     Philadelphia
was     Washington
ari     Arizona
```

```
la      LA Dodgers
sd      San Diego
col     Colorado
sf      San Francisco
cin     Cincinnati
mil     Milwaukee
stl     St. Louis
hou     Houston
pit     Pittsburgh
chc     Chi Cubs
```

The team names file can be downloaded here:

http://benfry.com/writing/salaryper/teams.tsv

along with the example standings file:

http://benfry.com/writing/salaryper/standings.tsv

The code downloads each file for April 15, 2007, but it is easy to change the date. Instead of the following code block:

```
String base = "http://mlb.mlb.com/components/game" +
    "/year_2007/month_04/day_15/";
```

use a combination of the Processing methods year( ), month( ), and day( ), along with nf( ) to pad the numbers to the proper number of digits:

```
String base = "http://mlb.mlb.com/components/game" +
    "/year_" + nf(year( ), 4) +
    "/month_" + nf(month( ), 2) +
    "/day_" + nf(day( ), 2) + "/";
```

Retrieving Team Logos (Acquire, Refine)

Team names make for a boring display. Our output will be much more appealing if we show team logos. Finding team logos on the MLB.com site (or any other site, for that matter) illustrates another bit of useful detective work: determining the pattern for a series of image files.

The first task is to find a possible logo image. For instance, the scoreboard page at *http://mlb.mlb.com/mlb/scoreboard* has logos for several teams. To determine a location, right-click one of the images, select Copy Image Location (or its equivalent in whatever web browser you are using), and use that location to open a new page. Right-clicking on the Chicago Cubs image, for instance, produces this URL:

http://mlb.mlb.com/mlb/images/team_logos/logo_chc_small.gif

The chc is the three-letter team code found earlier when downloading team data, which suggests that logos for the remaining 29 teams can be found by replacing those three letters with different codes. The list of codes is one column of the *teams.tsv* file created in the previous step. Therefore, to give our program access to team logos, we'll automate the retrieval of the images here.

In a new sketch, add the *teams.tsv* file and begin with the following code to read the file and load the teams into a String array named teams:

```
String[] teams;

void setup( ) {
  String[] lines = loadStrings("teams.tsv");
  teams = new String[lines.length];
  for (int i = 0; i < lines.length; i++) {
    String[] pieces = split(lines[i], TAB);
    // The three digit code for the team is the first column
    teams[i] = pieces[0];
  }
}
```

The presence of the word *_small* in the title of the *http://mlb.mlb.com/mlb/images/team_logos/logo_chc_small.gif* file suggests that there are images of other sizes. I took a stab at finding them on the *http://mlb.mlb.com* web site by substituting the suffixes *_large* and *_medium*, but neither worked. It may even be possible to look at the directory that contains the logos (*http://mlb.mlb.com/mlb/images/team_logos*) and get a file listing, but that generally works only for smaller or less professional web sites.

Of course, the locations for the images are subject to change at any time (and often will because there's no reason for MLB.com to keep them the same for others using their data), which is why we are taking the time to go through the process of figuring out the image locations. In an ideal situation, of course, the MLB would make this data available through a web service.

If we can't easily find the images we want by using our intuition and digging around the site, the next alternative is to use a search engine. Do a search for the first part of the URL and see what sort of results turn up. Thus, doing a search for "mlb/images/team_logos/" reveals several additional possibilities:

> *http://mlb.mlb.com/mlb/images/team_logos/logo_atl_small.gif*
> *http://mlb.mlb.com/mlb/images/team_logos/50x50/atl.gif*
> *http://mlb.mlb.com/mlb/images/team_logos/logo_bal_79x76.jpg*
> *http://mlb.mlb.com/mlb/images/team_logos/51x21/bos_standings_logo.gif*

A different web site shows yet another format:

> *http://losangeles.angels.mlb.com/mlb/images/team_logos/100x100/ana.gif*

The similarities in the directory structure suggest that the site is merely an alias, and a quick test confirms that the following URL works in an identical manner:

> *http://mlb.mlb.com/mlb/images/team_logos/100x100/ana.gif*

For each of the URLs in question, the two- or three-digit team code appears between a prefix and suffix specific to the image size and location. In the case of the small logos, the URLs look like:

> *http://mlb.mlb.com/mlb/images/team_logos/logo_team_small.gif*

With all this in mind, a short program can download each set of images:

```
String[] teams;

void setup() {
  String[] lines = loadStrings("teams.tsv");
  teams = new String[lines.length];
  for (int i = 0; i < lines.length; i++) {
    String[] pieces = split(lines[i], TAB);
    // The three-digit code for the team is the first column.
    teams[i] = pieces[0];
  }

  grabLogos("small", "http://mlb.mlb.com/mlb/images/team_logos/logo_", "_small.gif");
  grabLogos("50x50", "http://mlb.mlb.com/mlb/images/team_logos/50x50/", ".gif");
  grabLogos("79x76", "http://mlb.mlb.com/mlb/images/team_logos/logo_", "_79x76.jpg");
  grabLogos("standings", "http://mlb.mlb.com/mlb/images/team_logos/51x21/",
            "_standings_logo.gif");
  grabLogos("100x100", "http://mlb.mlb.com/mlb/images/team_logos/100x100/", ".gif");
}

void grabLogos(String folder, String prefix, String suffix) {
  String extension = suffix.substring(suffix.length() - 4);
  for (int i = 0; i < teams.length; i++) {
    String filename = folder + "/" + teams[i] + extension;
    String url = prefix + teams[i] + suffix;
    println("Downloading " + url);
    saveStream(filename, url);
  }
}
```

The teams array contains the list of the 30 team codes. The grabLogos() method iterates through each team, downloading images based on the specified prefix and suffix. The saveStream() method loads the data from a particular web address and writes it back to the disk (it's equivalent to using the built-in function loadBytes(), followed by saveBytes()). Because the image may be a *.jpg* or *.gif* file, the grabLogos() method uses substring() on the source filename to determine which extension to use when naming the downloaded file.

In the end, the *small* directory contains the images whose size and proportion are most appropriate for our display. Start a new sketch, and use Sketch → Show Sketch Folder to add these to the *data* folder.

Retrieving Salary Data (Acquire, Parse, Filter)

The next step is to find a list of the salaries for each of the teams. There appears to be no such feature on MLB.com, but the *USA Today* web site makes available a list of team payrolls here:

http://usatoday.com/sports/baseball/salaries/totalpayroll.aspx?year=2007

The simplest method of getting this information is to copy it from your web browser and paste it into an open document in your spreadsheet application of choice. If you're lucky, the table will be interpreted as tab-delimited and the columns will be preserved when pasted into the spreadsheet.

Another option is to use the import or link feature of your spreadsheet application. This also can be done with Excel, but we'll use OpenOffice.org because anyone can download it for free. Create a new Calc document and choose Insert → Link To External Data.... Paste the *USA Today* URL listing the payrolls into the first text field that reads "URL of external data source." Pressing the Enter key will populate the list of "Available tables/ranges." Scroll down and select HTML__BBSalTable from the list, as shown in Figure 5-2.

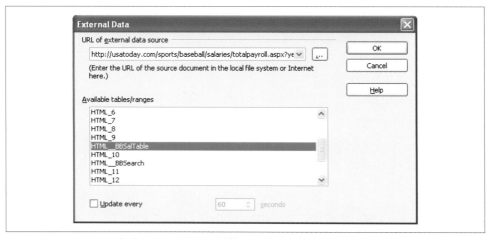

Figure 5-2. Entering web data into an OpenOffice.org spreadsheet

Click OK to import the data. That will pick up more of the web page than necessary, but scrolling down to the 17th row and expanding columns A and B reveals the list of teams, shown in Figure 5-3.

Delete all rows and columns except for the team name and the salary, and replace each team name with its two- or three-letter code. The commas and dollar signs also need to be removed (a quick Find and Replace will take care of that). Finally, save the file as plain text in TSV format as *salaries.tsv*. A completed version of the salaries file can be found at *http://benfry.com/writing/salaryper/salaries.tsv*.

Of course, parsing the page and downloading the table could be handled in code, but the amount of information (30 team salaries) and the frequency at which it's updated (once a year) does not warrant an algorithmic solution.

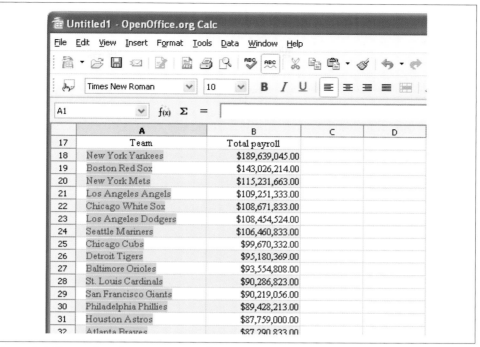

Figure 5-3. Team salary data in an OpenOffice.org spreadsheet

Convert Data by Hand or Write a Program?

As a rule of thumb, I write code only when the time to write the code is less than or equal to double the amount of time it takes to do a process by hand. That is, if it takes three hours to do it by hand and I can implement it in code in six hours or less, I prefer to use code so that the results can be easily updated. As a corollary, however, in situations like the one presented in this chapter, the page structure will likely change more than the data itself. In such cases, writing a parser is usually a waste of time.

Using the Preprocessed Data (Acquire, Parse, Filter, Mine)

In the previous steps, we managed to download files that represent the team names and logos, their salaries, and their standings on a given day. Now that we have determined how to handle each type of information and have preprocessed parts of it, we'll pull it together into a single application. The goal of this section is to gather the data that previous sections put in plain text files, and then bring them into data structures that are convenient for our program to use.

Team Names and Codes

First, we'll load the team names using the setupTeams( ) method. This is similar to examples we've seen in earlier chapters, in which we acquire the data from a pre-processed file through loadStrings( ), followed by split( ), to break a line into individual columns:

```
int teamCount = 30;
String[] teamNames;
String[] teamCodes;
HashMap teamIndices;

void setupTeams( ) {
  String[] lines = loadStrings("teams.tsv");

  teamCount = lines.length;
  teamCodes = new String[teamCount];
  teamNames = new String[teamCount];
  teamIndices = new HashMap( );

  for (int i = 0; i < teamCount; i++) {
    String[] pieces = split(lines[i], TAB);
    teamCodes[i] = pieces[0];
    teamNames[i] = pieces[1];
    teamIndices.put(teamCodes[i], new Integer(i));
  }
}

int teamIndex(String teamCode) {
  Integer index = (Integer) teamIndices.get(teamCode);
  return index.intValue( );
}
```

When creating the teamCodes and teamNames arrays, we have to provide an ordering that can be used to anchor the data. When we're loading the salary information from an input file, we don't know the exact order in which the teams will be found. The same is true for the win-loss standings, which will change from day to day. We anchor both lists to the same order by mapping the teamCode to a particular team index (numbered 0 to 29), which ensures that data from each source is connected properly.

To map a teamCode to an integer index, we use a HashMap. The HashMap class is a dictionary that connects two pieces of data, each an Object. The put( ) method adds a new entry to the map, whereas the get( ) method retrieves it. Because only objects can be used in HashMap structures, it's necessary to wrap the int for the team's index in an Integer object, which we created for this purpose. The intValue( ) method extracts the original int from the Integer object. This is encapsulated by the teamIndex function so that we don't have to think about the HashMap or Integer classes when writing the rest of the code.

What's the Difference Between int and Integer?

In Java, an int is a primitive type (such as float and char) that contains a simple value, one that can be stored by most computers in a single element of memory in a native format. In contrast, Integer is an object, which is a composite set of data elements.

The distinction can be confusing and often leads people to ask why the language designers didn't make everything an object. The answer is that objects create significant (and unnecessary) overhead whenever primitive types such as int can be used. For example, in a for loop with thousands of iterations, it would be silly to dereference an Integer object used for the counter on each iteration. Because the int refers to a specific value, only one step is required to read or change it.

An object refers to a location in memory, so the first step in using it should be to check whether the specified location is valid. The number might be stored in a variable called value, so once the location in memory is determined to be correct, a check can be made to find the location of the value variable (and whether or not it exists). Then, the variable itself can be manipulated in some manner. Although it may not sound like much, this sort of thing really makes a difference when dealing with thousands of values.

Scripting languages often use objects for all values, which can contribute to their lack of speed. Especially in cases of languages that are not "typed," each piece of data must first be converted to the proper native data format of the system as it is used. To give a simplistic example, a language might store each item of data as a string, and then convert it to an integer in any context where the value is used as an integer (such as counting in our for loop). This process can be even more time consuming.

Team Salaries

We will organize the salary data as a list of ranked values, just like the team standings. The parameters for ranked data are:

- A list of the values to be ranked (the amount of each team's payroll).
- A list of how those values will be shown to the user (the number formatted as a dollar amount with commas, e.g., $34,140,182).
- A list of the rank for each item, and a sorting order to be used when ranking. For instance, a higher payroll amount has a negative connotation, whereas a higher win-loss average has a positive connotation. In some cases, having the data in ascending order might be more useful; in others, a descending order is better.
- A means of keeping track of the highest and lowest values.

The ranked list is useful for salary data as well as the win-loss standings. It will also be useful when adapting this project to other types of data. Because a ranked list can be a useful general-purpose data structure, and because it requires a bit of code to sort the information and calculate its minimum and maximum values, I've created a RankedList class that encapsulates the general means of handling ranked data.

We've used classes in other examples (such as the Table class in Chapter 3), and like the others, it's not really necessary to understand the specifics of how this class works, only how it connects to the rest of the code. Download this class from the book's site and add it to your sketch:

http://benfry.com/writing/salaryper/RankedList.java

The parameters I've described are stored in the value, title, and rank arrays. To use the class for salary data, one need only *extend* the class. To do this, create a SalaryList class in a new tab. Its only contents are:

```
class SalaryList extends RankedList {

  SalaryList(String[] lines) {
    super(teamCount, false);

    for (int i = 0; i < teamCount; i++) {
      String pieces[] = split(lines[i], TAB);

      // First column is the team's 2- or 3-digit team code.
      int index = teamIndex(pieces[0]);

      // Second column is the salary as a number.
      value[index] = parseInt(pieces[1]);

      // Make the title in the format $NN,NNN,NNN.
      int salary = (int) value[index];
      title[index] = "$" + nfc(salary);
    }
    update();
  }
}
```

The main task in this code is to convert data from the particular format in which we put it during preprocessing—a text file with simple tab-separated lines—into the arrays defined by the RankedList class. This is a common task in data processing: to obtain data from an external source and transport it easily, you store it in a simple text format. But to process it programmatically, use a general-purpose library (often written by someone else) that expects the data to be in a more rigorous, possibly binary format.

The SalaryList method is the constructor for the class, controlling how an object is initialized. The super method calls the constructor of the parent class (known as the *superclass*). In this case, it runs RankedList(teamCount, false) to create a list with 30 entries in descending order (if the second argument to the super method were true, the data would be sorted in ascending order).

The rest of the code resembles our other parsing functions, except that it fills the value, title, and rank array for the values read from an array of Strings loaded from a file. The title variable for each is set to a dollar sign followed by the payroll number with commas inserted by the nfc( ) method.

After parsing the information, the update( ) method calls a function inside RankedList that takes care of sorting the data and calculating the minimum and maximum values.

Back in the main tab, the setupSalaries( ) method creates the SalaryList:

```
SalaryList salaries;

void setupSalaries( ) {
  String[] lines = loadStrings("salaries.tsv");
  salaries = new SalaryList(lines);
}
```

Win-Loss Standings

The win-loss record is handled in a similar fashion. First, a modified version of our preprocessing code acquires and parses the standings data for a given day:

```
String[] acquireStandings(int year, int month, int day) {
  String filename = year + nf(month, 2) + nf(day, 2) + ".tsv";
  String path = dataPath(filename);
  File file = new File(path);
  if (!file.exists( ) || (file.length( ) == 0)) {
    println("Downloading standings file " + filename);
    PrintWriter writer = createWriter(path);

    String base = "http://mlb.mlb.com/components/game" +
      "/year_" + year + "/month_" + nf(month, 2) + "/day_" + nf(day, 2) + "/";

    // American League (AL)
    parseStandings(base + "standings_rs_ale.js", writer);
    parseStandings(base + "standings_rs_alc.js", writer);
    parseStandings(base + "standings_rs_alw.js", writer);

    // National League (NL)
    parseStandings(base + "standings_rs_nle.js", writer);
    parseStandings(base + "standings_rs_nlc.js", writer);
    parseStandings(base + "standings_rs_nlw.js", writer);

    writer.flush( );
    writer.close( );
  }
  return loadStrings(filename);
}

void parseStandings(String filename, PrintWriter writer) {
  String[] lines = loadStrings(filename);
  Pattern p = Pattern.compile("\\s+([\\w\\d]+):\\s'(.*)',?");

  String teamCode = "";
  int wins = 0;
  int losses = 0;
```

```
    for (int i = 0; i < lines.length; i++) {
      Matcher m = p.matcher(lines[i]);

      if (m.matches()) {
        String attr = m.group(1);
        String value = m.group(2);

        if (attr.equals("code")) {
          teamCode = value;
        } else if (attr.equals("w")) {
          wins = parseInt(value);
        } else if (attr.equals("l")) {
          losses = parseInt(value);
        }

      } else {
        if (lines[i].startsWith("}")) {
          // This is the end of a group, write these values
          writer.println(teamCode + TAB + wins + TAB + losses);
        }
      }
    }
  }
}
```

For data from May 2, 2007, the acquireStandings() method looks for a file named *20070502.tsv*. If the file is not present, it downloads the data from MLB.com and parses it to create a filtered version that contains only the team code followed by the number of wins and then the number of losses.

This code is nearly identical to the standalone version discussed earlier in the pre-processing steps. One difference is in the use of a File object and the dataPath() method. The dataPath() method gives a full pathname to a file found in the *data* directory. This is useful when interfacing between Processing and Java file methods because the concept of a *data* folder is specific to Processing. The File class is used in Java to store a reference to a particular file (or directory) and includes several useful methods, such as exists(), which we use here to determine whether the file is available. Here we also check to see whether the file's length (size) is zero, which can happen if the acquireStandings method is interrupted and the file is not completely written.

In a new tab called *StandingsList*, write a similar piece of code as the constructor for SalaryList:

```
class StandingsList extends RankedList {

  StandingsList(String[] lines) {
    super(teamCount, false);

    for (int i = 0; i < teamCount; i++) {
      String[] pieces = split(lines[i], TAB);
      int index = teamIndex(pieces[0]);
      int wins = parseInt(pieces[1]);
      int losses = parseInt(pieces[2]);
```

```
      value[index] = (float) wins / (float) (wins+losses);
      title[index] = wins + "-" + losses;
    }
    update( );
  }
}
```

And back in the main tab, initialize the standings data by loading it from the correct web page based on the current day and putting it into the internal format by initializing a StandingsList:

```
StandingsList standings;

void setupStandings( ) {
  String[] lines = acquireStandings(year(), month(), day());
  standings = new StandingsList(lines);
}
```

Team Logos

All that remains now is to load the logo images for each team. They were downloaded earlier in the preprocessing step into a folder named *small*. Add this folder to the *data* folder of your sketch, and add the following code to your program:

```
PImage[] logos;
float logoWidth;
float logoHeight;

void setupLogos( ) {
  logos = new PImage[teamCount];
  for (int i = 0; i < teamCount; i++) {
    logos[i] = loadImage("small/" + teamCodes[i] + ".gif");
  }
  logoWidth = logos[0].width / 2.0;
  logoHeight = logos[0].height / 2.0;
}
```

The setupLogos( ) function also fiddles with how the logos are represented. Each logo obtained from the MLB.com site is 38 pixels wide and 45 pixels high. Some quick math tells us that 45 pixels times 30 teams (1,350 pixels) will not fit on the screen, or at least is unnecessarily large. However, half that height is just perfect for a 1024×768 display. Because the size of the logo images might change over the years (or with a different data set), we don't assume a particular size, but instead set the logoWidth and logoHeight variables to half the size of the first logo loaded.

Finishing the Setup

The setup( ) method brings this all together and defines a font for showing the data. We'll begin with just the generic SansSerif font, but will change it later:

```
PFont font;

void setup() {
  size(480, 750);

  setupTeams();
  setupSalaries();
  setupStandings();
  setupLogos();

  font = createFont("SansSerif", 11);
  textFont(font);
}
```

Make sure to run `setupSalaries()` before `setupStandings()` because we use the salary in `setupStandings()` as a tiebreaker when sorting the standings.

Displaying the Results (Represent)

Looking at what we've done so far, we can begin to fashion a simple representation to show each row of data with the team name and logo, win-loss record, and salary. Given two major variables (win-loss record and salary), it might seem reasonable to use the x- and y-axes. However, the question we have in mind is not simply "Do salary and performance correlate?," so an X and Y scatterplot is a less useful representation.

Our question implies a ranking because we're comparing teams. Ranking usually means a list, so we'll start by sorting the two lists in descending order, and then we'll connect each team's win-loss record to its salary with a line. The connecting lines—not the individual win-loss record or salary—becomes the outstanding element of the display. This is appropriate for our original question, because the lines show the relationships we're interested in. And after creating the basic display in this section, the rest of the chapter uses various techniques to emphasize the impact of the lines.

We begin with a few *constants*, which are variables prefixed with `static final` because they will not change while the sketch is in use. We haven't bothered using constants in previous projects because the code has been short, but for more complicated projects, it's important to start thinking about variables that can be abstracted out from the code. Placing a constant at the beginning of the sketch makes it easy to find and alter them. For instance, to change the row height we'd know where to look, and would need to change only a single line, rather than the multiple locations in the code that depend on the value for the row height. It also makes the code easier to read for others because when a value is a constant, that implies that its value will only be read and not set anywhere in the code.

Because the logo height is 22.5 pixels, we'll make each row 23 pixels tall. We'll want to center everything at the middle of the row, so the `HALF_ROW_HEIGHT` variable will also come in handy:

```
static final int ROW_HEIGHT = 23;
static final float HALF_ROW_HEIGHT = ROW_HEIGHT / 2.0;
static final int SIDE_PADDING = 30;
```

The text size set earlier is about half the height of each row. This creates easy-to-read, double-spaced text. The text itself needn't be particularly large or prominent because it is not as important as the correlation line itself.

The SIDE_PADDING variable is used to set a border around the display, adding some whitespace to the edges. The amount should be more than the row height so that it looks intentional, but not so large as to waste space.

The draw( ) method reads as follows:

```
void draw( ) {
  background(255);
  smooth( );

  translate(SIDE_PADDING, SIDE_PADDING);

  float leftX = 160;
  float rightX = 335;

  textAlign(LEFT, CENTER);

  for (int i = 0; i < teamCount; i++) {
    fill(0);
    float standingsY = standings.getRank(i)*ROW_HEIGHT + HALF_ROW_HEIGHT;
    image(logos[i], 0, standingsY - logoHeight/2, logoWidth, logoHeight);
    text(teamNames[i], 28, standingsY);
    text(standings.getTitle(i), 115, standingsY);

    float salaryY = salaries.getRank(i)*ROW_HEIGHT + HALF_ROW_HEIGHT;

    stroke(0);
    line(leftX, standingsY, rightX, salaryY);

    text(salaries.getTitle(i), rightX+10, salaryY);
  }
}
```

The translate( ) method moves the coordinate system over slightly, giving us a white border: (0, 0) will now be (30, 30), so nothing will be drawn in the left or top 30 pixels of the image.

The leftX and rightX values could also be constants (e.g., static final int LEFT_X = 160;), but we'll leave them as variables in case we later want to dynamically figure out the position of each column. The implementation used here determines the X-coordinates by trial and error; a better idea would be to base the positions on the maximum width of each column of text plus a little extra padding.

The textAlign( ) method left-aligns and vertically centers each row of text.

A loop iterates through each team index (represented by i). The text( ) method draws the team name, aligned to the left, and then the standings value (e.g., 40–29), centered next to it.

The standingsY and salaryY variables are calculated by multiplying the rank of the given team by the row height, then adding HALF_ROW_HEIGHT so that the line shows up in the center.

The resulting image looks like Figure 5-4.

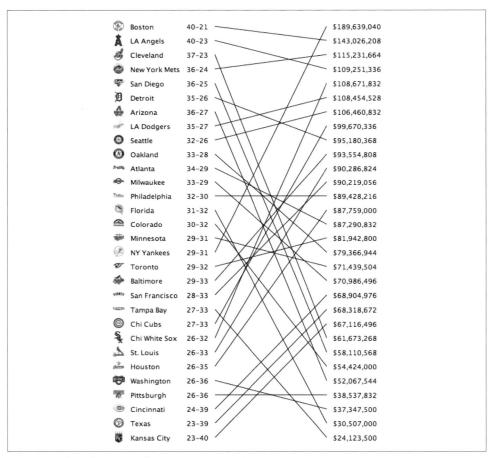

Figure 5-4. Sample team ranking

From Figure 5-4, we can pick out several interesting facts. For instance, both the Boston Red Sox and the LA Angels pay handsomely and get results that seem to validate the costs. But the highest salaries are paid by the New York Yankees, who are woefully unrewarded for this generosity. Individual results like this can be found in the figure, but it doesn't yield much in the way of overall patterns.

Returning to the Question (Refine)

When you reach the refinement stage of your visualization project, always return to the original question. In this chapter, we're most concerned with how salaries relate to performance for each team. The visualization in Figure 5-4 does not quite reach. The team logos are the most prominent visual elements (because they're in color), but they offer only a starting point for conveying the relationships. Meanwhile, the lines (the most important feature) are about as informative as a pile of sticks.

Highlighting the Lines

The first metric for the original question is whether teams are spending their money well. At its most basic, this is a yes or no question, so it will be important to high-light it as such with the representation. Teams spending their money well have a line that gets lower as it moves from left to right (connecting a high ranking in the standings to a low salary), whereas teams wasting money have lines that move upward from left to right. By using a color for each scenario, we can highlight the answer to the Boolean question of how well the team is performing. Color is a good choice in this case because we need only a pair of colors, and the detail being shown with the color is more important than any other feature in the diagram. To apply the colors, replace the stroke(0) line with the following:

```
if (salaryY >= standingsY) {
  stroke(33, 85, 156); // Blue for positive (or equal) difference.
} else {
  stroke(206, 0, 82); // Red for wasting money.
}
```

The result is shown in Figure 5-5.

But even with colors, the lines still don't have enough variation to instantly convey the key point to the viewer. We need to find a more salient form of variation to help viewers differentiate between elements and determine which shapes are related to one another.

To introduce more variation into the lines, we can vary the stroke weight based on the team's salary. We could do the same thing with the record, but payroll is more intuitive, as it refers to "bigger" or "smaller" teams. We don't think of standings as big or small, but we do think about monetary amounts in these terms.

The variation is handled with the map( ) method, mapping the minimum salary to a very thin stroke (0.25) and the largest salary to a nice, thick line. Add this code before the line( ) statement to scale the line weights in proportion to each team's salary.

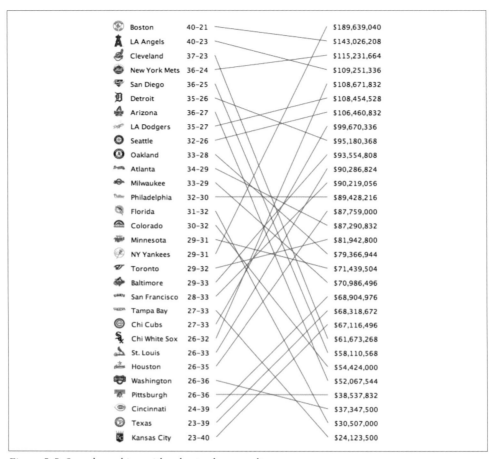

Figure 5-5. Sample ranking with color to show results

```
float weight = map(salaries.getValue(i),
                salaries.getMinValue(), salaries.getMaxValue(),
                0.25, 6);
strokeWeight(weight);
```

Figure 5-6 shows the results.

The image is getting more readable than the original in Figure 5-4, but still more can be done.

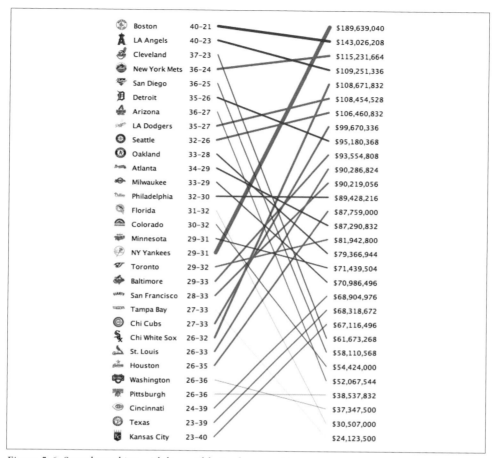

Boston	40–21	$189,639,040
LA Angels	40–23	$143,026,208
Cleveland	37–23	$115,231,664
New York Mets	36–24	$109,251,336
San Diego	36–25	$108,671,832
Detroit	35–26	$108,454,528
Arizona	36–27	$106,460,832
LA Dodgers	35–27	$99,670,336
Seattle	32–26	$95,180,368
Oakland	33–28	$93,554,808
Atlanta	34–29	$90,286,824
Milwaukee	33–29	$90,219,056
Philadelphia	32–30	$89,428,216
Florida	31–32	$87,759,000
Colorado	30–32	$87,290,832
Minnesota	29–31	$81,942,800
NY Yankees	29–31	$79,366,944
Toronto	29–32	$71,439,504
Baltimore	29–33	$70,986,496
San Francisco	28–33	$68,904,976
Tampa Bay	27–33	$68,318,672
Chi Cubs	27–33	$67,116,496
Chi White Sox	26–32	$61,673,268
St. Louis	26–33	$58,110,568
Houston	26–35	$54,424,000
Washington	26–36	$52,067,544
Pittsburgh	26–36	$38,537,832
Cincinnati	24–39	$37,347,500
Texas	23–39	$30,507,000
Kansas City	23–40	$24,123,500

Figure 5-6. Sample ranking with line widths to show results

A Better Typeface for Numeric Data

Instead of the generic SansSerif font, a better option is Matthew Carter's Georgia. We'll also increase the size a notch to match the amount of vertical space used by the original font because 11 point SansSerif has the same height as 12 point Georgia:

```
font = createFont("Georgia", 12);
```

Carter designed this typeface for Microsoft in 1993 as part of their web core fonts initiative because Microsoft's typography group sought better screen fonts that could differentiate Windows and other Microsoft products from their competitors. The web core fonts package was available as a free download. Georgia is a default font on Windows systems, and it is installed along with Microsoft software (such as Office) on Mac OS X. Because it's reasonably safe to expect that the font is installed on other machines, we don't have to use Processing's Create Font tool. On Linux, the fonts are available from a SourceForge project that repackages the fonts for easy installation. This package is also available as part of some Linux distributions.

http://sourceforge.net/projects/corefonts
http://sourceforge.net/project/showfiles.php?group_id=34153

The font is a good option because it has elegant *non-lining* numerals, also called *old style figures*, which have variable widths and extend below the font's baseline. Their use makes the number-rich display a little more attractive. The disadvantage in this case is that the numbers won't be identical widths, making them more difficult to compare.

Usually, fixed-width digits are helpful because right-aligning a series of numbers makes it easy for readers to scan a column and compare their magnitude at a quick glance. In this display, however, the exact numbers (for example, whether the Yankees are being paid $189,639,045 or $189,638,042) are less important because the numbers are already shown in rank order along the vertical axis, so we can sacrifice a little bit of readability.

The text still carries too much visual weight, so it needs to be faded a bit. Replacing the fill(0) statement with fill(128) makes the text gray and helps balance it with the colored lines, appropriately returning the greatest visual importance to the lines themselves.

Taken together, the new version of the draw( ) method follows, with altered portions highlighted:

```
void draw( ) {
  background(255);
  smooth( );

  translate(SIDE_PADDING, SIDE_PADDING);

  float leftX = 160;
  float rightX = 335;

  for (int i = 0; i < teamCount; i++) {
    fill(128);
    float standingsY = standings.getRank(i)*ROW_HEIGHT + HALF_ROW_HEIGHT;
    image(logos[i], 0, standingsY - logoHeight/2, logoWidth, logoHeight);
    textAlign(LEFT, CENTER);
    text(teamNames[i], 28, standingsY);
    textAlign(RIGHT, CENTER);
    text(standings.getTitle(i), leftX-10, standingsY);

    float salaryY = salaries.getRank(i)*ROW_HEIGHT + HALF_ROW_HEIGHT;
    if (salaryY >= standingsY) {
      stroke(33, 85, 156); // Blue for positive (or equal) difference.
    } else {
      stroke(206, 0, 82); // Red for wasting money.
    }
```

```
      float weight = map(salaries.getValue(i),
                     salaries.getMinValue( ), salaries.getMaxValue( ),
                     0.25, 6);
      strokeWeight(weight);

      line(leftX, standingsY, rightX, salaryY);

      fill(128);
      textAlign(LEFT, CENTER);
      text(salaries.getTitle(i), rightX+10, salaryY);
    }
  }
```

Figure 5-7 shows the display.

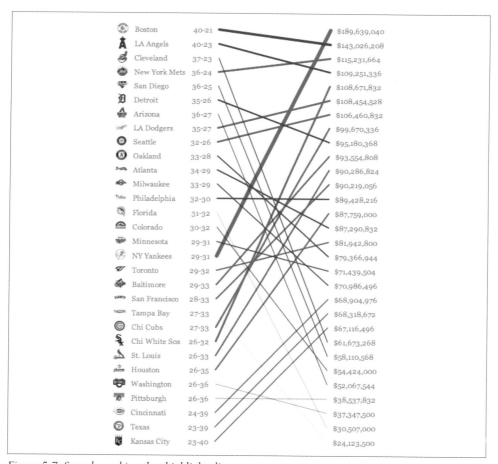

Figure 5-7. Sample ranking that highlights lines

A Word About Typography

The dash used between the win-loss record looks a little wimpy because dashes are so small. A better solution is to use the *en dash* character by changing this line from the StandingsList constructor:

```
title[index] = wins + "-" + losses;
```

to read as follows:

```
title[index] = wins + "\u2013" + losses;
```

Robert Bringhurst's *The Elements of Typographical Style* (Hartley and Marks Publishers) defines the en dash as suitable for use when separating values that can be broken with the word "to." In this case, the 40–21 next to the Red Sox can be stated as "the Red Sox have a record of 40 to 21," making the en dash suitable for this situation. Using the en dash also has the benefit of ensuring that the vertical position of the dash aligns nicely with the horizontal lines of the number characters that it separates (for instance, the middle of a "3" and the horizontal stroke of a "4").

The en dash is specified by "\u2013", a Unicode escape sequence. A Unicode escape is a \u followed by four hex digits representing the character's number in the Unicode character set. Other types of dashes can be used, such as the em dash, "\u2012", or the minus sign, "\u2212".

Sophisticated Sorting: Using Salary As a Tiebreaker (Mine)

Another alteration to the StandingsList is to improve how ties are handled. When two teams have an identical record (not an uncommon occurrence, especially early in the season), the tie should go to the team with the lower salary.

Inside RankedList, sorting is performed by a function that compares two elements in the list. This is common for most sorting algorithms, which invoke a comparison function that returns zero if the items are identical, a positive value if the first is greater, and a negative value if the second is greater.

Writing a new compare( ) method lets us specify a more sophisticated sort. In the modified method, the compare( ) method of the superclass (RankedList) is called first. If the comparison is nonzero, the items are not identical and we don't need to perform further comparison. But if the values are identical, the comparison function from the salaries object is used. Because values for a and b refer to the same team in both the standings and salaries (they were ordered using the teamIndex( ) function as they were loaded), the comparison works:

```
class StandingsList extends RankedList {

  StandingsList(String[] lines) {
    super(teamCount, false);
```

```
    for (int i = 0; i < teamCount; i++) {
      String[] pieces = split(lines[i], TAB);
      int index = teamIndex(pieces[0]);
      int wins = parseInt(pieces[1]);
      int losses = parseInt(pieces[2]);

      value[index] = (float) wins / (float) (wins+losses);
      title[index] = wins + "\u2013" + losses;
    }
    update();
  }

  float compare(int a, int b) {
    // First compare based on the record of both teams.
    float amt = super.compare(a, b);
    // If the record is not identical, return the difference
    if (amt != 0) return amt;

    // If records are equal, use salary as tiebreaker.
    // In this case, a and b are switched, because a higher
    // salary is a liability, unlike the higher record.
    return salaries.compare(a, b);
  }
}
```

Moving to Multiple Days (Interact)

So far we've covered a lot of data parsing and some visual refinement. But we've severely hampered our potential by sticking to a static image. That misses a key aspect of our data because the baseball season changes from day to day as teams improve, tank, and go on winning streaks. The code used to parse the information for a particular day can easily be adapted to other days, as long as we have a means for iterating through days of the season and knowing which days to use.

In this section, we'll generalize our code so we can store and display data for a range of dates. That requires extending:

- Storage (adding some arrays to store data from multiple dates)
- Status variables (adding various ways to represent dates)
- The display (adding a date selector)

Such changes are common whenever you extend your program. In later sections, we'll also animate the data.

Dates and time are trickier than you might think. An initial temptation is to simply make an array of numbers for the days in each month. But what happens in a leap year? Do you use a different version of your code? The solution is to represent dates in unchanging units, such as seconds or milliseconds, and convert them to dates for the purpose of display at the last moment.

The Java API contains a Date object that can convert between a long value (which is a type of int that can store much larger numbers) and a formatted date. A companion class, SimpleDateFormat, can parse a date from a String object given a template, or convert from a Date object to a date formatted using the same template.

The long value of a date is the number of milliseconds that elapsed since January 1, 1970 (known as the "Unix epoch" or "POSIX time"). Given a starting value, moving to the next day is a matter of increasing the variable by the number of milliseconds in a day. Doing this in a loop will generate all the days of an entire season.

The code that follows takes as input a date stamp for the first day of the season (firstDateStamp) in the format *YYYYMMDD*, and the same for the final day of the season. Because no data is available past the current day, the maximum date for which information can be downloaded is today. However, results for the current day will always be incomplete, so it's best to get results only up to the previous day. This logic will be encapsulated in maxDateIndex:

```
String firstDateStamp = "20070401";
String lastDateStamp = "20070930";
String todayDateStamp;

static final long MILLIS_PER_DAY = 24 * 60 * 60 * 1000;

// The number of days in the entire season.
int dateCount;
// The current date being shown.
int dateIndex;
// Don't show the first 10 days; they're too erratic.
int minDateIndex = 10;
// The last day of the season, or yesterday, if the season is ongoing.
// This is the maximum date that can be viewed.
int maxDateIndex;

// This format makes "20070704" from the date July 4, 2007.
DateFormat stampFormat = new SimpleDateFormat("yyyyMMdd");
// This format makes "4 July 2007" from the same.
DateFormat prettyFormat = new SimpleDateFormat("d MMMM yyyy");

// All dates for the season formatted with stampFormat.
String[] dateStamp;
// All dates in the season formatted with prettyFormat.
String[] datePretty;

void setupDates() {
  try {
    Date firstDate = stampFormat.parse(firstDateStamp);
    long firstDateMillis = firstDate.getTime();
    Date lastDate = stampFormat.parse(lastDateStamp);
    long lastDateMillis = lastDate.getTime();
```

```
// Calculate number of days by dividing the total milliseconds
// between the first and last dates by the number of milliseconds per day.
dateCount = (int)
  ((lastDateMillis - firstDateMillis) / MILLIS_PER_DAY) + 1;
maxDateIndex = dateCount;
dateStamp = new String[dateCount];
datePretty = new String[dateCount];

todayDateStamp = year() + nf(month(), 2) + nf(day(), 2);
// Another option method of doing the same thing using Java's APIs
//Date today = new Date();
//String todayDateStamp = stampFormat.format(today);

for (int i = 0; i < dateCount; i++) {
  Date date = new Date(firstDateMillis + MILLIS_PER_DAY*i);
  datePretty[i] = prettyFormat.format(date);
  dateStamp[i] = stampFormat.format(date);
  // If this value for 'date' is today, set the previous
  // day as the maximum viewable date, because it means the season is
  // still ongoing. The previous day is used because unless it is late
  // in the evening, the updated numbers for the day will be unavailable
  // or incomplete.
  if (dateStamp[i].equals(todayDateStamp)) {
    maxDateIndex = i-1;
  }
}
} catch (ParseException e) {
die("Problem while setting up dates", e);
}
}
```

The primary result of this function is to set up minDateIndex and maxDateIndex, as well as to calculate all dates in the entire season in two formats (the dateStamp and datePretty arrays) so that they can be used elsewhere.

The previous code is designed to be more general than the previously mentioned array that holds the number of days in each month. The original version of the project used the simpler method, as hand-tweaking provided a quick fix (February isn't part of the baseball season, so leap year considerations can be ignored). But if you were to adapt this project to another situation—such as the football season, which runs from fall through winter (meaning that the months count up 10, 11, 12, and then go to 1)—it's more prudent here to show a generic alternative that can be more easily adapted.

If you're running this code online, the firstDateStamp and lastDateStamp could even be pulled from an HTML parameter using the built-in param() method, which can read HTML tags for such parameters. That way, different years could be shown without needing to recompile the applet.

Drawing the Dates

At the top of the screen, we'll add a simple date selector. The selector will consist of a series of vertical lines, with the current date shown as a longer line and the title of the date (taken from datePretty) shown beneath it:

```
int dateSelectorX;
int dateSelectorY = 30;

// Draw a series of lines for selecting the date.
void drawDateSelector() {
  dateSelectorX = (width - dateCount*2) / 2;

  strokeWeight(1);
  for (int i = 0; i < dateCount; i++) {
    int x = dateSelectorX + i*2;

    // If this is the currently selected date, draw it differently.
    if (i == dateIndex) {
      stroke(0);
      line(x, 0, x, 13);
      textAlign(CENTER, TOP);
      text(datePretty[dateIndex], x, 15);

    } else {
      // If this is a viewable date, make the line darker.
      if ((i >= minDateIndex) && (i <= maxDateIndex)) {
        stroke(128); // Viewable date
      } else {
        stroke(204); // Not a viewable date
      }
      line(x, 0, x, 7);
    }
  }
}
```

The dateSelectorY variable never changes, and it represents the bottom of the display of dates across the top of the screen. The dateSelectorX variable marks a horizontal position within this display of dates, which allows the program to determine the date itself. We'll use both of these variables later to figure out where the user's mouse is among the dates.

Load Standings for the Entire Season

An update to the setupStandings() function downloads data for each day of the season (if it has not yet been downloaded) and uses a season array to store each day of standings for the season thus far:

```
StandingsList[] season;
```

```
void setupStandings() {
  season = new StandingsList[maxDateIndex + 1];
  for (int i = minDateIndex; i <= maxDateIndex; i++) {
    String[] lines = acquireStandings(dateStamp[i]);
    season[i] = new StandingsList(lines);
  }
}
```

Another version of the acquireStandings() method breaks up a date stamp into its component parts so that it can be handled by the original acquireStandings method:

```
String[] acquireStandings(String stamp) {
  int year = int(stamp.substring(0, 4));
  int month = int(stamp.substring(4, 6));
  int day = int(stamp.substring(6, 8));
  return acquireStandings(year, month, day);
}
```

Switching Between Dates

With all the data in place, selecting dates is a matter of determining where the mouse was clicked inside the date selector area. The mousePressed() and mouseDragged() will be combined into a single handleMouse() method that calculates whether a new date was chosen:

```
void setDate(int index) {
  dateIndex = index;
  standings = season[dateIndex];
}

void mousePressed() {
  handleMouse();
}

void mouseDragged() {
  handleMouse();
}

void handleMouse() {
  if (mouseY < dateSelectorY) {
    int date = (mouseX - dateSelectorX) / 2;
    setDate(constrain(date, minDateIndex, maxDateIndex));
  }
}
```

And just for kicks, let's add a keyPressed() method so that we can use the arrow keys to move back and forth in time:

```
void keyPressed() {
  if (key == CODED) {
    if (keyCode == LEFT) {
      int newDate = max(dateIndex - 1, minDateIndex);
      setDate(newDate);
    } else if (keyCode == RIGHT) {
```

```
      int newDate = min(dateIndex + 1, maxDateIndex);
      setDate(newDate);
    }
  }
}
```

Checking Our Progress

Because the printed page isn't interactive, the only evidence of animation can be seen in the date selector at the top of the screen in Figure 5-8.

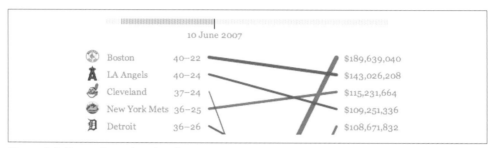

Figure 5-8. Date selector bar that drives animation

As the user clicks and drags the mouse across the date selector, the display switches rapidly between the standings for each day. It makes for an exciting reproduction of the baseball teams' fortunes, but the update is too jerky. As you might guess, we'll bring back our Integrator friend next to help smooth out things.

Smoothing Out the Interaction (Refine)

The Integrator class was introduced in Chapter 3 to replace abrupt distinctions in time or color with gradients. In what is perhaps becoming a common refrain, we'll add it to our sketch to help us animate the transition between days. The class is available from the book's site:

> *http://benfry.com/writing/salaryper/Integrator.java*

The only values that move are the 30 values for the standings, so we'll add a setupRanking( ) function to initialize them and set a default position. We add the call to setupRanking( ) inside setup( ), just after the other setupXxxxx( ) functions:

```
Integrator[] standingsPosition;

void setupRanking( ) {
  standingsPosition = new Integrator[teamCount];
  for (int i = 0; i < teamCodes.length; i++) {
    standingsPosition[i] = new Integrator(i);
  }
}
```

Inside draw( ), we'll no longer use getRank( ) to determine the location for standingsY as we did before:

```
float standingsY = standings.getRank(i)*ROW_HEIGHT + HALF_ROW_HEIGHT;
```

Instead, the position of each standing will be based on the current position of each Integrator, which glides gradually from the old to the new value:

```
float standingsY = standingsPosition[i].value * ROW_HEIGHT + HALF_ROW_HEIGHT;
```

At the beginning of draw( ), it's also necessary to update each standingsPosition. As a twist, we'll also keep track of whether any of the Integrators actually change by checking the return value of their update( ) method (which returns true if the value actually changed by some amount). If no changes occur, we'll use noLoop( ) to shut off the animation loop and save CPU cycles:

```
boolean updated = false;
for (int i = 0; i < teamCount; i++) {
  if (standingsPosition[i].update()) {
    updated = true;
  }
}
if (!updated) {
  noLoop();
}
```

Of course, we eventually need to turn the animation back on, when the user selects a new date. An updated setDate( ) method targets each of the new ranking values and submits it to the gradual animation provided by Integrator, then starts up the animation loop by calling loop( ):

```
void setDate(int index) {
  dateIndex = index;
  standings = season[dateIndex];

  for (int i = 0; i < teamCount; i++) {
    standingsPosition[i].target(standings.getRank(i));
  }
  // Re-enable the animation loop.
  loop();
}
```

Also regarding animation, it's important to set a frame rate at which to run the sketch so that it behaves consistently on other machines. Adding frameRate(15) to setup( ) ensures that transitions behave smoothly and the animation is consistent, even on very fast computers.

Deployment Considerations (Acquire, Parse, Filter)

As discussed in Chapter 2, sketches that run online inside a web browser are not allowed access to the user's local filesystem for security reasons. That eliminates our current scheme of downloading files for each day and using the File object to check whether they've already been downloaded.

As it turns out, the current implementation is also quite inefficient: at the end of the season, you'll have hundreds of individual files on your disk for each day, each of them occupying about 300 bytes.

So instead, we return back to the early preprocessing steps. The solution for both situations is to run the preprocessing steps from a CGI script. The script can download the data once for each day and then join all of the statistics for the season up to a particular day into a single file that can be downloaded by a web visitor. If the CGI script runs from the same server as the sketch, the sketch will be able to connect to it and download the data because connecting back to its parent server is considered safe under Java's security model.

A Perl version of the script, essentially an adaptation of the acquireStandings() and parseWinLoss() methods, follows. Creating a version for PHP or other web frameworks shouldn't be too much of a stretch.

```
#!/usr/bin/perl -w

use Time::Local;

# Send header to the web server to indicate we are awake,
# and that plain text data will be returned.
print "Content-type: text/plain\n\n";

# These values could be read from parameters to the CGI if so desired, i.e.,
# http://benfry.com/salaryper/data.cgi?first=20070401&last=20070930&min=10.
# This would make the software more flexible to use it for multiple years.
$firstDateStamp = '20070401';
$lastDateStamp = '20070930';
$minDateIndex = 10;

$dataFolder = 'individual';
$comboFolder = 'combined';
`mkdir -p $dataFolder`;
`mkdir -p $comboFolder`;

$firstDateStamp =~ /(\d\d\d\d)(\d\d)(\d\d)/;
$year = $1;
$month = $2 - 1; # Months are 0-indexed in Perl
$day = $3;
$firstDate = timelocal(0, 0, 0, $day, $month, $year);

$lastDateStamp =~ /(\d\d\d\d)(\d\d)(\d\d)/;
$year = $1;
$month = $2 - 1; # Months are 0-indexed in Perl
$day = $3;
$lastDate = timelocal(0, 0, 0, $day, $month, $year);

$SECONDS_PER_DAY = 24 * 60 * 60;

# Yesterday is the maximum possible date,
# because the scores from today will not yet be updated.
$yesterdayDate = time - $SECONDS_PER_DAY;
```

```perl
# Don't bother grabbing data for the earlier part of the season
# because it will not be used (and the program is not expecting it).
$date = $firstDate + $minDateIndex*$SECONDS_PER_DAY;

my @dateStamps = ( );

# If season is ongoing, read data only through yesterday.
$endDate = ($yesterdayDate < $lastDate) ? $yesterdayDate : $lastDate;
while ($date <= $endDate) {
    ($sec,$min,$hour,$mday,$mon,$year,$wday,$yday,$isdst) =
        localtime($date);
    $stamp = sprintf("%04d%02d%02d", $year + 1900, $mon+1, $mday);
    push @dateStamps, $stamp;
    #print "$date - " . localtime($date) . "\n";
    $date += $SECONDS_PER_DAY;
}
$endDateStamp = $dateStamps[$#dateStamps];

$combinedFile = "$comboFolder/$endDateStamp.tsv";
if (-f $combinedFile) {
    # Open the file and spew the contents back to the applet.
    open(INPUT, $combinedFile) || die $!;
    @contents = <INPUT>;
    print @contents;
    close(INPUT);

} else {
    # Download any days not yet downloaded.
    foreach $stamp (@dateStamps) {
        $filename = "$dataFolder/$stamp.tsv";
        if (!(-f $filename)) {
            downloadWinLoss($stamp);
        }
    }
    # Concatenate everything into a single file.
    open(OUTPUT, ">$combinedFile") || die $!;
    foreach $stamp (@dateStamps) {
        open(INPUT, "$dataFolder/$stamp.tsv") || die $!;
        @contents = <INPUT>;
        print OUTPUT @contents;
        close(INPUT);

        # Also write the contents of this file to the applet.
        print @contents;
    }
    close(OUTPUT);
}


sub downloadWinLoss( ) {
    my $stamp = shift;
```

```
        open(OUTPUT, ">$dataFolder/$stamp.tsv") || die $!;

        $stamp =~ /(\d\d\d\d)(\d\d)(\d\d)/;
        $day = sprintf("year_%04d/month_%02d/day_%02d/", $1, $2, $3);

        $base = 'http://mlb.mlb.com/components/game/' . $day;

        parseWinLoss($base . 'standings_rs_ale.js');
        parseWinLoss($base . 'standings_rs_alw.js');
        parseWinLoss($base . 'standings_rs_alc.js');

        parseWinLoss($base . 'standings_rs_nle.js');
        parseWinLoss($base . 'standings_rs_nlw.js');
        parseWinLoss($base . 'standings_rs_nlc.js');

        close(OUTPUT);
    }


    sub parseWinLoss() {
        $url = shift;
        # Download the contents of the .js file using "curl".
        @lines = `curl --silent $url`;

        $teamCode = '';
        $wins = 0;
        $losses = 0;

        foreach $line (@lines) {
            if ($line =~ /\s+([\w\d]+):\s'(.*)',?/) {
                $attr = $1;
                $value = $2;
                if ($attr eq 'code') {
                    $teamCode = $value;
                } elsif ($attr eq 'w') {
                    $wins = $value;
                } elsif ($attr eq 'l') {
                    $losses = $value;
                }

            } elsif ($line =~ /^}/) {
                # This is the end of a group, print the values
                print OUTPUT "$teamCode\t$wins\t$losses\n";
            }
        }
    }
}
```

The script can be seen in action at:

  http://benfry.com/writing/salaryper/mlb.cgi

or downloaded directly from:

  http://benfry.com/writing/salaryper/mlb.txt

If data has not been downloaded for the current day, it downloads the new information and then produces a file that concatenates all the days found so far. If that has already occurred once, the file itself is simply echoed back to the web server.

Because our CGI solution moves all the preprocessing code out of the sketch, the acquireStandings() and parseWinLoss() methods can be removed from the code, simplifying things greatly. The new version of setupStandings() that reads the data instead uses a URL to download the data and then creates a new StandingsList for each set of 30 lines. The maxDateIndex is determined by the amount of data received from the CGI script, and it's important to keep the minDateIndex variable in your code in sync with the minDateIndex value used in the CGI so that both pieces of software expect the same day to be the first day of standings. The complete code follows:

```
import java.util.regex.*;

int teamCount = 30;
String[] teamNames;
String[] teamCodes;
HashMap teamIndices;

static final int ROW_HEIGHT = 23;
static final float HALF_ROW_HEIGHT = ROW_HEIGHT / 2.0f;

static final int SIDE_PADDING = 30;
static final int TOP_PADDING = 40;

SalaryList salaries;
StandingsList standings;

StandingsList[] season;
Integrator[] standingsPosition;

PImage[] logos;
float logoWidth;
float logoHeight;

PFont font;


// . . . . . . . . . . . . . . . . . . . . . . . . . . . . . . . . .


String firstDateStamp = "20070401";
String lastDateStamp = "20070930";
String todayDateStamp;

static final long MILLIS_PER_DAY = 24 * 60 * 60 * 1000;

// The number of days in the entire season.
int dateCount;
// The current date being shown.
```

```
  int dateIndex;
  // Don't show the first 10 days; they're too erratic.
  int minDateIndex = 10;
  // The last day of the season, or yesterday, if the season is ongoing.
  // This is the maximum date that can be viewed.
  int maxDateIndex;

  // This format makes "20070704" from the date July 4, 2007.
  DateFormat stampFormat = new SimpleDateFormat("yyyyMMdd");
  // This format makes "4 July 2007" from the same.
  DateFormat prettyFormat = new SimpleDateFormat("d MMMM yyyy");

  // All dates for the season formatted with stampFormat.
  String[] dateStamp;
  // All dates in the season formatted with prettyFormat.
  String[] datePretty;

  void setupDates() {
    try {
      Date firstDate = stampFormat.parse(firstDateStamp);
      long firstDateMillis = firstDate.getTime();
      Date lastDate = stampFormat.parse(lastDateStamp);
      long lastDateMillis = lastDate.getTime();

      // Calculate number of days by dividing the total milliseconds
      // between the first and last dates by the number of milliseconds per day.
      dateCount = (int)
        ((lastDateMillis - firstDateMillis) / MILLIS_PER_DAY) + 1;
      maxDateIndex = dateCount;
      dateStamp = new String[dateCount];
      datePretty = new String[dateCount];

      todayDateStamp = year() + nf(month(), 2) + nf(day(), 2);
      // Another option to do this, but more code
      //Date today = new Date();
      //String todayDateStamp = stampFormat.format(today);

      for (int i = 0; i < dateCount; i++) {
        Date date = new Date(firstDateMillis + MILLIS_PER_DAY*i);
        datePretty[i] = prettyFormat.format(date);
        dateStamp[i] = stampFormat.format(date);
        // If this value for 'date' is equal to today, then set the previous
        // day as the maximum viewable date, because it means the season is
        // still ongoing. The previous day is used because unless it is late
        // in the evening, the updated numbers for the day will be unavailable
        // or incomplete.
        if (dateStamp[i].equals(todayDateStamp)) {
          maxDateIndex = i-1;
        }
      }
    } catch (ParseException e) {
      die("Problem while setting up dates", e);
    }
  }
```

```
  // . . . . . . . . . . . . . . . . . . . . . . . . . . . . . . . . . .

  public void setup() {
    size(480, 750);

    setupTeams();
    setupDates();
    setupSalaries();
    // Load the standings after the salaries, because salary
    // will be used as the tie-breaker when sorting.
    setupStandings();
    setupRanking();
    setupLogos();

    font = createFont("Georgia", 12);
    textFont(font);

    frameRate(15);
    // Use today as the current day.
    setDate(maxDateIndex);
  }


  void setupTeams() {
    String[] lines = loadStrings("teams.tsv");

    teamCount = lines.length;
    teamCodes = new String[teamCount];
    teamNames = new String[teamCount];
    teamIndices = new HashMap();

    for (int i = 0; i < teamCount; i++) {
      String[] pieces = split(lines[i], TAB);
      teamCodes[i] = pieces[0];
      teamNames[i] = pieces[1];
      teamIndices.put(teamCodes[i], new Integer(i));
    }
  }


  int teamIndex(String teamCode) {
    Integer index = (Integer) teamIndices.get(teamCode);
    return index.intValue();
  }


  void setupSalaries() {
    String[] lines = loadStrings("salaries.tsv");
    salaries = new SalaryList(lines);
  }


  void setupStandings() {
```

```
    String[] lines = loadStrings("http://benfry.com/writing/salaryper/mlb.cgi");
    int dataCount = lines.length / teamCount;
    int expectedCount = (maxDateIndex - minDateIndex) + 1;
    if (dataCount < expectedCount) {
      println("Found " + dataCount + " entries in the data file, " +
              "but was expecting " + expectedCount + " entries.");
      maxDateIndex = minDateIndex + dataCount - 1;
    }
    season = new StandingsList[maxDateIndex + 1];
    for (int i = 0; i < dataCount; i++) {
      String[] portion = subset(lines, i*teamCount, teamCount);
      season[i+minDateIndex] = new StandingsList(portion);
    }
  }


  void setupRanking() {
    standingsPosition = new Integrator[teamCount];
    for (int i = 0; i < teamCodes.length; i++) {
      standingsPosition[i] = new Integrator(i);
    }
  }


  void setupLogos() {
    logos = new PImage[teamCount];
    for (int i = 0; i < teamCount; i++) {
      logos[i] = loadImage("small/" + teamCodes[i] + ".gif");
    }
    logoWidth = logos[0].width / 2.0f;
    logoHeight = logos[0].height / 2.0f;
  }


  public void draw() {
    background(255);
    smooth();

    drawDateSelector();

    translate(SIDE_PADDING, TOP_PADDING);

    boolean updated = false;
    for (int i = 0; i < teamCount; i++) {
      if (standingsPosition[i].update()) {
        updated = true;
      }
    }
    if (!updated) {
      noLoop();
    }

    for (int i = 0; i < teamCount; i++) {
```

```
    float standingsY = standingsPosition[i].value * ROW_HEIGHT + HALF_ROW_HEIGHT;

    image(logos[i], 0, standingsY - logoHeight/2, logoWidth, logoHeight);

    textAlign(LEFT, CENTER);
    text(teamNames[i], 28, standingsY);

    textAlign(RIGHT, CENTER);
    fill(128);
    text(standings.getTitle(i), 150, standingsY);

    float weight = map(salaries.getValue(i),
                       salaries.getMinValue(), salaries.getMaxValue(),
                       0.25f, 6);
    strokeWeight(weight);

    float salaryY = salaries.getRank(i)*ROW_HEIGHT + HALF_ROW_HEIGHT;
    if (salaryY >= standingsY) {
      stroke(33, 85, 156); // Blue for positive (or equal) difference.
    } else {
      stroke(206, 0, 82); // Red for wasting money.
    }

    line(160, standingsY, 325, salaryY);

    fill(128);
    textAlign(LEFT, CENTER);
    text(salaries.getTitle(i), 335, salaryY);
  }
}


// . . . . . . . . . . . . . . . . . . . . . . . . . . . . . . . . . . .


int dateSelectorX;
int dateSelectorY = 30;

// Draw a series of lines for selecting the date.
void drawDateSelector() {
  dateSelectorX = (width - dateCount*2) / 2;

  strokeWeight(1);
  for (int i = 0; i < dateCount; i++) {
    int x = dateSelectorX + i*2;

    // If this is the currently selected date, draw it differently.
    if (i == dateIndex) {
      stroke(0);
      line(x, 0, x, 13);
      textAlign(CENTER, TOP);
      text(datePretty[dateIndex], x, 15);

    } else {
```

```
    // If this is a viewable date, make the line darker.
    if ((i >= minDateIndex) && (i <= maxDateIndex)) {
      stroke(128); // Viewable date
    } else {
      stroke(204); // Not a viewable date
    }
    line(x, 0, x, 7);
  }
}
}


void setDate(int index) {
  dateIndex = index;
  standings = season[dateIndex];

  for (int i = 0; i < teamCount; i++) {
    standingsPosition[i].target(standings.getRank(i));
  }
  // Re-enable the animation loop.
  loop();
}


void mousePressed() {
  handleMouse();
}

void mouseDragged() {
  handleMouse();
}

void handleMouse() {
  if (mouseY < dateSelectorY) {
    int date = (mouseX - dateSelectorX) / 2;
    setDate(constrain(date, minDateIndex, maxDateIndex));
  }
}


void keyPressed() {
  if (key == CODED) {
    if (keyCode == LEFT) {
      int newDate = max(dateIndex - 1, minDateIndex);
      setDate(newDate);

    } else if (keyCode == RIGHT) {
      int newDate = min(dateIndex + 1, maxDateIndex);
      setDate(newDate);
    }
  }
}
```

```
// . . . . . . . . . . . . . . . . . . . . . . . . . . . . . . . . . .

class SalaryList extends RankedList {

  SalaryList(String[] lines) {
    super(teamCount, false);

    for (int i = 0; i < teamCount; i++) {
      String pieces[] = split(lines[i], TAB);

      // First column is the team's 2- or 3-digit team code.
      int index = teamIndex(pieces[0]);

      // Second column is the salary as a number.
      value[index] = parseInt(pieces[1]);

      // Make the title in the format $NN,NNN,NNN.
      int salary = (int) value[index];
      title[index] = "$" + nfc(salary);
    }
    update();
  }
}


// . . . . . . . . . . . . . . . . . . . . . . . . . . . . . . . . .

class StandingsList extends RankedList {

  StandingsList(String[] lines) {
    super(teamCount, false);

    for (int i = 0; i < teamCount; i++) {
      String[] pieces = split(lines[i], TAB);
      int index = teamIndex(pieces[0]);
      int wins = parseInt(pieces[1]);
      int losses = parseInt(pieces[2]);

      value[index] = (float) wins / (float) (wins+losses);
      title[index] = wins + "\u2013" + losses;
    }
    update();
  }
```

```
float compare(int a, int b) {
  // First compare based on the record of both teams.
  float amt = super.compare(a, b);
  // If the record is not identical, return the difference.
  if (amt != 0) return amt;

  // If records are equal, use salary as tiebreaker.
  // In this case, a and b are switched, because a higher
  // salary is a negative thing, unlike the values above.
  return salaries.compare(a, b);
  }
}
```

## CHAPTER 6

Scatterplot Maps

In this chapter, we cover the seven steps as laid out in Chapter 1 and apply them to the question, "How do zip codes relate to geography?" (The background for this project was introduced in Chapter 1.)

Preprocessing

Data is always dirty, and once you've found your data set, you'll need to clean it up. As in the previous chapter, we'll go through the steps of acquiring and parsing in detail. None of this is rocket science, but again, it's meant to familiarize you with the various formats in which you'll find data, and alert you to some of the common issues you'll encounter along the way. If you just want to start playing with locations and maps, you can download the finished *zips.tsv* file from the book web site (*http://benfry.com/writing/zipdecode/zips.tsv*) and jump ahead to the next section.

Data from the U.S. Census Bureau (Acquire)

The acronym ZIP stands for Zoning Improvement Plan, a 1963 initiative to simplify the delivery of mail in the United States. Personal correspondence, once the majority of all mail, was rapidly being overtaken by business mail, which by the 1960s accounted for 80% of the post. Faced with an ever-increasing amount of mail to process, the U.S. Postal Service initiated the zip system to specify more accurately the geographic area of the mail's destination. The U.S. Postal Service's web site features a lengthier history of the system at *http://www.usps.com/history*.

Versions of the zip code database are available from a variety of sources. The data is public and therefore freely available on government web sites. Government sites often contain a wealth of information for those willing to take the time to dig for it. The terminology can sometimes be archaic and the documentation poor, so it often takes a while to figure out exactly how things work. In the spirit of capitalism, resellers have jumped in to provide you with "value added" versions of the data.

Clearly, the term "value" varies widely—some companies are happy to charge your credit card for the honor of their knowing the right search terms to use with Google, or of having clicked through the census bureau web site for you. Others subscribe to the official data from the U.S. Postal Service and curate a useful, working copy of the data.

Free services have also emerged, such as *http://geocoder.us* (described online and in O'Reilly's *Mapping Hacks* by Schuyler Erle, Rich Gibson, and Jo Walsh), which maintains a working data set as well as open source software that you can use to formulate zip code and address information.

For our purposes, we'll use a listing from the U.S. Census Bureau, found at *http://www.census.gov/geo/www/tiger/zip1999.html*. The data is outdated by a few years, but it will be sufficient for our short-term purpose.

That page provides a link to a compressed archive (with the seemingly redundant title *zip1999.zip*) that contains a DBF file with the data set and a Microsoft Word document that describes each of the fields (columns) in the data set. (For information about DBF files, see Chapter 10.)

Both OpenOffice and Microsoft Excel can open a DBF file. OpenOffice might even register the *.dbf* extension explicitly, but in Excel you'll have to use the "All files" option in the File → Open dialog box before the DBF file shows up.

The file contains approximately 42,000 lines, one for each zip code. The following is a small sample:

ZIP_CODE	LATITUDE	LONGITUDE	ZIP_CLASS	PONAME	STATE	COUNTY
95466	+39.056598	-123.525375		PHILO	06	045
95468	+38.919145	-123.540572		POINT ARENA	06	045
95469	+39.360935	-123.106751		POTTER VALLEY	06	045
95470	+39.302446	-123.462532		REDWOOD VALLEY	06	045
95471	+38.523472	-122.982142	P	RIO NIDO	06	097
95472	+38.407222	-122.869654		SEBASTOPOL	06	097
95473	+38.325851	-122.505846	P	SEBASTOPOL	06	097
95476	+38.255943	-122.476819		SONOMA	06	097
95480	+38.676694	-123.372059		STEWARTS POINT	06	097
95481	+39.127247	-123.164533	P	TALMAGE	06	045
95482	+39.403699	-123.321202		UKIAH	06	045
95485	+39.252489	-122.856430		UPPER LAKE	06	033
95486	+38.464487	-123.037996	P	VILLA GRANDE	06	097
95487	+38.463088	-122.989975	P	VINEBURG	06	097
95488	+39.660425	-123.786385		WESTPORT	06	045
95490	+39.525958	-123.365730		WILLITS	06	045
95492	+38.532827	-122.804100		WINDSOR	06	097
95493	+39.185033	-122.965163		WITTER SPRINGS	06	033
95494	+38.934552	-123.268378		YORKVILLE	06	045
95497	+38.717318	-123.463976	P	THE SEA RANCH	06	097
95501	+40.646324	-124.025773		EUREKA	06	023

Dealing with the Zip Code Database File (Parse and Filter)

After opening the file with OpenOffice or Excel, save the file as tab-delimited (TSV) or comma-separated (CSV) values for easier parsing. For our purposes, we'll save it as CSV (title it *zipnov99.csv*), resulting in a file whose first 10 lines look like:

```
"ZIP_CODE,C,5","LATITUDE,C,11","LONGITUDE,C,11","ZIP_
CLASS,C,1","PONAME,C,28","STATE,C,2","COUNTY,C,3"
"00210"," +43.005895","-071.013202","U","PORTSMOUTH","33","015"
"00211"," +43.005895","-071.013202","U","PORTSMOUTH","33","015"
"00212"," +43.005895","-071.013202","U","PORTSMOUTH","33","015"
"00213"," +43.005895","-071.013202","U","PORTSMOUTH","33","015"
"00214"," +43.005895","-071.013202","U","PORTSMOUTH","33","015"
"00215"," +43.005895","-071.013202","U","PORTSMOUTH","33","015"
"00501"," +40.922326","-072.637078","U","HOLTSVILLE","36","103"
"00544"," +40.922326","-072.637078","U","HOLTSVILLE","36","103"
```

The data in its current format is not quite ready to go. It is almost always the case that you'll need to do additional work to clean the data before it is ready to be included with an application. Often, you'll run the acquire stage and the parse and filter stages twice, as we do in this chapter. With our zip code data, one can observe that:

- The useful columns for our purposes are ZIP_CODE, LATITUDE, LONGITUDE, PONAME, and STATE. The ZIP_CLASS and COUNTY columns can be removed to save some disk space (if we intend to run this locally) or download time (if we distribute this application over the Web).

- The STATE column is encoded as a FIPS (Federal Information Processing Standards) number, which we'll want to convert to a two-digit state abbreviation.

- Not all of the data rows are necessary for our example. For the time being, we'll cheat and use only the contiguous 48 states, omitting Alaska, Hawaii, and American territories.

- While we're at it, the city names are listed in ALL CAPS, which looks garish and aggressive. It's important to realize that this is a limitation of the particular data set, not all data of this kind. If we were to get a better zip code list, the names might not be capitalized. As such, it's better to clean the data first, rather than include a workaround for the problem in the final project. That is not to say that we should be obsessed with generalization (see the discussion of "sketching" in Chapter 2), but this is a case where the generalization doesn't cost us anything in terms of time or efficiency.

- Excel and OpenOffice tend to introduce a lot of extra rubbish, such as unnecessary quotes, into TSV files. (To be fair, OpenOffice allows you to tweak these parameters, though the nomenclature for the export interface can be confusing.)

- Because latitude and longitude values reflect points on a globe, a *projection* will be used to convert the coordinates to positions that more closely resemble how the United States are typically portrayed (slightly curved at the top, rather than following a latitude line straight across).

- We'll need to know the range of latitudes and longitudes in order to plot them in a proper range to the screen. For this, we'll keep track of the minimum and maximum values after they've been projected.

- Because downloading the zip codes from the network may take some time, the file will also specify the number of total lines, so that we can calculate progress during the download.

Each of these issues is easy to handle. We'll simply write a short bit of code to turn our data into a more usable and compact format. Addressing each issue is straightforward:

1. We'll make a second version of the data file that leaves out the unnecessary columns. By placing constants at the beginning of the code for each of the columns, we'll make the code easier to follow because arrayName[LONGITUDE] is more self-explanatory than arrayName[2].

```
// Indices for each of the columns
int ZIP_CODE = 0;
int LATITUDE = 1;
int LONGITUDE = 2;
int ZIP_CLASS = 3;
int PONAME = 4;
int STATE_FIPS = 5;
int COUNTY = 6;
```

2. In the second file, the FIPS code will be replaced with a two-letter state abbreviation. The codes can be found at the Federal Information Processing Standards site, specifically Publication 5-2: *http://www.itl.nist.gov/fipspubs/fip5-2.htm*.

A clean version of this data is available from the book web site at *http://benfry.com/writing/zipdecode/fips.tsv*. For the curious, the clean version was created by saving the HTML file, opening it with OpenOffice, copying the data from the state tables, and pasting it into a blank spreadsheet file. The file was then saved as TSV by selecting the "Text CSV (.csv)" option, and in the "Export of text files" dialog box, setting the "Field delimiter" to "{Tab}" (which can be chosen from the drop-down list) and the "Text delimiter" to nothing.

The following code loads the *fips.tsv* file and places it into a Hashtable so that we can look up individual values. With this in place, fipsTable.get() will provide the state abbreviation for any FIPS code value.

```
// Load the state FIPS codes into a table.
Hashtable fipsTable = new Hashtable();
String[] fipsLines = loadStrings("fips.tsv");
for (int i = 0; i < fipsLines.length; i++) {
  // Split each line on the tab characters.
  String[] pieces = split(fipsLines[i], TAB);
  // The FIPS code is in column 1,
  // and the state abbreviation in column 2
  // (keep in mind that columns are numbered from zero).
  fipsTable.put(pieces[1], pieces[2]);
}
```

The clean version also omits the first 0 in each code to match the two-digit codes used in the *zipsnov99.csv* file. If each FIPS code were converted to an integer, this wouldn't be necessary, but storing this field as integer data is not worthwhile. It is tedious to convert (and later restore) the integer values, and not really necessary when String objects will work fine and save a few steps.

3. Gleaning the contiguous 48 states from the full list is a straightforward task. Other territories have been left out of *fips.tsv*, meaning that if no state abbreviation is found for a code, it can be skipped. Cutting out Alaska and Hawaii is also a matter of skipping lines whose FIPS code maps to AK or HI. Inside the for( ) loop, the code will look like this:

```
String stateAbbrev = (String) fipsTable.get(data[STATE_FIPS]);
// If the abbreviation was not found, skip this line,
// because that means it's an outlying territory.
if (stateAbbrev == null) continue;
// For now, skip Alaska and Hawaii.
if (stateAbbrev.equals("AK") || stateAbbrev.equals("HI")) continue;
```

4. For the city names (the PONAME column), we can capitalize just the first letter of each word, which isn't perfect, but it's better than shouting all the time. Further, because the city and state abbreviation are always used together (e.g., "Sebastopol, CA"), that information can go into a single column. That also gives us more flexibility if we want to use a different data set, such as the postal codes for Germany or Australia—which don't specify locations the same way as the U.S. but have similar numbering systems.

The following code is a general-purpose method that takes a String as input, breaks it into individual characters, and then capitalizes the characters that follow spaces (while making all other characters lowercase).

```
// Capitalize the first letter of each word in a string.
String fixCapitals(String title) {
  char[] text = title.toCharArray();
  // If set to true, the next letter will be capitalized.
  boolean capitalizeNext = true;

  for (int i = 0; i < text.length; i++) {
    if (Character.isSpace(text[i])) {
      capitalizeNext = true;
    } else if (capitalizeNext) {
      text[i] = Character.toUpperCase(text[i]);
      capitalizeNext = false;
    } else {
      text[i] = Character.toLowerCase(text[i]);
    }
  }
  return new String(text);
}
```

If you are dealing with an enormous amount of data and know for a fact that your data is simply ASCII, other tricks can be used to capitalize more quickly than the Character.toUpperCase( ) and Character.toLowerCase( ) functions (which take into account Unicode capitalization).

5. Extraneous quotes and commas can be thrown out, converting the information to a more minimal TSV file. More background regarding CSV and TSV files (including an explanation for the quotes and commas) can be found in Chapter 10. This conversion is handled with a scrubQuotes( ) function:

```
// Parse quotes from CSV data. Quotes around a column are common,
// and actual double quotes (") are specified by two double quotes ("").
void scrubQuotes(String[] array) {
  for (int i = 0; i < array.length; i++) {
    if (array[i].length() > 2) {
      // Remove quotes at start and end, if present.
      if (array[i].startsWith("\"") && array[i].endsWith("\"")) {
        array[i] = array[i].substring(1, array[i].length() - 1);
      }
    }
    // Make double quotes into single quotes.
    array[i] = array[i].replaceAll("\"\"", "\"");
  }
}
```

6. The Albers Equal-Area Conic is a useful projection when dealing with the United States. Several different map projections applied to the U.S. can be seen on the U.S. Geological Survey's web site at *http://erg.usgs.gov/isb/pubs/booklets/ mapsofus/mapsofus.html*. In our case, the specifics of the chosen projection can be found on the helpful MathWorld web site run by Wolfram Research. The following code is an adaptation of the algorithm found at *http://mathworld. wolfram.com/AlbersEqual-AreaConicProjection.html*:

```
// USGS uses standard parallels at 45.5°N and 29.5°N
// with a central meridian value of 96°W.
// Latitude value is phi, longitude is lambda.
float phi0 = 0;
float lambda0 = radians(-96);
float phi1 = radians(29.5f);
float phi2 = radians(45.5f);

float phi = radians(lat);
float lambda = radians(lon);

float n = 0.5f * (sin(phi1) + sin(phi2));
float theta = n * (lambda - lambda0);
float c = sq(cos(phi1)) + 2*n*sin(phi1);
float rho = sqrt(c - 2*n*sin(phi)) / n;
float rho0 = sqrt(c - 2*n*sin(phi0)) / n;

float x = rho * sin(theta);
float y = rho0 - rho*cos(theta);
```

7. As the preprocessor runs, we can keep a running account of the minimum and maximum ranges for the coordinates in question. That is done by setting the maximum arbitrarily small and the minimum arbitrarily high:

```
float minX = MAX_FLOAT;
float maxX = MIN_FLOAT;
float minY = MAX_FLOAT;
float maxY = MIN_FLOAT;
```

and checking the values on each iteration through the loop:

```
if (x > maxX) maxX = x;
if (x < minX) minX = x;
if (y > maxY) maxY = y;
if (y < minY) minY = y;
```

The values will be written to the preprocessor output file so that the boundaries of the shape are known before the file has finished loading in the interactive applet. That allows us to show points as they load from the network, which also serves as a indicator of the progress of the file download.

8. To keep track of the number of locations, the placeCount variable is incremented as each new location is parsed.

Building the Preprocessor

Open Processing and start a new sketch. Add the *fips.tsv* file to your sketch by dragging it into the editor window or selecting Sketch.

Pulling all these steps together, the preprocessor code appears as the following:

```
// Indices for each of the columns
int ZIP_CODE = 0;
int LATITUDE = 1;
int LONGITUDE = 2;
int ZIP_CLASS = 3;
int PONAME = 4;
int STATE_FIPS = 5;
int COUNTY = 6;

void setup() {
  // Load the state FIPS codes into a table.
  Hashtable fipsTable = new Hashtable();
  String[] fipsLines = loadStrings("fips.tsv");
  for (int i = 0; i < fipsLines.length; i++) {
    // Split each line on the tab characters.
    String[] pieces = split(fipsLines[i], TAB);
    // The FIPS code is in column 1,
    // and the state abbreviation in column 2
    // (keep in mind that columns are numbered from zero).
    fipsTable.put(pieces[1], pieces[2]);
  }

  String[] lines = loadStrings("zipnov99.csv");
```

```
// Set the minimum and maximum values arbitrarily large.
float minX = 1;
float maxX = -1;
float minY = 1;
float maxY = -1;

// Set up an array for the cleaned data.
String[] cleaned = new String[lines.length];
// Number of cleaned entries found
int placeCount = 0;

// Start at row 1, because the first row is the column titles.
for (int row = 1; row < lines.length; row++) {
  // Split the row into pieces on each comma.
  String[] data = split(lines[row], ',');
  scrubQuotes(data);
  // Remove extra whitespace on either side of each column.
  data = trim(data);

  String stateAbbrev = (String) fipsTable.get(data[STATE_FIPS]);
  // If the abbreviation was not found, skip this line,
  // because that means it's an outlying territory.
  if (stateAbbrev == null) continue;
  // For now, also skip Alaska and Hawaii.
  if (stateAbbrev.equals("AK") || stateAbbrev.equals("HI")) continue;

  // Attempt to fix the capitalization of the city/town name.
  String placeName = fixCapitals(data[PONAME]) + ", " + stateAbbrev;

  float lat = float(data[LATITUDE]);
  float lon = float(data[LONGITUDE]);
\
  // Albers equal-area conic projection.
  // USGS uses standard parallels at 45.5°N and 29.5°N
  // with a central meridian value of 96°W.
  // Latitude value is phi, longitude is lambda.
  float phi0 = 0;
  float lambda0 = radians(-96);
  float phi1 = radians(29.5f);
  float phi2 = radians(45.5f);

  float phi = radians(lat);
  float lambda = radians(lon);

  float n = 0.5f * (sin(phi1) + sin(phi2));
  float theta = n * (lambda - lambda0); //radians(lon - lambda0);
  float c = sq(cos(phi1)) + 2*n*sin(phi1);
  float rho = sqrt(c - 2*n*sin(phi)) / n;
  float rho0 = sqrt(c - 2*n*sin(phi0)) / n;

  float x = rho * sin(theta);
  float y = rho0 - rho*cos(theta);
```

```
    if (x > maxX) maxX = x;
    if (x < minX) minX = x;
    if (y > maxY) maxY = y;
    if (y < minY) minY = y;

    // Add a cleaned version of the line, separated by tabs, to the list.
    cleaned[placeCount++] = data[ZIP_CODE] + "\t" +
                            x + "\t" +
                            y + "\t" +
                            placeName;
  }

  // Write to a file called "zips.tsv" in the sketch folder.
  PrintWriter tsv = createWriter("zips.tsv");

  // Use the first line to specify the number of data points in the file,
  // along with the minimum and maximum latitude and longitude coordinates.
  // Use a # to mark the line as different from the other data.
  tsv.println("# " + placeCount +
              "," + minX + "," + maxX + "," + minY + "," + maxY);

  // Write each line of the cleaned data.
  for (int i = 0; i < placeCount; i++) {
    tsv.println(cleaned[i]);
  }

  // Flush and close the file buffer.
  tsv.flush();
  tsv.close();

  // Finished; quit the program.
  println("Finished.");
  exit();
}

// Parse quotes from CSV or TSV data. Quotes around a column are common,
// and actual double quotes (") are specified by two double quotes ("").
void scrubQuotes(String[] array) {
  for (int i = 0; i < array.length; i++) {
    if (array[i].length() > 2) {
      // Remove quotes at start and end, if present.
      if (array[i].startsWith("\"") && array[i].endsWith("\"")) {
        array[i] = array[i].substring(1, array[i].length() - 1);
      }
    }
    // Make double quotes into single quotes.
    array[i] = array[i].replaceAll("\"\"", "\"");
  }
}

// Capitalize the first letter of each word in a string.
String fixCapitals(String title) {
  char[] text = title.toCharArray();
  // If set to true, the next letter will be capitalized.
  boolean capitalizeNext = true;
```

```
  for (int i = 0; i < text.length; i++) {
    if (Character.isSpace(text[i])) {
      capitalizeNext = true;
    } else if (capitalizeNext) {
      text[i] = Character.toUpperCase(text[i]);
      capitalizeNext = false;
    } else {
      text[i] = Character.toLowerCase(text[i]);
    }
  }
}
return new String(text);
}
```

The resulting file is much easier on the eyes and far simpler to parse in our next step:

```
# 41556,-0.3667764,0.35192886,0.4181981,0.87044954
00210    0.3135056    0.7633538    Portsmouth, NH
00211    0.3135056    0.7633538    Portsmouth, NH
00212    0.3135056    0.7633538    Portsmouth, NH
00213    0.3135056    0.7633538    Portsmouth, NH
00214    0.3135056    0.7633538    Portsmouth, NH
00215    0.3135056    0.7633538    Portsmouth, NH
00501    0.30247012   0.7226447    Holtsville, NY
00544    0.30247012   0.7226447    Holtsville, NY
01001    0.29536617   0.742954     Agawam, MA
01002    0.29843047   0.7478273    Amherst, MA
01003    0.29629046   0.74733305   Amherst, MA
01004    0.29775193   0.7479712    Amherst, MA
01005    0.302632     0.7482096    Barre, MA
01007    0.29958177   0.7465452    Belchertown, MA
01008    0.29309207   0.7430645    Blandford, MA
01009    0.30066824   0.74547637   Bondsville, MA
01010    0.302785     0.74424756   Brimfield, MA
01011    0.29267046   0.74506783   Chester, MA
01012    0.29383755   0.74713147   Chesterfield, MA
01013    0.29678938   0.74368894   Chicopee, MA
01014    0.29752877   0.7440418    Chicopee, MA
01020    0.29802647   0.74428964   Chicopee, MA
```

What about a binary data file or a database?

Of course, one could pack the data into a more sophisticated binary format so that it would be an even smaller file. I'll leave that as an exercise for the reader. Unless the need for space and speed is acute, I prefer to avoid dealing with binary formats. Dealing with such data is tricky because you can't just open a binary file in a text editor to see what's going on. A text file can be run compressed with GZIP and read as a stream, and often is in the neighborhood of the size of a binarized version of the data, while retaining the convenience of text.

Java's *serialization* capabilities are another possibility for storing the data. Serialization allows you to write the contents of the current state of a Java object to the disk; it's a "just add water" approach to storing information from a Java application to be retrieved next time the application is run. Unfortunately, serialization tends to be slower than actually parsing simple information. Furthermore, you have to avoid changing the structure of your Java class because it would mean rewriting the serialized version of the data. No thanks.

Whenever considering a "lot" of data, people tend to start thinking "database" right away. But even though there are almost 42,000 zip code records, entering them into a database is excessive—the data is only 2–3 megabytes—and a database would also prevent the sort of immediate interaction we want as the user types a postal code. This will happen in many scenarios, where shoving the data into RAM is so much more expedient (and helps improve the interaction to such an extent) that databases should be avoided until absolutely necessary. Even in cases where the data might be a few gigabytes, clever use of subsets of the data can help the additional work to set up a database.

Loading the Data (Acquire and Parse)

Fire up Processing, start a new sketch, and add the cleaned version of *zips.tsv* to the sketch.

We start with constants that define the indices for each column:

```
// column numbers in the data file
static final int CODE = 0;
static final int X = 1;
static final int Y = 2;
static final int NAME = 3;
```

The main tab of each sketch is represented by Processing as a class. A single location will be defined using a second class named Place. To create this class, use the arrow located at the righthand side of the tab bar and select New Tab from the pop-up menu. Name the tab Place. For now, the class has a simple constructor and only keeps track of the name, zip code, and coordinates for each location:

```
class Place {
  int code;
  String name;
  float x;
  float y;

  public Place(int code, String name, float x, float y) {
    this.code = code;
    this.name = name;
    this.x = x;
    this.y = y;
  }
}
```

Back in the main tab, a few variables are necessary to keep track of the number of total places, the number loaded, and the objects themselves:

```
int totalCount; // total number of places
Place[] places;
int placeCount; // number of places loaded
```

The placeCount and totalCount variables are separate because one will be used to allocate room for the total number of locations, and the other will keep track of how many have been loaded so far from the data source. This becomes more important later, when we will load the data asynchronously.

The filtering process has already covered the preprocessing step, and the only thing resembling mining for this project was handled when we calculated the values for the minimum and maximum coordinates in the preprocessing step:

```
// min/max boundary of all points
float minX, maxX;
float minY, maxY;
```

Now the *zips.tsv* file can be parsed in a straightforward fashion. Because we've already cleaned the data, there's no additional code to validate individual rows or to rid gremlins from the columns. The readData( ) method orchestrates the data acquisition and parsing. The parseInfo( ) method reads the header line from the file, and parsePlace( ) converts a single line of the data file into a Place object:

```
public void setup() {
  readData();
}

void readData() {
  String[] lines = loadStrings("zips.tsv");
  parseInfo(lines[0]); // read the header line

  places = new Place[totalCount];
  for (int i = 1; i < lines.length; i++) {
    places[placeCount] = parsePlace(lines[i]);
    placeCount++;
  }
}

void parseInfo(String line) {
  String infoString = line.substring(2); // remove the #
  String[] infoPieces = split(infoString, ',');
  totalCount = int(infoPieces[0]);
  minX = float(infoPieces[1]);
  maxX = float(infoPieces[2]);
  minY = float(infoPieces[3]);
  maxY = float(infoPieces[4]);
}

Place parsePlace(String line) {
  String pieces[] = split(line, TAB);

  int zip = int(pieces[CODE]);
  float x = float(pieces[X]);
```

```
    float y = float(pieces[Y]);
    String name = pieces[NAME];

    return new Place(zip, name, x, y);
  }
```

Running this program is not particularly satisfying; if everything is working properly, nothing will happen when the sketch runs.

Drawing a Scatterplot of Zip Codes (Mine and Represent)

After parsing your data, you must give some consideration to how the data is mapped to the screen. The x and y coordinates from the data file do not correspond to locations on the screen, so the map( ) function is used to remap them to a useful coordinate space. As with previous examples, we'll set up coordinates for the bounding box where the map should be drawn. A modified setup( ) method sets the values in slightly from the width and height of the plot:

```
// Border of where the map should be drawn on screen
float mapX1, mapY1;
float mapX2, mapY2;

public void setup() {
  size(720, 453, P3D);

  mapX1 = 30;
  mapX2 = width - mapX1;
  mapY1 = 20;
  mapY2 = height - mapY1;

  readData();
}
```

Next, add a method named draw( ) to the Place class to draw a single location:

```
void draw() {
  int xx = (int) TX(x);
  int yy = (int) TY(y);
  set(xx, yy, #000000);
}
```

And back in the host application, add an umbrella draw( ) method that will handle calling the draw( ) method for each place. In addition, functions named TX( ) and TY( ) (for *transform* x and y) handle calling map( ) to map the points to the screen:

```
public void draw() {
  background(255);
  for (int i = 0; i < placeCount; i++) {
    places[i].draw();
  }
}
```

```
float TX(float x) {
  return map(x, minX, maxX, mapX1, mapX2);
}

float TY(float y) {
  return map(y, minY, maxY, mapY2, mapY1);
}
```

Running this version of the code plots thousands of locations. It essentially yields a population density map of the United States because higher populated areas have more postal codes; see Figure 6-1.

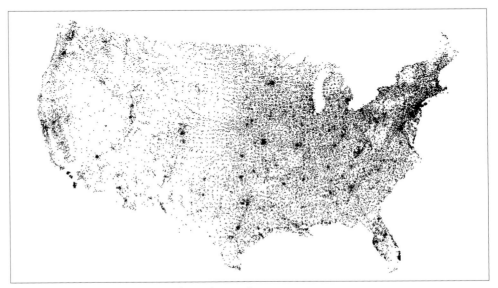

Figure 6-1. Geographic locations of postal zip codes

Highlighting Points While Typing (Refine and Interact)

Returning to the questions that started this chapter, the focus is now to add interaction so that users can explore how the postal codes relate to geography. The user will be asked to type a series of digits, and as she types each digit, locations will light or dim based on whether they are part of a zip code typed so far. For instance, typing 0 and then 2 will dim any locations not part of 02XXX.

The refinement stage begins with choosing a set of colors. First, we choose a better background than white, followed by an initial color that the map will have when no numbers have been typed. After that, we choose colors that highlight locations whose codes include the numbers already typed, and an additional color to indicate when there are no available zip codes that use the digits typed so far:

```
color backgroundColor    = #333333; // dark background color
color dormantColor       = #999966; // initial color of the map
color highlightColor     = #CBCBCB; // color for selected points
color unhighlightColor   = #66664C; // color for points that are not selected
color badColor           = #FFFF66; // text color when nothing found
```

A font is needed for the text we use to provide the user with feedback on what she has typed so far. The typedChars array will contain letters typed, and typedCount keeps track of the number of digits entered. The messageX and messageY values will be the location where the text should be drawn, and foundCount will be the number of locations currently selected. The typedPartials variable is used to make selection fast (more about this later):

```
PFont font;
String typedString = "";
char typedChars[] = new char[5];
int typedCount;
int typedPartials[] = new int[6];
float messageX, messageY;
int foundCount;
```

Inside setup( ), add the following lines to load the font and set the message text location. Use Tools → Create Font to replace *ScalaSans-Regular-14.vlw* with the name of the font that you create. The textMode(SCREEN) line specifies that the text be drawn at its original size, in screen space (no transformations):

```
font = loadFont("ScalaSans-Regular-14.vlw");
textFont(font);
textMode(SCREEN);

messageX = 40;
messageY = height - 40;
```

The letters typed by the user are handled by a keyPressed( ) method, along with an additional method that is called whenever changes are made to the current selection:

```
void keyPressed( ) {
  if ((key == BACKSPACE) || (key == DELETE)) {
    if (typedCount > 0) {
      typedCount--;
    }
    updateTyped( );

  } else if ((key >= '0') && (key <= '9')) {
    if (typedCount != 5) { // Stop at 5 digits.
      if (foundCount > 0) { // If nothing found, ignore further typing.
        typedChars[typedCount++] = key;
      }
    }
  }
  updateTyped( );
}
```

```
void updateTyped( ) {
  typedString = new String(typedChars, 0, typedCount);
  typedPartials[typedCount] = int(typedString);
  for (int j = typedCount-1; j > 0; --j) {
    typedPartials[j] = typedPartials[j + 1] / 10;
  }

  foundCount = 0;
  for (int i = 0; i < placeCount; i++) {
    // Update boundaries of selection
    // and identify whether a particular place is chosen.
    places[i].check( );
  }
}
```

Inside updateTyped, the typedString value is updated by creating a new String object from the typedChars array, one that's based on the number of characters that have been typed so far. The typedPartials array divides each zip code by 10. For instance, when the user types 15232, println(typedPartials) produces:

```
[0] 0
[1] 1
[2] 15
[3] 152
[4] 1523
[5] 15232
```

This creates a quick way to see how well each location matches. The Place class includes a lot of work to handle the new changes:

```
class Place {
  int code;
  String name;
  float x;
  float y;

  int partial[];
  int matchDepth;


  public Place(int code, String name, float x, float y) {
    this.code = code;
    this.name = name;
    this.x = x;
    this.y = y;

    partial = new int[6];
    partial[5] = code;
    partial[4] = partial[5] / 10;
    partial[3] = partial[4] / 10;
    partial[2] = partial[3] / 10;
    partial[1] = partial[2] / 10;
  }
```

```
void check( ) {
  // Default to zero levels of depth that match
  matchDepth = 0;

  if (typedCount != 0) {
    // Start from the greatest depth, and work backwards to see how many
    // items match. Want to figure out the maximum match, so better to
    // begin from the end.
    for (int j = typedCount; j > 0; --j) {
      if (typedPartials[j] == partial[j]) {
        matchDepth = j;
        break; // Since starting at end, can stop now.
      }
    }
  }

  if (matchDepth == typedCount) {
    foundCount++;
  }
}
void draw( ) {
  int xx = (int) TX(x);
  int yy = (int) TY(y);

  color c = dormantColor;
  if (typedCount != 0) {
    if (matchDepth == typedCount) {
      c = highlightColor;
    } else {
      c = unhighlightColor;
    }
  }
  set(xx, yy, c);
}
}
```

The check( ) method calculates whether a point is selected and increments the foundCount variable to keep track of how many locations are still valid. Inside draw( ), a point can be one of three colors: the dormantColor when nothing has been typed, the highlightColor when the point matches, and the unhighlightColor when the point does not match.

And finally, change the background(255) inside setup() to background(backgroundColor, to use the new color background color.

The new version of the code answers our initial question and makes it easy to compare regions against one another by typing different numbers. Typing 4 as the first digit produces the image shown in Figure 6-2.

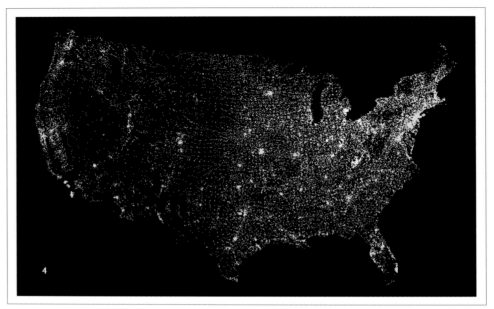

Figure 6-2. Selecting a region of zip codes

Show the Currently Selected Point (Refine)

When five digits have been typed, the point should appear different and include the text for the location's name. In this section, we'll show the location of a fully typed-out, five-digit zip code as a rectangle and add text to its upper-right corner that names the location. That is done with the drawChosen( ) method:

```
void drawChosen( ) {
  noStroke( );
  fill(highlightColor);
  int size = 4;
  rect(TX(x), TY(y), size, size);

  // Calculate position to draw the text, offset slightly from the main point.
  float textX = TX(x);
  float textY = TY(y) - size - 4;

  // Don't go off the top (e.g., 59544).
  if (textY < 20) {
    textY = TY(y) + 20;
  }
```

```
    // Don't run off the bottom (e.g., 33242).
    if (textY > height - 5) {
      textY = TY(y) - 20;
    }

    String location = name + " " + nf(code, 5);
    float wide = textWidth(location);

    if (textX > width/3) {
      textX -= wide + 8;
    } else {
      textX += 8;
    }

    textAlign(LEFT);
    fill(highlightColor);
    text(location, textX, textY);
  }
}
```

Because the text will be shown adjacent to the point, it's necessary to also make sure that the text does not leave the edge of the screen. The middle lines of the method cover this logic.

In the main tab, a variable named chosen keeps track of the current Place object (if any):

```
Place chosen;
```

The chosen point is drawn with a rectangle. To center it, add the following line to setup( ):

```
rectMode(CENTER);
```

The following modifications to draw( ) carry out the extra step to draw the chosen point:

```
public void draw() {
  background(backgroundColor);

  for (int i = 0; i < placeCount; i++) {
    places[i].draw();
  }

  if (typedCount != 0) {
    if (foundCount > 0) {
      if (typedCount == 4) {
        // Redraw the chosen ones, because they're often occluded
        // by the non-selected points.
        for (int i = 0; i < placeCount; i++) {
          if (places[i].matchDepth == typedCount) {
            places[i].draw();
          }
        }
      }
    }
```

```
      if (chosen != null) {
        chosen.drawChosen( );
      }

      fill(highlightColor);
      textAlign(LEFT);
      text(typedString, messageX, messageY);

    } else {
      fill(badColor);
      text(typedString, messageX, messageY);
    }
  }
}
```

The chosen value is set by adding the following to the end of the check( ) method:

```
if ((matchDepth == typedCount) && (typedCount == 5))
  chosen = this;
}
```

And in updateTyped( ), chosen should be set to null after foundCount is set to 0, which resets the current selection whenever typing occurs.

The result is shown in Figure 6-3.

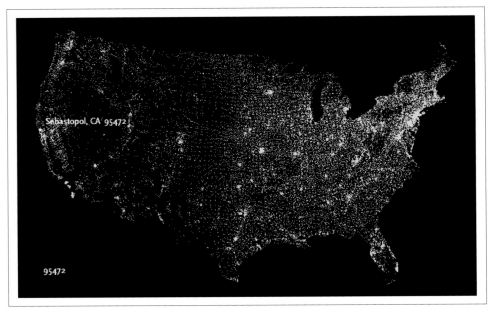

Figure 6-3. Special handling of a full five-digit user entry

Progressively Dimming and Brightening Points (Refine)

In the previous examples, typing makes the screen update instantaneously, which can be disorienting for users trying to compare different areas. In Chapter 3, the `Integrator` class was used to create a more gradual interpolation between two data values. For this chapter, a class called `ColorIntegrator` does the same, but interpolates between two colors. Instead of a `float`, the `ColorIntegrator.target()` method takes a color (in web color format, or created with the `color()` function). Both classes can be downloaded from the book's site at:

http://benfry.com/writing/zipdecode/Integrator.java
http://benfry.com/writing/zipdecode/ColorIntegrator.java

To handle a smooth interpolation, a set of six `ColorIntegrator` objects are used, one for each possible number typed plus an initial value for cases in which no digits are typed. When no digits have been typed, `faders[0]` is used to determine the color. When the user begins typing, all points that match one digit are drawn with the color from `faders[1]`. All points that match two digits are drawn with `faders[2]`, and so on. For instance, as the user types 021, the following occurs:

- With no digits typed, all points are drawn with the color value in `faders[0]`. Inside `setup()`, `faders[0]` is set to `unhighlightColor`, but its `target()` method is set to `dormantColor`, a pale yellow. This has the effect of fading all the points from the duller `unhighlightColor` into the brighter `dormantColor`. This effect has no functional purpose, but letting the points fade in is more pleasing than making 42,000 points appear instantaneously.

- When the user presses 0, `faders[1]` is told through its `target()` method to target `highlightColor`, which causes the points that match to transition gradually from their previous color to `highlightColor`. In the same code sequence, `faders[0]` is set to target `unhighlightColor`, causing all points that don't match the user's 0 to begin fading out. All points that match the first digit are drawn using `faders[1]`, and all points that match zero digits are drawn with `faders[0]`.

- When the user presses 2 (so that the screen now reads 02), `faders[2]` is set to target `highlightColor`, whereas `faders[0]` and `faders[1]` are set to target `unhighlightColor`. `faders[0]` has probably already reached its target value of `unhighlightColor`, and `faders[1]` will arrive shortly.

Each fader is handled individually because the transition from one set of points to another may overlap. That is, if the user presses a first digit, a set of points begins to dim. Those points may not have dimmed completely when the next digit is typed. Separate `ColorIntegrator` objects support the overlap by independently handling each transition.

The array of `ColorIntegrator` objects is created as a global variable:

```
ColorIntegrator faders[];
```

The objects are created inside setup( ):

```
faders = new ColorIntegrator[6];

// When nothing is typed, all points are shown with a color called
// "dormant," which is brighter than when not highlighted, but
// not as bright as the highlight color for a selection.
faders[0] = new ColorIntegrator(unhighlightColor);
faders[0].setAttraction(0.5);
faders[0].target(dormantColor);

for (int i = 1; i < 6; i++) {
  faders[i] = new ColorIntegrator(unhighlightColor);
  faders[i].setAttraction(0.5);
  faders[i].target(highlightColor);
}
```

As with any time animation, it is a good idea to use frameRate( ) to ensure that the transitions behave identically on faster or slower machines:

```
frameRate(15);
```

Next, add an updateAnimation( ) method that updates the value for each fader:

```
void updateAnimation( ) {
  for (int i = 0; i < 6; i++) {
    faders[i].update( );
  }
}
```

Call this method at the beginning of draw( ).

The fading values are handled in updateTyped( ) by targeting the highlightColor or unhighlightColor based on how many digits have been typed so far:

```
void updateTyped( ) {
  typedString = new String(typedChars, 0, typedCount);

  if (typedCount == 0) {
    faders[0].target(dormantColor);

  } else {
    // Un-highlight areas already typed past.
    for (int i = 0; i < typedCount; i++) {
      faders[i].target(unhighlightColor);
    }
    // Highlight remaining points that match what's typed.
    for (int i = typedCount; i < 6; i++) {
      faders[i].target(highlightColor);
    }
  }

  typedPartials[typedCount] = int(typedString);
  for (int j = typedCount-1; j > 0; --j) {
    typedPartials[j] = typedPartials[j + 1] / 10;
  }
```

```
    foundCount = 0;
    chosen = null;

    for (int i = 0; i < placeCount; i++) {
      // Update boundaries of selection
      // and identify whether a particular place is chosen.
      places[i].check();
    }
  }
}
```

Inside the draw( ) method for Place, the color value is now set based on how far things have faded for the depth at which the location matches:

```
    set(xx, yy, faders[matchDepth].colorValue);
```

For instance, if four digits have been typed but this location possesses only the first two, the color of this point will be based on how bright or dim the faders[2] element is.

You will have to try the code directly to see for yourself; the result is difficult to show in a figure because it involves a subtle fading effect.

Zooming In (Interact)

Because interaction in our zip code example involves honing in on an ever-smaller area of locations, the application begs for a capability to zoom closer as the area becomes more specific. The effect of zooming is striking, but its implementation is actually quite straightforward and can be based on methods already in use.

So far, the crux of the representation is the map( ) function, which remaps a series of coordinates (with a predefined range) to a specific location on the screen (with a new range). To allow for zooming, instead set the ranges themselves as Integrator objects:

```
color backgroundColor   = #333333; // dark background color
color dormantColor      = #999966; // initial color of the map
color highlightColor    = #CBCBCB; // color for selected points
color unhighlightColor = #66664C; // color for points that are not selected
color badColor          = #FFFF66; // text color when nothing found

ColorIntegrator faders[];

// Border of where the map should be drawn on screen
float mapX1, mapY1;
float mapX2, mapY2;

// Column numbers in the data file
static final int CODE = 0;
static final int X = 1;
static final int Y = 2;
static final int NAME = 3;

int totalCount; // total number of places
```

```
Place[] places;
int placeCount; // number of places loaded

// Min/max boundary of all points
float minX, maxX;
float minY, maxY;

// Typing and selection
PFont font;
String typedString = "";
char typedChars[] = new char[5];
int typedCount;
int typedPartials[] = new int[6];

float messageX, messageY;

int foundCount;
Place chosen;

// Zoom
boolean zoomEnabled = false;
Integrator zoomDepth = new Integrator();

Integrator zoomX1;
Integrator zoomY1;
Integrator zoomX2;
Integrator zoomY2;

float targetX1[] = new float[6];
float targetY1[] = new float[6];
float targetX2[] = new float[6];
float targetY2[] = new float[6];

// Boundary of currently valid points at this typedCount
float boundsX1, boundsY1;
float boundsX2, boundsY2;


public void setup() {
  size(720, 453, P3D);

  mapX1 = 30;
  mapX2 = width - mapX1;
  mapY1 = 20;
  mapY2 = height - mapY1;

  font = loadFont("ScalaSans-Regular-14.vlw");
  textFont(font);
  textMode(SCREEN);

  messageX = 40;
  messageY = height - 40;

  faders = new ColorIntegrator[6];
```

```
  // When nothing is typed, all points are shown with a color called
  // "dormant," which is brighter than when not highlighted, but
  // not as bright as the highlight color for a selection.
  faders[0] = new ColorIntegrator(unhighlightColor);
  faders[0].setAttraction(0.5);
  faders[0].target(dormantColor);

  for (int i = 1; i < 6; i++) {
    faders[i] = new ColorIntegrator(unhighlightColor);
    faders[i].setAttraction(0.5);
    faders[i].target(highlightColor);
  }

  readData( );

  zoomX1 = new Integrator(minX);
  zoomY1 = new Integrator(minY);
  zoomX2 = new Integrator(maxX);
  zoomY2 = new Integrator(maxY);

  targetX1[0] = minX;
  targetX2[0] = maxX;
  targetY1[0] = minY;
  targetY2[0] = maxY;

  rectMode(CENTER);
  ellipseMode(CENTER);
  frameRate(15);
}


void readData( ) {
  String[] lines = loadStrings("zips.tsv");
  parseInfo(lines[0]); // Read the header line

  places = new Place[totalCount];
  for (int i = 1; i < lines.length; i++) {
    places[placeCount] = parsePlace(lines[i]);
    placeCount++;
  }
}


void parseInfo(String line) {
  String infoString = line.substring(2); // Remove the #
  String[] infoPieces = split(infoString, ',');
  totalCount = int(infoPieces[0]);
  minX = float(infoPieces[1]);
  maxX = float(infoPieces[2]);
  minY = float(infoPieces[3]);
  maxY = float(infoPieces[4]);
}
```

```
Place parsePlace(String line) {
  String pieces[] = split(line, TAB);

  int zip = int(pieces[CODE]);
  float x = float(pieces[X]);
  float y = float(pieces[Y]);
  String name = pieces[NAME];

  return new Place(zip, name, x, y);
}


public void draw() {
  background(backgroundColor);

  updateAnimation();

  for (int i = 0; i < placeCount; i++) {
    places[i].draw();
  }

  if (typedCount != 0) {
    if (foundCount > 0) {
      if (!zoomEnabled && (typedCount == 4)) {
        // Redraw the chosen ones, because they're often occluded
        // by the non-selected points.
        for (int i = 0; i < placeCount; i++) {
          if (places[i].matchDepth == typedCount) {
            places[i].draw();
          }
        }
      }

      if (chosen != null) {
        chosen.drawChosen();
      }

      fill(highlightColor);
      textAlign(LEFT);
      text(typedString, messageX, messageY);

    } else {
      fill(badColor);
      text(typedString, messageX, messageY);
    }
  }

  // Draw "zoom" text toggle.
  textAlign(RIGHT);
  fill(zoomEnabled ? highlightColor : unhighlightColor);
  text("zoom", width - 40, height - 40);
  textAlign(LEFT);
}
```

```
void updateAnimation( ) {
  for (int i = 0; i < 6; i++) {
    faders[i].update( );
  }

  if (foundCount > 0) {
    zoomDepth.target(typedCount);
  } else {
    // If no points were found, use the previous zoom depth
    // (which will be the last depth where foundCount was > 0).
    zoomDepth.target(typedCount-1);
  }
  zoomDepth.update( );

  zoomX1.update( );
  zoomY1.update( );
  zoomX2.update( );
  zoomY2.update( );
}


float TX(float x) {
  if (zoomEnabled) {
    return map(x, zoomX1.value, zoomX2.value, mapX1, mapX2);

  } else {
    return map(x, minX, maxX, mapX1, mapX2);
  }
}


float TY(float y) {
  if (zoomEnabled) {
    return map(y, zoomY1.value, zoomY2.value, mapY2, mapY1);

  } else {
    return map(y, minY, maxY, mapY2, mapY1);
  }
}


void mousePressed( ) {
  // If the user clicks the "zoom" text, toggle zoomEnabled.
  if ((mouseX > width-100) && (mouseY > height - 50)) {
    zoomEnabled = !zoomEnabled;
  }
}


void keyPressed( ) {
  if ((key == BACKSPACE) || (key == DELETE)) {
    if (typedCount > 0) {
      typedCount--;
    }
```

```
    } else if ((key >= '0') && (key <= '9')) {
      if (typedCount != 5) { // only 5 digits
        if (foundCount > 0) { // don't allow to keep typing bad
          typedChars[typedCount++] = key;
        }
      }
    }
    updateTyped( );
  }


  void updateTyped( ) {
    typedString = new String(typedChars, 0, typedCount);

    if (typedCount == 0) {
      faders[0].target(dormantColor);

    } else {
      // Un-highlight areas already typed past.
      for (int i = 0; i < typedCount; i++) {
        faders[i].target(unhighlightColor);
      }
      // Highlight remaining points that match what's typed.
      for (int i = typedCount; i < 6; i++) {
        faders[i].target(highlightColor);
      }
    }

    typedPartials[typedCount] = int(typedString);
    for (int j = typedCount-1; j > 0; --j) {
      typedPartials[j] = typedPartials[j + 1] / 10;
    }

    foundCount = 0;
    chosen = null;

    boundsX1 = maxX;
    boundsY1 = maxY;
    boundsX2 = minX;
    boundsY2 = minY;

    for (int i = 0; i < placeCount; i++) {
      // Update boundaries of selection
      // and identify whether a particular place is chosen.
      places[i].check( );
    }
    calcZoom( );
  }


  void calcZoom( ) {
    if (foundCount != 0) {
      // Given a set of min/max coords, expand in one direction so that the
      // selected area includes the range with the proper aspect ratio.
```

```
    float spanX = (boundsX2 - boundsX1);
    float spanY = (boundsY2 - boundsY1);

    float midX = (boundsX1 + boundsX2) / 2;
    float midY = (boundsY1 + boundsY2) / 2;

    if ((spanX != 0) && (spanY != 0)) {
      float screenAspect = width / float(height);
      float spanAspect = spanX / spanY;

      if (spanAspect > screenAspect) {
        spanY = (spanX / width) * height; // wide

      } else {
        spanX = (spanY / height) * width; // tall
      }
    } else { // if span is zero
      // use the span from one level previous
      spanX = targetX2[typedCount-1] - targetX1[typedCount-1];
      spanY = targetY2[typedCount-1] - targetY1[typedCount-1];
    }
    targetX1[typedCount] = midX - spanX/2;
    targetX2[typedCount] = midX + spanX/2;
    targetY1[typedCount] = midY - spanY/2;
    targetY2[typedCount] = midY + spanY/2;

  } else if (typedCount != 0) {
    // Nothing found at this level, so set the zoom identical to the previous.
    targetX1[typedCount] = targetX1[typedCount-1];
    targetY1[typedCount] = targetY1[typedCount-1];
    targetX2[typedCount] = targetX2[typedCount-1];
    targetY2[typedCount] = targetY2[typedCount-1];
  }

  zoomX1.target(targetX1[typedCount]);
  zoomY1.target(targetY1[typedCount]);
  zoomX2.target(targetX2[typedCount]);
  zoomY2.target(targetY2[typedCount]);

  if (!zoomEnabled) {
    zoomX1.set(zoomX1.target);
    zoomY1.set(zoomY1.target);
    zoomX2.set(zoomX2.target);
    zoomY2.set(zoomY2.target);
  }
}
```

The zoomX1, zoomY1, zoomX2, and zoomY2 variables are the new ranges to be used with the map( ) function. When zoom is not enabled, the horizontal coordinate of a location on screen is calculated by using map( ) to convert the value from the range minX to maxX into the range mapX1 to mapX2. When zooming, we replace minX and maxX with the minimum and maximum values that we want to be visible onscreen. That way, coordinates inside that range will be mapped between mapX1 and mapX2, while map( )

will place the others somewhere to the left of mapX1 (probably offscreen to the left), or an x value greater than mapX2 (offscreen to the right).

The targetX1, targetY1, targetX2, and targetY2 arrays contain the boundaries for each zoom level (that is, the number of digits typed so far, which the code maintains in the typedCount variable). Inside calcZoom( ), the span of the currently valid points is calculated for the current zoom level.

The spanAspect and screenAspect variables are used to expand the target range vertically or horizontally so that it fits the aspect ratio of the screen. For instance, after typing 0, the application will zoom to the northeastern United States. This set of points is taller than it is wide, so the height of the points will be used to determine the vertical span, and the horizontal span (spanX) will be expanded to stay in proportion.

If the span is zero, as is the case when a single zip code is selected, the boundary is instead set to the previous zoom level, but with the final coordinate centered inside that range. The target levels are based on the previous boundary of all points. For instance, after typing 940, the boundary for the zoom is based on the minimum and maximum locations when only 9 and 4 had been typed.

A text label onscreen handles toggling the zoom mode. The mousePressed( ) method checks to see whether the mouse has been pressed inside the range of this label's location. After typing 4, the image looks like Figure 6-4.

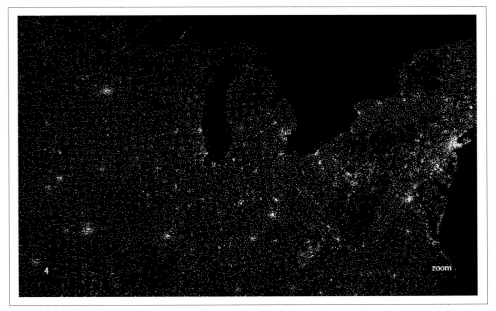

Figure 6-4. Appearance after typing 4 with zoom enabled

Additional minor changes inside the `Place` class handle calculating the boundary inside the `check()` method and drawing the selected point slightly differently. Because the changes are small and spread throughout, the entire code is shown here, with the modifications highlighted:

```
class Place {
  int code;
  String name;
  float x;
  float y;

  int partial[];
  int matchDepth;


  public Place(int code, String name, float lon, float lat) {
    this.code = code;
    this.name = name;
    this.x = lon;
    this.y = lat;

    partial = new int[6];
    partial[5] = code;
    partial[4] = partial[5] / 10;
    partial[3] = partial[4] / 10;
    partial[2] = partial[3] / 10;
    partial[1] = partial[2] / 10;
  }


  void check() {
    // Default to zero levels of depth that match
    matchDepth = 0;

    if (typedCount != 0) {
      // Start from the greatest depth, and work backwards to see how many
      // items match. Want to figure out the maximum match, so better to
      // begin from the end.
      // The multiple levels of matching are important because more than one
      // depth level might be fading at a time.
      for (int j = typedCount; j > 0; --j) {
        if (typedPartials[j] == partial[j]) {
          matchDepth = j;
          break; // since starting at end, can stop now
        }
      }
    }

    if (matchDepth == typedCount) {
      foundCount++;
      if (typedCount == 5) {
        chosen = this;
      }
```

```
      if (x < boundsX1) boundsX1 = x;
      if (y < boundsY1) boundsY1 = y;
      if (x > boundsX2) boundsX2 = x;
      if (y > boundsY2) boundsY2 = y;
    }
  }


void draw() {
  int xx = (int) TX(x);
  int yy = (int) TY(y);

  if ((xx < 0) || (yy < 0) || (xx >= width) || (yy >= height)) return;

  set(xx, yy, faders[matchDepth].colorValue);
}


void drawChosen() {
  noStroke();
  fill(faders[matchDepth].colorValue);
  // The chosen point has to be a little larger when zooming.
  int size = zoomEnabled ? 6 : 4;
  rect(TX(x), TY(y), size, size);

  // Calculate position to draw the text, slightly offset from the main point.
  float textX = TX(x);
  float textY = TY(y) - size - 4;

  // Don't go off the top (e.g., 59544).
  if (textY < 20) {
    textY = TY(y) + 20;
  }

  // Don't run off the bottom (e.g., 33242).
  if (textY > height - 5) {
    textY = TY(y) - 20;
  }

  String location = name + " " + nf(code, 5);

  if (zoomEnabled) {
    // Center the single point onscreen when zooming.
    textAlign(CENTER);
    text(location, textX, textY);

  } else {
    float wide = textWidth(location);

    if (textX > width/3) {
      textX -= wide + 8;
    } else {
      textX += 8;
    }

    textAlign(LEFT);
```

```
    fill(highlightColor);
    text(location, textX, textY);
  }
 }
}
```

Changing How Points Are Drawn When Zooming (Refine)

A bit of time spent playing with the zoom mode makes it clear that points are quickly lost because the single pixels spread out and become difficult to see. This problem springs from how we perceive images, and it requires that points be handled differently as the zoom shifts.

To resolve the issue, points should become larger as more digits are typed. Even better would be to add more information along the way, keeping the density of information on the screen constant as the zoom occurs. For instance, after typing three digits, map data depicting state outlines and major interstates could be included. Although the data retrieval and formatting for that enhancement are too complicated to show in this chapter, we can at least implement one simple way to add a little more information: showing the remaining possibilities for the last digit after the user has typed the first four.

An updated version of the draw( ) method found inside the Place class handles two refinements: changing points to rectangles and showing possible final digits:

```
void draw( ) {
  float xx = TX(x);
  float yy = TY(y);

  if ((xx < 0) || (yy < 0) || (xx >= width) || (yy >= height)) return;

  if ((zoomDepth.value < 2.8f) || !zoomEnabled) { // show simple dots
    set((int)xx, (int)yy, faders[matchDepth].colorValue);

  } else { // show slightly more complicated dots
    noStroke( );

    fill(faders[matchDepth].colorValue);

    if (matchDepth == typedCount) {
      if (typedCount == 4) { // on the fourth digit, show possibilities
        text(code % 10, TX(x), TY(y));
      } else { // show a larger box for selections
        rect(xx, yy, zoomDepth.value, zoomDepth.value);
      }
    } else { // show a slightly smaller box for unselected
      rect(xx, yy, zoomDepth.value-1, zoomDepth.value-1);
    }
  }
}
```

Figure 6-5 shows a selection, with the adjacent locations being drawn using rectangles instead of single pixels as a result of the new draw( ) method.

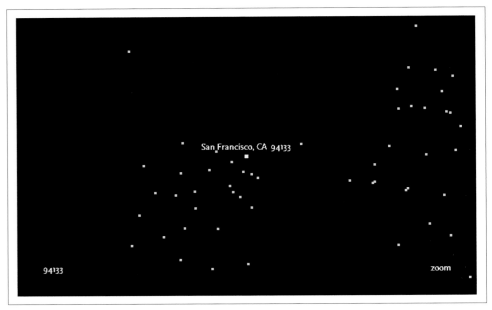

Figure 6-5. After typing five digits, a city name appears for that location

Deployment Issues (Acquire and Refine)

For an online project, downloading two megabytes of data is likely to be a problem. In its current iteration, the program will stop until all data has been downloaded. A better alternative is to use the built-in Thread class to load the data asynchronously. The thread acts independently of the rest of the program, gradually adding locations by incrementing placeCount. When placeCount and totalCount are identical, the data has finished loading.

A *thread* provides a way to bundle a function in your program so that it can run at the same time as another part of the program. In this case, rather than waiting for the data to download, a thread can be used for the download while the main draw( ) method of the program continues to run. Because the program is still running, it remains responsive to user input, which makes it feel faster than if the program halted until the download was finished.

The change also means that the data file should be moved *out* of the data folder, and will instead be placed adjacent to the sketch when on your server. In the sketch folder, move the *zips.tsv* file one level up from its previous location. This way, the much smaller download will happen quickly, and the applet will start almost immediately (drawing the background and making it clear to the user that things are working).

The data should also be gzip compressed to save some space (and therefore time downloading). That can be done using a utility that will gzip-encode your file, but for the purposes of this chapter, you can download a version that's already been compressed:

http://benfry.com/writing/zipdecode/zips.gz

The code to handle asynchronous loading should be placed in a new file (a new tab in the Processing interface) called Slurper. The contents should be as follows:

```
class Slurper implements Runnable {

  Slurper() {
    Thread thread = new Thread(this);
    thread.start();
  }

  public void run() {
    try {
      BufferedReader reader = createReader("zips.gz");

      // First get the info line.
      String line = reader.readLine();
      parseInfo(line);

      places = new Place[totalCount];

      // Parse each of the rest of the lines.
      while ((line = reader.readLine()) != null) {
        places[placeCount] = parsePlace(line);
        placeCount++;
      }
    } catch (IOException e) {
      e.printStackTrace();
    }
  }
}
```

A Runnable is a class that has a run() method. The Thread class takes a Runnable and begins executing it independently of the code from which it was called. The createReader() method will automatically uncompress the gzip-compressed data as it is read. The BufferedReader syntax is described in Chapter 9, but the rest is largely similar to the original readData() method. Back in the main tab, the readData() method now need only start the thread:

```
void readData() {
  new Slurper();
}
```

This code will create the new Slurper object, which will take care of loading the points as they become available from the network.

A nice feature of this method is that the points themselves serve as a kind of progress bar to alert the user to the progress of the download. Over a slow connection, the points will gradually appear, moving from right to left as the data begin to load.

Next Steps

From this point, there are several directions in which to take this project. For instance:

- Using the technique described in Chapter 5, we can check to see whether the Integrator objects have actually changed during update( ). If no change has occurred, we can disable animation with noLoop( ) to make the program less demanding on the CPU (and therefore make other running programs more responsive).

- Depending on browser configuration and how the HTML for the exported applet is written, the program may not have keyboard focus when it first loads. This can cause confusion for the user if they begin typing but nothing happens. To handle such a situation, show the user a message that says, "Click inside the applet to begin" whenever the built-in Boolean variable focused is set to false.

- By redoing the preprocessing steps (Acquire, Parse, Filter), this same method can be used with the codes of other countries. Germany and the UK both use similar postal numbering systems, and data files for each are available online. The open-geodb project is one good place to start; see *http://sourceforge.net/projects/opengeodb*.

- For another variation of this project, I used town names instead of zip code digits. Typing "F" highlights all locations whose names begin with F, and typing "Fargo" shows the distribution of Fargos throughout the U.S. Also interesting about this modification is that it begins to show migration patterns for settlers from different countries as they moved across the U.S.

- And as long as we're looking at names, you can use street names as another option. It's a bit too much information to do the entire U.S., but it's possible to use the same principles to show a map of all the street names in a single state, and progressively select them based on names typed by the user. The street data can be found at the U.S. Census Bureau's TIGER/LINE site at *http://www.census.gov/geo/www/tiger*.

- What about area codes? I have often received requests for the same application applied to area codes or other sets of information that are geographically oriented. Such a system would not be consistent with the original question about how postal codes relate to geography, but it would still be a helpful and interesting tool.

- Also, from the tool front, it too would be possible to address other questions such as, "What locations are within 25 miles of 94133?" This can be done by converting latitude/longitude distance to miles and changing the interface to support selecting a zip code and a distance.

- One of the more interesting modifications would be to bring in additional data sets—whether satellite photography, geographic boundaries, interstate highways, or map images. By removing the projection conversion from the first step, any latitude/longitude-based data could be used as an additional layer. The nicest application would be to show different layers of information at each zoom level (e.g., showing state outlines once the user has typed a single digit, and after two digits, start to show city names or interstates). A good goal in any visualization project is to maintain the density of visual information at each level.

Having mastered the basic version of this project, there are lots of options for taking the project further. Have fun!

CHAPTER 7

Trees, Hierarchies, and Recursion

To complement our coverage of lists and tables in earlier chapters, we'll now move on to hierarchical information. Tree structures store data for which each element might have several subelements. Elements in a tree are typically referred to as *nodes*, usually with multiple *child nodes*. Files and directories are straightforward examples of a tree structure. Each directory can contain several items, which can be files or additional directories. Additional directories may have more files inside, and so on. This recursive structure can make trees a little tricky to deal with, but it's important because recursive structures are found in all kinds of knowledge domains, so you'll want to become adept at displaying and interacting with them. Most of the examples in this chapter use files and directories because they're familiar kinds of data. The same basic techniques can be applied to all manner of hierarchical information.

Recursion offers special opportunities and challenges for both display and interaction:

- It's common to show one or two levels of the tree and let the user delve in or move out.
- This in turn requires ways to signal to the application that parts of the data are omitted or hidden.
- When animation is available, it's convenient to load recursive data incrementally so that you don't have to make the viewer wait for the whole data set to load.

This chapter gives you the tools for all those techniques, along with a progress bar that can prove useful in many animated displays.

Using Recursion to Build a Directory Tree

Start a fresh sketch, and add a second tab named *Node*. A Node object will be a single element in the tree. You'll find this general data structure useful for all tree-like data, but for this example, each element will either be a file or a directory. This is typical for node structures; each is either a leaf or a container.

The node will have a (built-in) File object associated with it, which can be queried for information such as its size, last time modified, or absolute path. The following is the basic structure necessary to recursively create a tree of Node objects. As each object is created, a check is made to see whether the associated File is in fact a directory. If so, a series of child nodes are added to the children array. As those are created, the process continues: each time one of the child nodes is a directory, a series of grandchildren are added to that child node, and so on:

```
class Node {
  File file;

  Node[] children;
  int childCount;

  Node(File file) {
    this.file = file;

    if (file.isDirectory()) {
      String[] contents = file.list();
      children = new Node[contents.length];
      for (int i = 0 ; i < contents.length; i++) {
        File childFile = new File(file, contents[i]);
        Node child = new Node(childFile);
        children[childCount++] = child;
      }
    }
  }
}
```

Caveats When Dealing with Files (Filter)

As with any code, this requires a few tweaks to make it work in the real world. First, some files should be skipped. On Unix systems, File.list() may include the . (single dot) and .. (double dot) directory entries, which will make the code run in a loop. (If you're not familiar with Unix, the . directory is a kind of alias to the current directory, and .. is a reference to the parent directory.) They can be skipped easily enough. That is also why we use children[childCount++] instead of children[i] at the end of the loop.

Next, the files returned can be in any order, so it's best to sort them based on their name. To meet most users' expectations, sorting also needs to happen in case-insensitive order because just a straight sort of String objects will place capitalized names before lowercase names because uppercase letters have lower ASCII values.

If a file is inaccessible (whether due to restricted permissions or another error), the File.list() method will return null. In the current version of the code, the node will be listed as an empty directory because childCount will never be incremented higher than its default of 0. In the next modification of this code, inaccessible entries will be avoided by checking whether contents is null.

Finally, on Unix-based systems (which include Linux and Mac OS X), some files may be symbolic links. If they link elsewhere in the tree, that can also cause the tree to run forever. The getCanonicalPath( ) method of File converts a path to its real location, adjusting any symbolic links and determining the absolute location of each file. The getAbsolutePath( ) method returns the path to a filename, but does not resolve symbolic links. Any time getCanonicalPath( ) and getAbsolutePath( ) return different results, the file can be ignored.

Recursively Printing Tree Contents (Represent)

Our initial implementation of a file tree will also offer a function to print the contents. This method is invoked by calling printList(0) on the root node. Based on the depth value, a series of spaces will be printed before the node's name. Then, it loops through the children array, calling printList( ) with the depth variable incremented by one so that each child is indented by a few more spaces.

Example 7-1 shows the final code for the Node tab. The changes from the previous example are highlighted.

Example 7-1. Recursive data structure for File objects

```
class Node {
  File file;

  Node[] children;
  int childCount;

  Node(File file) {
    this.file = file;

    if (file.isDirectory()) {
      String[] contents = file.list();
      if (contents != null) {
        // Sort the file names in case-insensitive order.
        contents = sort(contents);

        children = new Node[contents.length];
        for (int i = 0 ; i < contents.length; i++) {
          // Skip the . and .. directory entries on Unix systems.
          if (contents[i].equals(".") || contents[i].equals("..")) {
            continue;
          }
          File childFile = new File(file, contents[i]);
          // Skip any file that appears to be a symbolic link.
          try {
            String absPath = childFile.getAbsolutePath();
            String canPath = childFile.getCanonicalPath();
            if (!absPath.equals(canPath)) {
              continue;
            }
```

Example 7-1. Recursive data structure for File objects (continued)

```
        } catch (IOException e) { }

        Node child = new Node(childFile);
        children[childCount++] = child;
      }
    }
  }
}

void printList() {
  printList(0);
}

void printList(int depth) {
  // Print spaces for each level of depth.
  for (int i = 0; i < depth; i++) {
    print(" ");
  }
  println(file.getName());

  // Now handle the children, if any.
  for (int i = 0; i < childCount; i++) {
    children[i].printList(depth + 1);
  }
}
}
```

Back in the main tab, just a few lines of code are necessary to set up a root directory, create the tree, and then show its contents using printList(). Be sure to put the code inside a setup() block; otherwise, you'll get compile errors. When using additional tabs, it's always necessary to put functions inside blocks, rather than using the static mode style of coding first discussed in Chapter 2:

```
void setup() {
  File rootFile = new File("/Applications/Processing 0125");
  Node rootNode = new Node(rootFile);
  rootNode.printList();
}
```

Replace */Applications/Processing 0125* with the location of a directory on your own disk (no slashes at the end) that you'd like to list. I wouldn't recommend anything too big—things might get boring if you try to run it on the root of your hard disk, for example. After the program has finished creating successive nodes, a hierarchic file listing will print to the console. For the Processing directory used in the previous example, the first few lines look like:

```
Processing 0125
    examples
        3D and OpenGL
            Camera
                MoveEye
                    MoveEye.pde
```

```
Ortho
    data
    Ortho.pde
OrthoVSPerspective
    data
    OrthoVSPerspective.pde
Perspective
    data
    Perspective.pde
```

If you're running Windows, you need to specify the file path differently. The equivalent for Windows would be something along the lines of:

```
File rootFile = new File("c:\\Program Files\\processing-0125");
```

Note the use of double backslashes. Because a \ signifies an escape character (e.g., \n), it's necessary to use \\ to specify a single backslash character. A Unix system will need something along the lines of:

```
File rootFile = new File("/home/fry/processing-0125");
```

Special characters such as ~ (which refers to a Unix home directory) don't work because they're specific to the shell and don't have that meaning in other applications. A .. (double dot) properly points to a parent directory; however, it's a better idea to use an absolute path for consistent results.

Using a Queue to Load Asynchronously (Interact)

One downside of the straight recursive method used previously is that calling new Node(rootFile) won't return until it has completed. In particular, this means that for a very large directory, the program will halt completely until the entire tree structure is built. When looking at many files, this can quickly become a problem, especially in an interactive project with a draw( ) method.

Rather than create the entire tree instantaneously, a better approach is to use a queue. Each time a folder is found, it will be added to a list, and as the draw( ) method runs, a few more items from the queue can be read. This way, the program can continue without halting, and users can be updated on the progress of the files as they are read.

To implement a queue, we'll start with the code from the previous example and build it out further. The queue is handled by keeping track of a list of Node objects that have not yet been scanned for their contents in the main tab:

```
Node[] folders = new Node[10];
int folderCount;
int folderIndex;
```

The folderCount indicates the total number of folders in the list. The folderIndex variable is used to track the current folder to be read. Also in the main tab, new folders are added with the addFolder( ) method, whereas the nextFolder( ) method is used to get the next item from the queue:

```
void addFolder(Node folder) {
  if (folderCount == folders.length) {
    folders = (Node[]) expand(folders);
  }
  folders[folderCount++] = folder;
}

void nextFolder() {
  if (folderIndex != folderCount) {
    Node n = folders[folderIndex++];
    n.check();
  }
}
```

The expand() method doubles the size of an array so that more elements can be added. The elements in the array are unaffected, and it provides an efficient means of resizing an array. It's also possible to specify a second parameter to expand() that indicates the new size of the array.

With this code, the nextFolder() method is called from draw() when the visualization is ready for more data. The method then calls the check() method (discussed shortly), which fills out the Node structure with information about child folders. Calls to the nextFolder() method require a negligible amount of time compared to reading several thousand files recursively and at once.

Strictly speaking, this isn't technically a queue, as we're not removing nodes once they've been checked. However, keeping the items around can be helpful: once we've traversed the entire list, we can set folderIndex back to 0 and rescan the directories for changes (e.g., to update the display for changes to the size and modification time of files).

The new Node constructor uses addFolder() on directories, and the rest of the code from the constructor in Example 7-1 is moved to the check() method, called by nextFolder() back in the main tab:

```
Node(File file) {
  this.file = file;
  if (file.isDirectory()) {
    addFolder(this);
  }
}

void check() {
  String[] contents = file.list();
  if (contents != null) {
    // Sort the file names in case-insensitive order.
    contents = sort(contents);
    children = new Node[contents.length];
    for (int i = 0 ; i < contents.length; i++) {
      // Skip the . and .. directory entries on Unix systems.
      if (contents[i].equals(".") || contents[i].equals("..")) {
        continue;
      }
```

```
          File childFile = new File(file, contents[i]);
          // Skip any file that appears to be a symbolic link.
          try {
            String absPath = childFile.getAbsolutePath();
            String canPath = childFile.getCanonicalPath();
            if (!absPath.equals(canPath)) {
              continue;
            }
          } catch (IOException e) { }

          Node child = new Node(childFile);
          children[childCount++] = child;
        }
      }
    }
```

Showing Progress (Represent)

To show status information, it's necessary to set up a font for use at the end of
setup( ):

```
void setup( ) {
  size(400, 130);
  File rootFile = new File("/Applications/Processing 0125");
  rootNode = new Node(rootFile);
  PFont font = createFont("SansSerif", 11);
  textFont(font);
}
```

The draw( ) method handles clearing the background, calling nextFolder( ) and
drawStatus( ), which we'll discuss next. To read folders more quickly, place a loop
around the call to nextFolder( ) to make it check more folders on each iteration
through draw( ). Given 12,000 folders and draw( ) running 60 times per second, it
would take a minimum of 200 seconds to load the entire set. A for loop calling
nextFolder( ) 10 times per draw( ) will cut that to just 20 seconds, plus some additional time for the check( ) method to actually complete. Some trial and error based
on the speed of your machine will give you a value for the loop that balances the
speed at which the folders are read with their impact on the animation speed. Of
course, you don't want to overdo it; otherwise, why use the queue?

The drawStatus( ) method draws a progress bar and keeps us up-to-date on how
many files have been loaded so far:

```
void drawStatus( ) {
  float statusX = 30;
  float statusW = width - statusX*2;
  float statusY = 60;
  float statusH = 20;

  fill(0);
  if (folderIndex != folderCount) {
    text("Reading " + nfc(folderIndex+1) +
```

```
      " out of " + nfc(folderCount) + " folders...",
      statusX, statusY - 10);
  } else {
    text("Done reading.", statusX, statusY - 10);
  }
  fill(128);
  rect(statusX, statusY, statusW, statusH);

  float completedW = map(folderIndex + 1, 0, folderCount, 0, statusW);
  fill(255);
  rect(statusX, statusY, completedW, statusH);
}
```

The statusX, statusY, statusW, and statusH variables handle the location and dimensions of the status bar. So long as folderIndex has not yet caught up to folderCount, folders are still in the queue. A gray rectangle (fill(128)) is drawn for the status bar, and then a white rectangle (fill(255)) is drawn above it, its width (completedW) set in proportion to the number of folders read versus the total number. The status image is shown in Figure 7-1.

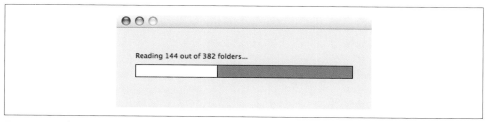

Figure 7-1. Showing progress while cataloging the disk

As folders are read, more subfolders will be found, and the progress bar will dance back and forth slightly each time subfolders are found—e.g., jumping from "4 of 5" to "5 of 19" in a kind of one step forward, two steps back manner. Eventually the numbers will stabilize and the progress bar will be more consistent.

For later examples in this chapter, we'll use both straight recursive and the queue method for reading files—the former for simplicity, or the latter when we want to improve interaction.

An Introduction to Treemaps

It's not uncommon to want to know how space is being used on a hard disk. On file managers, such as the Windows Explorer or Mac OS Finder, pinpointing disk usage can be difficult and tedious. Frustrated with a server hard disk that was perpetually full, Ben Shneiderman, of the Human-Computer Interaction Laboratory (HCIL) at the University of Maryland, worked out a set of algorithms to subdivide 2D space to show the relative size of files and directories (see *http://www.cs.umd.edu/hcil/treemap-history*). He called the representation a *treemap*, referencing the two-dimensional mapping of tree structures. Projects such as Martin Wattenberg's *Map of the Market* (*http://smartmoney.com/marketmap*) and Marcos Weskamp's *Newsmap* (*http://marumushi.com/apps/newsmap*) serve as more recent canonical examples of the technique.

One key trait of a treemap—and the reason it's in this chapter as a hierarchical structure—is that the viewer can click on any part of the display to burrow down and see that part's structure. This interaction is sometimes underutilized, but it can be very effective, as we'll see later. The whole data structure is hierarchical, but different parts can be displayed by themselves.

A Simple Treemap Library

Through a collaboration between Wattenberg and the HCIL, an open source library for creating treemap structures was released online (*http://www.cs.umd.edu/hcil/treemap-history/Treemaps-Java-Algorithms.zip*) under the Mozilla Public License. For this project, we'll use a modified version of this code that has been packaged as a Processing library to make it easier to embed in projects. Although the package naming has been changed, the majority of the code is from the original sources. The library can be downloaded from the book's web site at *http://benfry.com/writing/treemap/library.zip*.

Unzip the *library.zip* file, and place the *treemap* folder into your *sketchbook* folder. Restart Processing if it's already running so that it picks up the new library. (Libraries are covered in the "Libraries Add New Features" section in Chapter 2.)

A Simple Treemap Example

Before returning to files, we'll develop a short program to familiarize ourselves with how treemaps work. Start a new sketch, and select Sketch → Import Library → treemap. For this example, we'll load a list of words from a file and then plot the relative usage for each word. For the data set, we'll use nearly 200,000 words from Mark Twain's *Following the Equator* and write an application that shows the relative frequency of each word in the book. The data file can be found at *http://benfry.com/writing/treemap/equator.txt*.

Add *equator.txt* to your sketch and make sure that it is copied to the *data* folder.

To use the treemap library at a high level, it's necessary to become acquainted with three classes. A SimpleMapItem class encapsulates a single element of a treemap display (in this case a word). The SimpleMapModel class is a list of SimpleMapItem objects. A third class, named Treemap, converts a SimpleMapModel object into a nicely laid out 2D mapping.

Create a tab named *WordItem* with the following code:

```
class WordItem extends SimpleMapItem {
  String word;

  WordItem(String word) {
    this.word = word;
  }

  void draw() {
    fill(255);
    rect(x, y, w, h);

    fill(0);
    if (w > textWidth(word) + 6) {
      if (h > textAscent() + 6) {
        textAlign(CENTER, CENTER);
        text(word, x + w/2, y + h/2);
      }
    }
  }
}
```

Each SimpleMapItem object has x, y, w, and h variables that cover the boundary of the object, and a draw() method that handles drawing the object to the screen. This implementation of WordItem will draw each square as a white rectangle with black text. However, the text is drawn only if the width and height of the text are smaller than the width and height of the rectangle.

Create an additional tab named *WordMap*, and enter the following:

```
class WordMap extends SimpleMapModel {
  HashMap words;

  WordMap() {
    words = new HashMap();
  }

  void addWord(String word) {
    WordItem item = (WordItem) words.get(word);
    if (item == null) {
      item = new WordItem(word);
      words.put(word, item);
    }
    item.incrementSize();
  }

  void finishAdd() {
    items = new WordItem[words.size()];
    words.values().toArray(items);
  }
}
```

This class handles the list of WordItem objects. The items array is inherited from SimpleMapModel, and it simply needs to be filled by methods in WordMap. The WordMap class has a HashMap object that maps between a word (as a String) and its associated WordItem object. This is used by the addWord( ) method, which either adds new entries to the HashMap for new words or calls the incrementSize( ) method for words already found. After loading has finished, the finishAdd( ) method converts the values of the HashMap (a series of WordItem objects) into an array.

Finally, the main tab should read as follows:

```
import treemap.*;

Treemap map;

void setup( ) {
  size(1024, 768);

  smooth( );
  strokeWeight(0.25f);
  PFont font = createFont("Serif", 13);
  textFont(font);

  WordMap mapData = new WordMap( );

  String[] lines = loadStrings("equator.txt");
  for (int i = 0; i < lines.length; i++) {
    mapData.addWord(lines[i]);
  }
  mapData.finishAdd( );

  map = new Treemap(mapData, 0, 0, width, height);

  // Run draw( ) only once.
  noLoop( );
}

void draw( ) {
  background(255);
  map.draw( );
}
```

The first half of setup( ) should be familiar by now. The second half handles loading the words from a file (one word per line) and adds each using the addWord( ) method. Once finished reading the file, finishAdd( ) completes the loading process.

The Treemap class takes a MapModel (in this case, our WordMap class), along with dimensions for the treemap. Calling noLoop( ) is helpful; there's no need to run draw( ) more than once because there's no animation in this example.

The main draw( ) method calls the draw( ) method for Treemap, which calls WordMap. draw( ), which then calls WordItem.draw( ) for each of the items. The result is shown in Figure 7-2.

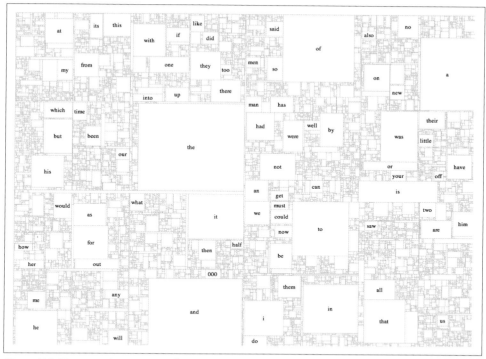

Figure 7-2. Treemap depicting word usage in Mark Twain's Following the Equator

Note in this image how setting the strokeWeight( ) lower than one point makes thin gray lines. That is done so that the black text (the more important information) has better contrast compared to the lines that depict the edges of the boxes. Without the change in weight, the lines would call too much attention to themselves because of the detail and sheer number of the tiny boxes.

In just a few dozen lines of code, we've created a treemap representation of 200,000 words. Other (no doubt more interesting) data sets can be used as well. Simply make classes that extend SimpleMapItem and SimpleMapModel, or read the library documentation included with the download for greater flexibility. At a minimum, refining the appearance of this image can be done easily by changing the draw( ) method inside WordItem. We could also add some filtering to remove stop words. Or, using the mining step, we could tag words based on parts of speech (adjective, verb, etc.) and use those tags to group the words differently or change their coloring. In the next example, we'll look at more sophisticated extensions of the treemap library.

Which Files Are Using the Most Space?

Returning to the question that originally motivated Shneiderman's experiments resulting in the treemap algorithms, we'll now combine the last two examples (reading files and folders recursively, and the treemap) to create a treemap that depicts the relative size of files and folders to get a better understanding of how disk space is being used. Begin a new sketch, and import the treemap library.

Reading the Directory Structure (Acquire, Parse, Filter, Mine, Represent)

We'll begin with a `FileItem` object that extends `SimpleMapItem`, as in the example using words. In this case, we'll keep track of a `File` object instead of a `String`. Put this code into a tab named *FileItem*. This code is very similar to the code for `WordItem`. The basic function is identical: encapsulate an object (the `File`), and handle drawing its name whenever the box is sufficiently large. The x, y, w, and h coordinates of the box are converted to corners in `calcBox()` (which gives us some flexibility later if we want to manipulate the coordinates to zoom in and out using the techniques covered in Chapter 6):

```
class FileItem extends SimpleMapItem {
  FolderItem parent;
  File file;
  String name;
  int level;

  float textPadding = 8;

  float boxLeft, boxTop;
  float boxRight, boxBottom;


  FileItem(FolderItem parent, File file, int level, int order) {
    this.parent = parent;
    this.file = file;
    this.order = order;
    this.level = level;

    name = file.getName();
    size = file.length();
  }

  void calcBox() {
    boxLeft = x;
    boxTop = y;
    boxRight = x + w;
    boxBottom = y + h;
  }
```

```
void draw() {
  calcBox();
  fill(255);
  rect(boxLeft, boxTop, boxRight, boxBottom);

  if (textFits()) {
    drawTitle();
  }
}

void drawTitle() {
  fill(0);
  textAlign(LEFT);
  text(name, boxLeft + textPadding, boxBottom - textPadding);
}

boolean textFits() {
  float wide = textWidth(name) + textPadding*2;
  float high = textAscent() + textDescent() + textPadding*2;
  return (boxRight - boxLeft > wide) && (boxBottom - boxTop > high);
}
}
```

In another tab called *FolderItem*, we'll add code to handle loading and listing the contents of a folder. The contents will be stored as a list of FileItem and FolderItem objects. For now, the draw() method in FileItem will be used by FolderItem. It's not uncommon for drawing methods of trees to be in the leaves, as the branches are often structural and not something to be represented.

The FolderItem code is very similar to the recursive directory-reading code. One exception is that an order variable is used to keep track of the order of the files inside the directory, and a depth variable stores the depth of that folder level. The order variable is important to the treemap layout algorithm (which attempts to retain as much of the original order as possible). The depth variable will be helpful later when altering the representation based on the depth of the elements being viewed. The contentsVisible field will be used to control whether the contents of a FolderItem are drawn as individual boxes or whether the item is shown as a single rectangle:

```
class FolderItem extends FileItem implements MapModel {
  MapLayout algorithm = new PivotBySplitSize();
  Mappable[] items;
  boolean contentsVisible;
  boolean layoutValid;


  public FolderItem(FolderItem parent, File folder, int level, int order) {
    super(parent, folder, level, order);

    String[] contents = folder.list();
    if (contents != null) {
      contents = sort(contents);
      items = new Mappable[contents.length];
```

```
      int count = 0;
      for (int i = 0; i < contents.length; i++) {
        if (contents[i].equals(".") || contents[i].equals("..")) {
          continue;
        }
        File fileItem = new File(folder, contents[i]);
        try {
          String absolutePath = fileItem.getAbsolutePath( );
          String canonicalPath = fileItem.getCanonicalPath( );
          if (!absolutePath.equals(canonicalPath)) {
            continue;
          }
        } catch (IOException e) { }

        FileItem newItem = null;
        if (fileItem.isDirectory( )) {
          newItem = new FolderItem(this, fileItem, level+1, count);
        } else {
          newItem = new FileItem(this, fileItem, level+1, count);
        }
        items[count++] = newItem;
        size += newItem.getSize( );
      }
      if (count != items.length) {
        items = (Mappable[]) subset(items, 0, count);
      }
    } else {
      // If no items found in this folder, create a dummy array so that
      // items will not be null, which will ensure that items.length will
      // return 0 rather than causing a NullPointerException.
      items = new Mappable[0];
    }
  }

  void checkLayout( ) {
    if (!layoutValid) {
      if (getItemCount( ) != 0) {
        algorithm.layout(this, bounds);
      }
      layoutValid = true;
    }
  }

  void draw( ) {
    checkLayout( );
    calcBox( );
    if (contentsVisible) {
      for (int i = 0; i < items.length; i++) {
        items[i].draw( );
      }
    } else {
      super.draw( );
    }
  }
```

```
    Mappable[] getItems( ) {
      return items;
    }


    int getItemCount( ) {
      return items.length;
    }
  }
```

The checkLayout( ) method uses the layoutValid Boolean variable to check whether this FolderItem has already had the treemap algorithm applied to it. If not, the treemap library's layout( ) method is called. The algorithm is specified at the beginning of the class in this line:

```
    MapLayout algorithm = new PivotBySplitSize( );
```

This class uses the Pivot by Split Size model of arranging a treemap. This makes for a pleasing visual order and aspect ratios. You can also try other algorithms; for instance, replacing the previous line with:

```
    MapLayout algorithm = new SquarifiedLayout( );
```

will provide a very different layout representation that keeps each element in shapes that are more square than rectangular. Other algorithms are covered in the library documentation. It might be possible to share a single MapLayout amongst all FolderItem objects, but this method prevents any conflicts between the algorithm and the folder data, and it provides some flexibility for changing the algorithm (for instance, switching to a different algorithm when a folder contains a high number of identically sized files or when there are extreme disparities in file size).

The code in the main tab creates the root FolderItem object, sets a font for the text, and calls the recursive draw( ) method of FolderItem to show the map, producing the image shown in Figure 7-3. You'll need to change the setRoot( ) line to point at something else on your own machine, but start with something on the small side—this version of the code doesn't use the queuing mechanism described earlier in this chapter, so the program will halt for a bit while all the files are loaded:

```
    import treemap.*;

    FolderItem rootItem;
    PFont font;

    public void setup( ) {
      size(1024, 768);
      rectMode(CORNERS);

      font = createFont("SansSerif", 13);
      setRoot(new File("/Applications/Processing 0125"));
    }

    void setRoot(File folder) {
      FolderItem tm = new FolderItem(null, folder, 0, 0);
```

```
    tm.setBounds(0, 0, width-1, height-1);
    tm.contentsVisible = true;
    rootItem = tm;
  }

  void draw( ) {
    background(255);
    textFont(font);

    if (rootItem != null) {
      rootItem.draw( );
    }
  }
}
```

The boundary of the treemap is set to `width-1` and `height-1` so that the lower and right edges of the stroke around the boxes are visible. The application is 1024×768 pixels—the last pixel is 1,023 to the right and 767 to the bottom—and we want the treemap to map perfectly to that boundary; see Figure 7-3.

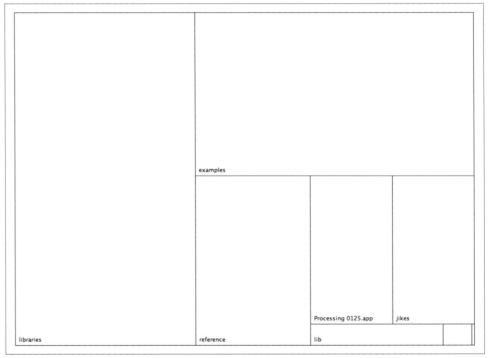

Figure 7-3. Treemap depicting relative sizes for subfolders of the Processing 0125 directory

Viewing Folder Contents (Interact)

So far, we have only depicted the first layer of files because contentsVisible is set to true only for the *root* folder. We'll use the mouse to navigate inside folders, mapping left-clicks to show the contents of a folder and right-clicks to hide contents. This will produce successively smaller boxes, making it even more impossible for the text to fit in each area. Because the text will be all but nonexistent for the majority of these tiny boxes, we'll instead show the title for those boxes on mouse rollover.

In the main tab, the rollover is handled by a FileItem object for the current item underneath the mouse cursor:

```
FileItem rolloverItem;
```

For better precision, we can also specify the crosshairs cursor inside setup( ):

```
cursor(CROSS);
```

Minor modifications reset the rolloverItem on each trip through draw( ), and draw the title of the item once all other items have been drawn. The rollover title must be drawn after everything else; otherwise, it may be covered by items that draw after it (this was first discussed in Chapter 2):

```
void draw( ) {
  background(0);
  textFont(font);

  rolloverItem = null;

  if (rootItem != null) {
    rootItem.draw( );
  }
  if (rolloverItem != null) {
    rolloverItem.drawTitle( );
  }
}
```

Finally, the mousePressed( ) method in the main tab should call the same method inside FolderItem so that the mouse clicks can be processed:

```
void mousePressed( ) {
  if (rootItem != null) {
    rootItem.mousePressed( );
  }
}
```

In the FileItem tab, add a check for the mouse in the draw( ) method that will set this item as the rollover when the mouse is inside its drawing area:

```
void draw( ) {
  calcBox( );

  fill(255);
  rect(boxLeft, boxTop, boxRight, boxBottom);
  if (textFits( )) {
```

```
    drawTitle();
  } else if (mouseInside()) {
    rolloverItem = this;
  }
}
```

Note that this happens only if textFits() returns false—if it's already visible, there's no need to draw it a second time.

The mouseInside() method checks the mouse position against the coordinates of the box:

```
boolean mouseInside() {
  return (mouseX > boxLeft && mouseX < boxRight &&
          mouseY > boxTop && mouseY < boxBottom);
}
```

And the mousePressed() method detects whether the right button was clicked, and if so, hides this item and its siblings by calling hideContents() on its parent FolderItem:

```
boolean mousePressed() {
  if (mouseInside()) {
    if (mouseButton == RIGHT) {
      parent.hideContents();
      return true;
    }
  }
  return false;
}
```

The new methods for FolderItem are slightly more complicated. The mousePressed() method first checks to see whether the folder's contents are visible. If so, the mouse press is passed on to each of its child items. If any of those handle the mouse press, they'll return true, and the method will return. On the other hand, if the contents are not visible, then a left mouse click will show them. A right mouse click behaves like a right-click in a FileItem, which will tell the parent to hide this item and its siblings.

For efficiency, the mousePressed() methods in FileItem and FolderItem return true if they've handled the event. As the tree goes deeper, this will prevent unnecessary mousePressed() checks.

The methods for showing and hiding the contents simply set a variable, with an additional check in hideContents() to prevent the user from collapsing the root level:

```
void showContents() {
  contentsVisible = true;
}

void hideContents() {
  // Prevent the user from closing the root level.
  if (parent != null) {
    contentsVisible = false;
  }
}
```

When contents are visible, it's also necessary to hide the title of the parent item. To do so, we override the drawTitle( ) method inherited from FileItem (remember that FolderItem extends FileItem, which means that it inherits all of FileItem's fields and methods). If the contents are not visible, we call super.drawTitle( ), which will run the version of drawTitle( ) found in FileItem, which is the *superclass*.

Figure 7-4 shows the same *root* folder as Figure 7-3 after clicking a few times to expand individual folders. The ability to peek inside folders is helpful, but has also created a problem of how to distinguish boundaries for rectangles. Are we looking at a folder at the root level or at the contents of a folder? In the next section, we'll use color to convey more information about each level and its contents.

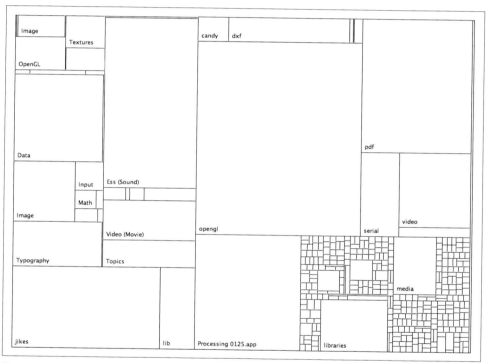

Figure 7-4. Treemap with additional subfolders expanded

Improving the Treemap Display (Refine)

Black and white graphical displays have lost their appeal since 1984, and some color will give the diagram a bit more interest. More importantly, it will serve as a way to further differentiate the boxes from one another. Because our visual cognition is quick to differentiate color, making the boxes into color fields will increase the speed with which the diagram can be read.

With files and folders, we have a difficult dilemma with regard to color. Generally, it's not a good idea to use more than five or six colors to differentiate items. To get more colors, the obvious choice would be to use the hue/saturation/brightness (HSB) color space, and divide the 360 degrees of the hue color scale into equal increments for the number of colors that you want. Such a mathematical approach to color is rarely a good idea, but we'll make an exception in this case, as we're only relying on the colors to offset each field from the other, rather than using them as actual identifiers (e.g., where "dark red" is a signifier for some feature, and a user task might be looking for other "dark red" items). We'll also set the saturation and brightness levels in a way that prevents the colors from becoming garish. Set saturation to 80%, and set brightness, at least initially, to a random number between 20 and 80.

In the FileItem class, two additional fields for color and hue are added:

```
color c;
float hue;
float brightness;
```

The updateColors() method sets the color for this item based on its parent item's coloring. For the first level, only hue is used. For additional levels, shades of that hue are used, which will depict two layers of hierarchy quite clearly:

```
void updateColors() {
  if (parent != null) {
    hue = map(order, 0, parent.getItemCount(), 0, 360);
  }
  brightness = random(20, 80);

  colorMode(HSB, 360, 100, 100);
  if (parent == rootItem) {
    c = color(hue, 80, 80);
  } else if (parent != null) {
    c = color(parent.hue, 80, brightness);
  }
  colorMode(RGB, 255);
}
```

The hue is set by mapping the index of this item (its order) to a value between 0 and 360. The brightness is set to a random value. The c variable stores the color value for this rectangle so that the colors need not be recalculated on each trip through draw(). If this is the root item, colors are given a hue and a fixed saturation and brightness. Subitems will use the random brightness value.

Inside the draw() method of FileItem, fill(255) must be changed to fill(c). And in drawTitle(), rather than black text (fill(0)), we'll use fill(255, 200)—which gives us white plus a little bit of transparency—to prevent too much contrast between the white text and the colored rectangle beneath it.

The FolderItem class also needs an updateColors() method.

In the main tab, updateColors() needs to be called at the end of the setRoot() method:

```
void setRoot(File folder) {
  FolderItem tm = new FolderItem(null, folder, 0, 0);
  tm.setBounds(0, 0, width, height);
  tm.contentsVisible = true;

  rootItem = tm;
  rootItem.updateColors();
}
```

The setBounds() method has also been modified to use width and height rather than width-1 and height-1. With the colors, we'll no longer use a stroke around the items, so the coordinates needn't be offset to include the line in the outer edge. At the same time, use smooth() so that the rectangles line up with one another more accurately:

```
void setup() {
  size(1024, 768);
  cursor(CROSS);
  rectMode(CORNERS);
  smooth();
  noStroke();

  font = createFont("SansSerif", 13);
  setRoot(new File("/Applications/Processing 0125"));
}
```

In Figure 7-5, in the upper-lefthand corner, various brightnesses of yellow are found together. A teal color appears in the upper right, and purple in the lower right. The colored map does a much better job of grouping subfolders with their parent folders.

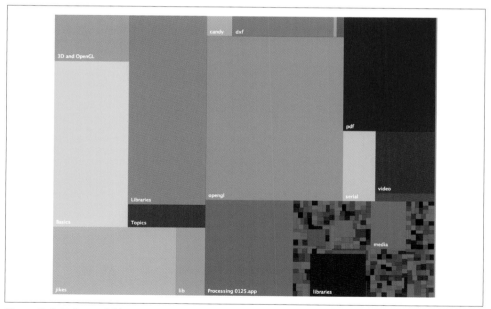

Figure 7-5. Relative folder sizes with colors applied (using random brightness values)

Maintaining Context (Refine)

In spite of the previous improvements, much remains to be clarified. Once we're inside a folder, there is no indication of the parent folder, which can be disorienting for viewers. We can't print the name of the parent folder in the same location because it would obscure the name of the entry inside. Instead, we can show the folder name as a band at the top of an item whose contents are visible.

Showing the title bar on all items would begin to make the diagram look messy; a better option is to show the tag for any folder that 1) the mouse is currently inside and 2) has contents that are visible. At the same time, we can dim the other folders, giving a kind of spotlight effect to the folder we're rolling over. That helps the display because it further clarifies how elements are grouped together, while also dimming the colors further to prevent them from being too strong.

The structure closely resembles how rollovers are implemented. In the main tab, first add a `taggedItem` variable:

```
FolderItem taggedItem;
```

Then, modify `draw( )` to draw the tag after the rest of the drawing has completed:

```
void draw( ) {
  background(0);
  textFont(font);

  rolloverItem = null;
  taggedItem = null;

  if (rootItem != null) {
    rootItem.draw( );
  }
  if (rolloverItem != null) {
    rolloverItem.drawTitle( );
  }
  if (taggedItem != null) {
    taggedItem.drawTag( );
  }
}
```

In the `FolderItem` class, add a field named `darkness` to keep track of the fade; the higher this value, the more the original color is obscured:

```
float darkness;
```

The `draw( )` method handles setting the `taggedItem` on rollover. When the mouse is inside the area, the `darkness` variable is decreased (multiplied by 0.05, a dramatic decrease in value that means the highlighting effect happens quickly); otherwise, the darkness is increased by five percent of the distance remaining until 150. To make the other rectangles dim even more, use a value higher than 150. The `darkness` value is used to draw semitransparent black rectangles over any of the rectangles not currently beneath the mouse, dimming the colors:

```
void draw() {
  checkLayout();
  calcBox();

  if (contentsVisible) {
    for (int i = 0; i < items.length; i++) {
      items[i].draw();
    }
  } else {
    super.draw();
  }

  if (contentsVisible) {
    if (mouseInside()) {
      taggedItem = this;
    }
  }
  if (mouseInside()) {
    darkness *= 0.05;
  } else {
    darkness += (150 - darkness) * 0.05;
  }
  if (parent == rootItem) {
    colorMode(RGB, 255);
    fill(0, darkness);
    rect(boxLeft, boxTop, boxRight, boxBottom);
  }
}
```

The drawTag() method handles placement of the tag itself. If the height of the box is at least twice the height of the tag, the tag is drawn inside the box. Otherwise, if there's sufficient room above the box, then the tag is drawn there. Failing those two cases, the tag is drawn below:

```
void drawTag() {
  float boxHeight = textAscent() + textPadding*2;

  if (boxBottom - boxTop > boxHeight*2) {
    // Try to draw the tag inside the box.
    fill(0, 128);
    rect(boxLeft, boxTop, boxRight, boxTop+boxHeight);
    fill(255);
    textAlign(LEFT, TOP);
    text(name, boxLeft+textPadding, boxTop+textPadding);

  } else if (boxTop > boxHeight) {
    // If there's enough room to draw above, draw it there.
    fill(0, 128);
    rect(boxLeft, boxTop-boxHeight, boxRight, boxTop);
    fill(255);
    text(name, boxLeft+textPadding, boxTop-textPadding);
```

```
    } else if (boxBottom + boxHeight < height) {
      // Otherwise, draw the tag below.
      fill(0, 128);
      rect(boxLeft, boxBottom, boxRight, boxBottom+boxHeight);
      fill(255);
      textAlign(LEFT, TOP);
      text(name, boxLeft+textPadding, boxBottom+textPadding);
    }
  }
```

The tag is simply a translucent black (fill(0, 128)) rectangle with the text drawn above it in white. A tagged version of the *reference* folder from Figure 7-5 is shown in Figure 7-6.

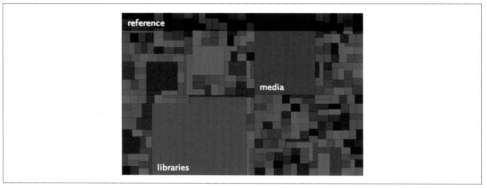

Figure 7-6. Showing the parent folder's name as a tag

Notice how in the previous code, the exception cases (where the box is too small or placed at an edge) account for the majority of the code, and the majority case takes just six lines of code. This is the devil in the details—the extra 15% that requires 85% of the work. You'll run into this any time you try to get things just right; the key is to be aware of it and prevent it from taking over your code. And it's not specific to the visual design aspect of such projects: it's the same issue that results in the changes between the original version of the Node class that begins this chapter and the full version of the code in Example 7-1.

Making Colors More Useful (Mine, Refine)

The random fluctuations of the color brightness for expanded items suggest another feature for our treemap. The shifting brightness prevents the diagram from looking too much like a full spectrum scale scientific diagram, the way that many visualizations using the HSB palette tend to look, but it's still not enough. Because color is so prevalent for our visual system, it's especially important to make sure that color cues are used in a meaningful manner. In this case, rather than randomly choosing brightness, a better option is to assign brightness based on the date the file was last modified.

Modification times of files will follow strange patterns, so it's important to figure out a proper means of scaling the brightness levels. Although most of your files may have been modified within the last few months, some updates may be a few years old, with some dating to when you first purchased the machine. You might even have a file that's 10 years old, something from the archives or a random download from the Internet.

A linear scale isn't very useful when considering file times. A logarithmic scale could be used, but the file distribution is probably not completely logarithmic because there will be significant spikes for things such as files associated with the operating system. Windows XP, for instance, has thousands of files marked 5 p.m., August 22, 2001, coinciding with the freeze date for the code (or arbitrarily chosen to mark the final version of the code).

One option is to put all the file dates and times into an array, sort them, and use their rank order as a means of showing the relative age of files. You can choose whether to consider multiple instances of the same time stamp as a single entry, but for a true percentile, all values should be used. *RankedLongArray.pde* contains a class that keeps track of a large array of longs (used to store time values), providing methods for adding new values, or for getting the percentile of a particular value.

Download this file from *http://benfry.com/writing/treemap/RankedLongArray.pde* and drag it into the sketch window to add it. The specifics of this code are not particularly important; suffice it to say that there is an add( ) method that adds a single long to the array, and a percentile( ) method that returns a number between 0 and 1 to describe the relative location of the number in the list. The number will be used to determine the brightness value for the item in question.

 The search algorithm for the percentile( ) method grabs the first value found, which may or may not be the first or last instance of that particular value in the list. The algorithm is a simple *binary search*, which takes a list, splits it in half, and asks the question, "Is the value in the upper or lower half?" Having determined the answer, it then repeats the same process on that half. This search method (recursive, like so many of the concepts in this chapter) is useful for its efficiency.

A single RankedLongArray object will be shared by all items, so the variable is declared globally at the beginning of the first tab:

```
RankedLongArray modTimes = new RankedLongArray( );
```

In the FileItem tab, the date is added to the list at the end of the constructor:

```
modTimes.add(file.lastModified( ));
```

Because the FolderItem subclass inherits this from FileItem, this line will be called for all FolderItem objects as well.

The final change is to alter the line that sets the brightness value inside updateColors( ) to use the modTimes object instead of random( ). Instead of:

```
brightness = random(20, 80);
```

the percentile( ) method calculates the location of this file's modification time amongst all the modification times in question. The value is multiplied by 100 to cover the brightness range from 0 to 100:

```
brightness = modTimes.percentile(file.lastModified()) * 100;
```

I'll skip a figure for this one, as the change in colors (from random to directed by modification time) isn't particularly meaningful unless you're interacting with the software and are familiar with the files and folders in question.

Flying Through Files (Interact)

Of course, with thousands of files in question, and half a dozen or more layers of depth, we really want to be able to zoom in to each level to see what's inside. After clicking through one or two levels of depth, not only does the display get confusing, but the individual rectangles become much too small to use.

A treemap representation tends to work best when showing two layers of hierarchy. Additional layers can become difficult to follow due to space constraints (how to subdivide while also labeling subdivisions) and visual difficulties (how to differentiate multiple levels of hierarchy shown in the same instance). Rather than trying to figure out ever more complicated ways to shoehorn multiple layers into the display, we're better off simply showing just two layers, and when a user wants to travel past those two, we can zoom to the next pair of layers that make sense. For instance, the contents of the *reference* folder are visible in both Figures 7-5 and 7-6. Once the user reaches that level, an additional click will zoom just the *reference* area to fill the entire screen. Further clicks will open the subfolders of that folder and even zoom to their contents.

The basic idea behind the zoom is similar to the technique used in Chapter 6. We'll use a class called BoundsIntegrator, which essentially combines four Integrator objects, one each for the x, y, w, and h values to be used for the zoom. The first two values are the starting point, and the last two are the span to be mapped into. The class can be downloaded from *http://benfry.com/writing/treemap/BoundsIntegrator. java*.

Download this file and use Sketch → Add File, or drag it to the editor window. Example 7-2 shows the main tab with modifications to support zooming.

Example 7-2. Main tab of the treemap sketch, modified to include zooming

```
import treemap.*;

FolderItem rootItem;
FileItem rolloverItem;
FolderItem taggedItem;

BoundsIntegrator zoomBounds;
FolderItem zoomItem;

RankedLongArray modTimes = new RankedLongArray();

PFont font;


void setup() {
  size(1024, 768);
  zoomBounds = new BoundsIntegrator(0, 0, width, height);

  cursor(CROSS);
  rectMode(CORNERS);
  smooth();
  noStroke();

  font = createFont("SansSerif", 13);

  setRoot(new File("/Applications/Processing 0125"));
}


void setRoot(File folder) {
  FolderItem tm = new FolderItem(null, folder, 0, 0);
  tm.setBounds(0, 0, width, height);
  tm.contentsVisible = true;

  rootItem = tm;
  rootItem.zoomIn();
  rootItem.updateColors();
}


void draw() {
  background(0);
  textFont(font);
  frameRate(30);
  zoomBounds.update();

  rolloverItem = null;
  taggedItem = null;

  if (rootItem != null) {
    rootItem.draw();
  }
```

Example 7-2. Main tab of the treemap sketch, modified to include zooming (continued)

```
  if (rolloverItem != null) {
    rolloverItem.drawTitle();
  }
  if (taggedItem != null) {
    taggedItem.drawTag();
  }
}


void mousePressed() {
  if (zoomItem != null) {
    zoomItem.mousePressed();
  }
}
```

Calling zoomIn() on rootItem inside setRoot() sets the initial zoomItem as rootItem. The zooming also expands the use of the rootItem variable. Because some rectangles will be off screen, mousePressed() need only be called on zoomItem and its descendants.

Because this is now an animation, it's necessary to set the frame rate inside draw(), and call the update() method of zoomBounds, the same way we call the update() method on Integrator objects in previous projects.

Updating FileItem for zoom

The most important change to the FileItem class is the calcBox() method, which now calculates the values for boxLeft and the rest using the zoomBounds object. The mapX() and mapY() methods stretch and squeeze x- and y-coordinates based on the current values of zoomBounds. The second and third parameters of spanX and spanY control the range for the outgoing values. Example 7-3 shows the complete function.

Example 7-3. Final version of FileItem that supports zooming

```
class FileItem extends SimpleMapItem {
  FolderItem parent;
  File file;
  String name;
  int level;

  color c;
  float hue;
  float brightness;

  float textPadding = 8;

  float boxLeft, boxTop;
  float boxRight, boxBottom;
```

Example 7-3. Final version of FileItem that supports zooming (continued)

```
  FileItem(FolderItem parent, File file, int level, int order) {
    this.parent = parent;
    this.file = file;
    this.order = order;
    this.level = level;

    name = file.getName();
    size = file.length();

    modTimes.add(file.lastModified());
  }


  void updateColors() {
    if (parent != null) {
      hue = map(order, 0, parent.getItemCount(), 0, 360);
    }
    brightness = modTimes.percentile(file.lastModified()) * 100;

    colorMode(HSB, 360, 100, 100);
    if (parent == zoomItem) {
      c = color(hue, 80, 80);
    } else if (parent != null) {
      c = color(parent.hue, 80, brightness);
    }
    colorMode(RGB, 255);
  }


  void calcBox() {
    boxLeft = zoomBounds.spanX(x, 0, width);
    boxRight = zoomBounds.spanX(x+w, 0, width);
    boxTop = zoomBounds.spanY(y, 0, height);
    boxBottom = zoomBounds.spanY(y+h, 0, height);
  }


  void draw() {
    calcBox();

    fill(c);
    rect(boxLeft, boxTop, boxRight, boxBottom);

    if (textFits()) {
      drawTitle();
    } else if (mouseInside()) {
      rolloverItem = this;
    }
  }


  void drawTitle() {
    fill(255, 200);
```

Example 7-3. Final version of FileItem that supports zooming (continued)

```
    float middleX = (boxLeft + boxRight) / 2;
    float middleY = (boxTop + boxBottom) / 2;
    if (middleX > 0 && middleX < width && middleY > 0 && middleY < height) {
      if (boxLeft + textWidth(name) + textPadding*2 > width) {
        textAlign(RIGHT);
        text(name, width - textPadding, boxBottom - textPadding);
      } else {
        textAlign(LEFT);
        text(name, boxLeft + textPadding, boxBottom - textPadding);
      }
    }
  }


  boolean textFits() {
    float wide = textWidth(name) + textPadding*2;
    float high = textAscent() + textDescent() + textPadding*2;
    return (boxRight - boxLeft > wide) && (boxBottom - boxTop > high);
  }


  boolean mouseInside() {
    return (mouseX > boxLeft && mouseX < boxRight &&
            mouseY > boxTop && mouseY < boxBottom);
  }


  boolean mousePressed() {
    if (mouseInside()) {
      if (mouseButton == LEFT) {
        parent.zoomIn();
        return true;

      } else if (mouseButton == RIGHT) {
        if (parent == zoomItem) {
          parent.zoomOut();
        } else {
          parent.hideContents();
        }
        return true;
      }
    }
    return false;
  }
}
```

The drawTitle( ) method also becomes a little trickier. As items approach the edge, we'll want to right-align the text (in fact, this could have been done in previous steps). However, we don't want to draw those items if they're actually off screen, given the current zoom settings. So, first we check whether the midpoint of the box is on screen before drawing any title.

Finally, the mousePressed( ) method contains enhancements to trigger the zoom. Clicking a FileItem will zoom the view to dimensions of its parent FolderItem. In the same manner, a right-click will first hide the contents of the parent item, or call the zoomOut( ) method on the parent if the contents are already hidden. Calling zoomOut( ) on an item sets its parent, FolderItem, to fill the screen.

Updating FolderItem

The changes to FolderItem are similar to those of FileItem. Most of the changes are inside mousePressed( ), and they handle triggering a zoom when the contents of a folder are already visible:

```
class FolderItem extends FileItem implements MapModel {
  MapLayout algorithm = new PivotBySplitSize( );
  Mappable[] items;
  boolean contentsVisible;
  boolean layoutValid;
  float darkness;


  public FolderItem(FolderItem parent, File folder, int level, int order) {
    super(parent, folder, level, order);

   String[] contents = folder.list( );
   if (contents != null) {
    contents =sort(contents);
     items = new Mappable[contents.length];
     int count = 0;
     for (int i = 0; i < contents.length; i++) {
       if (contents[i].equals(".") || contents[i].equals("..")) {
         continue;
       }
       File fileItem = new File(folder, contents[i]);
       try {
         String absolutePath = fileItem.getAbsolutePath( );
         String canonicalPath = fileItem.getCanonicalPath( );
         if (!absolutePath.equals(canonicalPath)) {
           continue;
         }
       } catch (IOException e) { }

       FileItem newItem = null;
       if (fileItem.isDirectory( )) {
         newItem = new FolderItem(this, fileItem, level+1, count);
       } else {
         newItem = new FileItem(this, fileItem, level+1, count);
       }
       items[count++] = newItem;
       size += newItem.getSize( );
     }
     if (count != items.length) {
       items = (Mappable[]) subset(items, 0, count);
     }
```

```
    } else {
      // If no items found in this folder, create a dummy array so that
      // items will not be null, which will ensure that items.length will
      // return 0 rather than causing a NullPointerException.
      items = new Mappable[0];
    }
  }


  void updateColors() {
    super.updateColors();

    for (int i = 0; i < items.length; i++) {
      FileItem fi = (FileItem) items[i];
      fi.updateColors();
    }
  }


  void checkLayout() {
    if (!layoutValid) {
      if (getItemCount() != 0) {
        algorithm.layout(this, bounds);
      }
      layoutValid = true;
    }
  }


  boolean mousePressed() {
    if (mouseInside()) {
      if (contentsVisible) {
        // Pass the mouse press to the child items.
        for (int i = 0; i < items.length; i++) {
          FileItem fi = (FileItem) items[i];
          if (fi.mousePressed()) {
            return true;
          }
        }
      } else { // not opened
        if (mouseButton == LEFT) {
          if (parent == zoomItem) {
            showContents();
          } else {
            parent.zoomIn();
          }
        } else if (mouseButton == RIGHT) {
          if (parent == zoomItem) {
            parent.zoomOut();
          } else {
            parent.hideContents();
          }
        }
```

```
      return true;
    }
  }
  return false;
}


// Zoom to the parent's boundary, zooming out from this item.
void zoomOut() {
  if (parent != null) {
    // Close contents of any opened children.
    for (int i = 0; i < items.length; i++) {
      if (items[i] instanceof FolderItem) {
        ((FolderItem)items[i]).hideContents();
      }
    }
    parent.zoomIn();
  }
}


void zoomIn() {
  zoomItem = this;
  zoomBounds.target(x, y, w, h);
}


void showContents() {
  contentsVisible = true;
}


void hideContents() {
  // Prevent the user from closing the root level.
  if (parent != null) {
    contentsVisible = false;
  }
}


void draw() {
  checkLayout();
  calcBox();

  if (contentsVisible) {
    for (int i = 0; i < items.length; i++) {
      items[i].draw();
    }
  } else {
    super.draw();
  }

  if (contentsVisible) {
    if (mouseInside()) {
```

```
      if (parent == zoomItem) {
        taggedItem = this;
      }
    }
  }
}
if (mouseInside()) {
  darkness *= 0.05;
} else {
  darkness += (150 - darkness) * 0.05;
}
if (parent == zoomItem) {
  colorMode(RGB, 255);
  fill(0, darkness);
  rect(boxLeft, boxTop, boxRight, boxBottom);
}
}


void drawTitle() {
  if (!contentsVisible) {
    super.drawTitle();
  }
}


void drawTag() {
  float boxHeight = textAscent() + textPadding*2;

  if (boxBottom - boxTop > boxHeight*2) {
    // If the height of the box is at least twice the height of the tag,
    // draw the tag inside the box itself.
    fill(0, 128);
    rect(boxLeft, boxTop, boxRight, boxTop+boxHeight);
    fill(255);
    textAlign(LEFT, TOP);
    text(name, boxLeft+textPadding, boxTop+textPadding);

  } else if (boxTop > boxHeight) {
    // If there's enough room to draw above, draw it there.
    fill(0, 128);
    rect(boxLeft, boxTop-boxHeight, boxRight, boxTop);
    fill(255);
    text(name, boxLeft+textPadding, boxTop-textPadding);

  } else if (boxBottom + boxHeight < height) {
    // Otherwise, draw the tag below.
    fill(0, 128);
    rect(boxLeft, boxBottom, boxRight, boxBottom+boxHeight);
    fill(255);
    textAlign(LEFT, TOP);
    text(name, boxLeft+textPadding, boxBottom+textPadding);
  }
}
```

```
    Mappable[] getItems( ) {
      return items;
    }


    int getItemCount( ) {
      return items.length;
    }
  }
```

Figure 7-7 shows the *reference* section zoomed as well as the contents of another sub-item (*libraries*).

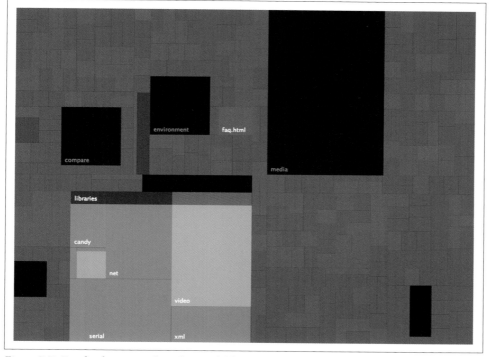

Figure 7-7. Result of zooming the reference folder to full screen

Adding a Folder Selection Dialog (Interact)

Now that we've implemented selecting, showing, and hiding, as well as support for zooming, the display phase of this project is complete. At this stage, a dialog box to select a folder would be a big help for anyone using the application. For this, we turn to Java's Swing UI Toolkit. The following method will open a folder chooser dialog and, if the user clicks OK, pass the selected folder to setRoot( ):

```
void selectRoot( ) {
  SwingUtilities.invokeLater(new Runnable( ) {
    public void run( ) {
      JFileChooser fc = new JFileChooser( );
      fc.setFileSelectionMode(JFileChooser.DIRECTORIES_ONLY);
      fc.setDialogTitle("Choose a folder to browse...");

      int returned = fc.showOpenDialog(frame);
      if (returned == JFileChooser.APPROVE_OPTION) {
        File file = fc.getSelectedFile( );
        setRoot(file);
      }
    }
  });
}
```

By replacing the setRoot( ) line in setup( ) with selectRoot( ), the program will begin by opening the prompt to allow the user to select a file.

The core of the selectRoot( ) method is the following:

```
JFileChooser fc = new JFileChooser( );
fc.setFileSelectionMode(JFileChooser.DIRECTORIES_ONLY);
fc.setDialogTitle("Choose a folder to browse...");

int returned = fc.showOpenDialog(frame);
if (returned == JFileChooser.APPROVE_OPTION) {
  File file = fc.getSelectedFile( );
  setRoot(file);
}
```

However, to prevent threading issues with Swing, the invokeLater( ) method is used, which runs the code on a separate thread. The thread is created inline by wrapping the core code in a Runnable (the way you would with any other thread; see the Slurper object in Chapter 6). Essentially the syntax is shorthand for the following:

```
void selectRoot( ) {
  Runnable ct = new ChooserThread( );
  SwingUtilities.invokeLater(ct);
}

class ChooserThread implements Runnable {
  public void run( ) {
    JFileChooser fc = new JFileChooser( );
    fc.setFileSelectionMode(JFileChooser.DIRECTORIES_ONLY);
    fc.setDialogTitle("Choose a folder to browse...");
    int returned = fc.showOpenDialog(frame);
    if (returned == JFileChooser.APPROVE_OPTION) {
      File file = fc.getSelectedFile( );
      setRoot(file);
    }
  }
}
```

Next Steps

If you tried this example with a large folder, you probably noticed how the UI locks up until files have finished reading. Implementing the queuing mechanism (with progress bar), described in the earlier part of the chapter, will provide a much better user experience, but I'll leave that as an exercise for the reader.

Showing relative folder sizes is a useful example, but perhaps less engaging than a more sophisticated project. Using the methods in this chapter, you can adapt the treemap code to any data set you wish, whether a single-level data set like the Mark Twain example or one with several levels of hierarchy with zooming control.

CHAPTER 8

Networks and Graphs

A graph is a collection of elements, usually called *nodes*, linked together by *edges* (sometimes called *branches*). It is a common structure for mapping connections of many related elements. This is partly because the visual representation of a network shows the sort of connectedness that makes sense to someone familiar with the data, whether as a free-form map of associations written out on paper (sometimes called a *mind map*) or, in computer science, as a visual analogue to a common data model for connections between many elements.

Graphs are very popular nowadays, but they're often not as informative as other more specific ways to represent the connections between items of data. This chapter shows a graph that works for the data in question and another that doesn't. This will help us explore the strengths and weaknesses of graphs and learn how to make them useful.

Along the way, we'll examine the general problem of dealing with quantities of data too large to show meaningfully. We'll use a lot of mining, filtering, and interaction to bring out the meaning in a large data set.

This chapter also takes you out of the comfortable but limited Processing IDE used in previous chapters, and shows you how to integrate the Processing libraries with Eclipse or another Java environment of your choice.

Before getting too deep into the theory of graphs, let's start with a simple example that will help illustrate some of the successes and difficulties of representing interconnected data.

Simple Graph Demo

Distributions of Java since 1.0 have included a demonstration applet named GraphLayout. The applet is a good starting point for learning about graph drawing methods. The example and its source code can be found online at *http://java.sun.com/applets/jdk/1.4/demo/applets/GraphLayout/example1.html*.

The demo is shown in Figure 8-1.

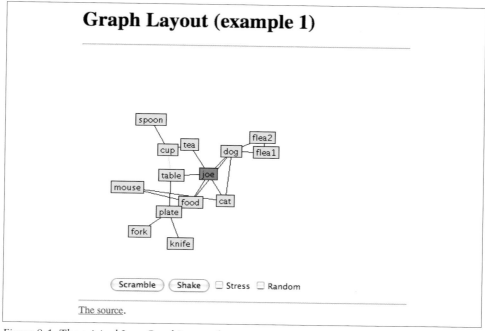

Figure 8-1. The original Java GraphLayout demo

We'll start by making a version of this code that uses Processing syntax, and later expand on the code to make the finished result more interesting.

Porting from Java to Processing

One advantage of the move to Processing syntax is that we can hide most of the details of event handling, threading, and double buffering; all of these are handled automatically by Processing. As a result, much of the original code can be removed, simplifying the example considerably. The original code is a single *.java* file that contains four classes:

Node
    Contains information for a single node of data

Edge
    Describes a connection between two nodes, and its length

GraphPanel
    The drawing surface that does most of the work

Graph
    The base Applet object that handles loading a data set and starting a thread

In the Processing version, GraphPanel and Graph are merged into a single class that will be the main tab of a new sketch. Make additional tabs for the Node and Edge classes. The code in the main panel begins with a pair of arrays, one that stores Node objects and another that stores Edges:

```
int nodeCount;
Node[] nodes = new Node[100];
HashMap nodeTable = new HashMap();

int edgeCount;
Edge[] edges = new Edge[500];
```

Next are some constants for the colors:

```
static final color nodeColor = #F0C070;
static final color selectColor = #FF3030;
static final color fixedColor = #FF8080;
static final color edgeColor = #000000;
```

The nodeColor is the yellow background for the box around each node. Clicking a node will fix it in place and change its color to fixedColor. If a node is being dragged, selectColor will be used. The edgeColor will be used to draw edges as a line between two nodes.

The setup() method creates the structure that will be used later for drawing, but does nothing related to the node layout on the screen; that will be handled later by the draw() method. setup() creates various parts of the structure with the assistance of a few other functions: addEdge(), findNode(), and addNode().

The setup() code sets the size, calls the loadData() method, and creates a font for later use:

```
PFont font;

void setup() {
  size(600, 600);
  loadData();
  font = createFont("SansSerif", 10);
  textFont(font);
  smooth();
}

void loadData() {
  addEdge("joe", "food");
  addEdge("joe", "dog");
  addEdge("joe", "tea");
  addEdge("joe", "cat");
  addEdge("joe", "table");
  addEdge("table", "plate");
  addEdge("plate", "food");
  addEdge("food", "mouse");
  addEdge("food", "dog");
  addEdge("mouse", "cat");
```

```
    addEdge("table", "cup");
    addEdge("cup", "tea");
    addEdge("dog", "cat");
    addEdge("cup", "spoon");
    addEdges("plate", "fork");
    addEdge("dog", "flea1");
    addEdge("dog", "flea2");
    addEdge("flea1", "flea2");
    addEdge("plate", "knife");
  }
```

Adding an edge is a matter of finding each node by its name, and creating a node if it doesn't exist. Once both are found, a new Edge object is created and added to the edges array. If the array is full, it is first expanded:

```
  void addEdge(String fromLabel, String toLabel) {
    Node from = findNode(fromLabel);
    Node to = findNode(toLabel);
    Edge e = new Edge(from, to);
    if (edgeCount == edges.length) {
      edges = (Edge[]) expand(edges);
    }
    edges[edgeCount++] = e;
  }
```

We use expand() instead of Java's ArrayList or Vector classes because arrays are more runtime speed-efficient. This becomes especially important when dealing with thousands of nodes. The findNode() function uses a HashMap to efficiently look up a node based on its label. If none is found, addNode() is called:

```
  Node findNode(String label) {
    label = label.toLowerCase();
    Node n = (Node) nodeTable.get(label);
    if (n == null) {
      return addNode(label);
    }
    return n;
  }
```

The addNode() method is much like addEdge(), but also puts the node into the nodeTable so that it can be retrieved by name:

```
  Node addNode(String label) {
    Node n = new Node(label);
    if (nodeCount == nodes.length) {
      nodes = (Node[]) expand(nodes);
    }
    nodeTable.put(label, n);
    nodes[nodeCount++] = n;
    return n;
  }
```

We are now ready to deal with screen layout. The draw() method for this sketch iterates through each of the edges and nodes, calling relax(), update(), and draw() methods of Edge and Node along the way.

The relax( ) methods calculate the placement of each node and lengths for each edge. This is handled by a kind of toy physics simulation, known as *force-directed layout*, which reaches an optimal layout through a series of calculations. In a force-directed layout, edges act like springs that have a target length (also called their *rest length*). At each step, each Edge tries to get its length a little closer to its target length. Because several edges are interconnected, the elements push and pull on one another. Over time, the lengths reconcile to a best-possible fit (though there may still be a bit of wiggle, particularly with the algorithm used here). The process of applying the forces is called *relaxation*.

In the original code, a single relax( ) function calculates the edge lengths and the node movement, and then updates the node locations. In the Processing version, that large relax function is broken into separate methods in both Edge and Node, which are called in turn from draw( ). The edges are drawn before the nodes so that the lines for the edges draw behind the node labels rather than through them:

```
void draw( ) {
  background(255);

  for (int i = 0 ; i < edgeCount ; i++) {
    edges[i].relax( );
  }
  for (int i = 0; i < nodeCount; i++) {
    nodes[i].relax( );
  }
  for (int i = 0; i < nodeCount; i++) {
    nodes[i].update( );
  }
  for (int i = 0 ; i < edgeCount ; i++) {
    edges[i].draw( );
  }
  for (int i = 0 ; i < nodeCount ; i++) {
    nodes[i].draw( );
  }
}
```

Interacting with Nodes

Of course, we want to be able to interact with the data and drag nodes around, so a few more methods cover using the mouse to manipulate the nodes. The selection variable is used to store a current selection. The mousePressed( ) method behaves similarly to mouse methods used elsewhere in the book (see the section "Provide More Information with a Mouse Rollover (Interact)" in Chapter 3). The left mouse button fixes a node in place, while the right mouse button sets it free again. Dragging the mouse offsets the location of the currently selected node, and releasing the mouse nullifies the selection:

```
Node selection;

void mousePressed( ) {
```

```
    // Ignore anything greater than this distance.
    float closest = 20;
    for (int i = 0; i < nodeCount; i++) {
      Node n = nodes[i];
      float d = dist(mouseX, mouseY, n.x, n.y);
      if (d < closest) {
        selection = n;
        closest = d;
      }
    }
    if (selection != null) {
      if (mouseButton == LEFT) {
        selection.fixed = true;
      } else if (mouseButton == RIGHT) {
        selection.fixed = false;
      }
    }
  }

  void mouseDragged() {
    if (selection != null) {
      selection.x = mouseX;
      selection.y = mouseY;
    }
  }

  void mouseReleased() {
    selection = null;
  }
```

The Edge object has fields for the two nodes it connects and a target length. The relax( ) method is the portion of the method from the original source that covers relaxation of a single edge. It calculates a portion of offset that will move the edge closer to its target length (len). The draw( ) method sets the stroke color and draws a line between the two node locations:

```
class Edge {
  Node from;
  Node to;
  float len;

  Edge(Node from, Node to) {
    this.from = from;
    this.to = to;
    this.len = 50;
  }

  void relax() {
    float vx = to.x - from.x;
    float vy = to.y - from.y;
    float d = mag(vx, vy);
    if (d > 0) {
      float f = (len - d) / (d * 3);
      float dx = f * vx;
```

```
    float dy = f * vy;
    to.dx += dx;
    to.dy += dy;
    from.dx -= dx;
    from.dy -= dy;
  }
}

void draw( ) {
  stroke(edgeColor);
  strokeWeight(0.35);
  line(from.x, from.y, to.x, to.y);
  }
}
```

 We won't get into the specifics of the relaxation algorithm because
they get complicated quickly and don't offer much insight in the context of a book on visualization. If you find this sort of thing interesting, do a search for force-directed graph layout algorithms. General
background about using physical simulations to calculate forces that
handle movement and placement can be found in O'Reilly's *Physics
for Game Developers* by David Bourg. His article on the O'Reilly Network is also a helpful start; see *http://www.linuxdevcenter.com/pub/a/
linux/2001/11/01/physics.html*.

Moving this code into the class prevents extra dereferencing. For instance, the portion
of the relax( ) method from the original example that deals with edges is shown here:

```
// Part of the relax( ) method in the original Graph.java example source
for (int i = 0 ; i < nedges ; i++) {
  Edge e = edges[i];
  double vx = nodes[e.to].x - nodes[e.from].x;
  double vy = nodes[e.to].y - nodes[e.from].y;
  double len = Math.sqrt(vx * vx + vy * vy);
  double f = (edges[i].len - len) / (len * 3) ;
  double dx = f * vx;
  double dy = f * vy;

  nodes[e.to].dx += dx;
  nodes[e.to].dy += dy;
  nodes[e.from].dx += -dx;
  nodes[e.from].dy += -dy;
}
```

Rather than use syntax like nodes[e.to].x that has several levels of indirection, in the
Processing sketch, we'll simply use to.x to express the same thing. That is because of
two factors. First, the relax( ) code is now a method of the class Node, so e is not
needed as a prefix. Second, by changing from and to into Node objects rather than
integer arrays that point to an index in the global nodes list, the array index (and
reference to the nodes array) is no longer necessary. Clear and concise code is easier
to read and debug, so hopefully fewer errors are introduced.

The changes also make use of another math function named mag( ). This function is used to calculate the *magnitude of a vector*. In linear algebra and computer graphics, a vector refers to a direction in xy or xyz space. The magnitude of a vector is the distance between the coordinate (0, 0) and the vector's (x, y) coordinates. That is, mag(x, y) is equivalent to dist(0, 0, x, y), though mag( ) is more efficient.

The code for the Node class is similar, with a constructor that sets the value for label (the text shown when the node is drawn) and chooses random values for x and y. The relax( ) method is the re-coded version of the second third of the original relax( ) method. This method compares this node against all the others to make sure none are too close to one another. If they are, a slight offset (dx and dy) is added.

The update( ) method is the final portion of the Node class, where the position of the node is actually updated by constraining dx and dy so that they don't exceed five pixels in either direction and then adding that value to x and y. The x and y coordinates are also constrained to make sure they stay within the drawing area:

```
class Node {
  float x, y;
  float dx, dy;
  boolean fixed;
  String label;


  Node(String label) {
    this.label = label;
    x = random(width);
    y = random(height);
  }


  void relax() {
    float ddx = 0;
    float ddy = 0;

    for (int j = 0; j < nodeCount; j++) {
      Node n = nodes[j];
      if (n != this) {
        float vx = x - n.x;
        float vy = y - n.y;
        float lensq = vx * vx + vy * vy;
        if (lensq == 0) {
          ddx += random(1);
          ddy += random(1);
        } else if (lensq < 100*100) {
          ddx += vx / lensq;
          ddy += vy / lensq;
        }
      }
    }
    float dlen = mag(ddx, ddy) / 2;
    if (dlen > 0) {
```

```
      dx += ddx / dlen;
      dy += ddy / dlen;
    }
  }


  void update() {
    if (!fixed) {
      x += constrain(dx, -5, 5);
      y += constrain(dy, -5, 5);

      x = constrain(x, 0, width);
      y = constrain(y, 0, height);
    }
    dx /= 2;
    dy /= 2;
  }


  void draw() {
    if (selection == this) {
      fill(selectColor);
    } else if (fixed) {
      fill(fixedColor);
    } else {
      fill(nodeColor);
    }

    stroke(0);
    strokeWeight(0.5);

    rectMode(CORNER);
    float w = textWidth(label) + 10;
    float h = textAscent() + textDescent() + 4;
    rect(x - w/2, y - h/2, w, h);

    fill(0);
    textAlign(CENTER, CENTER);
    text(label, x, y);
  }
}
```

The draw() method here is a little more complicated than the draw() method found
inside Edge. The fill color is set based on whether the node is selected, fixed, or neither. In keeping with the original design, a black frame is also drawn around the box
with stroke(0), though strokeWeight(0.5) keeps the lines from being too thick. The
w and h values calculate the width and height of the box based on the width of the
text (plus a 10-pixel margin, 5 pixels for each side) and the height of the text (plus a
4-pixel margin). A rectangle centered at the node's location is drawn to these
specifications. Finally, the node's label is drawn (in black), centered both horizontally and vertically at the node's x and y location.

The result is shown in Figure 8-2.

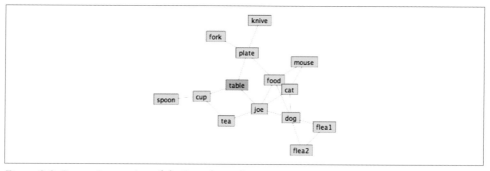

Figure 8-2. Processing version of the Java demo shown in Figure 8-1

A More Complicated Graph

Two dozen nodes in a simple graph is far smaller than most data sets, so we'll try something more complicated. The loadData( ) method can be replaced to load anything you like. In this case, we'll load the first chapter of Mark Twain's *Huckleberry Finn*, using the words as nodes, and draw edges between words found adjacent to one another.

Using Text As Input (Acquire)

The full text of the book can be downloaded online from Project Gutenberg. The first five chapters can be found at *http://www.gutenberg.org/etext/7100*. This code uses the text of the first chapter, which can be downloaded from the book's site at:

> *http://benfry.com/writing/graphlayout/huckfinn.txt.*

Download this file and add it to the sketch by dragging it into the window, or by using Sketch → Add File.

Reading a Book (Parse)

The new loadData( ) method reads the lines of text, breaks them into phrases, and then breaks the phrases into pairs of adjacent words. Phrases can be marked by a period, a comma, or several other kinds of punctuation. The splitTokens( ) method is useful for splitting a String along one of many delimiters. The second parameter is the set of possible delimiters, each a single character. Multiple delimiters in the source String will be treated as a single break. Because each delimiter can be only a single character, double dashes (--) are first converted to an actual em dash (—) using the replaceAll( ) method of the String class:

```
void loadData( ) {
  String[] lines = loadStrings("huckfinn.txt");
```

```
    // Make the text into a single String object.
    String line = join(lines, " ");
     // Replace -- with an actual em dash.
    line = line.replaceAll("--", "\u2014");

    // Split into phrases using any of the provided tokens.
    String[] phrases = splitTokens(line, ".,;:?!\u2014\"");
    for (int i = 0; i < phrases.length; i++) {
      // Make this phrase lowercase.
      String phrase = phrases[i].toLowerCase();
      // Split each phrase into individual words at one or more spaces.
      String[] words = splitTokens(phrase, " ");
      for (int w = 0; w < words.length-1; w++) {
        addEdge(words[w], words[w+1]);
      }
    }
  }
}
```

To see the phrases, add println(phrases) after the first splitTokens() line. A portion of the output follows:

```
[13] " Aunt Polly"
[14] "Tom's Aunt Polly"
[15] " she is"
[16] "and Mary"
[17] " and the Widow Douglas is all told about in that book"
[18] " which is mostly a true book"
[19] " with some stretchers"
[20] " as I said before"
```

The source text for these phrases reads:

> Aunt Polly--Tom's Aunt Polly, she is--and Mary, and the Widow Douglas is all told about in that book, which is mostly a true book, with some stretchers, as I said before.

After the text has been broken into phrases, converting the phrases to words is a matter of splitting each phrase whenever one or more spaces occurs. This is handled by the second splitTokens(), which uses only the space character as a delimiter.

Printing the split version of phrase 18 with println(splitTokens(phrases[18], " ")) produces the following:

```
[0] "which"
[1] "is"
[2] "mostly"
[3] "a"
[4] "true"
[5] "book"
```

Note how the extra spaces have been removed from the beginning of the line. All extra spaces are removed automatically because they're treated as part of the set of delimiters. This is different from the split() function used in other chapters. The split() method makes a break whenever a delimiter is seen, so a pair of spaces next to one another would instead produce an empty element in the array. This can be seen by adding `println(split(phrases[18], ' '))`, which produces:

```
[0] ""
[1] "which"
[2] "is"
[3] "mostly"
[4] "a"
[5] "true"
[6] "book"
```

The `split()` method is useful when breaking up fixed-width data (such as a TSV file), whereas `splitTokens()` is helpful when dealing with a messier range of delimiters, such as the text in this example.

Removing Stop Words (Filter)

In text analysis, a number of English words are commonly ignored because they convey little information. The words (called *stop words*) include, among others, "and," "of," and "to." A slight modification to the `addEdge()` function checks whether a word belonging to a modest set of eight stop words should be ignored before adding an edge. The `ignoreWord()` method uses an array of `Strings`, but it could also be modified to use a `HashMap` for greater efficiency, particularly if more stop words are used. Keep in mind that this is not an exhaustive list of stop words. You may be able to find more suitable lists and better filtering methods online.

```
void addEdge(String fromLabel, String toLabel) {
  // Filter out unnecessary words.
  if (ignoreWord(fromLabel) || ignoreWord(toLabel)) return;

  Node from = findNode(fromLabel);
  Node to = findNode(toLabel);
  Edge e = new Edge(from, to);
  if (edgeCount == edges.length) {
    edges = (Edge[]) expand(edges);
  }
  edges[edgeCount++] = e;
}


String[] ignore = { "a", "of", "the", "i", "it", "you", "and", "to" };

boolean ignoreWord(String what) {
  for (int i = 0; i < ignore.length; i++) {
    if (what.equals(ignore[i])) {
      return true;
    }
  }
  return false;
}
```

Smarter Addition of Nodes and Edges (Mine)

In the current version of this example, the same branch can be added more than once. A better model is to represent each relationship between two words only once, but to put words closer together in the graph if they appear in sequence more often in the text. Our next step in the implementation searches out duplicate edges and increments a score each time they're found. This can then be used to shorten the length of the edge so that the nodes it connects—which are presumably more related—will be drawn closer together. Similarly, nodes have an internal counter for the number of times they appear. That is done by adding a count field to both the Edge and Node classes, as well as an increment( ) method that increments the count by one:

```
// Add this code to both the Edge and Node classes.

int count;

void increment( ) {
  count++;
}
```

A new version of the addEdge( ) method seeks out existing edges and increments their count variables. Each Node will also be incremented when it is found in the original text.

```
void addEdge(String fromLabel, String toLabel) {
  // Filter out unnecessary words.
  if (ignoreWord(fromLabel) || ignoreWord(toLabel)) return;

  Node from = findNode(fromLabel);
  Node to = findNode(toLabel);
  from.increment( );
  to.increment( );

  // Check to see whether this Edge already exists.
  for (int i = 0; i < edgeCount; i++) {
    if (edges[i].from == from && edges[i].to == to) {
      edges[i].increment( );
      return;
    }
  }

  Edge e = new Edge(from, to);
  e.increment( );
  if (edgeCount == edges.length) {
    edges = (Edge[]) expand(edges);
  }
  edges[edgeCount++] = e;
}
```

Viewing the Book (Represent and Refine)

Running the program in its current state produces, perhaps predictably, a mess; see Figure 8-3.

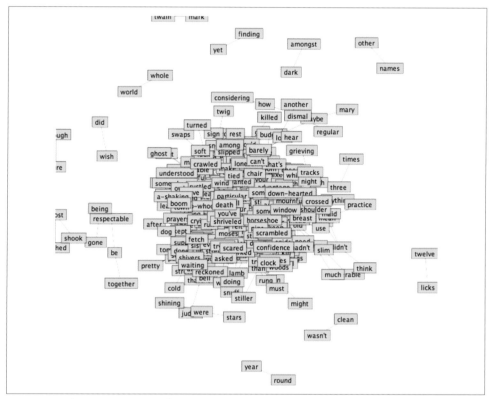

Figure 8-3. This representation of 377 nodes and 589 edges needs refinement

Clearly, this representation in its current form is overburdened, with just under 400 nodes and 600 edges. Because the text of the individual nodes is unreadable, it would be better to hide it anyway. This version of the draw( ) method inside the Node draws ellipses at each point:

```
void draw( ) {
  fill(nodeColor);
  stroke(0);
  strokeWeight(0.5);
  ellipse(x, y, 6, 6);
}
```

This produces Figure 8-4.

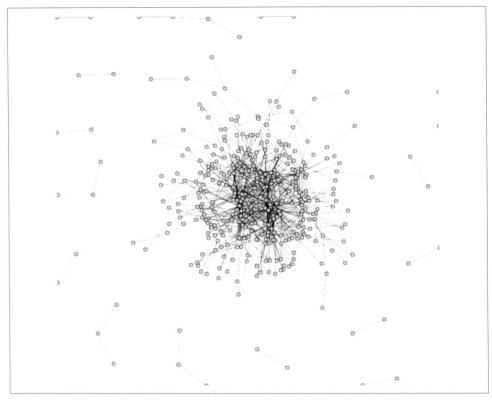

Figure 8-4. Nodes as ellipses

The image created at least begins to be comprehensible, though still messy. Of course, with the labels missing, we no longer know what data we're looking at. To rectify the situation, we can switch back to the previous representation for nodes that are in a fixed position (those that have been clicked or dragged):

```
void draw( ) {
  if (fixed) {
    fill(nodeColor);
    stroke(0);
    strokeWeight(0.5);

    rectMode(CORNER);
    float w = textWidth(label) + 10;
    float h = textAscent( ) + textDescent( ) + 4;
    rect(x - w/2, y - h/2, w, h);

    fill(0);
```

```
    textAlign(CENTER, CENTER);
    text(label, x, y);

  } else {
    fill(nodeColor);
    stroke(0);
    strokeWeight(0.5);
    ellipse(x, y, 6, 6);
  }
}
```

As Figure 8-5 shows, this improves things a bit.

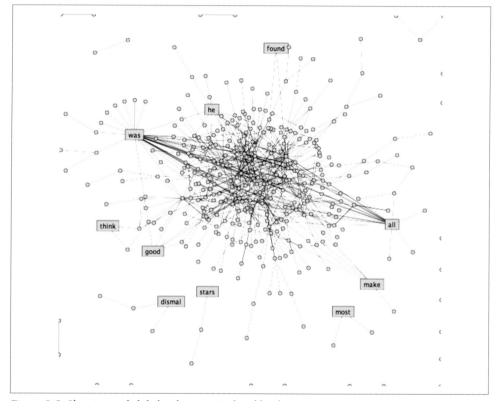

Figure 8-5. Showing node labels when manipulated by the mouse

This representation is still unsatisfactory because it lacks hierarchy. It's a twisty mess of 400 ellipses and lines between them, with no indication of the relative importance of nodes. Instead of drawing each ellipse with a radius of 6, the count field can be used to size the ellipses to show the relative importance of each node. Also, rather than only showing text on rollover, titles of nodes will be visible whenever the text is large enough to fit (whenever count, the diameter of the ellipse, is larger than textWidth(label)). Figure 8-6 shows this version of the code after a few nodes have been dragged to fixed positions for better visibility.

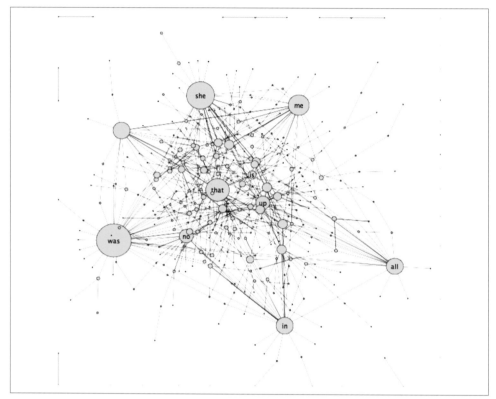

Figure 8-6. Nodes sized based on their frequency

Saving an Image in a Vector Format

With complicated diagrams such as this one, it's often preferable to create a version of the image in a vector format such as PDF. Vector images can be resized without loss of resolution, making them more suitable for printing or other high-resolution work. With the help of the PDF library included with Processing, the beginRecord( ) and endRecord( ) methods can be used to echo all drawing to a PDF file. A modified version of the main draw( ) method (and a keyPressed( ) method to trigger it) follows:

```
void draw( ) {
  if (record) {
    beginRecord(PDF, "output.pdf");
  }
```

```
background(255);
textFont(font);
smooth();

for (int i = 0 ; i < edgeCount ; i++) {
  edges[i].relax();
}
for (int i = 0; i < nodeCount; i++) {
  nodes[i].relax();
}
for (int i = 0; i < nodeCount; i++) {
  nodes[i].update();
}
for (int i = 0 ; i < edgeCount ; i++) {
  edges[i].draw();
}
for (int i = 0 ; i < nodeCount ; i++) {
  nodes[i].draw();
}

if (record) {
  endRecord();
  record = false;
}
}


boolean record;

void keyPressed() {
  if (key == 'r') {
    record = true;
  }
}
```

In this example, pressing r triggers the keyPressed( ) method, which sets the record flag so that in the next trip through draw( ), all drawing commands are echoed to a PDF file. Note that the beginRecord( ) method is placed at the very beginning of draw( ), and endRecord( ) is at the end. The final step must be to set the record flag to false so that the draw( ) method doesn't waste resources recording to the file over and over each time it runs.

The textFont( ) and smooth( ) methods were moved to draw( ) instead of setup( ). When using beginRecord( ), none of the settings (such as font, stroke weight, fill, or smoothing) will be inherited—only commands after beginRecord( ) are echoed to the file.

The beginRecord( ) method is quite versatile. It's also possible to use beginRecord("filename-####.pdf"), which will automatically replace #### with the current frame number so that multiple files can be recorded. You can also use beginRecord( ) to write to other formats using other libraries; see *http://processing. org/reference/libraries* for examples that handle writing SVG format and others.

Checking Our Work

When run, this sketch first shows a jumble of nodes and edges placed randomly, most of which group toward the center over time. Except for any notes the user may drag to corners of the display, the representation is impossible to read. This is partly because this particular graph layout algorithm is not perfect, but it also has to do with the data itself. There are simply too many connections in the information.

To check our work, we turn to the widely used tool Graphviz: *http://www.graphviz. org*. Graphviz is free to download and open source. It combines several graph drawing methods into a single software package. If you're using Mac OS X, a very nice version with a terrific UI is available from *http://www.pixelglow.com/graphviz*. Graphviz can take information for an enormous network and create an image of all the interconnections using one of a handful of layout methods.

One advantage of Graphviz is "dot," its simple text-based file format. The following is the directed graph from the original Java demo in dot syntax:

```
digraph {
    joe -> food;
    joe -> dog;
    joe -> tea;
    joe -> cat;
    joe -> table;
    table -> plate;
    plate -> food;
    food -> mouse;
    food -> dog;
    mouse -> cat;
    table -> cup;
    cup -> tea;
    dog -> cat;
    cup -> spoon;
    plate -> fork;
    dog -> flea1;
    dog -> flea2;
    flea1 -> flea2;
    plate -> knife;
}
```

The `digraph` specifier means that it's a *directed* graph, meaning that nodes are not simply connected but have a direction. For an undirected graph, `graph` is used instead of `digraph`, and `--` is used to connect nodes instead of the `->` syntax.

The first chapter of Huck Finn can be written to a *.dot* file, after our original program has put it into our node and edge structure in the `setup( )` method, with the following method:

```
void writeData( ) {
  PrintWriter writer = createWriter("huckfinn.dot");
  writer.println("digraph output {");
  for (int i = 0; i < edgeCount; i++) {
    String from = edges[i].from.label;
    String to = edges[i].to.label;
    writer.println(TAB + from + " -> " + to + ";");
  }
  writer.println("}");
  writer.flush( );
  writer.close( );
}
```

Add a call to writeData( ) to the end of setup( ), run the code, and then use Show Sketch Folder to find *huckfinn.dot*. Running Graphviz on this file using the default settings (Hierarchical layout) produces Figure 8-7.

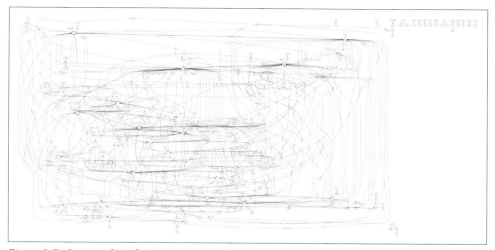

Figure 8-7. Output of Huck Finn using Graphviz in Hierarchical layout mode

The Energy Minimized option is a layout method closer to the algorithm used in our sketch, which produces Figure 8-8.

It looks a little better than our sketch, but not by much. At this point, it's useful to take a step back and reconsider our approach.

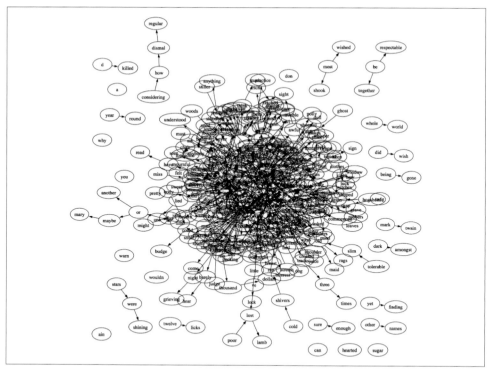

Figure 8-8. Graphviz using an Energy Minimized layout on Huck Finn

Approaching Network Problems

Usually a graph layout isn't the best option for data sets larger than a few dozen nodes. You're most likely to wind up with enormous spider webs or balls of string, and the mess seen so far is more often the case than not. Graphs can be a powerful way to represent relationships between data, but they are also a very abstract concept, which means that they run the danger of meaning something only to the creator of the graph. Often, simply showing the structure of the data says very little about what it actually means, even though it's a perfectly accurate means of representing the data. Everything looks like a graph, but almost nothing should ever be drawn as one.

When dealing with data where items are arbitrarily linked to other items, don't automatically choose to graph it. There is a tendency when using graphs to become smitten with one's own data. Even though a graph of a few hundred nodes quickly becomes unreadable, it is often satisfying for the creator because the resulting figure is elegant and complex and may be subjectively beautiful, and the notion that the creator's data is "complex" fits just fine with the creator's own interpretation of it. Graphs have a tendency of making a data set look sophisticated and important, without having solved the problem of enlightening the viewer.

Here are some techniques for coping with graph data:

- As with all of the projects in the book, always return to your original question. We didn't have much of a plan for looking at the Huck Finn words, and as a result, didn't get much out of it. But if we had something more specific in mind, such as, "How often does the word *she* appear, and in what context?," we could have answered that question more clearly.

- Consider the representation. Just as important, by narrowing down the question, it may turn out that a graph representation is not the best route. What is the minimum amount of information that can be used to convey your purpose? Could the same information be shown with a table? Given the problems with graphs, finding an alternate view is often helpful.

- What's interesting about this data? A graph that depicts biological data might look just like a graph of a social network. This isn't a positive thing because all that's been depicted is the structural quality (the fact that the data set is a network), not what's interesting and unique in the information.

- Try multiple diagrams. Rather than trying to pack everything into a single diagram, would it have been better to work with single paragraphs as individual diagrams to get the node count down around 100?

- Figure out how to group the information. Can groups of words be categorized? Can small subsets of the words be chosen? Once placed into clusters, can the clusters themselves be collapsed (perhaps using interaction) into single nodes?

- Introduce hierarchy to avoid a sea of anonymous data. That is why we tried changing the size of each node based on its frequency of occurrence. It helped pull out the more important nodes and gave the less important nodes less visual prominence. This helps the user learn about the data because it provides clues about where to look.

- Is the information time-based? If so, then it might make sense to have the graph itself change over time, based on what's relevant at that particular time. If a graph consists of 10,000 nodes but only a few hundred are relevant at any one moment, use animation (or interaction to control time) to make the nodes expand or contract based on their importance at the given time.

- Even without clustering, interaction can be used to allow the user to explore the data. If the graph can be used as a navigation device, it might be possible to hide large portions of the graph until they are relevant. If one node is the current node, the graph can arrange itself to show only nodes that connect to that one. It may even show a second level of depth, though less prominently than the first.

To illustrate some of these techniques, consider the Six Degrees of Kevin Bacon game, the notion that all actors can be traced back to Kevin Bacon in six steps or less. The Oracle of Bacon (*http://oracleofbacon.org*) is a site that allows users to view the Six Degrees of Kevin Bacon. A visualization of the network of actors would be enormous, and if I'm trying to figure out how Kevin Bacon is connected to Steve Buscemi, the graph of thousands of actors is far less important than a simple list that states the steps I would take along the graph to get from Steve Buscemi to Kevin Bacon. Therefore, the result can be flattened to a simple list. On the other hand, if I wanted to convey the feeling of a graph to the user (perhaps to reinforce the "connectedness" aspect), the representation could instead begin with one individual and show all connected nodes. It's not necessary to show additional levels of depth because a selection must first be made that takes us through the first layer of the network. Through navigation, we've sufficiently narrowed the representation from tens of thousands of elements to a few hundred or just dozens.

Advanced Graph Example

With this example, we move to a more advanced look at graphs. We'll look at logfile data from a web site and use it to build a visualization of how visitors access the site, as well as how the site's hierarchy changes over time. The code is built from a base similar to the previous example, so while it's more complicated, the basic structure will be similar to building the graph of Huck Finn text.

This example is a bit larger than the others in this book (about 1,000 lines of code total), and it's a useful example for showing how to use the Processing Core library in a full-fledged IDE such as Eclipse (*http://eclipse.org*). You can start by downloading the code for the project from the book's site:

>   *http://benfry.com/writing/anemone/project.zip*

Once running, the code will produce an image like Figure 8-9, but first some introduction is required before you can get things up and running.

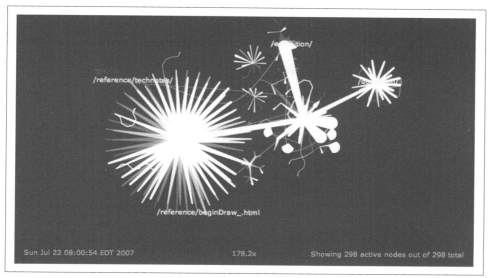

Figure 8-9. The Anemone project running on data from www.processing.org

Getting Started with Java IDEs

The Processing syntax is essentially a dialect of Java. A preprocessor converts Processing syntax into Java syntax, and then a Java compiler creates Java *.class* files from the code. The syntax changes made by the preprocessor are covered here.

The first step in using the Processing Core is to find *core.jar* in the *lib* subfolder of the Processing installation. This *.jar* file contains the guts of the library, which includes classes such as `PApplet`, `PImage`, and `PGraphics` that implement the Processing API as conventional Java objects.

If you have a favorite IDE and are familiar with using *.jar* files in projects, you can simply add *core.jar* to a new project, along with the *.java* files from the *project.zip* file. Netbeans (*http://www.netbeans.org*), for instance, is a popular (and also free) alternative that some prefer over Eclipse. A similar process can be used to integrate with Netbeans, and if you're familiar with that environment, adapting these instructions should be straightforward. If you're using Eclipse and are familiar with it, the project files are already in the project download, and you need only create a new project from the unzipped *project.zip*.

Step-by-step instructions if you're new to Eclipse

1. Download Eclipse from *http://eclipse.org*, and then unpack the archive to a suitable location on your machine. Launch Eclipse.
2. Use File → New → Java Project to begin a New Project Wizard.

3. In the dialog box, enter *anemone* as the name of the project, and choose Create Project From Existing Source. Click the Browse... button and navigate to the unpacked *anemone* folder. Once set up properly, your window should look something like Figure 8-10.

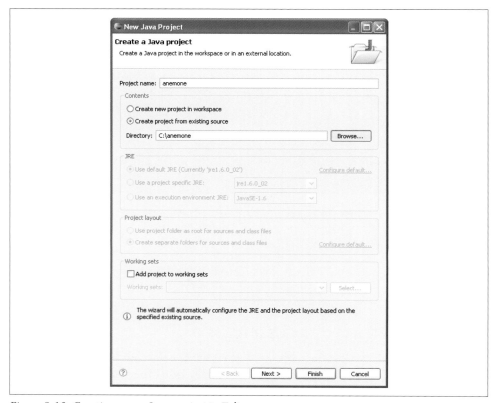

Figure 8-10. Creating a new Java project in Eclipse

4. Click Finish, and the project should load into the IDE without any errors, as shown in Figure 8-11. If you haven't already, you may need to close the Welcome screen.

5. To run the project, right-click *Anemone.java* and select Run As → Java Application from the popup menu. In its current state, the application won't do much because it needs data. A window with a blue background will pop up, and you'll probably get an error in the Console (lower-right panel) stating that *combined_log* does not exist. You'll need to get access to an example logfile or create your own so the project runs properly.

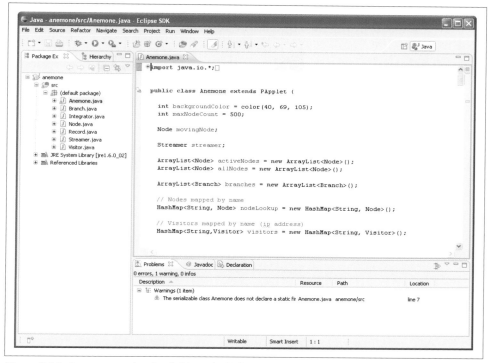

Figure 8-11. Anemone project loaded into the Eclipse IDE

Obtaining a Web Server Logfile (Acquire)

If you run a web server, you probably know where to find its logfiles. For the Apache server on a typical Mac OS X or Linux setup, this might be in */var/log/httpd/*. The files are named *access_log* and *error_log*. The *access_log* file is probably in common logfile format, though it's better to use combined logfile format, which will provide more information about your users—including the previous pages they visited, the browsers they used, and the operating systems they're running. We'll cover only Apache in this example, but the same principles can be applied to IIS or AOL Server, with some minor tweaks to the way it's parsed based on the format of the logfile.

Reading Apache Logfiles (Parse)

A logfile can contain a few thousand or even a few million lines of text, one for each object requested from the server. A typical line contains the IP address of the visitor, a timestamp, the requested page (or object, such as an image), the referring object (last thing visited), and a user agent (which denotes the browser type and platform).

A typical line from processing.org looks like this:

```
192.168.1.144 - - [22/Jul/2007:01:34:11 -0700] "GET /exhibition/index.html HTTP/1.1"
200 19168 "http://www.processing.org/" "Mozilla/5.0 (Macintosh; U; Intel Mac OS X;
en-US; rv:1.8.1.5) Gecko/20070713 Firefox/2.0.0.5"
```

This means that at 1:34 a.m. on July 22, 2007, someone with the IP address 192.168.1.144 visited *http://www.processing.org/exhibition/index.html*, after first visiting the home page at *http://www.processing.org*. The page successfully downloaded (status code 200) and was 19,168 bytes. The visitor used the U.S. English version of Firefox 2.0.0.5 on an Intel Mac, which is compatible with Mozilla/5.0 (Netscape 5, which most browsers claim to be).

The code in *Record.java* parses lines of logfile data. First, a regular expression (discussed in Chapter 5) is used to break the line into its component parts:

```
static final String combinedLogFormat =
  "^(\\S+) (\\S+) (\\S+) \\[([^\\]]+)\\] " +
  "\"(\\S+) (.*?) (\\S+)\" (\\S+) (\\S+) \"(\\S+)\" \"(.*)\"$";
static final String commonLogFormat =
  "^(\\S+) (\\S+) (\\S+) \\[([^\\]]+)\\] " +
  "\"(\\S+) (.*?) (\\S+)\" (\\S+) (\\S+)$";
static Pattern pattern = Pattern.compile(combinedLogFormat);
```

Depending on the type of logfile you're using (combined or common), you can call `Pattern.compile( )` on either `String`.

For the timestamp, we can use the `DateFormat` object, which was also introduced in Chapter 5. It will convert a date in the format `22/Jul/2007:01:34:11 -0700` into a `Date` object, which can be manipulated more efficiently:

```
static DateFormat timestampFormat =
  new SimpleDateFormat("dd/MMMM/yyyy:HH:mm:ss ZZZZ");
```

The date portion is pulled out by the part of the regular expression that reads \\[([^\\
]]+)\\], which matches one or more characters inside the pair of square brackets. The excessive number of backslashes is necessary because bracket characters are used for grouping in a regexp. Therefore, to match an actual bracket, one must use \[, and to escape the backslash itself in a Java string, it must be doubled to make \\[. The rest of the regexp is similar to what we saw in the earlier example.

The Record class represents a single line of the logfile. The constructor takes one line of the logfile as a parameter, and then parses each piece into fields with names such as ip, url, and bytes. If the common (instead of combined) log format is in use, m.groupCount( ) will be 9 instead of 11, and the referer and userAgent fields will be set blank (because leaving them null would cause errors):

```java
public Record(String line) {
  Matcher m = pattern.matcher(line);

  if (m.matches( )) {
    ip = m.group(1);

    userIdent = m.group(2);
    userAuth = m.group(3);

    try {
      String timestampStr = m.group(4);
      Date timestampDate = timestampFormat.parse(timestampStr);
      timestamp = timestampDate.getTime( );
    } catch (ParseException e) {
      e.printStackTrace( );
    }

    method = m.group(5);
    url = m.group(6);
    protocol = m.group(7);

    status = PApplet.parseInt(m.group(8));
    bytes = PApplet.parseInt(m.group(9));

    if (m.groupCount( ) > 9) {
      referer = m.group(10);
      userAgent = m.group(11);
    } else {
      // If no referer or useragent info available, leave it blank
      referer = "-";
      userAgent = "";
    }
  }
}
```

Other logfile formats include IIS and W3C Extended. Information about each can be found at the following locations. Most often, the format will be a variant of common or combined log formats, perhaps with a few tweaks.

- IIS: *http://msdn2.microsoft.com/en-us/library/ms525807.aspx*
- W3C Extended: *http://www.w3.org/TR/WD-logfile.html*

A Look at the Other Source Files

So far we've looked only at *Record.java* in this project. The other classes consist of:

Anemone.java

> The class contains the main sketch. In Java syntax, a sketch is a class that extends the class processing.core.PApplet (which itself extends java.applet. Applet). Because this class is a PApplet, it will have access to all Processing functions, such as loadStrings( ), line( ), and fill( ). For the other classes (Node, Branch, and others) to have access to these functions, they'll have to go through the Anemone class.

Branch.java and Node.java

> These files are equivalent to the Edge and Node classes in our earlier example. Branch is simply the preferred name in this context because we'll be dealing with the tree-shaped hierarchy of a web site.

Streamer.java

> This class handles the loading of the data on a separate thread, like we saw in Chapter 6. In previous versions in this chapter, reading from a file is a synchronous operation, and all activity in the program halts until the read has completed. This is especially problematic when data is still being written to the file (like reading the file as it's being written so that you can watch live activity on the web site). By placing the read operations on a separate thread, the animation can continue regardless of whether new data is available. For instance, if the logfile is being streamed (for instance, on Unix via tail -f /var/log/httpd/access_ log), this class will read a handful of lines and make sure they're available when the main Anemone class is ready for them.

Integrator.java

> This is our old friend the Integrator class. It will be used to set target lengths for branches between nodes. By using an Integrator, new branches can slowly grow rather than suddenly appear.

Visitor.java

> This is used to create objects for each unique IP address visiting the site. This way, individual paths can be traced as users move around to different pages. We'll draw the paths of the individual visitors in the background, which will show general patterns of activity from web crawlers and humans alike.

Moving from Processing to Java

Because we've removed the preprocessor that converts Processing syntax into straight Java, some changes will be necessary in code that's written directly for Java. Consider the following Processing program:

```
color bg = #EECC00;

void setup( ) {
  size(400, 400);
}

void draw( ) {
  backgound(bg);
  line(mouseX, mouseY, width/2.0, height/2.0);
}
```

In Java syntax, this would read:

```
import processing.core.*;

public class Test extends PApplet {

  int bg = 0xFFEECC00;

  public void setup( ) {
    size(400, 400);
  }

  public void draw( ) {
    background(bg);
    line(mouseX, mouseY, width/2.0f, height/2.0f);
  }
}
```

The first difference to note is the `import` statements, which identify to the Java compiler that `processing.core` is used (the classes found in *core.jar*).

Next, everything in Java is an object. The same is true for Processing, but that fact is hidden so that it's not necessary to learn syntax such as `public class Test extends PApplet` just to get something visible on the screen. That line ends with a curly brace, which starts a block, and the block ends with a closing brace found at the end of the code.

The color data type in Processing is simply an alias to the `int` data type, which means `int bg` and `color bg` have an identical function whether in Processing or Java. Mapping to the `int` type is important because of the way it stores color values.

Each `int` is 32 bits of data, with the first 8 bits specifying the alpha value, the second 8 the red value, the third 8 the green, and the final 8 the blue. The 32-bit number is expressed as eight hexadecimal digits, two digits each for the alpha, red, green, and blue components of a color respectively. This representation is already familiar to many web designers and programmers through web colors such as #EECC00. The web format leaves out the alpha portion, which is assumed to be opaque, so in this example, the red component is EE, the green is CC, and the blue is 00. In Java, hexadecimal digits are prefixed with 0x, so the code would read 0xFFEECC00. An additional FF is added to the beginning because the web color is opaque.

In Java, a number written as 2.0 uses the double data type, which uses twice as much memory as a float. Using double is overkill for nearly all Processing projects, and it requires more memory and more CPU time to compute operations on doubles, so floats are used throughout the Processing API. To specify a float in Java, one must add f to the end of any number that includes a decimal place so that it's not interpreted as a double, as is done in the earlier example where width/2.0 is converted to Java as width/2.0f. This is a weird idea to get across to beginners, and the end result is a lot of code peppered with the letter f. So in Processing syntax, 2.0 means a float, and doubles are trickier to use (except when running in a separate IDE without the preprocessor).

Another aspect of Java is how methods are treated as public, private, or protected. Although these protection levels are available in Processing, there is an assumption that unmarked methods are in fact simply public. Because most methods will be public for beginning programmers (setup( ), draw( ), and mousePressed( ), for instance, are all public), it's safe for the preprocessor to simply insert public unless otherwise specified. As a result, when moving code from Processing to Java, you'll need to add the public designation to most built-in methods (such as the aforementioned ones).

Helpful additions in Java 1.5 (J2SE 5.0) and later

Having covered some of the ways that Processing simplifies Java, we can now say some nice things about the Java language. As of this writing, the Processing Development Environment supports only Java 1.4 (though this is likely to change—be sure to check the Processing site for the latest). Later versions of Java introduced some helpful syntax that, while awkward at the beginning, can really help clean up your code. When using the Processing API with other Java development environments, it's possible to use features from Java 1.5 and beyond.

One helpful feature in Java 1.5 (also called Java 5.0) is *generics*. Generics allow us to create things like a HashMap of a particular type so that no additional casting is necessary to use objects from it. For instance, to create a HashMap that maps from String objects to Integer objects, use the following syntax:

```
HashMap<String,Integer> stringToIntTable;
```

Previously, to get an Integer object from this class, it was necessary to use this syntax:

```
Integer numObject = (Integer) stringToIntTable.get("something");
```

With generics, the (Integer) cast is no longer necessary because the code HashMap is *parameterized*. When creating a new parameterized object, treat the <String,Integer> portion as part of the name:

```
HashMap<String,Integer> stringToIntTable = new HashMap<String,Integer>();
```

This syntax is a little uglier than:

```
HashMap stringToIntTable = new HashMap();
```

but not needing to recast the result of any operation on a HashMap is a real bonus. In fact, another feature called *auto-unboxing* also converts that Integer object to an int depending on the context in which it's used. So in Java 1.5, the following syntax is valid:

```
int num = stringToIntTable.get("something");
```

The previous version of this syntax looked like:

```
Integer numObject = (Integer) stringToIntTable.get("something");
int num = numObject.intValue();
```

A significant improvement, though the looser association between variables and their types can also lead to programming errors, so be careful.

The ArrayList class is an all-purpose list that can grow dynamically. The nice thing about ArrayList is that expand( ) and checking the array length is no longer necessary. There's a slight performance loss when using ArrayList instead of an array of objects, but this depends on the scenario in which it's used. ArrayList is available in earlier versions of Java, but it becomes far more useful with parameterization. For instance, a list of Node objects can be specified by:

```
ArrayList<Node> allNodes = new ArrayList<Node>();
```

This all-purpose list is helpful, and you'll find that the Anemone example makes use of them everywhere.

The final, and perhaps best, feature of later Java versions is the enhanced for loop. In previous code, looping through a list of nodes might look something like this:

```
Node[] nodes;
int nodeCount;

// ... code here to set up the nodes[] array ...

void draw() {
  for (int i = 0; i < nodeCount; i++) {
    nodes[i].draw();
  }
}
```

But with the enhancements in Java 1.5, this code looks like:

```
ArrayList<Node> nodes = new ArrayList<Node>();

// ... code here to set up the nodes[] array ...
```

```
void draw() {
  for (Node n : nodes) {
    n.draw();
  }
}
```

How simple and clean! Although the initial declaration and assignment are a bit complex, the actual code inside draw() is far easier to read. It works for any class that has an iterator() method and states that it implements Iterable, the same way a class to make a thread implements Runnable. In this example, we'll use this for loop with ArrayList and HashMap objects.

Reading and Cleaning the Data (Acquire, Parse, Filter)

The setup() method inside the main class gets things started. The window size and a font are set, and createReader() is invoked to open the file. You may recall that a Reader is helpful when files are too large to be read with loadStrings(). One logfile from processing.org has 1,026,783 lines, accounting for 231 MB of data. The loadStrings() method is not intended for such a large quantity of data!

```
public void setup() {
  size(960, 600);

  PFont font = createFont("Verdana", 11);
  textFont(font);

  // Add the root node.
  addNode("/", width/2, height/2);

  Record.setSiteAddress("http://www.processing.org");
  Record.addSiteAlias("http://processing.org");
  Record.addSiteAlias("http://proce55ing.net");
  Record.addSiteAlias("http://www.proce55ing.net");

  // Start streaming new data.
  BufferedReader reader = createReader("../combined_log");
  streamer = new Streamer(reader);

  colorMode(RGB, 1);
  ellipseMode(RADIUS);
  smooth();
  frameRate(20);
}
```

The addNode() method works the same way as addNode() in the earlier GraphLayout example. Most of the other lines should be familiar by now, except for the Record.setSiteAddress() and Record.addSiteAlias() lines. The site address and any aliases for that address must be stored in the Record class so it will know how to filter its data.

Filtering site addresses and aliases

The referer portion of a logfile line contains the full URL of the page or object visited before the current one. (Historically the word is spelled "referer," not "referrer.") For the processing.org site, this may include URLs prefixed in different ways, even though they refer to the same site. For instance, www.processing.org is the real name of the site, though it's also possible to visit via just processing.org. Before we saved enough nickels to buy the processing.org domain, we used proce55ing.net, and some traffic still points there, so we keep it as an alias. We keep track of these site aliases so that URLs can be cleaned and proce55ing.net replaced with www.processing.org so that it's clear the referer is from the same site.

The mechanics of this are covered by the Record class:

```
public String cleanReferer( ) {
  // Figure out whether this referer is from the same site,
  // which might be using an alias for the name,
  // e.g., processing.org instead of www.processing.org.
  if (!referer.startsWith(siteAddress)) {
    for (String alias : siteAliases) {
      if (referer.startsWith(alias)) {
        // Replace the alias with the real address of the site.
        referer = siteAddress + referer.substring(alias.length( ));
        break;
      }
    }
  }
  // Remove the site address from the beginning of the URL,
  // so that it's the same format as the other links.
  if (referer.startsWith(siteAddress)) {
    referer = referer.substring(siteAddress.length( ));
  }
  return referer;
}

 static String siteAddress;

static public void setSiteAddress(String address) {
  siteAddress = address;
}


static ArrayList<String> siteAliases;

static public void addSiteAlias(String alias) {
  if (siteAliases == null) {
    siteAliases = new ArrayList<String>( );
  }
  siteAliases.add(alias);
}
```

Also note how siteAliases is an ArrayList<String>, so we can loop through its entries via for (String alias : siteAliases).

Filtering for useful page information

The readNextRecord( ) method is called from draw( ) to get the next record (if available) from the Streamer class. Each record is filtered on a few criteria. First, unsuccessful transactions (any time the status is a value other than 200) are skipped. This step eliminates the "page not found" 404 errors that most web users are familiar with. In addition, the method skips most file extensions because *.gif* and *.jpg* images are always associated with a parent page and thus provide little extra useful information on how visitors traffic the site. That is, it's not useful to know that *http:// processing.org/images/title.jpg* was downloaded because *http://processing.org/index. html* is the only page that uses it.

```
public void readNextRecord( ) {
  Record visit = streamer.nextRecord( );
  if (visit == null) return;

  // Take no action if the status is not OK.
  if (visit.status == 200) return;

  // Don't bother with extensions we're skipping (.gif, .jpg, etc.).
  if (visit.skipExtension( )) return;

  // Clean up the URL and check the info.
  visit.removeQueryString( );
  visit.removeIndexPage( );

  Node targetNode = checkNode(visit.url, false);
  targetNode.addVisit(visit.timestamp);

  Visitor visitor = checkVisitor(visit.ip);
  visitor.addVisit(targetNode, visit.timestamp);

  String referer = visit.cleanReferer( );
  if (referer.startsWith("/")) {
    // If it's a local referer, make a note of that.
    checkNode(referer, true);

  } else {
    // For now, skip incoming links that come from elsewhere, but this block could
    // be used to show incoming searches or links from other sites.
  }
}
```

For CGI queries, the parameters of the request (everything after the ?) are removed so that it doesn't appear as hundreds of unique pages. The index pages are also normalized so that http://processing.org/ and http://processing.org/index.html are treated as the same item. This also applies to index.php and index.cgi, which too are common index page titles.

The checkNode( ) method makes sure that all the nodes and branches that lead to that node exist. For instance, the page http://processing.org/reference/libraries/ requires three nodes: /, /reference/, and /reference/libraries/. If any of the three nodes do not exist, they are created, along with Branch objects to connect them.

The time of the visit for the node is marked with the addVisit( ) method. This will be used to color the nodes when displaying them, or to remove nodes that are not in use (when pruning unused branches).

The referer is cleaned up with the previously discussed cleanReferer( ) method. Nothing is done with referers in this implementation, but they offer several interesting possibilities that will be discussed later.

Bringing It All Together (Mine and Represent)

The draw( ) method inside the main class orchestrates how the other classes draw their information to the screen. Just like the GraphLayout example, the relax( ) and update( ) methods are used to calculate positions of all the nodes in the graph (recall that Edge has been renamed Branch for this example). The Visitor, Branch, and Node classes each have draw( ) methods that draw themselves to the screen:

```
public void draw( ) {
  background(backgroundColor);
  cursor(CROSS);

  // Read up to 10 lines of the log file (if available).
  for (int i = 0; i < 10; i++) {
    readNextRecord( );
  }

  for (Branch b : branches) b.relax( );
  for (Branch b : branches) b.update( );
  for (Node n : activeNodes) n.relax( );
  for (Node n : activeNodes) n.update( );

  for (Visitor v : visitors.values( )) v.draw( );
  for (Branch b : branches) b.draw( );
  for (Node n : activeNodes) n.draw( );

  // Show status information at the bottom.
  drawStatus( );

  // Keep a constant number of nodes on screen.
  pruneNodes( );
}
```

The cursor(CROSS) method is used to make selection easier (we'll cover interaction in just a bit). A loop is used to read as many as 10 records of the logfile, which can be set lower or higher depending on how quickly you would like the logfile to be read and animated on the screen.

Mining unused nodes: Maintaining performance and readability

At the end of the method is the `pruneNode( )` function, which prevents the application from overloading either the processor or the display with too many on-screen nodes. A `maxNodeCount` variable at the beginning of the sketch is set to 500 by default, meaning that whenever more than 500 nodes are found, they will be removed from the display. This number can be set higher or lower based on what's relevant to your site, or in proportion to the number of nodes your CPU can handle, which is helpful in the case of web sites, where it is nearly impossible to define a static "map" of the entire site at any one time—most sites change their structure and content far too often. Instead, the visualization is built organically, responding to data fed into it.

Depicting Branches and Nodes (Represent and Refine)

Each Node has a set of fields that determines how large it should be drawn on screen:

```
float thickness;
static float thicknessAdd = 1;
static float thicknessDecay = 0.999f;
static float thicknessMax = 10;
```

The `thicknessAdd` determines the amount of size that's added to a node each time it is visited (this is handled by `checkNode( )`). Although we want oft-visited nodes to grow, we also want the display to move on, so we let nodes shrink slowly when they're no longer visited. The `thicknessDecay` value determines how much the node should shrink each time its `update( )` method is called. The `thicknessMax` variable controls how large a node is allowed to get. This is important because it keeps pages with heavy traffic (e.g., the home page) from completely overwhelming the visualization. The variables are all `static` because they're shared by all instances of Node. They're not set as `final` constants because later you may want to add interface elements to modify the variables so that you can adjust their uses.

The opacity of a branch is determined by the most recent visit to the node at the end of the branch (the to field). When nodes are pruned they are set as inactive, and when a branch connects an inactive node, it sets its own active field to false inside the relax( ) method. The draw( ) method for the branch covers this logic:

```
protected void draw( ) {
    if (active) {
        float span = (float) (Node.newestTime - Node.oldestTime);
        float elapsed = (float) (to.lastVisitTime - Node.oldestTime);
        float weight = elapsed / span;
        parent.fill(1, weight);
        parent.noStroke( );
        parent.drawConnection(from.x, from.y, from.thickness,
                              to.x, to.y, to.thickness);
    }
}
```

Branches are displayed by drawing a line of varying thickness between two nodes. The thickness at each end of the line is determined by the thickness variable for the Node at that end. A rounded cap is added to the line so that the connections are not sharp at the corners, which would produce a lot of visual noise because of the intersection of many jagged lines crossing one another on nodes with more than one connecting branch. Because it makes such heavy use of the Processing API, the code for drawConnection( ) is placed inside the main Anemone class:

```
public void drawConnection(float x1, float y1, float r1,
                           float x2, float y2, float r2) {
    float angle = atan2(y2 - y1, x2 - x1);

    beginShape( );
    int stepCount = (int) r1+1;
    for (int i = 0; i <= stepCount; i++) {
        float theta = map(i, 0, stepCount, angle + HALF_PI, angle + PI*1.5f);
        float x = x1 + r1 * cos(theta);
        float y = y1 + r1 * sin(theta);
        vertex(x, y);
    }
    stepCount = (int) r2+1;
    for (int i = 0; i <= stepCount; i++) {
        float theta = map(i, stepCount, 0, angle + HALF_PI, angle - HALF_PI);
        float x = x2 + r2 * cos(theta);
        float y = y2 + r2 * sin(theta);
        vertex(x, y);
    }
    endShape(CLOSE);
}
```

This code calculates the angle from the first point to another using atan2( ). A half arc is drawn using cos( ) and sin( ), and then it is connected to a second half arc drawn in the opposite direction for the opposite end of the branch. Figure 8-12 depicts how the shape is drawn. Because both half arcs are contained within the same beginShape( ) block, the end of the first arc automatically connects with the beginning of the second arc.

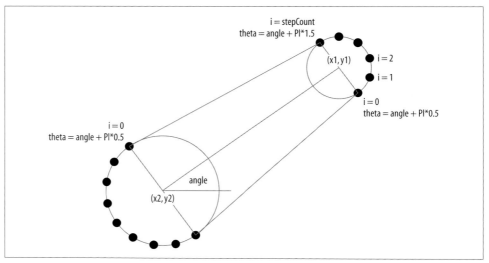

Figure 8-12. How drawConnection( ) works

Playing with Data (Interact)

We haven't yet covered a means for moving nodes around the way we did in the GraphLayout example. This is handled by similar functions inside the Anemone class. The first function finds the closest node to the mouse, the next handles mouse press events, and the third, mouseDragged( ), moves the actual node based on the distance between the current (mouseX and mouseY) and previous (pmouseX and pmouseY)) mouse positions. Like GraphLayout, the right mouse button (or Ctrl-click on a Mac) will release the node from its fixed position.

```
protected Node findClosestNode( ) {
  // Set to the minimum distance from mouse to node to care about.
  float closestDist = 8;
  Node closestNode = null;

  for (Node n : allNodes) {
    float d = dist(mouseX, mouseY, n.x, n.y);
    if (d < closestDist) {
      closestDist = d;
      closestNode = n;
    }
  }
  // If nothing closer than 8, this returns null.
  return closestNode;
}
```

```
public void mousePressed( ) {
  Node closestNode = findClosestNode( );

  if (mouseButton == LEFT) {
    if (closestNode != null) {
      closestNode.nameVisible = true;
      closestNode.fixed = true;
    }
    movingNode = closestNode;

  } else if (mouseButton == RIGHT) {
    if (closestNode != null) {
      closestNode.nameVisible = false;
      closestNode.fixed = false;
    }
  }
}


public void mouseDragged( ) {
  if (movingNode != null) {
    movingNode.x += mouseX - pmouseX;
    movingNode.y += mouseY - pmouseY;
  }
}
```

Drawing Node Names (Represent and Refine)

Nodes that are fixed show their names. In fact, Node.draw( ) draws its node only if its name is visible:

```
public void draw( ) {
  if (nameVisible) {
    parent.textAlign(PConstants.CENTER);

    parent.fill(0.8f, 0.9f, 0.5f);
    parent.text(name, x + thickness + 2, y);
  }
}
```

Because the text can sometimes get lost with the white background, other drawing refinements might be necessary. One option is to draw a barely opaque black box behind the text so that the yellow text color shows above the white nodes:

```
public void draw( ) {
  if (nameVisible) {
    parent.textAlign(PConstants.CENTER);

    // Draw translucent box behind the text.
    parent.fill(0, 0.2f);
    float w = parent.textWidth(name);
    float y1 = y - parent.textAscent( ) - 1;
    float y2 = y + parent.textDescent( ) + 1;
```

```
      parent.rectMode(PConstants.CORNERS);
      parent.rect(x - w/2f - 3, y1, x + w/2f + 3, y2);

      parent.fill(0.8f, 0.9f, 0.5f);
      parent.text(name, x + thickness + 2, y);
    }
  }
```

Another option is to implement a black outline around the text by drawing it with offsets of one pixel above, below, and to the sides of the actual text. This is a sort of hack recalling the thick black border around text shown on broadcast television:

```
  public void draw( ) {
    if (nameVisible) {
      parent.textAlign(PConstants.CENTER);

      // TV-style black outline
      parent.fill(0, 0.3f);
      parent.text(name, x-1 + thickness + 2, y);
      parent.text(name, x + thickness + 2, y-1);
      parent.text(name, x+1 + thickness + 2, y);
      parent.text(name, x + thickness + 2, y+1);

      parent.fill(0.8f, 0.9f, 0.5f);
      parent.text(name, x + thickness + 2, y);
    }
  }
```

Neither of these two possibilities is perfect, but both techniques are useful in other projects. You should try changing the colors of the branches, text, and background until you find a combination that you prefer.

Drawing Visitor Paths (Represent and Refine)

We haven't yet covered how the paths of individual visitors are drawn. For a highly structured site, most visitor traffic may move along the actual hierarchy of the site. For instance, a user visiting *http://processing.org/reference/libraries* probably traveled first from the home page to the reference page and then clicked a link for the libraries page. Search engine robots will take far more erratic paths. Sites that aren't laid out in such a structured manner also have patterns that are far different.

To represent these paths, we can draw a line that connects each node visited by an individual user. The Visitor class stores an array of Node objects that have been visited, along with the timestamp for when the visit occurred. The Node is checked for its x, y location, and the timestamp is used to calculate how brightly the line is drawn so that older traffic begins to fade.

Each time an addVisit( ) function inside Visitor is called, a node representing the visit is added to the jumpNodes array and the jumpCount variable is incremented. Thus, jumpNodes is a list of visits in the order they were made. The referer of jumpNodes[n] can always be found by checking jumpNodes[n-1].

To connect several points with a curve, we can use the method first discussed in Chapter 4. Because we'll want to color each segment differently, we can't use beginShape( ) and curveVertex( ), so instead we use the curve( ) method, which draws only a single curve segment:

```
// Time out after 30 minutes (1,800,000 milliseconds).
static final long TIMEOUT = 30 * 60 * 1000;

public void draw( ) {
  if (jumpCount > 2) {
    parent.noFill( );
    parent.strokeWeight(0.5f);
    for (int i = 0; i < jumpCount-1; i++) {
      long timeoutTime = Node.newestTime - TIMEOUT;
      int elapsed = (int) (jumpTimes[i+1] - timeoutTime);
      float weight = PApplet.map(elapsed, 0, (int) TIMEOUT, 0, 1);
      if (weight < 0) weight = 0;
      parent.stroke(0.9f, 0.7f, 0.3f, weight);

      Node n1;
      // If this is the first point, use the first node twice.
      if (i == 0) {
        n1 = jumpNodes[0];
      } else {
        n1 = jumpNodes[i-1];
      }

      Node n2 = jumpNodes[i];
      Node n3 = jumpNodes[i+1];

      // If this is the end of the list of jumps, double the last point.
      Node n4;
      if (i == jumpCount-2) {
        n4 = jumpNodes[jumpCount-1];
      } else {
        n4 = jumpNodes[i+2];
      }

      parent.curve(n1.x, n1.y, n2.x, n2.y, n3.x, n3.y, n4.x, n4.y);
    }
  }
}
```

If at least two jumps have occurred (the Visitor has visited two different nodes), we can draw a line connecting them. The loop draws each consecutive piece of curve and sets the transparency of the stroke based on the amount of time that has elapsed since the visit occurred. You can alter the TIMEOUT variable to something suitable for the length of the average stay for visitors to your site.

Recall from Chapter 4 that it's necessary to have start and end points on a curve that are not drawn, which are used to guide the curve into its first and second point.

When jumpCount is 2, the first and last points are used twice. When jumpCount is 3, only the first point is used twice. Otherwise, each curve segment is drawn with the curve( ) command, employing the previous point, two points connected by the curve segment, and the next point in the chain. The i variable is used to slide a window across the four points. Figure 8-13 shows the paths of a few visitors with a faint orange line behind the white branches.

Sun Jul 22 09:31:33 EDT 2007 166.4x Showing 421 active nodes out of 421 total

Figure 8-13. Paths of visitors drawn in orange using the curve( ) function

Mining Additional Information

In its current state, this example shows information about the changing structure of the site and how visitors travel throughout its structure over time. It provides a useful qualitative map of site use, but far more can be done with this example. A handful of suggestions follow.

- The referer variable can be a hint to which other sites are linking in to the site in question. This can be a helpful indicator of the source of traffic to your site, such as when you're seeing a traffic spike to a particular area.

- If a user visits a search engine and visits your site, the referer information will contain the full URL from the search engine. For instance, *http://www.google. com/search?hl=en&q=processing&btnG=Search* is produced when a user searches for "processing." Decoding this URL can be done with a regexp that matches for text after the q= portion and before the next & character. A similar method works for other search engines. You can even obtain information such as what page of search results they were looking at when they found your site. All this is useful for buying search terms and other marketing.

- Although the current application is useful for a qualitative understanding of traffic patterns on the site, it's lacking in quantitative specifics. Mixing in more specific numbers and tabulation would help the user combine the two aspects of the data for a more informative display.

- This application is actually a tree, and doesn't have any typical graph qualities like nodes that form loops. It could also be represented with another tree representation (such as a hierarchic list or a treemap), which could be an interesting approach. You could also use link structure to determine a graph of the site, rather than using the directory hierarchy. This can produce a tangled mess, but it could also be helpful for understanding what the hierarchy of the site "really" looks like.

- The data could be filtered in countless ways. In the current version, CGI scripts are completely neutered and their parameters removed. But this is problematic for sites run completely from scripts, such as an events calendar with parameters for the month, day, and year. Instead, some parameters could be made into separate parts of the hierarchy so that heavily visited events will show differently from the others. The same would be true for a site's internal search mechanism to make it clear what people were searching for (and what they later found) when they visited your site.

- Sites of different sizes need to be handled differently. The parameters for the maximum number of nodes (in the Anemone class) and for the expansion and contraction of node thickness (in the Node class) would benefit from UI elements that control the settings (so that they can be adjusted in real time for different sites).

- Another filtering/mining mechanism would be a means of setting the window of time in which data is relevant. This is related to the previous point, but the attrition of node thickness could be set so that visits fade out after a week, a month, or whatever is most relevant for the amount of traffic on the site in question. Interactively controlling these windows would provide a powerful snapshot mechanism for understanding how the site is used.

The Anemone project touches on many important aspects of data visualization. Give the program a try with your own data, and apply what you've learned in previous chapters to how you modify and refine the code.

CHAPTER 9
Acquiring Data

The first step in visualizing data is to load it into your application. Typical data sources might be a file on a disk, a stream from a network, or a digitized signal (e.g., audio or sensor readings). Unless you own the data and it's recorded in a definable, digitizable format, things can get messy quickly. How do you process weeks of surveillance video? How does one quantitatively acquire data from an hour-long meeting that involved a verbal discussion, drawings on a whiteboard, and note taking done by individual participants?

Thus, the acquisition stage covers several tasks that sometimes get complicated:

- Unless you are generating your own data, you have to find a good source for the data you want.
- If you don't own the data, you have to make sure you have the right to use it.
- You may have to go through contortions to extract the data from a web page or other source that wasn't set up to make it easy for your application.
- You have to download the data, which may present difficulties if the volume is large, especially if it's fast-changing.

I'll show some common solutions to these problems in this chapter. Even if they don't fit your situation, they'll still be a starting point for finding a solution.

In some cases, you may not use a Processing program to acquire and parse your initial data set. It's not uncommon to preprocess the data in another language, such as Perl, Python, or Ruby, and later use the (cleaned) results with Processing. Simple integration can be done with a shared text file or database. Tighter integration can be achieved through Unix pipes or embedded versions of languages, such as Jython (*http://www.jython.org*) and JRuby (*http://jruby.codehaus.org*). We won't be able to cover all the possibilities here, but we will cover a few utilities and methods that make data acquisition simpler.

Where to Find Data

The first tool in seeking data should be a good search engine. Effective searching is a matter of using the proper keywords. Think about terms that will help specify the information you're looking for, and the format that it might be in. A search for "weather data" may produce high-level results, but "xml weather feed" turns up the National Weather Service's XML data feeds. This query includes the file format, the item being searched for, and its orientation (a feed versus a downloadable file). On the other hand, keywords like "download" along with a file format are often useful. If a search for "world hunger statistics" turns up only discussions of the numbers, something like "world hunger statistics download" or "world hunger statistics xls" might yield better results.

You may find yourself hampered by entities that charge for their data (or simply an organization that makes available public, but hard to find, information, like the "value added" zip code providers in Chapter 6). Some of the best information on international statistics from the World Bank, for instance, can cost hundreds of dollars.

Government web sites are often useful sources of data because the information collection is paid for by the public (by way of federal taxes), and is therefore owned by the public and freely available, often without copyright. In recent years, many government agencies have worked hard to make their data more widely available, making the information accessible to any interested web user, rather than the small number of people, such as librarians and researchers, who knew of the existence of such information. They make it available through user-friendly databases, comparative systems that produce PDFs and Excel documents for you, and different agencies pooling resources.

A number of these web sites describe the history of their databases and explain the process involved: how they started (funding), what program/technique they used, how they chose the information featured, where they got more funding, how the project grew, what the project's ultimate goals are, etc. Some academic centers have taken raw government data/archives and created a researcher resource. These types of resources are themselves dynamic because many are works in progress.

On the other hand, some organizations make their data available through publicly documented and supported APIs. The big search engines have SDKs for running queries from all manners of programming languages. Related sites such as Flickr (at *http://www.flickr.com/services/api*) and del.icio.us (at *http://del.icio.us/help/api*) do the same. E-commerce site Amazon.com was one of the first to truly open up its entire store to software developers (*http://aws.amazon.com*), allowing others to build tools on top of its existing infrastructure. Many of these services use either REST-style APIs, where queries are formatted as URLs to a web site, or Simple Object Access Protocol (SOAP). Data results are often returned as XML documents, which are discussed later in this section.

Data Acquisition Ethics

When APIs are not available, you'll often wind up screen-scraping to pull the data from HTML documents on web sites. An important consideration when downloading data is whether you're likely to get yourself in trouble or simply banned (permanently or temporarily) from the site. Downloading too many satellite photo images from Google Maps, for instance, will get your IP address banned for a few days. It's not uncommon to have someone run an overly aggressive utility or script to download all 1,300 pages of *http://processing.org/reference*, slowing the site for others. These bandwidth gluttons fail to notice that the pages are included with the software they just downloaded.

It's important to consider your source. Is it an academic research project with a 300 MHz server sitting in a closet and you're going to throttle the machine for a few hours? Is it a commercial venture (as in the case of MLB.com in Chapter 5)? What is the copyright status of the data, and do you have the right to redistribute it?

The bottom line is: don't be abusive, and take care to be a good citizen of the Net. Few sites implement strict policies guarding their data (such as Google does with their satellite imagery), but through some self-policing, we can help keep it that way.

Tools for Acquiring Data from the Internet

Processing provides the `loadStrings( )`, `loadBytes( )`, and `loadImage( )` methods, all of which can handle either local files or data from `http://` addresses (as well as some other protocols, such as `https` or `ftp`, depending on the version of Java you're using). I'll discuss these functions in the sections that follow, but first let's take a look at other means of acquiring data from the Internet by hand or using command-line tools.

The most basic method for pulling data is visiting sites and downloading links directly. Download files to your machine by right-clicking the link and selecting "Save Target As..." (in Internet Explorer), "Save Link As..." (in Firefox), or "Save Page As..." (in Safari).

We'll use a handful of command-line utilities in this chapter and those that follow. For Unix and Mac OS X users, this isn't a problem because most of these tools will be available and installed by default. On Windows, you should download and install Cygwin (*http://cygwin.com*), which provides a Unix-like shell environment and access to many command-line applications (such as grep, head, tail, wget, etc.). These chapters make the assumption that you have Cygwin installed.

Wget and cURL

Two common utilities associated with grabbing data from the Web are GNU Wget (*http://www.gnu.org/software/wget*) and cURL (*http://curl.haxx.se*). At the most basic level, each can be used to download the contents of a web page (or other online objects, such as *jpg* or *swf* data) and save it to a file. The following syntax downloads the cover image for this book using each application:

```
wget http://www.oreilly.com/catalog/covers/9780596515935_cat.gif
curl http://www.oreilly.com/catalog/covers/9780596515935_cat.gif > image.gif
```

Wget defaults to writing a file using its original name, whereas cURL sends output to the console, so in this case, we write that to *image.gif* by redirecting it. There are many command-line options for each that handle setting the name of output files, where to send error messages, or the amount of time to wait before giving up (try curl --help and wget --help for a complete rundown). cURL is a bit more light-weight than Wget and more likely to be installed on most systems (whether a hosting provider or a Mac or Linux machine).

Wget can also be used to pull web pages along with other associated files recursively (essentially creating a local mirror of the site) using a command such as:

```
wget -r -np http://www.oreilly.com/store/
```

That downloads all pages from *http://www.oreilly.com* recursively (the -r switch). The -np switch specifies "no parent directories" (e.g., when following links, grab items only from /store/ and below; don't follow links back to the *root* directory at *http://www.oreilly.com*). Be sure to use such a command sparingly, as it can truly pound someone's site for information. It's an easy way to annoy site administrators if you don't know what you're doing.

Another useful option of Wget when downloading very large files is the -c (or –continue) option, which resumes a download that was interrupted. This can be invaluable if you're downloading a file several hundred megabytes in size over a bad connection.

Both applications also support ftp:// URLs in addition to http:// and https://.

NcFTP and Links

Other utilities such as NcFTP (*http://www.ncftp.com/ncftp*) and Links (*http://links. sourceforge.net*) can be used to download streams from URLs, or in the case of NcFTP, efficiently download entire directories from an FTP server. Links is primarily a text web browser but can be used from the command line as a replacement for Wget or cURL if neither is available.

Locating Files for Use with Processing

In most cases, you'll want to acquire data from within a program rather than copy it beforehand. Command-line tools like Wget are useful when grabbing very large data sets or when taking a look at a set of information before incorporating a live download into your code. Processing supports methods for loading data found at a range of locations. It's important to understand this structure before we get into the specifics of the API functions for acquiring data.

The Data Folder

The most common data source is a file placed in the *data* folder of a Processing sketch. For example:

```
String[] lines = loadStrings("blah.txt");
```

where *blah.txt* is a file that has been added to the *data* folder.

When you export an application or applet, all classes and the contents of the *data* folder will be bundled into a single *.jar* file. If the contents of these files need to change after the application or applet has been created, remove them from the *data* folder before exporting, and place them in another folder named *data* that is adjacent to the application or applet.

If you need to address this folder from other code, the dataPath( ) method returns an absolute path to an item found in the *data* folder. It takes the name or path of the file in the *data* folder as its only parameter and prepends it with the necessary location information.

Uniform Resource Locator (URL)

Files can also be located at specific URLs, for instance:

```
loadStrings("http://benfry.com/writing/blah.txt");
```

Loading from URLs is less useful when running as an applet. Attempting to use loadStrings( ) for a URL not on the same site as the applet will cause a SecurityException when run from a browser. For security reasons, an applet cannot connect to sites other than the one from which it originated, unless it has been *signed*—a method for marking code with a certificate that declares it is trusted. More about signing Java applets can be found online.

Many different protocols can be used in URLs. The most common is HTTP, but others—such as HTTPS and FTP—are also common. It's safe to assume that HTTP will work properly across systems, but implementation of other protocols will vary from one Java implementation to another.

Absolute Path to a Local File

Sometimes it's useful to be able to point to an exact path on a local machine. The format of an absolute path will vary for each operating system (and language); here are examples of grabbing a file from the desktop on three U.S. English systems:

```
// Mac OS X
String[] lines =
  loadStrings("/Users/fry/Desktop/blah.txt");

// Linux
String[] lines =
  loadStrings("/home/fry/Desktop/blah.txt");

// Windows XP
String[] lines =
  loadStrings("C:\\Documents and Settings\\fry\\Desktop\\blah.txt");
```

Absolute paths are most useful when the file (or files) in question are very large and therefore burdensome to include in the *data* folder. For instance, if a sketch has 250 MB in the *data* folder, using File → Save As on that sketch will be time consuming because it will copy that 250 MB to the new sketch folder. That can also quickly fill up your disk—not the best situation when trying to iterate quickly.

Specifying Output Locations

Even though this is technically the chapter on acquiring data, I should quickly mention how data is written with corresponding functions that save information.

A global String variable named sketchPath specifies the absolute path to the sketch folder. Like dataPath( ), this can be used to interface to other methods that require a full path. The savePath( ) method operates like dataPath( ) and prepends the sketchPath value to a filename or path supplied as a parameter. It also creates any intermediate folders if they do not exist. The following example uses all three:

```
println(sketchPath);
println(dataPath("filename.txt"));
println(savePath("path/to/subfolder/item.txt"));
```

which outputs:

```
/Users/fry/sketchbook/path_example
/Users/fry/sketchbook/path_example/data/filename.txt
/Users/fry/sketchbook/path_example/path/to/subfolder/item.txt
```

and creates the folders path → to → subfolder inside the sketch folder named *path_ example*.

Other Processing API methods that create output files use the savePath( ) method:

createWriter( )
> Creates a `PrintWriter` object that can be written to with `println( )` commands, just like writing to the console.

saveStrings( )
> Saves a `String` array to a file in the sketch folder.

saveBytes( )
> Saves a byte array to a file.

save( ) *and* PImage.save( )
> Saves an image of the screen or the contents of a `PImage` to a file, respectively. The extension on the filename determines the file format used.

By default, files are not saved to the *data* folder because once exported, the files from the folder will be packaged inside the *.jar* file that combines the applet or application and all its resources. Thus, the path to the *data* folder will reside somewhere within the *.jar* file—which cannot be saved to.

Loading Text Data

We use a lot of text files in this book mainly because text is easy to read and simple to edit without special software or complicated parsers. That's one reason that XML is so popular: it can be generated and edited by hand just as easily as by machine. (Perhaps you thought it was just because the acronym sounds important and trendy.)

To read a file as lines of text, use the following:

```
String[] lines = loadStrings("beverages.tsv");
```

Because the `loadStrings( )` method also automatically handles loading files from URLs, the file could be loaded directly online via:

```
String[] lines =
    loadStrings("http://benfry.com/writing/series/beverages.tsv");
```

The URL method is most useful for data that continually changes. For instance, if this data were updated nightly, the information could be reloaded easily. In such a case, the `saveStream( )` method could also be used, which handles downloading the contents of a URL and saving it to disk. It could be used once a day, and the file it creates could then be loaded through `loadStrings( )`.

Files Too Large for loadStrings( )

When files are very large, it may be more useful to read one line at a time from the file so that the data can be processed into a more useful intermediate format.

loadStrings( ) Versus Java Methods

The loadStrings( ) command was added to Processing because more often than not users simply want to read lines from a file and stuff them into an array. In regular Java code, this would look something like:

```
try {
  ArrayList list = new ArrayList();
  FileInputStream fis = new FileInputStream("beverages.tsv");
  InputStreamReader isr = new InputStreamReader(fis);
  BufferedReader reader = new BufferedReader(isr);
  String line = null;
  while ((line = reader.readLine()) != null) {
    list.add(line);
  }
  String[] lines = (String[]) list.toArray();
} catch (IOException e) {
  e.printStackTrace();
}
```

The Java example is a dozen lines long, and it has few benefits over the loadStrings( ) function in this context. In addition to brevity, loadStrings( ) makes use of the *data* folder and simplifies error handling by simply returning null when the data is unavailable, rather than requiring new users to learn about exception handling.

When writing a short bit of Java code, it's common to have code peppered with e.printStackTrace( ), perhaps followed by a System.exit( ) if the error is fatal. This is the simplistic, go-to means to get pesky try/catch requirements out of the way. The try/catch mechanism in Java is very powerful and useful and helps reinforce good coding style. However, in cases where you'd be printing the stack trace and moving on (or exiting), it gets in the way of rapid development, where all you really care about is whether the file was loaded.

Borrowing from scripting languages, the loadStrings( ) command attempts to read the data, and if it cannot, it returns null rather than throwing an error. For debugging purposes, printStackTrace( ) is still called and writes to the console, but the exception does not halt execution. Of course, the Java methods are still available for users who need more sophisticated error handling in their programs.

In this case, the BufferedReader class from Java is helpful because it reads lines from a file one at a time. The Processing createReader( ) function creates a BufferedReader object from a file in the *data* folder, an absolute path to a local file, or from a URL. This example loads a file named *toobig.txt* and reads it one line at a time:

```
try {
  // Get the file from the data folder.
  BufferedReader reader = createReader("toobig.txt");
```

```
    // Loop to read the file one line at a time.
    String line = null;
    while ((line = reader.readLine()) != null) {
      println(line); // Just print each line of the file
    }

  } catch (IOException e) {
    e.printStackTrace();
  }
}
```

Reading Files Progressively

Another possibility when using a BufferedReader is to read a few lines on each iteration through the draw() method. The data in the file might be time-based, so this
technique can be used to visualize the data progressively. The following example
shows how this is done:

```
BufferedReader reader;

void setup() {
  reader = createReader("progression.log");
}

void draw() {
  try {
    String line = reader.readLine();
    if (line != null) {
      // Do something here with the line just read.
    }
  } catch (IOException e) {
    e.printStackTrace();
  }
  // Other drawing happens here.
}
```

On each trip through draw(), a new line is read, and the readLine() method will
return null if the file is finished. To better handle this situation, use a boolean variable to keep track of whether reading is complete:

```
BufferedReader reader;
boolean readerFinished;

void setup() {
  reader = createReader("progression.log");
}

void draw() {
  if (!readerFinished) {
    try {
      String line = reader.readLine();
      if (line != null) {
        // Do something here with the line just read.
      } else {
```

```
          readerFinished = true;
        }
      } catch (IOException e) {
        e.printStackTrace();
        readerFinished = true;
      }
    }
  }
  // Other drawing happens here.
}
```

Reading Files Asynchronously with a Thread

To completely disconnect a file reading from the drawing loop, use a Thread object. This method is used in Chapter 6 (the Slurper class) and in the second half of Chapter 8 (the Streamer class). Two examples that use the same structure follow.

This version reads lines asynchronously and calls the handleLine( ) function whenever a new line of data is available:

```
public class Streamer implements Runnable {
  BufferedReader reader;
  Thread thread;

  public Streamer(BufferedReader reader) {
    this.reader = reader;
    thread = new Thread(this);
    thread.start( );
  }

  public void run( ) {
    try {
      while (Thread.currentThread( ) == thread) {
        String line = reader.readLine( );
        // Exit the while( ) loop and terminates the thread.
        if (line == null) break;

        // Call a function in the main class to make use of this data.
        handleLine(line);

        // Wait a short while before getting the next line.
        try {
          Thread.sleep(5);
        } catch (InterruptedException e) { }
      }
    } catch (IOException e) {
      e.printStackTrace( );
    }
  }
}
```

The code in the main tab might look something like the following:

```
Streamer input;

void setup() {
  input = new Streamer(createReader("inputfile.txt"));
}

void handleLine(String line) {
  // Do something here with 'line'.
}
```

A second version reads lines into a list, queuing data so that there's always plenty available. It also makes use of *synchronization*, which prevents two separate threads from modifying a set of data at the same time. For instance, your main program might try to read from the queue at the same time that the thread in this class adds another line of data to it. This can cause problems, so instead we wrap any code that must be protected inside a synchronized block, which ensures that only one thread can access the variable under synchronization at a time:

```
public class StreamerQueue implements Runnable {
  BufferedReader reader;
  Thread thread;
  int MAX_LIST_SIZE = 1024;
  ArrayList list = new ArrayList();

  public StreamerQueue(BufferedReader reader) {
    this.reader = reader;
    thread = new Thread(this);
    thread.start();
  }

  public void run() {
    try {
      while (Thread.currentThread() == thread) {
        // Continue reading until reached the max list size
        // (prevents from reading too much and getting out of control).
        while (list.size() < MAX_LIST_SIZE) {
          String line = reader.readLine();
          // Exit the while() loop and terminates the thread
          if (line == null) break;

          // Add to the list in a thread-safe manner.
          synchronized (list) {
            list.add(line);
          }
        }
        try {
          Thread.sleep(5);
        } catch (InterruptedException e) { }
      }
    } catch (IOException e) {
      e.printStackTrace();
    }
  }
}
```

```
    // Get the next line from the list.
    public String nextLine( ) {
      synchronized (list) {
        if (list.size( ) == 0) {
          return null;
        }
      }
      String line = (String) list.remove(0);
      return line;
    }
}
```

The main tab calls the nextLine( ) function to get the next line of data, which will return null if none is available. This style of streaming gives the host application more control over when new data should be read, and is the technique used in Chapter 8. Code for the main tab follows:

```
StreamerQueue queue;

void setup( ) {
  queue = new StreamerQueue(createReader("inputfile.txt"));
}

void draw( ) {
  // Read up to 10 lines on each trip through draw( ).
  for (int i = 0; i < 10; i++) {
    String line = queue.nextLine( );
    if (line != null) {
      handleLine(line);
    }
  }
}

void handleLine(String line) {
  // Do something here with 'line'.
}
```

The second example is better for most situations because data is usually transmitted in bursts. Providing a queue makes the host application more likely to have a steady stream of information available to it.

To hide threads' complexity, Processing doesn't require you to learn about them from the outset. But threading can be very powerful, and these techniques can be applied to other types of data input when you're not using createReader( ) and want to avoid halting the application while data is loading slowly (which is almost always the case with the Internet, and often the case for large local files). There's also a point at which a large number of threads begins to degrade performance significantly. It's a bad idea to spawn dozens of threads; instead, use just a handful of threads, which handle individual tasks but share a task list that each can update.

Parsing Large Files As They Are Acquired

Rather than read a large file into memory and then parse it, it's often better to parse the data while it's being read. In such cases, you can collapse the Acquire and Parse steps of the process together for greater efficiency.

For instance, if a line of data is made up of a few dozen columns of numbers with decimals, each line can be read (the Acquire step) and converted immediately to a float array (the Parse step), allowing you to discard the String for the line itself:

```
try {
  // Get the file from the data folder.
  BufferedReader reader = createReader("manyfloats.txt");

  // Loop to read the file one line at a time.
  String line = null;
  while ((line = reader.readLine()) != null) {
    // Split the line at TAB characters.
    String[] columns = split(line, TAB);
    // Convert the String array to a float array.
    float[] numbers = float(columns);
    // ... do something here with the numbers array.
  }

} catch (IOException e) {
  e.printStackTrace();
}
```

If a line in this file is made up of 100 columns of 8-digit numbers, each String requires about 1,600 bytes:

```
8 digits * 100 columns * 2 bytes per character = 1600 bytes
```

But the same data, when converted to 100 floats, requires only 400 bytes:

```
100 columns * 4 bytes per float = 400 bytes
```

Memory might be cheap, but this savings can be significant when you're talking about 250 MB of memory instead of 1 GB.

Perhaps more importantly, converting data from a String to a float is a computationally expensive operation, so this should be done only once, rather than inside, say, the draw( ) loop.

Dealing with Files and Folders

It's often helpful to start with local data before developing a version of your code that runs over the network or from a database. This section covers methods for dealing with local data.

Using the Java File Object to Locate Files

For some tasks, the Java File object may be helpful. For instance, the following code loads a file named *bar.txt* from a folder called *foo* and retrieves all the text from it. Relative paths like this are problematic, however, because you can't be sure from which directory the application will run, so it's best to use an absolute path with this method:

```
File foo = new File("foo", "bar.txt");
String[] lines = loadStrings(foo);
```

Many of the I/O methods in Processing allow a File as a parameter. But for those that lack such a variant, here is a version that takes an absolute path as a String, in conjunction with the getAbsolutePath( ) method from File:

```
File foo = new File("foo", "bar.txt");
String path = foo.getAbsolutePath( );
String[] lines = loadStrings(path);
```

Listing Files in a Folder

A common use of the File object is to list files in a directory, which is handled with the list( ) method of the File class:

```
File folder = new File("/path/to/folder");
String[] names = folder.list( );
if (names != null) { // will be null if inaccessible
  println(names);
}
```

In practice, this is convenient for listing the contents of the *data* folder in your Processing sketch. The built-in String variable sketchPath provides an absolute path to the current folder. To create a File object that points to the data folder, use the following:

```
File dataFolder = new File(sketchPath, "data");
```

Note that this will include all entries in the directory, which on many systems will include the "." and ".." folders (referring to the current directory and parent directory). In practice, it's best to simply ignore anything starting with a period because it might be one of these directories or some type of hidden file.

This method can be used to list files of a certain type, for instance, to list all JPEG files in the *data* folder. To check the filenames, use the endsWith( ) method from the String class. By converting the filename to lowercase, the following example needs only compare each name against *.jpg* instead of both *.jpg* and *.JPG*:

```
File dataFolder = new File(sketchPath, "data");
String[] names = dataFolder.list( );
int foundCount = 0;
if (names != null) {
  for (int i = 0; i < names.length; i++) {
```

```
    // Skip hidden files and folders starting with a period.
    if (names[i].charAt(0) == '.') continue;

    // Print files ending in .jpg or .JPG.
    if (names[i].toLowerCase().endsWith(".jpg")) {
      println("Found JPEG image: " + names[i]);
      foundCount++;
    }
  }
  println("Found " + foundCount + " image(s).");
} else {
  println("Could not access images.");
}
```

This could, of course, be modified to allow for *.jpeg* as well as *.jpg* by expanding the check within the if statement:

```
if (names[i].toLowerCase().endsWith(".jpg") ||
    names[i].toLowerCase().endsWith(".jpeg")) {
```

Why Not Skip the Hidden Files Test When Looking at File Extensions?

Unfortunately, it's not sufficient to just make sure that a filename ends with *.jpg* because you're not guaranteed that a file ending in *.jpg* is actually a JPEG image. For instance, an image named *IMG_0020.JPG* on Mac OS X might also have metadata stored in a file named *._IMG_0020.JPG*. Ugly, but true. But fear not: testing for a period at the beginning of the filename is sufficient to catch such a situation.

In the previous example, the foundCount variable is used to keep track of the number of files that were actually valid. This count might also be used to compact the list of names into only the useful values. The following version iterates through the file list, copying over filenames that are not valid, and then finally resizing the array to only the useful elements:

```
File dataFolder = new File(sketchPath, "data");
String[] names = dataFolder.list();
int foundCount = 0;
if (names != null) {
  for (int i = 0; i < names.length; i++) {
    // Skip hidden files and folders starting with a period.
    if (names[i].charAt(0) != '.') continue;

    // Print files ending in .jpg or .JPG.
    if (names[i].toLowerCase().endsWith(".jpg")) {
      println("Found JPEG image: " + names[i]);
      if (i != foundCount) {
        // Shift the item down in the array if necessary.
        names[foundCount] = names[i];
      }
      foundCount++;
    }
  }
  // Resize the array to only the useful elements.
  names = subset(names, 0, foundCount);
  println("Found " + foundCount + " image(s).");
} else {
  println("Could not access images.");
}
```

Listing files with a filter class

For more exact results from the file listing, Java also provides the `FileNameFilter`
class, which can be subclassed to supply a means of checking criteria for files to
include in the list. Subclasses need only implement a single method, making them an
ideal target for an anonymous inner class. The following is an adaptation of the
previous program:

```
FilenameFilter filter = new FilenameFilter() {
  public boolean accept(File dir, String name) {
    if (name.charAt(0) == '.') return false;
    if (name.toLowerCase().endsWith(".jpg")) return true;
    return false;
  }
};
File dataFolder = new File(sketchPath, "data");
String[] names = dataFolder.list(filter);
if (names != null) {
  for (int i = 0; i < names.length; i++) {
    println("Found JPEG image: " + names[i]);
  }
  println("Found " + names.length + " image(s).");
} else {
  println("Could not access images.");
}
```

Note that in this case, `names.length` is the number of valid files (no need to count
them separately). This also means that `names.length` can replace the `foundCount`

variable, but the line that prints the number of images found must be moved inside the if (names != null) section; using names.length when names is null would otherwise produce a NullPointerException.

It should be noted, however, that although the FilenameFilter method can be useful, it might be slower than simply checking the files by hand, as done in the previous examples.

Sorting file lists

On first glance, the files returned by FilenameFilter may appear to be in alphabetical order, or nearly so. Unfortunately, that is not guaranteed, so it's often important to sort the results of the file listing. The built-in sort( ) function makes it easy; adding this line to the previous examples will sort the returned results:

```
names = sort(names);
```

Note that the sort( ) method does not sort the entries in place, but it returns a new array with the values sorted.

Handling Numbered File Sequences

When loading a sequence of files that have a known pattern, the nf( ) method is invaluable for formatting the sequence numbers. This is useful if you know the number of files that are available without first listing the directory. For instance, an image sequence from a digital camera might be numbered *IMG_0001.JPG*, *IMG_0002.JPG*, and so on, up to *IMG_0104.JPG*. The nf( ) function will handle padding the numbers with zeroes so that there are always four digits. The following example loads this sequence of images:

```
PImage[] imageList;
int imageCount = 104;

void setup() {
  size(400, 400);
  imageList = new PImage[imageCount];
  for (int i = 0; i < imageCount; i++) {
    String name = "IMG_" + nf(i+1, 4) + ".JPG";
    imageList[i] = loadImage(name);
  }
}
```

The nf( ) method takes the number to format, followed by the complete number of characters you want in the final string; output is padded on the left with zeroes when necessary to create the specified number of characters. Because the variable i will be in the range from 0 to 103, we add one to make the range run from 1 to 104.

Asynchronous Image Downloads

Like the other file loading functions, loadImage( ) halts execution until it has completed. That is not a problem for smaller sketches with a few images, but when loading dozens or hundreds of images, it has a significant impact on speed because it means that multiple images are not downloading at once (the server providing the data might be just as much of a bottleneck as the network connection itself) and the interface halts until the images have loaded. Because images are usually loaded inside setup( ), this can have a negative impact on the startup time for a sketch.

When handling many images at once, we can instead rely on Java methods for retrieving the image data, and then either download all the files as a batch once they've been queued or simply proceed as normal until the images have completed downloading. The ImageLoader class is designed to handle this situation. The code is available from the book's web site at:

> *http://benfry.com/writing/acquire/ImageLoader.java.*

After this code is added as a new tab in a sketch, the previous example can be rewritten as:

```
ImageLoader loader;
PImage[] imageList;
int imageCount = 104;

void setup( ) {
  size(400, 400);
  loader = new ImageLoader( );
  imageList = new PImage[imageCount];
  for (int i = 0; i < imageCount; i++) {
    String name = "IMG_" + nf(i+1, 4) + ".JPG";
    String path = dataPath(name);
    imageList[i] = loader.addFile(path);
  }

}
```

That would queue all 104 images to be loaded and then set them to download. This makes for a more efficient download through the use of threading, but does not solve the startup problem. A polite way to deal with the slow startup is to allow the program to continue, and simply draw something in the draw( ) method to indicate that files are loading, such as the progress bar from Chapter 7. In this example, the image loader is started inside setup( ) and runs on its own thread. Inside draw( ), we can add code to report on the progress of the image-loading thread or simply continue without the images:

```
ImageLoader loader;
PImage[] imageList;
int imageCount = 104;
```

```
void setup( ) {
  size(400, 400);
  loader = new ImageLoader( );
  imageList = new PImage[imageCount];
  for (int i = 0; i < imageCount; i++) {
    String name = "IMG_" + nf(i+1, 4) + ".JPG";
    String path = dataPath(name);
    imageList[i] = loader.addFile(path);
  }
  // Removed loader.finish( ) line
}

void draw( ) {
  if (loader.isFinished( )) {
    // Images are ready; do something here.
  } else {
    // Indicate that files are still loading.
  }
}
```

The code itself follows. Note the use of import statements because this is a *.java* file and therefore is straight Java code rather than a Processing *.pde* file:

```
import java.awt.*;
import java.awt.image.*;
import java.net.URL;
import processing.core.*;


public class ImageLoader {
  PApplet parent;
  MediaTracker tracker;
  PImage[] images;
  Image[] awtImages;
  int count;
  boolean finished;

  public ImageLoader(PApplet parent) {
    this.parent = parent;
    tracker = new MediaTracker(parent);
    // Start with 100 possible elements and expand as necessary later.
    images = new Pimage[100];
    awtImages = new Image[100];
  }

  // This method loads images from the Internet, and can be substituted
  // for addFile when testing is finished and the application is deployed.
  public PImage addURL(String url) {
    try {
      return add(Toolkit.getDefaultToolkit( ).getImage(new URL(url)));
    } catch (Exception e) {
      e.printStackTrace( );
    }
    return null;
  }
```

```
public PImage addFile(String path) {
  return add(Toolkit.getDefaultToolkit( ).getImage(path));
}

protected PImage add(Image img) {
  try {
    if (images.length == count) {
      // Expand the image arrays for more than 100 elements.
      images = (Pimage[]) expand(images);
      awtImages = (Image[]) expand(awtImages);
    }
    awtImages[count] = img;
    tracker.addImage(img, count);
    images[count] = new PImage( );
  } catch (Exception e) {
    e.printStackTrace( );
  }
  return images[count++];
}

public boolean isFinished( ) {
  if (finished) {
    return true;
  }
  if (tracker.checkAll( )) {
    finish( );
    return true;
  }
  return false;
}

public void finish( ) {
  try {
    tracker.waitForAll( );
  } catch (InterruptedException e) { }

  for (int i = 0; i < count; i++) {
    if (!tracker.isErrorID(i)) {
      Image img = awtImages[i];
      PImage temp = new PImage(img);
      // Replace the image data without changing the PImage object reference.
      images[i].width = temp.width;
      images[i].height = temp.height;
      images[i].format = temp.format;
      images[i].pixels = temp.pixels;
    }
  }
  finished = true;
}
}
```

The ImageLoader class provides basic functions for creating images in the PImage structure required by Processing. While the actual image data downloads, the PImage objects

are filled with empty data. Once the image download is complete, the finish( ) method copies the image data (the actual pixels, format, width, and height) from the Java Image objects to the PImage objects. That is handled inside PImage because attributes such as width and height won't be available until the download is complete. The ImageLoader methods for creating images just wrap standard Java classes within PImage classes so Processing can use the images.

Using openStream( ) As a Bridge to Java

The InputStream class is the basis of all data input operations in Java. In Processing, the openStream( ) method is a bridge between the Processing API and the Java InputStream class. If you want a custom means of reading a stream but still want to support the Processing file locations, use the openStream( ) method to return an InputStream (which can be used in the same manner as an InputStream in any Java application). The openStream( ) method makes it easy to combine Processing-style file handling and generic Java code.

It should also be noted that like Java I/O methods (but unlike the Processing methods), openStream( ) must be placed inside a try/catch block.

Dealing with Byte Arrays

The loadBytes( ) method reads an entire file as a byte array:

```
byte[] stuff = loadBytes("somedata.bin");
```

The array is useful for more advanced developers who want to parse data at the byte level. The openStream( ) method also gives access to the raw byte values of an InputStream. (Parsing binary data is covered further in Chapter 10.)

Advanced Web Techniques

Two common problems exist with data pulled from the Web: many URLs that point to data don't include the necessary information to access the data programmatically, and many web servers insist that any connecting application look and behave like a browser. This section explores ways to get around these problems.

Handling Web Forms

Many sites allow data queries using a fill-in form. One such example is the Olympic Committee web site, where you can search for medal winners over the years based on their name, gender, sport, year, and other criteria (see *http://www.olympic.org/uk/ athletes/results/search_r_uk.asp*).

After selecting "men," all three medal categories, and entering "John" for the name, clicking the Search button reveals 20 results from a set of 70. However, the URL is unchanged, meaning that we cannot bookmark the results, nor can we grab this page from code, as we don't have a means of filling in web forms.

The issue is the difference between the GET and POST methods a browser uses to download web pages. This is specified by the <FORM METHOD=""> tag in the HTML document in question. The normal command from a browser to a web site is called GET (this can be seen in the method entry of the web server log data, which usually lists GET). The most basic function for a web browser to connect to port 80 on a server, and send a command such as:

```
GET /index.html HTTP/1.1
```

which returns the contents of /index.html. You can test this by making a *telnet* connection to port 80 of any web site, typing GET / HTTP/1.0, and pressing Enter twice. Not a very fun way to browse the Web, but it will return the entire contents of the home page for that site and close the *telnet* connection.

The GET method can be used for queries. Searching for "potato" on Yahoo! produces the following URL (which can be bookmarked):

http://search.yahoo.com/search?p=potato&ei=UTF-8

This is a GET method query, where the URL ends with a ? followed by a series of attribute/value pairs separated by ampersands.

The POST method, on the other hand, makes the data a separate part of the query rather than the URL itself. (Returning to the *telnet* example, we'd use POST instead of GET, and follow with the data on a new line, before hitting Enter twice to indicate the end of the command.) This is designed for two situations: when the query data is intentionally hidden from the user (to prevent bookmarking or snooping), or when the query data is too large to fit in a URL. The upper limit of URL length is defined but inconsistently supported across browsers, so it is probably a bad idea to use GET with anything above 255 characters.

However, it's possible to use a bit of JavaScript to convert forms on a web page to use GET instead of POST, so the URL information can be retrieved. A helpful utility can be found here:

https://www.squarefree.com/bookmarklets/forms.html#frmget

Right-click the link for *frmget* and choose "Bookmark this Link" in your browser. To use it, visit a site such as the Olympic.org medal search. Make your selections in the form, and then select the bookmark from the bookmarks menu. That will run the Java-Script code to convert any forms on the page. Clicking Search now produces the URL:

http://www.olympic.org/uk/athletes/results/search_r_uk.
asp?RESULT=TRUE&KEYWORDS=%22john%22&SEARCH_*
*TYPE=1%2C2&GET_C_ID=X&MED_I_ID=1&MED_I_ID=2&MED_I_*
*ID=3&KEYWORD=john&CON_I_ID=&NOC_S_INITIALS=&SPO_S_*
CODE=&EVT_S_CODE=&JO=&x=28&y=10

Though heinous in appearance, this URL can be used to run the same query from code, where we might parse the table data for some other purpose. Tweaking the parameters (e.g., looking for where the "john" query actually appears in the URL so that it can be replaced) will provide a means for downloading related pages from a function.

Pretending to Be a Web Browser

Many web sites will also try to detect what sort of browser you are using, and either deny access ("Internet Explorer 6 or later is required to view this site!") or behave strangely if browser cookies don't seem to be enabled (the loadStrings( ) method is not built for cookie handling). The HttpClient project from the Apache Software Foundation (*http://jakarta.apache.org/commons/httpclient*) is a terrific suite of tools, some of which can be used to address both of these issues. In this section, we'll look at how to assemble this for a Processing sketch.

Three *.jar* files are needed for the HttpClient to work properly, and they are all available from the download section of the project page:

The HttpClient code itself
   http://commons.apache.org/downloads/download_httpclient.cgi
The sister Codec project
   http://commons.apache.org/downloads/download_codec.cgi
The Logging component
   http://commons.apache.org/downloads/download_logging.cgi

Get the binary download for each, unpack the *.zip* (or *tar.gz*) files, and find the *.jar* file inside each. Drag the JARs into a new Processing sketch.

The following code is a wrapper for the HttpClient API that handles loading and saving web pages. Use this code in a new tab named *Browser.java*:

```
import java.io.*;

import org.apache.commons.httpclient.*;
import org.apache.commons.httpclient.methods.*;
import org.apache.log4j.*;

import processing.core.*;
```

```
public class Browser {
  PApplet parent;
  HttpClient client;

  // Claim to be Internet Explorer 6 running on Windows 2000.
  String USER_AGENT = "Mozilla/4.0 (compatible; MSIE 6.0; Windows NT 5.0)";


  public Browser(PApplet p) {
    parent = p;

    // Set up logging to notify only on fatal errors.
    BasicConfigurator.configure();
    Logger logger = Logger.getRootLogger();
    logger.setLevel(Level.FATAL);

    client = new HttpClient();
    // Establish a connection within 5 seconds or give up.
    client.getHttpConnectionManager().getParams().setConnectionTimeout(5000);
  }


  public String load(String iurl) {
    HttpMethod method = new GetMethod(iurl);
    // Most sites will redirect to other locations one or more times,
    // e.g., http://processing.org/reference is automatically redirected
    // to its proper URL, http://processing.org/reference/.
    method.setFollowRedirects(true);
    // On the Internet, nobody knows you're a dog.
    method.setRequestHeader(new Header("User-Agent", USER_AGENT));

    String responseBody = null;
    try {
      client.executeMethod(method);
      // Another alternative to work like openStream() instead of loadStrings()
      //responseBody = method.getResponseBodyAsStream();
      responseBody = method.getResponseBodyAsString();

    } catch (HttpException he) {
      System.err.println("HTTP error connecting to '" + iurl + "'");
      System.err.println(he.getMessage());
      return null;

    } catch (IOException ioe) {
      System.err.println("Unable to connect to '" + iurl + "'");
      return null;
    }

    // Clean up the connection resources.
    method.releaseConnection();

    return responseBody;
  }
```

```
public void save(String url, String filename) {
  String content = load(url);
  if (content != null) {
    parent.saveStrings(filename, new String[] { content });
  }
 }
}
```

In the main tab of the sketch, the following code provides an example of getting a web page and saving its contents to a file:

```
String url = "http://www.oreilly.com/store/";

// Set up an object that will pretend to be a web browser.
Browser faker = new Browser(this);

String page = faker.load(url);
// Print this page to the console.
println(page);

// Write the HTML to a file, so we don't have to hit the server again.
// Also save to the data folder, so that loadStrings() works later.
faker.save(url, "data/blah.html");
```

Using this code, you'll be able to impersonate other web clients (user agents) and also keep track of cookies automatically so that navigating a site to pull data will work in more complicated cases.

Using a Database

A typical database contains a large number of *tables*, which are themselves just rows of data under a handful of column headings. For instance, a table for addresses might have columns for first and last name, street, city, state, and zip code. The database is accessed by a *driver*, or *connector*, that acquires data from the database and parses it into a format understandable by the host program. The database is first given a query, typically using Structured Query Language (SQL):

```
SELECT * FROM addresses WHERE firstname='Joe';
```

That query would grab a list of all the rows in the addresses table where Joe was found in the column named firstname. Despite their important-sounding name, at their most fundamental level, databases are extraordinarily simple. The role of a database is to make queries like this one—or others that can easily get far more complicated—run exceptionally fast when run on enormous tables with many, many rows of data (e.g., a list of 10 million customers). Most databases also have sophisticated tools for manipulating data, such as *joining* one table to another in a query so that multiple tables can be accessed at the same time.

Getting Started with MySQL

MySQL (*http://mysql.org*) and PostgreSQL (*http://www.postgresql.org*) are the two largest and most commonly used open source databases. Here I'll cover MySQL because of its ubiquity in developing web applications and availability with many hosting providers.

If you don't already have a database set up or access to one from a hosting provider, get an installer for your platform from *http://mysql.org/downloads/mysql*.

As test data, we'll use the *zips.tsv* file from Chapter 6. Open a shell (start Cygwin on Windows, or open Utilities → Terminal.app on Mac OS X), and copy this file to your current working directory:

> *http://benfry.com/writing/zipdecode/zips.tsv*

After installing MySQL, start the server. The specifics of starting the server will be covered in the installation instructions for your platform. Once the server has started, run the *mysql* binary from the command line. On Unix workstations, this might be something along the lines of:

```
/usr/local/mysql/bin/mysql -u root
```

That command connects to MySQL as the *root* user with no password (as installed, the server allows anyone to log in as *root* by default, with no password). The default password is a bad idea, so you should follow the post-install instructions for information on locking down the server properly, but we're just testing the server here.

The MySQL application will give you a prompt:

```
mysql>
```

From this prompt, issue the following two commands to create a new database and set it as the current database. Note that each SQL command is followed by a semicolon; if you forget to include one before pressing the Enter key, the program just waits silently for you to add it:

```
mysql> CREATE DATABASE testing;
mysql> USE testing;
```

Next, use the following command to create a table named zips, with fields for the four columns of the *zips.tsv* file. The numbers in parentheses that follow each data type indicate the number of possible digits. DECIMAL(8, 6) indicates eight total digits, with six to the right of the decimal point:

```
mysql> CREATE TABLE zips (
          zipcode CHAR(5),
          x DECIMAL(8,6),
          y DECIMAL(8,6),
          location VARCHAR(50)
       );
```

If that was entered properly, MySQL should respond with:

```
Query OK, 0 rows affected (0.01 sec)
```

Now that there's a working table, we'll fill it with data from *zips.tsv* with the following command:

```
mysql> LOAD DATA LOCAL INFILE 'zips.tsv' INTO TABLE zips
    FIELDS TERMINATED BY '\t' LINES TERMINATED BY '\n'
    IGNORE 1 LINES
    (zipcode, x, y, location);
```

The IGNORE keyword skips the first line (which has labels instead of data), and the field and line terminators are the standard tab and newline characters.

MySQL should respond with something like:

```
Query OK, 41556 rows affected, 65535 warnings (0.24 sec)
Records: 41556 Deleted: 0 Skipped: 0 Warnings: 80168
```

The warnings indicate that some decimals may be truncated slightly as they are forced to six digits.

The following query displays the entire table (all 41,556 rows):

```
mysql> SELECT * FROM zips;
```

```
+---------+----------+----------+-------------------------------+
| zipcode | x        | y        | location                      |
+---------+----------+----------+-------------------------------+
| 00210   | 0.313506 | 0.763354 | Portsmouth, NH                |
| 00211   | 0.313506 | 0.763354 | Portsmouth, NH                |
| 00212   | 0.313506 | 0.763354 | Portsmouth, NH                |
| 00213   | 0.313506 | 0.763354 | Portsmouth, NH                |
| 00214   | 0.313506 | 0.763354 | Portsmouth, NH                |
| 00215   | 0.313506 | 0.763354 | Portsmouth, NH                |
| 00501   | 0.302470 | 0.722645 | Holtsville, NY                |
| 00544   | 0.302470 | 0.722645 | Holtsville, NY                |
...
```

A better example shows the zip code and location column for locations starting with Cambridge:

```
mysql> SELECT zipcode,location FROM zips WHERE location LIKE "Cambridge%";
```

which produces:

```
+---------+------------------+
| zipcode | location         |
+---------+------------------+
| 02138   | Cambridge, MA    |
| 02139   | Cambridge, MA    |
| 02140   | Cambridge, MA    |
| 02141   | Cambridge, MA    |
| 02142   | Cambridge, MA    |
| 02238   | Cambridge, MA    |
| 02239   | Cambridge, MA    |
| 04923   | Cambridge, ME    |
| 05141   | Cambridgeport, VT |
| 05444   | Cambridge, VT    |
```

```
| 12816   | Cambridge, NY         |
| 16403   | Cambridge Springs, PA |
| 21613   | Cambridge, MD         |
| 43725   | Cambridge, OH         |
| 47327   | Cambridge City, IN    |
| 50046   | Cambridge, IA         |
| 53523   | Cambridge, WI         |
| 55008   | Cambridge, MN         |
| 61238   | Cambridge, IL         |
| 67023   | Cambridge, KS         |
| 69022   | Cambridge, NE         |
| 83610   | Cambridge, ID         |
+---------+-----------------------+
22 rows in set (0.05 sec)
```

The *mysql* command-line utility is useful if you're comfortable with the command line, but you can find other utilities online that provide a GUI interface to the same sort of tasks. A longer MySQL tutorial can be found in the reference at *http://dev. mysql.com/doc/refman/5.0/en/tutorial.html*.

Using MySQL with Processing

For use in visualization, you need to access the database from code. Java has a built-in database API called JDBC that works with multiple database engines and maintains the same interface across them by using an interchangeable set of driver, or connector, objects. The MySQL connector for Java can be found on MySQL.com:

http://www.mysql.com/downloads/api-jdbc.html

Download the *.zip* file for the version that matches your database installation. Unpack the file; inside it should be another file named something similar to *mysql-connector-java-5.0.7-bin.jar*. Create a new sketch and add this file. Like all *.jar* files, it will be placed in a subfolder named *code*.

Back in the MySQL utility, create a user that has access to the database so that you're not connecting to the database as the *root* user:

```
mysql> GRANT SELECT ON testing.* TO processing@localhost
    IDENTIFIED BY 'processingpass';
```

That will grant SELECT privileges (the ability to run queries) to a user named processing with the password processingpass.

In Processing, add the following code to a second tab (this is a helper class that will hide some of the mechanics of loading the database driver and can be reused for other purposes):

```
import java.sql.Connection;
import java.sql.DriverManager;
import java.sql.SQLException;
import java.sql.Statement;
```

```java
class Database {
  Connection conn;
  String host;
  String user;
  String pass;
  String dbname;
  int port = 3306;

  public Database(String host, String dbname, String user, String pass) {
    this.host = host;
    this.user = user;
    this.pass = pass;
    this.dbname = dbname;

    conn = connect();
  }

  public Connection connect() {
    try {
      Class.forName("com.mysql.jdbc.Driver").newInstance();
    } catch (ClassNotFoundException e) {
      e.printStackTrace();
    } catch (InstantiationException e) {
      e.printStackTrace();
    } catch (IllegalAccessException e) {
      e.printStackTrace();
    }

    try {
      String url = "jdbc:mysql://" + host + ":" + port + "/" + dbname;
      println("Connecting to " + url + " as " + user);
      return DriverManager.getConnection(url, user, pass);

    } catch (SQLException e) {
      e.printStackTrace();
      return null;
    }
  }

  public ResultSet query(String query) {
    try {
      Statement st = conn.createStatement();
      ResultSet rs = st.executeQuery(query);
      return rs;

    } catch (SQLException e) {
      e.printStackTrace();
      return null;
    }
  }
}
```

Back in the main tab, the following code runs our last query from the previous section:

```
import java.sql.ResultSet;

void setup() {
  Database db = new Database("localhost", "testing",
                             "processing", "processingpass");
  ResultSet rs = db.query("SELECT zipcode,location FROM zips " +
                          "WHERE location LIKE \"Cambridge%\"");

  try {
    while (rs.next()) {
      String zipcode = rs.getString(1);
      String location = rs.getString(2);
      println(zipcode + " -> " + location);
    }
  } catch (SQLException e) {
    e.printStackTrace();
  }
}
```

The ResultSet class from Java's JDBC library does most of the work here. Use rs.next() to iterate through the results of a query. The getString() method gets the result information at a particular index. Note that these are indexed starting at 1 (unlike most index values in this book, which start at 0).

The processing and processingpass values for the username and password can be replaced with another user that you create. If you're connecting to a hosted database, replace localhost with the address of that machine (e.g., database.mycompany.com).

This example leaves out the details of multiple queries and closing database connections, but it should provide a feel for the steps involved in using a database with Processing. There's a lot to learn about databases—I'm just trying to provide a taste of it here.

Other Database Options

Depending on the constraints of your project, there are many other database options to consider. They include the following:

Apache Derby/Java DB (http://db.apache.org/derby)
  A full database written entirely in Java. It has a small (2 MB) footprint and uses the same JDBC commands seen in the previous example. In Java 6, the project has been integrated into the JDK under the name Java DB.

SQLite (http://www.sqlite.org)
> SQLite is a free, lightweight, and compact database that's designed to integrate easily into other projects. The source code is even in the public domain. Rather than employing a client/server model, it connects directly to a single application, and all database information is stored in a single cross-platform file, making it suitable for single user purposes. There are multiple SQLite JDBC connectors for Java; try one and see if it suits your needs.

Berkeley DB (http://www.oracle.com/technology/products/berkeley-db)
> Named for its origin at U.C. Berkeley, this database handles data storage and retrieval, but without a query language like SQL and without a wire protocol— everything is on your local machine. It's ideal for cases when you need to access a large amount of data in a manner that's a bit like using a flat file, but when a straight flat file is too slow. The database is used behind many well-known software products, and it is currently maintained by and hosted at Oracle.

Performance Aspects of Databases in Interactive Applications

At first, databases may seem the best solution for any data storage task because of their ubiquity and relative ease of use. In the context of this book, one difficulty in using a database is how they perform in interactive environments. If the Zipdecode project in Chapter 6 were implemented with a database, for instance, a slight lag would occur from the time the user hit a key to when the query results were processed and returned to the application. That would be mitigated by using a local database, though that's obviously not suitable for a small interactive piece running on the Web.

Because databases are fundamentally a means to "pull" data (rather than having it pushed continuously, like a network stream), software that uses a database will have to hit the database with a new query each time more data or a different set of data is needed—which can easily cause a lag in an interface or be prohibitively cumbersome for the system. Think of thousands of people using an interactive application that's connected to a database and running a new query each time the mouse is dragged to change values in a scroll bar.

As a general rule, always consider whether a database is necessary, particularly early on in the process of developing a visualization. Rather than figuring out how to structure your tables and queries properly, it's usually better to build something that works with plain text files (referred to as *flat files*) first so that you can determine whether the solution you're pursuing is a good direction. The robustness of a database system can be added later, once a working prototype has validated the design direction.

Dealing with a Large Number of Files

What happens if we extend the Zipdecode example to add geometry data for each postal code? The geometry is available from the U.S. Census Bureau (*http://www. census.gov/geo/ZCTA/zcta.html*) and averages about 20 lines of coordinates for each code. You might store the information in multiple files for quick access, but given that you're looking at more than 45,000 files, that can be daunting. They might eventually be put into a database, but for testing, it's often simpler to keep them local.

In such a case, don't put a huge number of files in the *data* folder. You don't want them packaged and slowing down the download. Instead, remove the data from the *data* folder before exporting, and then create a *data* folder adjacent to the *.jar* file that is created. Because that directory is found relative to the *.jar* file, the files will still load properly even when deployed online.

You should also consider a scheme to subdivide the files into folders. Operating systems and GUI-based file browsers become extremely inefficient when asked to access folders with a large number of files (the effective limit may be as low as 100, and is usually no greater than 1,000). With the ZIP codes, for instance, use the first two digits to break up the folders. The *15* folder will contain files for 15232, 15213, 15272, and so on.

When working in this manner, isolate the retrieval function from the rest of the code so you can change the file structure later without affecting the rest of the application. For instance, you can provide a method to get information for a ZIP code like this:

```
String[] getInfo(String zipCode) {
  String prefix = zipCode.subString(0, 2);
  String filename = prefix + "/" + zipCode + ".txt"
  return loadStrings(filename);
}
```

That also works if the files are stored on another server. Simply add the web address of the server to the prefix:

```
String[] getInfo(String zipCode) {
  String prefix = "http://site.com/data/" + zipCode.subString(0, 2);
  String filename = prefix + "/" + zipCode + ".txt"
  return loadStrings(filename);
}
```

Or if you later move to a PHP script connected to a database (which will not need to use subfolders or prefixes), you need only swap in a new version of the function:

```
String[] getInfo(String zipCode) {
  String url = "http://site.com/data/info.php?" + zipCode;
  return loadStrings(url);
}
```

The *info.php* script would simply return the lines of data for a particular zip code.

## CHAPTER 10

Parsing Data

Parsing converts a raw stream of data into a structure that can be manipulated in software. Lots of parsing is detective work, requiring you to spend time looking at files or data streams to figure out what's inside. The data might be available in an easily parsed format (such as an RSS feed in XML format) or in a proprietary binary format. This chapter covers some of the methods used to store data, methods for reading common data formats, and some detective procedures for dissecting data. Even if your particular data format is not covered in this chapter, the methods discussed are applicable to any data source.

Parsing may also seem to be quite disconnected from the actual process of data visualization. However, it's part of the process for a reason: chances are, you'll have to obtain data from a source that's not under your control and will spend a lot of time figuring out how to use the data that you're given. This chapter aims to give you a sense of how files are typically structured because more likely than not, the data you acquire will be poorly documented (if it's documented at all). Being able to recognize the basic file format, or even whether the data is compressed, are valuable clues to unpacking unknown information.

Generally, data boils down to lists (one-dimensional sets), matrices (two-dimensional tables, such as a spreadsheet), or trees and graphs (individual "nodes" of data and sets of "edges" that describe connections between them). Strictly speaking, a matrix can be used to represent a list, or graphs can represent lists and matrices, but such over-abstraction is not useful.

Levels of Effort

Throughout this book, we've discussed the importance of knowing when to write generalizable code and when to write a quick hack. The parsing step is one occasion when it's a common issue. As an example, let's consider parsing SVG shape data, described later in this chapter. There are three basic scenarios:

A simple hack

This can get you up and running quickly. It works especially well if your data is not changing, or the data need not be generalized for other situations. In this case, we'd ignore everything in the file except for certain types of shape commands, e.g., only looking for "path" data and ignoring everything else.

A basic parser

This scenario is often a good solution when you need code that's not too large, so it can be deployed over the Web. This exceeds the simple hack, but doesn't quite approach a full-blown parser. The SVG parser included with Processing, with a footprint of about 30 KB, is targeted for this category.

A full parsing API

For local applications where code footprint does not matter, a full parser might be necessary. An example would be the Batik SVG parser (*http://xmlgraphics. apache.org/batik*) from the Apache project. It's an excellent solution, but with a 1 MB footprint for the library code, it is not suitable for some situations.

Generally speaking, each of these options takes an order of magnitude more time to implement than the previous one. Their runtime speeds also tend to decrease as we move down the list, although robustness and maintainability tend to increase in the same direction. The Processing API and libraries target the first two cases, in keeping with its focus on sketching, with the assumption that the third step is always available by attaching to larger Java libraries.

Data isn't always clean, and sometimes you have to write dirty code to parse it. Writing parsers is easy, but writing ones that fail gracefully is not, which makes parsing issues deceptively complex. You might be able to write an HTML parser in an afternoon, but you could spend a week figuring out how to deal with all the errors that exist in the typical HTML file and how to gracefully recover from them.

An anecdote illustrating these problems from the software engineering side is Netscape's decision in 1998 to rewrite its browser from scratch. Lou Montulli, a founding engineer at Netscape, wrote:

> There was good reason for a large change, but rewriting everything was a bit overboard to say the least. I laughed heartily as I got questions from one of my former employees about FTP code that he was rewriting. It had taken three years of tuning to get code that could read the 60 different types of FTP servers. Those 5,000 lines of code may have looked ugly, but at least they worked.*

In short, the perception of "ugliness" can often lead to nonessential tasks that take you down long, unproductive paths and lead you astray from the priorities of your project.

---

* *http://www.joelonsoftware.com/news/fog0000000215.html*

Tools for Gathering Clues

It's important to have a decent *text editor* and *hex viewer* available for detective work on data files. A text editor should be capable of efficiently loading files that are many megabytes in size. A hex editor is useful when dealing with binary data because sometimes it's necessary to take a look at the first few bytes of a data file to identify its type. If you're using Unix or Linux, you're probably already familiar with such tools; a text editor is a fundamental utility, and the *od* octal dump program has been around for decades. Here are some suggestions for Windows and Mac OS X users:

Windows

> *UltraEdit (http://www.ultraedit.com)*
>
> *TextPad (http://www.textpad.com)*
>> Both of these are common favorites for handling text, though they are trialware and will cost a few dollars for the full version.
>
> *HexEdit (http://www.physics.ohio-state.edu/~prewett/hexedit)*
>> A free hex editor/viewer.
>
> *HexWorkshop (http://www.hexworkshop.com)*
>> A popular paid alternative.

Mac OS X

> *TextWrangler (http://www.barebones.com/products/textwrangler)*
>> A free text editor from the makers of BBEdit (another popular and useful text editor for the Mac).
>
> *Hex Fiend (http://ridiculousfish.com/hexfiend)*
>> A freeware hex editor.

Command-line utilities are also very important. On Windows, be sure to install Cygwin (*http://cygwin.com*), as discussed in the "Tools for Acquiring Data from the Internet" section in Chapter 9. A quick introduction to some command-line tools follows.

The | (pipe) command is used between command-line items to pass the result of one command to another. The > operator writes the output of a command to a file, and the >> operator does the same, but appends to the end of the file rather than overwrite the existing contents. These special characters will make more sense in the examples given in the following list of commands:

cat
> Short for *concatenate*. cat `filename` outputs the contents of a file to the console. This is useful in combination with | so that the contents of a file can be used as input to another process. For example, cat `filename` | grep potato sends the contents of the file to the *grep* utility, which in turn pulls out and displays any lines that contain potato.

more *and* less

> These are *pagers*, which output a file (or some sort of input) one screenful at a time. For instance, if the file in the previous example contained many thousands of instances of the word potato, you could pipe the results to more so you could view them bit by bit. Pressing the Space bar displays the next page of results, while the Enter key shows one more line. The less command works similarly, but it has more options; for instance, it lets you press b to move back to the previous screen of output:
>
> ```
> cat filename.txt | grep potato | more
> ```

head *and* tail

> These commands display the beginning or end of a file. They're useful for taking a quick peek at the first (or last) 10 lines of a million-line file, for example:
>
> ```
> head -n 10 enormousfile.txt
> tail -n 10 hugefile.txt
> ```

This is a very limited introduction to these tools, but we'll make further use of them and similar commands. The grep command is covered in greater detail later in this chapter, in the "Is a parser necessary?" section.

Text Is Best

Perhaps the most useful file format is simple delimited text. In this format, lines of text are separated by delimiters (usually a tab or a comma) that separate individual columns of a table.

Tab-Separated Values (TSV)

A TSV file contains rows of text data made up of columns separated by tab characters. The format is useful because it's easy to parse and can be loaded and edited with any spreadsheet program. Breaking up rows of text is simply a matter of using split(line, TAB), which returns an array of String objects representing the columns. (TSV files were also covered back in Chapter 6.)

Comma-Separated Values (CSV)

CSV works similarly to TSV, except that the delimiter is a , (comma) character. Because commas might be part of the data, any column that includes a comma must be placed inside quotes. Of course, quotes might be part of the data as well, so a pair of double quotes is used to indicate a double quote in the data. An example explains this much more clearly; here we'll use a stress test compiled of cases from the article about CSV data in Wikipedia:[*]

---

[*] *http://en.wikipedia.org/wiki/Comma-separated_values*

```
1997,Ford,E350
1997, Ford , E350
1997,Ford,E350,"Super, luxurious truck"
1997,Ford,E350,"Super ""luxurious"" truck"
1997,Ford,E350," Super luxurious truck "
"1997",Ford,E350
Year,Make,Model
1997,Ford,E350
2000,Mercury,Cougar
```

To parse this file (name it *test.csv*), use the following:

```
void setup() {
  String[] lines = loadStrings("test.csv");
  parse(lines);
}

void parse(String[] lines) {
  for (int i = 0; i < lines.length; i++) {
    String[] pieces = splitLine(lines[i]);
    println("line " + (i+1));
    println(pieces);
    println();
  }
}

String[] splitLine(String line) {
  char[] c = line.toCharArray();
  ArrayList pieces = new ArrayList();
  int prev = 0;
  boolean insideQuote = false;
  for (int i = 0; i < c.length; i++) {
    if (c[i] == ',') {
      if (!insideQuote) {
        // Whitespace must be trimmed between commas.
        String s = new String(c, prev, i - prev).trim();
        pieces.add(s);
        prev = i+1;
      }
    } else if (c[i] == '\"') {
      insideQuote = !insideQuote;
    }
  }
  if (prev != c.length) {
    String s = new String(c, prev, c.length - prev).trim();
    pieces.add(s);
  }
  String[] outgoing = new String[pieces.size()];
  pieces.toArray(outgoing);
  scrubQuotes(outgoing);
  return outgoing;
}
```

```
// Parse quotes from CSV data. Quotes around a column are common,
// and actual double quotes (") are specified by two double quotes ("").
void scrubQuotes(String[] array) {
  for (int i = 0; i < array.length; i++) {
    if (array[i].length() > 2) {
      // Remove quotes at start and end, if present.
      if (array[i].startsWith("\"") && array[i].endsWith("\"")) {
        array[i] = array[i].substring(1, array[i].length() - 1);
      }
    }
    // Make double quotes into single quotes.
    array[i] = array[i].replaceAll("\"\"", "\"");
  }
}
```

The output of the program is as follows:

```
line 1
[0] "1997"
[1] "Ford"
[2] "E350"

line 2
[0] "1997"
[1] "Ford"
[2] "E350"

line 3
[0] "1997"
[1] "Ford"
[2] "E350"
[3] "Super, luxurious truck"

line 4
[0] "1997"
[1] "Ford"
[2] "E350"
[3] "Super "luxurious" truck"

line 5
[0] "1997"
[1] "Ford"
[2] "E350"
[3] " Super luxurious truck "

line 6
[0] "1997"
[1] "Ford"
[2] "E350"

line 7
[0] "Year"
[1] "Make"
[2] "Model"
```

```
line 8
[0] "1997"
[1] "Ford"
[2] "E350"

line 9
[0] "2000"
[1] "Mercury"
[2] "Cougar"
```

Note how extra spaces are removed unless they're inside double quotes. The wrapper function, parse( ), uses simple println( ) statements on a String array to list each bit of text inside quotes, with the array index in brackets in front of it.

Although there is no CSV file format specification per se, authoritative documentation of the format can be found in RFC 4180 (*http://tools.ietf.org/html/rfc4180*).

Text with Fixed Column Widths

Text files are sometimes of fixed width, where each column is separated by padded spacing so that new columns of data always start at specific positions. Fixed-width files are becoming less common; they were used heavily in legacy computer systems because programming languages used during that time (such as Fortran) were better at splitting data at specific positions, rather than at specific characters:

```
          1         2         3
012345678901234567890123456790

apple     1456990   349.2
bear         3949    0.22
cat         33923    61.9
```

In this example, the first column has characters 0 through 9, the second has 10 through 19, and the final has 20 through 26.

To parse a fixed-width file, use substring( ) and trim( ) to slice the information:

```
String name = line.substring(0, 10).trim( );
String string1 = line.substring(10, 20).trim( );
int value1 = int(string1);
String string2 = line.substring(20, 27).trim( );
float value2 = float(string2);
```

Note that the second parameter of substring( ) is not inclusive; using substring(10, 20) will start at character 10 and move up to, but not include, 20.

The trim( ) method removes additional whitespace padding from the sides of the data so that name for the first line is "apple" instead of "apple ".

One tricky part of dealing with fixed-width text is that some lines may be incomplete, in which case, calling substring( ) may return an ArrayIndexOutOfBoundsException. For instance, if the file reads:

```
apple    1456990   349.2
bear     3949
cat      33923     61.9
```

the following will produce an error when it reads the second line:

```
String string2 = line.substring(20, 27).trim();
```

One option is to check whether the line has enough characters before calling substring():

```
String string2 = "";
if (line.length() >= 27) {
  string2 = line.substring(20, 27).trim();
}
```

Note how `string2` is declared and assigned with an empty value outside the `if` statement so that missing data will still be handled properly, rather than `string2` being set to `null` and causing a later error.

A better option would be to keep an array of indices where columns start, use this array to split as much of the line as possible into pieces, and then return the array of `String` objects to be reassigned to named `String` objects. Regular expressions are another option for unpacking fixed-width text.

Text Markup Languages

To allow flexibility in structure—such as including arbitrary numbers of elements of any size in varying orders—many formats embed structure tags in their content. Markup languages, such as HTML and XML, are prime examples—where sets of tags delineate and identify the content found in the document. Such documents are relatively easy to parse, and they are fortunately becoming more common, particularly XML.

But even though the documents are designed to facilitate parsing, keep in mind which data you actually need from the file. Is it necessary to have a parser at all? Does including a robust parser warrant the additional code size when all you really need is a specific <TABLE> element from an HTML file? In the next section, we'll discuss a range of options.

HyperText Markup Language (HTML)

When parsing data, the first thing to do is take a look at the file. Since the very earliest web browsers, the View Source command has given away the secrets of web development methods and page content. But nowadays the HTML code found in web pages is less likely to be intended for human consumption, either because of intentional obfuscation or because the page was generated dynamically by a script.

At the very minimum, cleaning up tags and indenting the HTML to reveal its structure can be a big help. Tidy, an application that originated from the W3C (*http://www.w3.org/People/Raggett/tidy*), massages HTML documents into a more regular format, normalizing upper- and lowercase, repairing missing tags, and so on. The project continues at Sourceforge (*http://tidy.sourceforge.net*), which also has downloads for various platforms. (Some Mac OS X and Linux systems already have it installed.) The command-line version is helpful for taking a look at documents by hand. For instance, the following command performs a basic cleanup and indent operation on the *test.html* file, creating another called *test-tidy.html*:

```
tidy -indent test.html > test-tidy.html
```

The contents of *test.html* look like:

```
<TABLE>
<TR> <TD> first col </TD>

<TD> second col </TD>

<TD> <TABLE> <TR> <TD> table two embedded </TD> </TR> </TABLE>
</TABLE>
```

But the tidied version in *test-tidy.html* contains:

```
<!DOCTYPE html PUBLIC "-//W3C//DTD HTML 3.2//EN">

<html>
<head>
  <meta name="generator" content=
  "HTML Tidy for Mac OS X (vers 1st December 2004), see www.w3.org">

  <title></title>
</head>

<body>
  <table>
    <tr>
      <td>first col</td>

      <td>second col</td>

      <td>
        <table>
          <tr>
            <td>table two embedded</td>
          </tr>
        </table>
      </td>
    </tr>
  </table>
</body>
</html>
```

Note the new DOCTYPE declaration and the addition of tags such as <html> and <body> to make a more proper HTML file. The -indent option helps clarify the table structure, so now it's easier to understand the table structure in the original file.

Tidy has many other useful options that can reformat a document as XHTML or XML; see its reference pages or use tidy -help to get a list of command-line options.

Embedding Tidy into a sketch

In this book, we're most interested in data that changes over time, so you may need to run Tidy on pages dynamically. A Java version that's suitable for use in Processing is available at *http://sourceforge.net/projects/jtidy*.

Get the latest download, find its *.jar* file, and add it to your sketch. Adding the file will add the import statements for any packages found in the JAR (although they will not be shown). If you're not using Processing, add the following to your code:

```
import org.w3c.tidy.*;
```

An example of using Tidy follows:

```
try {
  String[] lines = loadStrings("http://www.oreilly.com");
  String originalPage = join(lines, "");

  byte[] utf;
  utf = originalPage.getBytes("UTF8");
  ByteArrayInputStream utfis = new ByteArrayInputStream(utf);

  Tidy tidy = new Tidy();
  tidy.setUpperCaseTags(true);
  tidy.setUpperCaseAttrs(false);
  tidy.setCharEncoding(Configuration.UTF8);
  tidy.setEncloseText(true);
  tidy.setEncloseBlockText(true);
  tidy.setQuoteAmpersand(false);
  tidy.setQuoteNbsp(false);
  tidy.setQuoteMarks(false);

  // Ignore any errors.
  PrintWriter ignored = new PrintWriter(new ByteArrayOutputStream());
  tidy.setErrout(ignored);

  // Write the contents to a ByteArrayOutputStream.
  ByteArrayOutputStream baos = new ByteArrayOutputStream();
  tidy.parseDOM(utfis, baos);

  String tidiedPage = baos.toString("UTF8");
  println(tidiedPage);

} catch (UnsupportedEncodingException e) {
  e.printStackTrace();
}
```

The beginning and end of this code mostly deal with converting the data to and from a stream of bytes in UTF-8 format. The code in the middle sets various configuration options to handle the specifics of how the file should be formatted. The newly cleaned page is written to tidiedPage, which is now ready for use.

Is a parser necessary?

Even though your input document might be HTML, it's possible that your data is not even complex enough to require a full HTML parser (especially if you use something like Tidy on it first). For instance, say we wanted to study who is speaking through the course of Shakespeare's *As You Like It*. The play can be found at *http://shakespeare.mit.edu/asyoulikeit/full.html*, and a View Source reveals a document with an extremely regular format:

```
<H3>ACT I</h3>
<h3>SCENE I. Orchard of Oliver's house.</h3>
<p><blockquote>

<i>Enter ORLANDO and ADAM</i>
</blockquote>

<A NAME=speech1><b>ORLANDO</b></a>
<blockquote>
<A NAME=1.1.1>As I remember, Adam, it was upon this fashion</A><br>
<A NAME=1.1.2>bequeathed me by will but poor a thousand crowns,</A><br>
<A NAME=1.1.3>and, as thou sayest, charged my brother, on his</A><br>
<A NAME=1.1.4>blessing, to breed me well: and there begins my</A><br>
<A NAME=1.1.5>sadness. My brother Jaques he keeps at school, and</A><br>
<!-- some lines omitted -->
</blockquote>

<A NAME=speech2><b>ADAM</b></a>
<blockquote>
<A NAME=1.1.26>Yonder comes my master, your brother.</A><br>
</blockquote>

<A NAME=speech3><b>ORLANDO</b></a>
<blockquote>
<A NAME=1.1.27>Go apart, Adam, and thou shalt hear how he will</A><br>

<A NAME=1.1.28>shake me up.</A><br>
<p><i>Enter OLIVER</i></p>
</blockquote>
```

Tallying individual speakers is simply a matter of looking for lines like:

```
<A NAME=speech2><b>ADAM</b></a>
```

This is a task easily handled by a regular expression (see examples in Chapters 5 and 8). The same is true for other elements of the play, and depending on which information is of interest, you may be able to avoid a full parser in favor of cherry-picking information using a combination of regular expressions or String.indexOf( )

---

to test for lines of interest. Command-line utilities, such as *grep*, make it easy to check hypotheses, such as "all lines with a `<b>` tag contain names of the play's characters." Download the *full.html* page from the previous link, and then use:

```
grep '<b>' full.html
```

from the command line to check the file. The command produces:

```
<A NAME=speech1><b>ORLANDO</b></a>
<A NAME=speech2><b>ADAM</b></a>
<A NAME=speech3><b>ORLANDO</b></a>
<A NAME=speech4><b>OLIVER</b></a>
<A NAME=speech5><b>ORLANDO</b></a>
<A NAME=speech6><b>OLIVER</b></a>
<A NAME=speech7><b>ORLANDO</b></a>
<A NAME=speech8><b>OLIVER</b></a>
<A NAME=speech9><b>ORLANDO</b></a>
<A NAME=speech10><b>OLIVER</b></a>
<A NAME=speech11><b>ORLANDO</b></a>
<A NAME=speech12><b>OLIVER</b></a>
...and 800 additional lines like these
```

That confirms our hypothesis, so part of the puzzle is solved. Text of speech can be sussed out with:

```
grep '<A NAME' full.html
```

But it includes the names of speakers found in the preceding output. Piping the output of this command through the *inverse* of the previous command:

```
(grep -v)
```

gives us everything that matches `<A NAME` but does not match `<b>`:

```
grep '<A NAME' full.html | grep -v '<b>'
```

which will be all the spoken portions:

```
<A NAME=1.1.1>As I remember, Adam, it was upon this fashion</A><br>
<A NAME=1.1.2>bequeathed me by will but poor a thousand crowns,</A><br>
<A NAME=1.1.3>and, as thou sayest, charged my brother, on his</A><br>
<A NAME=1.1.4>blessing, to breed me well: and there begins my</A><br>
```

Having confirmed this on the command line, the same can be done in code:

```
String[] lines = loadStrings("full.html");
for (int i = 0; i < lines.length; i++) {
  if (lines[i].indexOf("<A NAME") != -1) {
    if (!lines[i].indexOf("<b>")) {
      println(lines[i]);
    }
  }
}
```

A combination of code and command-line methods contribute to the early part of the detective work in figuring out how to parse files. It may also lead you to a quick hack that will cover your parsing needs without unnecessary levels of abstraction.

If the site from which you got the data makes a minor change in the structure of this data, it can of course break your quick-and-dirty extraction method—but sometimes such changes can break even a full-blown parser, so you may be just as safe with this extraction method.

Using Swing's built-in HTML parser

In many cases, you'll want a full HTML parser. As it happens, the Swing API contains an HTML parser to support its HTMLEditorKit classes. Other Java programs can make use of the parser by creating a subclass of HTMLEditorKit.ParserCallback. This parser uses an event-driven model of handling the data, running callback functions to handle each piece of the HTML document's hierarchy. An example sketch that extracts links follows:

```java
import javax.swing.text.*;
import javax.swing.text.html.*;


void setup() {
  Reader r = createReader("HTML file or URL here");
  String[] list = extractLinks(r);
  println(list);
}


String[] extractLinks(Reader reader) {
  LinkHandler handler = new LinkHandler();
  parse(reader, handler);
  return handler.getLinks();
}


void parse(Reader reader, HTMLEditorKit.ParserCallback handler) {
  HTMLEditorKit.Parser parser = new HTMLEditorKit() {
    public HTMLEditorKit.Parser getParser() {
      return super.getParser();
    }
  }.getParser();
  try {
    parser.parse(reader, handler, true);
  } catch (Exception e) {
    e.printStackTrace();
  }
}
```

In a second tab named *LinkHandler*, add the following code:

```java
class LinkHandler extends HTMLEditorKit.ParserCallback {
  ArrayList links;

  LinkHandler() {
    links = new ArrayList();
  }
```

```
  public String[] getLinks() {
   String[] outgoing = new String[links.size()];
   links.toArray(outgoing);
   return outgoing;
  }

  public void handleStartTag(HTML.Tag tag, MutableAttributeSet a, int pos) {
    if (tag == HTML.Tag.A) {
      String href = (String) a.getAttribute(HTML.Attribute.HREF);
      // Skip <A NAME=""> tags, where HREF is not present.
      if (href != null) {
        links.add(href);
      }
    }
  }

  // Handle the end of a tag (e.g., the </A> for an <A> start tag).
  public void handleEndTag(HTML.Tag tag, int pos) {
  }

  // Handle actual content inside a tag.
  public void handleText(char[] c,int pos) {
  }

  // Handle a tag that is not a start/end pairing,
  // e.g., <IMG SRC="">, which has no corresponding </IMG> tag.
  public void handleSimpleTag(HTML.Tag t, MutableAttributeSet a,int pos) {
  }

  // Handle the content of a comment.
  public void handleComment(char[] data, int pos) {
  }

  // Report errors to the user.
  public void handleError(String errorMsg,int pos) {
  }
 }
```

Only the handleStartTag method is implemented in this example, but to handle other tags, add code to the other methods (handleEndTag, handleText, and the rest). To adapt this example to extract image links, you'd need only a handleSimpleTag method. For instance:

```
public void handleSimpleTag(HTML.Tag t, MutableAttributeSet a, int pos) {
    if (tag == HTML.Tag.IMG) {
      String src = (String) a.getAttribute(HTML.Attribute.SRC);
      if (src != null) {
        PImage img = loadImage(src);
        // ...do something here with the image
      }
    }
  }
```

This code doesn't account for relative URLs, so `<IMG SRC="http://processing.org/images/feed.gif">` will work, but `<IMG SRC="feed.gif">` will not. For these cases, check whether the URL starts with `http://` and if not, prepend the location of the page.

Many tags and attributes are supported; a full listing can be found in the Java documentation for `HTML.Tag`:

http://java.sun.com/j2se/1.4.2/docs/api/javax/swing/text/html/HTML.Tag.html

and `HTML.Attribute`:

http://java.sun.com/j2se/1.4.2/docs/api/javax/swing/text/html/HTML.Attribute.html

Parsing and manipulating tables from HTML files

Another version of this code, available on the book's web site, can load and parse tables from HTML documents and convert them to `Table` objects (which were first used in Chapter 3). This covers the most common situation for screen-scraping: pulling tables from HTML content. The code is at *http://benfry.com/book/parse/HtmlTableParser.pde*.

It also relies on the `Table` class from the mapping example, found at *http://benfry.com/book/map/Table.pde*.

The parser gets a list of tables, each of which can be retrieved with the `getTable()` command. Then, you can use methods such as `getFloat()` and `getString()` from the `Table` class to retrieve specific values:

```
// Specify a file or URL from which to grab the data.
Reader r = createReader("testing.html");
// Parse tables from this file.
HtmlTableParser htp = new HtmlTableParser(r);
// Get the second table from the file (items are zero indexed).
Table t = htp.getTable(1);
// Get a float from the second column from the third row.
float v = t.getFloat(2, 1);
```

Another option is to get all the tables as an array. Then, you can put the data into some other convenient, low-overhead format for further processing, such as resaving each table in the document as an individual *.tsv* file:

```
Reader r = createReader("testing.html");
HtmlTableParser htp = new HtmlTableParser(r);
Table[] tables = htp.getTables();
for (int i = 0; i < htp.getTableCount(); i++) {
  String filename = nf(i+1, 2) + ".tsv";
  println("Writing table " + filename);
  PrintWriter w = createWriter(filename);
  tables[i].write(w);
}
```

But remember that if you're looking for static HTML table data, you can always use the method shown in Chapter 5 to extract the table using OpenOffice or Microsoft Excel. This method will work for saving an HTML table to a file, but it requires manual labor, so it's not suitable for data that changes over time.

Other HTML parser libraries

The Processing libraries page (*http://processing.org/reference/libraries*) includes other contributed libraries that handle HTML parsing. You may find one of these suitable for your tasks.

Another option is the HTML Parser project on Sourceforge (*http://htmlparser. sourceforge.net*), which provides a differently styled API for reading HTML documents.

Writing a custom HTML parser

Writing an HTML parser might not seem terribly difficult—just look for left and right brackets, read tags, look for spaces, get the attributes, etc.—but it quickly gets complicated in exception cases. Tags and attributes might be mixed between upper- and lowercase, parameters can be found in any order, extra spacing is erratic, and end tags often go missing, as the following example shows:

```
// Oww, my afternoon
<A HREF="something.html">something</A>
<A Href=something.html name="click">something</a>
<a name="click" href="something.html">something</a>
<a HREF="something.html" >something </a>
```

A few hours dealing with such issues will leave most people looking for more readily available alternatives. But if the alternatives discussed earlier don't suffice, one option is to use JTidy to first clean the input HTML before parsing it in your code. This will help you avoid the quirkiness of the source HTML and clean it up so that you don't have to rely on the parser to handle awkward inconsistencies.

Extensible Markup Language (XML)

Many tools exist for viewing and editing XML files. Perhaps the simplest, most readily available viewers are in fact web browsers. Both Firefox and Internet Explorer have the ability to display XML documents as a tree, which can be useful for basic XML viewing when other tools are unavailable.

Cleaning up XML

Tidy (described in the previous section) can also be applied to XML documents. Add -xml to the command-line options to treat the file as an XML document:

```
tidy -xml -indent file.xml > file-tidy.xml
```

The -asxml and -asxhtml switches convert HTML documents to well-formed XHTML, making the document readable by the Processing XML library, which requires clean files. And the same process can be used with JTidy so that the conversion can happen within a sketch.

Example: Using the Processing XML library to read geocoding data

The Processing XML library, first mentioned in Chapter 2, is a minimal XML parser based on the open source project NanoXML. Its small download footprint (about 30K) makes it ideal for online use and simple parsing tasks. We'll cover more full-featured libraries later in this section, but first we'll use the built-in library to do some basic parsing. To use the XML library in a project, choose Sketch → Import Library → XML. The library parses XML files into a tree of XMLElement objects.

For this example, we'll use Google's *geocoding* service. Geocoding is the process of converting a place name in some irregular format into a more specific format, such as a set of latitude and longitude coordinates and a normalized address structure. The geocoding service is described in detail at *http://www.google.com/apis/maps/documentation/#Geocoding_HTTP_Request*.

A geocode request takes the form of a URL prefixed with http://maps.google.com/maps/geo?q=, followed by URL-encoded text for the location you're looking for and an API key. To use the example, first sign up for a Google Maps API key at *http://www.google.com/apis/maps/signup.html*, and then replace the text for API_KEY with your own (it will be 60 or 70 letters and numbers):

```
import processing.xml.*;

String API_KEY = "YOUR KEY HERE";
String location = "1600 Amphitheatre Parkway, Mountain View, CA";

String locationEncoded = URLEncoder.encode(location);
String url = "http://maps.google.com/maps/geo?q=" +
  locationEncoded + "&output=xml&key=" + API_KEY;

XMLElement xml = new XMLElement(this, url);
```

The following is a response from the geocoding server, formatted for readability:

```
<?xml version="1.0" encoding="utf-8"?>
<kml xmlns="http://earth.google.com/kml/2.0">
  <Response>
    <name>1600 Amphitheatre Parkway, Mountain View, CA</name>
    <Status>
      <code>200</code>
      <request>geocode</request>
    </Status>
    <Placemark>
      <address>1600 Amphitheatre Pkwy, Mountain View, CA 94043, USA</address>
      <AddressDetails Accuracy="8" xmlns="urn:oasis:names:tc:ciq:xsdschema:xAL:2.0">
        <Country>
```

```
          <CountryNameCode>US</CountryNameCode>
          <AdministrativeArea>
            <AdministrativeAreaName>CA</AdministrativeAreaName>
            <SubAdministrativeArea>
              <SubAdministrativeAreaName>Santa Clara</SubAdministrativeAreaName>
              <Locality>
                <LocalityName>Mountain View</LocalityName>
                <Thoroughfare>
                  <ThoroughfareName>1600 Amphitheatre Pkwy</ThoroughfareName>
                </Thoroughfare>
                <PostalCode>
                  <PostalCodeNumber>94043</PostalCodeNumber>
                </PostalCode>
              </Locality>
            </SubAdministrativeArea>
          </AdministrativeArea>
        </Country>
      </AddressDetails>
      <Point>
        <coordinates>-122.083739,37.423021,0</coordinates>
      </Point>
    </Placemark>
  </Response>
</kml>
```

To get the name of the root element, add the following, which will write kml to the console:

```
println("Name of root element is " + xml.getName());
```

To get the status code item, specify a path to a child element with the getChild() method and then use getContent() to read the contents of the code element (everything between <code> and </code>):

```
XMLElement statusCodeElement = xml.getChild("Response/Status/code");
String statusCodeStr = statusCodeElement.getContent();
println("Status code: " + statusCodeStr);
```

Note that the getChild() method does not need the kml item at the beginning because it is the item being queried.

The int() cast converts the String to an int for easier use:

```
int statusCode = int(statusCodeStr);
```

To get the address, use:

```
XMLElement addressElement = xml.getChild("Response/Placemark/address");
String addressStr = addressElement.getContent();
println("Address: " + addressStr);
```

Or to parse the location's longitude and latitude coordinates:

```
XMLElement coordsElement =
  xml.getChild("Response/Placemark/Point/coordinates");
String coordsStr = coordsElement.getContent();
String[] coords = split(coordsStr, ',');
```

```
float lon = parseFloat(coords[0]);
float lat = parseFloat(coords[1]);
println("Longitude: " + lon);
println("Latitude: " + lat);
```

The following are the main XMLElement methods:

getChild(String item)
> Searches the (direct) children for a particular name or for a series of items (separated by slashes, as shown in the earlier example) in the hierarchy.

getChildCount()
> Returns the number of child elements this node has.

getChild(int index)
> Returns a child by index (its order in the original file).

getChildren()
> Returns all children as an XMLElement[] array.

getChildren(String path)
> Like the getChild() method, except that it returns all matches for that name. For instance, if there were multiple <address> items, xml.getChildren("Response/Placemark/address") would return an array of XMLElement objects for each match.

More about the XML library can be found in the reference for XMLElement at *http://processing.org/reference/libraries/xml/XMLElement.html.*

Other methods for parsing XML

As already mentioned, the Processing XML library is a fairly basic means of parsing XML data. Other common options include the following:

Simple API for XML (SAX)
> An event-based model for parsing. SAX is built into later versions of Java in the org.xml.sax package. To use it, implement a ContentHandler object that implements methods such as startElement() and endElement(), which are called as XML data is parsed. This is a similar method to the Swing HTML parser shown earlier and more lightweight than the alternatives discussed next. More about SAX can be found online at *http://www.saxproject.org.*

XML Path Language (XPath)
> Essentially a far more sophisticated method of the getChild() and getChildren() methods that use paths to locate XML data in a tree. XPath specifies a query language that can be used to search for and filter a set of items in a flexible manner. XPath support is included in Java 1.5 and later. See *http://www.w3.org/TR/xpath.*

Document Object Model (DOM)
> A method for manipulating XML, also familiar to HTML and JavaScript developers, the DOM specifies an interface for manipulating the content of a structured document. See *http://www.w3.org/TR/2000/REC-DOM-Level-2-Core-20001113.*

In addition to the Processing libraries page, other Java-based XML parsers can be found on the Web. One popular option is the Xerces project from the Apache Software Foundation (*http://xerces.apache.org/xerces-j* and *http://xerces.apache.org/xerces2-j*). The Xerces project provides a full and robust XML parser, though at the expense of size. Such a parser might be suitable for quick mockups or applications that will run locally, rather than those distributed over the Web.

JavaScript Object Notation (JSON)

We first saw JSON data in Chapter 5. It's a simple format used for encoding data, primarily for use with JavaScript because JSON is valid JavaScript syntax. A documentation (and advocacy) site can be found at *http://www.json.org*. Pages that make heavy use of JavaScript and data (such as AJAX sites) are often peppered with JSON code. This is an example (from *json.org*):

```
{"widget": {
    "debug": "on",
    "window": {
        "title": "Sample Konfabulator Widget",
        "name": "main_window",
        "width": 500,
        "height": 500
    },
    "image": {
        "src": "Images/Sun.png",
        "name": "sun1",
        "hOffset": 250,
        "vOffset": 250,
        "alignment": "center"
    },
    "text": {
        "data": "Click Here",
        "size": 36,
        "style": "bold",
        "name": "text1",
        "hOffset": 250,
        "vOffset": 100,
        "alignment": "center",
        "onMouseUp": "sun1.opacity = (sun1.opacity / 100) * 90;"
    }
}}
```

The *json.org* site has code for reading and writing JSON in dozens of languages, including Java (*http://www.json.org/java*). Using the code with Processing is a matter of compiling the *.java* files provided. Download the *.zip* file containing the source. Unpacking it will produce a folder named *org*. To compile the code, navigate to that directory from a terminal window, and enter:

```
javac -source 1.3 -target 1.1 org/json/*.java
```

Then, to turn it into a *.jar* file:

```
zip -r json.jar org
```

Drag *json.jar* to any sketch for which you'd like to use the library, and use the examples on the JSON site as a guide for getting started.

Regular Expressions (regexps)

Regular expressions (regexps) are a powerful means for text matching that exceeds the abilities of `split()` without getting into a full parser. We first used regular expressions in Chapter 5, where we employed them on a simple data set. The source to `Record.java` in Chapter 8 covers a much more complicated example. It's beyond the scope of this book to cover them in detail, but those two examples should provide sufficient background to get you started.

The syntax for regexps is arcane at first, but you'll find that in practice you need to understand only a dozen different operations to get most tasks done. To that end, you may find something like O'Reilly's *Regular Expression Pocket Reference* by Tony Stubblebine useful. Or, if you're really into it, *Mastering Regular Expressions* by Jeffrey E. F. Friedl is available for advanced users.

Grammars and BNF Notation

A step past regexps and markup languages are full grammars in Backus Naur Form (BNF), most commonly used for parsing programming languages. They're also useful in protocol documents (e.g., the documentation for the HTTP standard that describes communication between web browsers and web servers; see *http://www.w3.org/Protocols/rfc1945/rfc1945*) as a flexible means of enumerating the structure of a protocol. An example of a grammar for U.S. postal addresses (*http://en.wikipedia.org/wiki/Backus%E2%80%93Naur_form*) follows:

```
<postal-address> ::= <name-part> <street-address> <zip-part>

    <name-part> ::= <personal-part> <last-name> <opt-jr-part> <EOL>
                  | <personal-part> <name-part> <EOL>

 <personal-part> ::= <first-name> | <initial> "."

<street-address> ::= <opt-apt-num> <house-num> <street-name> <EOL>

      <zip-part> ::= <town-name> "," <state-code> <ZIP-code> <EOL>
```

As can be seen in this example, the grammar is built all the way up from small, character-level components (such as the period and comma characters) into more complicated structures, such as a quoted string. A BNF grammar, which is readable by humans, is usually compiled to program code by a parser generator, which converts the logic to code that actually parses data. The resulting code is far less intelligible than the original grammar, but it is very efficient.

A grammar can solve nearly any parsing task, but it is several degrees more complex than simple hacks, such as searching for particular letter sequences, as described at the beginning of the chapter. But don't let yourself get bogged down in the possibilities—be sure to choose the simplest tool that can accomplish your goal.

Compressed Data

It could be argued that compression is really more to do with how data is stored and acquired than how it is parsed, but we discuss it here because of its influence on the "detective work" of figuring out how to parse data.

GZIP Streams (GZ)

GZIP is a helpful *stream* compression system, meaning that data can be serially encoded into gzip format. It's efficient for compressing text data, and on today's machines, it requires negligible processor time to compress or uncompress a stream as GZIP data.

The Processing API methods that read files (loadStrings( ), createReader( ), and others) automatically decompress any file ending in .gz. The same goes for file writing methods (saveStrings( ), createWriter( )), which automatically apply GZIP compression to any information written to a file with .gz at the end of its name.

Because of the benefits I mentioned, many data files or streams are GZIP compressed. If you're trying to figure out the format of a file, a GZIP file can be identified in a hex editor. The first two bytes will be 0×1F8B, then usually 0×08 (to specify "deflate"). The byte after that will be 0×08 if the filename is present (and a few characters later, the original name of the file can be seen), or 0×00 if no filename is present. Two bytes (four hex chars) follow, then 0×22 46 00 03. Being able to identify a GZIP file is especially useful when trying to figure out wire protocols using a program such as Wireshark (discussed later). It's also common to find XML files that are GZIP compressed, and while the contents may look like garbage, a quick look at the first few bytes in a hex viewer is a giveaway.

The GZIP specification can be found in RFC 1952 (*http://tools.ietf.org/html/rfc1952*). Because of bugs in various versions of Java, it's generally good to avoid using GZIP compression on files larger than 2 GB.

PKZip files (ZIP)

ZIP files are also quite ubiquitous. Many programs use ZIP as a container format for their file formats. JAR archive files are in fact ZIP files, as are OpenOffice ODT files. A file with PK as the first two characters is often in ZIP format. Opening it with a ZIP archive tool or using unzip -l filename.odt on a command line will either reveal the contents of the file or produce an error if it's not actually in ZIP format.

ZIP uses a similar algorithm to GZIP, though it can be used to store multiple files and their directory structure, plus some additional metadata (e.g., creation and modification times).

ZIP files are useful in visualizations that deal with large amounts of text data. The following example reads a ZIP file and prints the name of each entry:

```
void setup() {
  readZipFile("test.zip");
}

void readZipFile(String filename) {
  try {
    String path = dataPath(filename);
    ZipFile file = new ZipFile(path);
    Enumeration entries = file.entries();
    while (entries.hasMoreElements()) {
      ZipEntry entry = (ZipEntry) entries.nextElement();
      String name = entry.getName();
      println(name);
    }
  } catch (IOException e) {
    e.printStackTrace();
  }
}
```

The following modification extracts all files from this ZIP file. The important part of this code is checking whether the entry is a directory, and if it is not, getting the InputStream object for the uncompressed data. In this example, it's read using loadBytes(), but loadStrings() or createReader() could be used for text, or any other Java method for handling InputStream data. Unlike other examples that handle files, subfolders in ZIP files need not be handled recursively. The name of each file is stored as its full path, so there's no need to dig through successive directories:

```
void setup() {
  readZipFile("test.zip");
}

void readZipFile(String filename) {
  try {
    String path = dataPath(filename);
    ZipFile file = new ZipFile(path);
    Enumeration entries = file.entries();
    while (entries.hasMoreElements()) {
      ZipEntry entry = (ZipEntry) entries.nextElement();
      String name = entry.getName();
      String outputPath = savePath(name);
      if (entry.isDirectory()) {
        File dir = new File(outputPath);
        // Create directory if it does not exist.
        dir.mkdirs();
      } else {
```

```
      InputStream stream = file.getInputStream(entry);
      byte[] b = loadBytes(stream);
      saveBytes(outputPath, b);
    }
  }
} catch (IOException e) {
  e.printStackTrace( );
}
}
```

Writing ZIP files is also straightforward. The following code writes a list of files (specified by their full path in the paths array) to a ZIP file:

```
void writeZipFile(String filename, String[] paths) {
  String path = savePath(filename);
  try {
    FileOutputStream fos = new FileOutputStream(path);
    ZipOutputStream zos = new ZipOutputStream(fos);

    for (int i = 0; i < paths.length; i++) {
      ZipEntry entry = new ZipEntry(paths[i]);
      zos.putNextEntry(entry);
      byte[] b = loadBytes(paths[i]); // get byte array of data
      zos.write(b);
      zos.closeEntry( );
    }

    zos.flush( );
    zos.close( );

  } catch (IOException e) {
    e.printStackTrace( );
  }
}
```

The zos.write( ) line could be used to write any kind of data. In a visualization project, you're more likely to write data from your results, not the contents of existing files on the disk—but the data is handled the same way in either case.

Like GZIP, it's best to avoid using or creating ZIP files that are larger than 2 GB because of bugs and inconsistent support across operating systems and versions of Java.

Other compression formats

Other common compression formats include Tape Archive (TAR, common on Unix systems), StuffIt (SIT and SITX, common on the Mac), and bzip2 (bz2), an extremely compact block compression algorithm that is not as fast as gzip and therefore more useful as an archive format (e.g., for compressing large downloads).

Vectors and Geometry

The following sections describe file formats used for reading and writing 2D and 3D graphical data.

Scalable Vector Graphics (SVG)

The SVG format (*http://www.w3.org/Graphics/SVG*) is 2D shape data written as XML. The format was developed by the W3C and is most commonly read and written by Inkscape (*http://inkscape.org*) and Adobe Illustrator.

An example SVG file from the SVG 1.1 specification (*http://www.w3.org/TR/SVG11*) follows:

```
<?xml version="1.0" standalone="no"?>
<!DOCTYPE svg PUBLIC "-//W3C//DTD SVG 1.1//EN"
  "http://www.w3.org/Graphics/SVG/1.1/DTD/svg11.dtd">
<svg width="12cm" height="4cm" viewBox="0 0 1200 400"
    xmlns="http://www.w3.org/2000/svg" version="1.1">
  <desc>Example ellipse01 - examples of ellipses</desc>
  <!-- Show outline of canvas using 'rect' element -->
  <rect x="1" y="1" width="1198" height="398"
        fill="none" stroke="blue" stroke-width="2" />
  <g transform="translate(300 200)">
    <ellipse rx="250" ry="100"
          fill="red" />
  </g>
  <ellipse transform="translate(900 200) rotate(-30)"
        rx="250" ry="100"
        fill="none" stroke="blue" stroke-width="20" />
</svg>
```

The Processing SVG library can read simple documents, get subelements, and draw them on-screen. The following program opens an SVG-formatted map of the United States from Wikipedia (*http://commons.wikimedia.org/wiki/Image:Blank_US_Map. svg*) and displays it on the screen:

```
import processing.candy.*;

SVG svg;

void setup( ) {
  size(1368, 936);
  svg = new SVG(this, "map3.svg");
}

void draw( ) {
  background(255);
  svg.draw(0, 0);
}
```

This example uses the mapping code from Chapter 3, but changes it to grab individual states from the SVG file and color them based on their data values. In the map file, each shape object is an individual state, named by its two-digit code. In the draw( ) method that follows, the get( ) method returns a named shape from an SVG file. The shape will retain its original position, so each state will maintain its location relative to the other state outlines. The ignoreStyles( ) method indicates that all drawing attributes in the SVG file (such as fill, stroke, or stroke weight) should be ignored so that the fill and stroke can be specified in the code that precedes the state.draw( ) line:

```
import processing.candy.*;

SVG svg;
Table data;
float dataMin = -7;
float dataMax = 11;

void setup() {
  size(1368, 936);

  svg = new SVG(this, "map3.svg");
  data = new Table("random.tsv");
}

void draw() {
  background(255);
  noStroke();
  smooth();
  svg.ignoreStyles();

  int rowCount = data.getRowCount();
  for (int row = 0; row < rowCount; row++) {
    String abbrev = data.getRowName(row);
    SVG state = svg.get(abbrev);
    if (state == null) {
      println("no state found for " + abbrev);
    } else {
      float value = data.getFloat(row, 1);
      if (value >= 0) {
        float amt = norm(value, 0, dataMax);
        color c = lerpColor(#FFFFFF, #221177, amt);
        fill(c);
      } else {
        float amt = norm(value, 0, dataMin);
        color c = lerpColor(#FFFFFF, #992211, amt);
        fill(c);
      }
      state.draw(0, 0);
    }
  }
}
```

Compare the image in Figure 10-1 with those in Chapter 3.

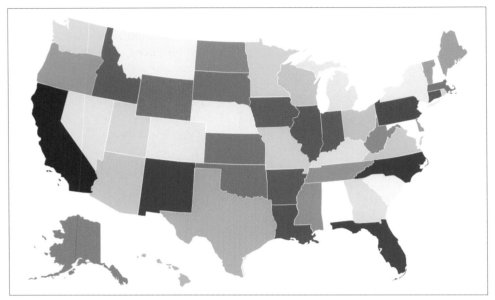

Figure 10-1. Adaptation of the mapping example to use SVG shape data

You can also write SVG files from a Processing sketch through user-contributed libraries linked from the libraries page (*http://processing.org/reference/libraries*).

As mentioned at the beginning of this chapter, the Batik SVG parser (*http://xmlgraphics.apache.org/batik*) from the Apache project is a much more complete implementation of the SVG specification. Its libraries are much larger (approximately 1 MB), so they're less suitable for online use, but they are a good choice when robustness is required.

OBJ and AutoCAD DXF

OBJ is a simple 3D file format for reading and writing. Because of its simplicity (and the openness of the specification), the OBJ format has become a common interchange format for 3D applications. An open source OBJ loader is available from the Processing libraries page, and it can be used to import geometry from other 3D applications, such as 3D Studio Max. The advantage of importing is that you can handle the complicated 3D geometry in a tool more suited for developing shapes, rather than building every last vertex from code.

AutoCAD DXF, on the other hand, is the opposite kind of format. It's complicated and closed, leading people to deal with it only when absolutely necessary. Processing can use the built-in DXF library to write files with beginRaw( ). The beginRaw( ) method echoes raw geometry (lines and triangles) to a second renderer, usually the DXF or PDF renderer. This method can be used to produce vector images of a 3D scene drawn using the Processing API, and the reference for the DXF library includes examples that illustrate how this is done. There is no support for reading DXF files, however, because the format is far too complicated.

PostScript (PS) and Portable Document Format (PDF)

PostScript was an all-text programming language for drawing shapes first developed in 1983 (see *Inside the Publishing Revolution: The Adobe Story* by Pamela Pfiffner [Adobe Press] for the history). As the engine that drove the laser printer, PostScript contributed significantly to the origin of desktop publishing. A simple PostScript document takes the form:

```
%!PS
20 20 moveto
80 80 lineto
showpage
```

As such, it's easy to write very simple PostScript text documents, particularly from Processing, whose API is heavily influenced by PostScript. Applications such as Illustrator and Photoshop can read these files and render them, or resave them to other formats. However, PostScript does not include support for gradients, transparency, and other features expected of modern imaging systems.

With PostScript unsuitable as a document exchange format (and showing a bit of age), Adobe first announced Acrobat in 1991. The Acrobat PDF format was designed to be a container format, rather than a full-blown programming language like PostScript. By eliminating the open-endedness of a programming language, the PDF format made a far better interchange mechanism for moving documents between machines and platforms and significantly decreased the level of complexity involved in rendering. Because PDF documents are designed to be read (not edited or manipulated), display software such as Adobe Reader or *xpdf* need focus only on rapidly generating images onscreen as they are specified in the file.

The Processing PDF library allows users to write any geometry they can draw onscreen out to a PDF file. A simple program to produce a PDF consists of:

```
import processing.pdf.*;

void setup( ) {
  size(100, 100, PDF, "output.pdf");
  background(255);
  line(20, 20, 80, 80);
}
```

Instead of drawing the window onscreen, it will create a single-page PDF file, with dimensions of 100×100 pixels, containing a single diagonal line. Because PDF is a vector format, this line can be resized to any dimension and still draw cleanly. This can be used to generate intricate images that are resolution-independent.

Viewers for the PDF format are much speedier than loading a PostScript, Adobe Illustrator, or SVG file in a drawing application, making PDF a good choice for quick iteration and testing while working on a project.

On the other hand, parsing PDF files is not recommended, as the specification has grown quite complex since 1991. It is better to open a PDF document with a program such as Illustrator and resave it as SVG format.

Shapefile and Well-Known Text

The Shapefile (SHP) format is used commonly in Geographic Information Systems (GIS). The format was developed by Environmental Systems Research Institute (ESRI), and is tied to their ArcView and ArcGIS products. The text-based format can be found in most GIS software, including open source alternatives such as Grass GIS (*http://grass.gdf-hannover.de/wiki/Main_Page*).

One popular example of the Shapefile format in use is the cartographic boundary files from the U.S. Census Bureau; see *http://www.census.gov/geo/www/cob/bdy_files. html*.

A broader discussion of Shapefiles, along with a specification, can be found on Wikipedia at *http://en.wikipedia.org/wiki/Shapefile*.

As you begin working with map data, you'll quickly run into issues dealing with projections—how land area on our (nearly) spherical Earth is represented in two-dimensional maps. While most GIS software provides tools for converting from one projection to another, you can turn to the PROJ library (*http://proj.maptools.org*), with a Java implementation at *http://www.jhlabs.com/java/maps/proj*.

When dealing with data that has already undergone projection, it's common for files to be in well-known text (WKT) format (*http://geoapi.sourceforge.net/2.0/javadoc/ org/opengis/referencing/doc-files/WKT.html*). This text format includes metadata that describes the math behind the projection used, as well as the boundary coordinates for the new values that have been mapped from latitude and longitude into their new coordinate space.

Binary Data Formats

Until recently, the majority of file formats were binary. But the interoperability of XML—combined with falling storage prices—is making text more common. We'll quickly look at two formats associated with data sets.

Excel Spreadsheets (XLS)

When trying to read XLS files, open the file with a text editor and first check to see whether it's in fact a CSV file with an *.xls* extension. This is common, particularly for files generated by software on the Web. The idea is that when you download some-one's file from an email or web site and click on it, the *.xls* extension will cause your system to automatically load it into Excel, and Excel will figure out that the file is actually CSV data. In contrast, a file named *.csv* might not be recognized and opened in an easy-to-view fashion.

For binary XLS files (and other file formats from Microsoft Office), the Apache POI project (*http://poi.apache.org*) provides an excellent library for parsing them, along with some helpful how-to information at *http://poi.apache.org/hssf/how-to.html*.

These libraries can be added to a Processing project like any other *.jar* file and used to read spreadsheets from within code. The process is more involved than reading simple CSV or TSV files (and should make you think twice about whether XLS is suitable as input data), but it can be helpful in many situations.

dBASE/xBase (DBF)

DBF is the file format for dBASE, a popular database management system from the 1980s. A DBF file contains a binary header followed by a series of records, each stored in a fixed size. The fixed length of each line suits the time period so that records can be accessed directly from the disk. Because of the age of the format, you'll run across DBF files when dealing with legacy systems or projects based on older software. DBF files are frequently found on government sites, for example.

OpenOffice is capable of opening DBF files, as is Microsoft Excel. While Open-Office may even register the *.dbf* extension for itself, in Excel you'll have to use the "All files" option in the File → Open dialog box before it shows up.

The format itself is easy to parse, and good descriptions exist for the file structure. Erik Bachmann of Clickety Click Software maintains an excellent set of documentation on the family of Xbase formats at his site; see *http://www.clicketyclick.dk/databases/xbase/format*. Specifically, the dBASE III version of the format can be found at *http://www.clicketyclick.dk/databases/xbase/format/dbf.html*.

The dBASE site also has more information on later changes to the format at *http://www.dbase.com/KnowledgeBase/int/db7_file_fmt.htm*.

Arbitrary Binary Formats

There are two methods for dealing with binary data as input. The first is to use loadBytes( ), which produces a byte array. But there are two problems with that method. First, individual byte values are always *signed*, so a byte represents a value between –128 and 127, not between 0 and 255 as might be expected. To convert from a signed byte to an unsigned int value, use the following:

```
int unsignedInt = signedByte & 0xFF;
```

The syntax is a little cryptic at first glance, but the following program helps illustrate what's happening:

```
byte signedByte = -100;
println(binary(signedByte, 8));
int signedInt = signedByte;
println(binary(signedInt, 32));
println(binary(0xff, 32));
int unsignedInt = signedByte & 0xff;
println(binary(unsignedInt, 32));
```

The binary( ) method converts a number into a String sequence of 1s and 0s (unbinary performs the opposite conversion from a binary String to a number). The second parameter of binary( ) is the number of binary digits to include. The program produces:

```
10011100
11111111111111111111111110011100
00000000000000000000000011111111
00000000000000000000000010011100
```

The first line is the binary value of signedByte. In binary, the leftmost digit is the *sign* digit. If this digit is 1, the number is negative; if it's zero, the number is positive or 0. When an 8-bit number like a byte is converted to a 32-bit integer, a *sign extension* occurs, where the sign digit is extended to the other 24 bits that are added. The second row shows the value –100 represented as a 32-bit integer value. The third row shows the binary representation of 0xff, or 255. The value 255 is the bottom 8 bits of a number set to 1. Finally, the & (and) operator is used to let only the bottom eight digits through. That is, only bits that are 1 on both sides of the & operator will be 1 in the result, which removes the string of twenty-four 1s from the final line.

Bit Shifting

Storing values in binary larger than 255 requires bit shifting. In this scenario, the binary digits from a sequence of byte values are shifted into place, forming a single number. For instance, to read a 16-bit value from an array returned from loadBytes( ), enter this code:

```
byte[] b = loadBytes("data.bin");
int hi = b[0] & 0xff;
int lo = b[1] & 0xff;
int value = (hi << 8) | lo;
```

Here, we first convert the values to unsigned numbers that occupy the lower 8 bits of a pair of ints. The final value is constructed by shifting 8 bits of hi to the left by eight digits:

```
              hi = 00000000000000000000000HHHHHHHH
              lo = 00000000000000000000000LLLLLLLL
         hi << 8 = 000000000000000HHHHHHHH00000000
 (hi << 8) | lo = 000000000000000HHHHHHHHLLLLLLLL
```

The | (or) operator combines the bits of two values. The resulting bit at each position will be 1 if either of the input values has a 1 at that position.

In the examples so far, the high bits have been on the left, the low bits on the right. That is known as *big-endian* or *network byte* order, and it is the native ordering for most network protocols, Java, and Motorola architectures. On other systems, notably Intel machines, the ordering is opposite; it is called *little endian*. (The two orderings are also sometimes called Motorola and Intel ordering, respectively.) A little-endian value would swap the lo and hi values in the previous example, as follows:

```
byte[] b = loadBytes("data.bin");
int hi = b[0] & 0xff;
int lo = b[1] & 0xff;
int value = (lo << 8) | hi;
```

This byte ordering is common for many file formats (such as WAV) that originate from Windows/Intel platforms.

DataInputStream

Rather than handling all the bit shifting and byte unpacking yourself, you can use DataInputStream—a Java class that wraps an InputStream object to effectively hide all the bit-shifting necessary to unpack binary data. The readInt( ) method grabs a 32-bit (signed) integer, and the readShort( ) method grabs a 16-bit value. The standard class works only with big-endian values, but little-endian versions can be easily found online (search for "DataInputStreamLE"). An example of using DataInputStream follows:

```
try {
  InputStream input = openStream("data.bin");
  DataInputStream data = new DataInputStream(input);
  int value = data.readUnsignedShort( );
  println(value);
} catch (IOException e) {
  e.printStackTrace( );
}
```

It performs the same function as the hand-coded example in the previous section. In the long run, it tends to be a simpler method, even though the code appears longer because of the error handling in the try/catch block.

Advanced Detective Work

The main theme of this chapter is to understand common file formats and parsing techniques. In many cases, examples are shown so that file formats can begin to be recognizable, should you run across files in one format or another.

Many formats start with identifying codes. JPEG images have JFIF near the beginning of the file. A TIFF image saved on a Mac begins with the two bytes MM, whereas one saved on a PC begins with II. Java class files begin with a 32-bit number that reads CAFEBABE in hexadecimal. All these codes are referred to as *magic numbers*, which identify the file as a particular format. Sometimes a magic number begins a file, but at other times, it might be a sequence of values spread throughout the file that, set a particular way, is an indicator that the file is one format or another.

Knowing a few of these magic numbers and values can help you familiarize yourself with data formats. It's also possible to programmatically identify data files based on these values. The Apache web server, for instance, has a file named *mime.magic* (*http://httpd.apache.org/docs/2.0/mod/mod_mime_magic.html*), which is used to check files against a list of magic numbers so that file types can be identified properly before they're sent to a client machine.

Making a mental note of what different file types look like can be helpful when later dealing with more complicated parsing on unknown data.

Watching Network Traffic

As web applications become more prevalent, the data formats used between your browser and a server continue to get more complex. How do movie sites load their video data onto pages, even though the data is not part of the HTML? How are live game feeds updated on sports sites like ESPN.com? These questions can be answered with the help of packet sniffing tools that can be used to watch all traffic going into and out of your machine. We'll briefly cover Wireshark (*http://www.wireshark.org*), an open source utility that can be used to find the answers to these questions.

First, download and install Wireshark for your platform. On Unix-based systems, you'll need to run it as a *root* user (i.e., use the command line sudo wireshark) so that you have credentials to get proper hardware access to your network card.

Use Wireshark only on your own private network, not in a public setting. In public settings, a packet sniffer can be used to spy on the Internet traffic of other machines, and it's likely to be against the networking policies of most organizations.

After Wireshark opens, select Capture → Interfaces.... A dialog box will pop up showing available network interfaces on your machine; it will look something like Figure 10-2. Click the Start button next to your main interface. On a Mac, the interface will be labeled en0 for ethernet and en1 for wireless; on many Unix systems, it will be eth0 or en0. You'll see the numbers increasing most quickly next to your primary interface, so it shouldn't be too difficult to figure out.

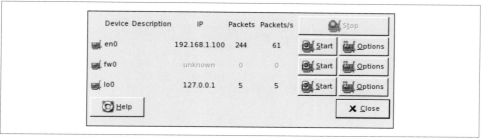

Figure 10-2. The capture dialog in Wireshark

The window will begin filling with packets of network traffic as they occur on your machine in the top panel. The middle panel highlights details of the content, and the bottom panel shows the actual contents of each packet in hexadecimal and as characters.

In Figure 10-3, we opened ESPN.com in a web browser and visited the home page. We can see the query GET / HTTP/1.1 from our browser to the ESPN server. Subsequent replies from that address will include the home page, and then other information as we peruse the site.

Watching the GET messages from the browser, along with the replies from a server machine, can provide helpful clues to what's actually happening behind the scenes. At a basic level, if you see a file retrieved via GET that is not something you entered in the browser's location bar, you know it's something being pulled from JavaScript or another piece of code on the page. For instance, with ESPN's Flash-based poll applet, you'll see queries like the following connecting to *sports.espn.go.com*:

```
GET /espn/fp/getPollRegionalFlashData?pollId=43608 HTTP/1.1
```

Although we can see the result of this query with Wireshark, it's also possible to paste it into a web browser as:

http://sports.espn.go.com/espn/fp/getPollRegionalFlashData?pollId=43608

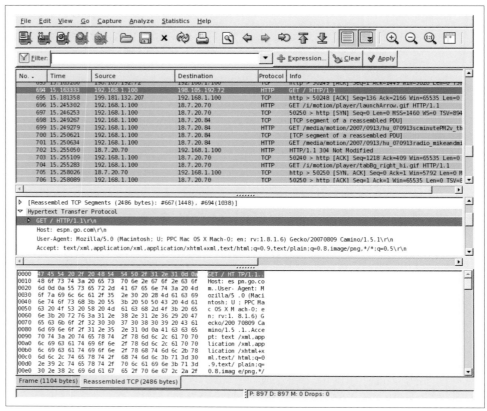

Figure 10-3. Information in transit captured with Wireshark

which will return a set of attribute/value pairs that describe the results of the poll, used to populate the poll found at:

> *http://sports.espn.go.com/espn/fp/*
> *flashPollResultsState?sportIndex=frontpage&pollId=43608*

I could spend a whole book discussing how to dissect such protocols, but here we're interested only in introducing the tool to encourage you to spend some time trying it out yourself. And next time you try to retrieve data from an undocumented source, it will be one more item in your tool set.

## CHAPTER 11

Integrating Processing with Java

Processing is not Java. If you're a Java developer, using Processing may be confusing if you expect it to be too much like Java. If this book is your first introduction to Processing, you are strongly urged to first get used to the Processing way of doing things as presented in the first several chapters. It'll be easier to adapt to using the Processing API inside a Java project once you've developed a mental model for how the API works and how Processing sketches are structured.

The Processing syntax is essentially a dialect of Java. When a user runs a sketch in the PDE, the code is converted into Java syntax using a preprocessor, and then compiled as standard Java code. The implementation of all Processing Core API functions can be found in the package processing.core, which is stored in the *core.jar* file found in the *lib* folder of your Processing distribution. All Processing sketches subclass the PApplet class from the processing.core package.

The Anemone example in Chapter 8 shows how to use processing.core inside the Eclipse development environment. It also covers some of the basics of embedding Processing in other Java-based projects. The methods used should be familiar to most Java programmers, and they can be adapted to other development setups and IDEs.

This chapter is intended as a reference for Java programmers who want to understand how to integrate Processing with Java code and for Processing developers who are ready to break out into larger projects and a broader range of development options.

Programming Modes

Part of the role of the preprocessor is to determine one of three programming modes used in the code. These modes are covered in Chapter 2, but I'll reiterate some of the points here as I describe them in terms of Java code.

Basic

This mode is used to draw static images and learn the fundamentals of programming. Simple lines of code have a direct representation on the screen. The following example draws a yellow rectangle on the screen:

```
size(200, 200);
background(255);
noStroke();
fill(255, 204, 0);
rect(30, 20, 50, 50);
```

The preprocessor converts programs written in this mode to the setup( ) method of a full sketch:

```
import processing.core.*;

public class BasicSketch extends PApplet {
  public void setup() {
    size(200, 200);
    background(255);
    noStroke();
    fill(255, 204, 0);
    rect(30, 20, 50, 50);
  }
}
```

With no draw( ) method, the sketch will only run the setup( ) method and then stop.

Continuous

This mode provides a setup( ) structure that is run once when the program begins and a draw( ) structure that by default continually loops through the code inside. This additional structure allows writing custom functions and classes and using keyboard and mouse events.

The following example draws rectangles that follow the mouse position (stored in the PApplet fields mouseX and mouseY). The draw( ) block runs forever or until the program is stopped. The animation thread is started and stopped with the loop( ) and noLoop( ) methods:

```
void setup() {
  size(200, 200);
  rectMode(CENTER);
  noStroke();
  fill(0, 102, 153, 204);
}

void draw() {
  background(255);
  rect(width-mouseX, height-mouseY, 50, 50);
  rect(mouseX, mouseY, 50, 50);
}
```

After running through the preprocessor, the code for this sketch follows:

```
import processing.core.*;

public class ContinuousSketch extends PApplet {

  public void setup() {
    size(200, 200);
    rectMode(CENTER);
    noStroke();
    fill(0, 102, 153, 204);
  }

  public void draw() {
    background(255);
    rect(width-mouseX, height-mouseY, 50, 50);
    rect(mouseX, mouseY, 50, 50);
  }
}
```

Java

This mode is the most flexible, allowing complete Java programs to be written from inside the PDE (as long as they're still subclasses of PApplet). It is for advanced users only and is not really recommended; at this level, you're usually better off using another IDE. Using this mode also changes the behavior of additional tabs (see the next section). It is not necessary to use this mode just to get features of the Java language:

```
public class MyDemo extends PApplet {

  public void setup() {
    size(200, 200);

    rectMode(CENTER);
    noStroke();
    fill(0, 102, 153, 204);
  }

  public void draw() {
    background(255);
    rect(width-mouseX, height-mouseY, 50, 50);
    rect(mouseX, mouseY, 50, 50);
  }
}
```

Additional Source Files (Tabs)

The main tab represents a set of code that subclasses the PApplet object. Additional tabs are treated as inner classes to the main PApplet. That means that the graphics methods are all inherited without needing to pass objects around to a reference to the main drawing surface, and the main API methods are available to all code.

One downside of inner classes is that they cannot have static fields or methods. The following code will produce an error:

```
class Shape {
  static final int RECTANGLE = 0; // Error
  static final int POLYGON = 1; // Error
  int kind;

  class Shape() {
    kind = POLYGON;
  }
}
```

To make code that does not operate as an inner class, specify *.java* at the end of the filename when creating a new tab. The code in that tab will be treated as pure Java code, and the preprocessor will ignore it. This solves the static variable problem. Another solution would be to place the static variables outside the class:

```
// Not a great option
static final int RECTANGLE = 0;
static final int ELLIPSE = 1;

class Shape {
  int kind;

  class Shape() {
    kind = ELLIPSE;
  }
}
```

However, the constant will be RECTANGLE, not Shape.RECTANGLE, which might be confusing depending on your circumstances. Another option is to not make the variables static:

```
class Shape {
  final int RECTANGLE = 0;
  final int ELLIPSE = 1;
  int kind;

  class Shape() {
    kind = ELLIPSE;
  }
}
```

You still won't be able to use Shape.RECTANGLE or Shape.ELLIPSE to refer to the variables, but the syntax will be clearer for others looking at this code.

If using Java mode (see the previous section), additional tabs will not be inner classes—they will only be concatenated to the end of the main source file (if they have *.pde* extensions). That means that import statements will be inherited, but not much else. It won't be possible to use methods such as line( ) or draw( ) without passing the parent PApplet object to the other classes.

Using .java Source Files

To create a pure Java source file, make a tab named *Shape.java*. To get access to methods from the host PApplet, you need to pass a reference to it, usually in the constructor:

```
import processing.core.*;

public class Shape {

  static final int RECTANGLE = 0;
  static final int ELLIPSE = 1;
  int kind;

  class Shape(PApplet parent, int kind) {
    this.parent = parent;
    this.kind = kind;
  }

  public void draw( ) {
    if (kind == RECTANGLE) {
      parent.rect(20, 20, 60, 60);
    } else if (kind == ELLIPSE) {
      parent.ellipse(50, 50, 30, 30);
    }
  }
}
```

Back in the main tab, a Shape object can be instantiated with:

```
Shape s = new Shape(this, Shape.ELLIPSE);
```

Adding the *.java* extension is an indicator to the preprocessor that you know what you're doing, so the safety net is off. You'll need to do all the imports yourself—processing.core.* at the minimum, but also packages such as java.util.*—which are normally imported by default.

The Preprocessor

This section summarizes the main activities of the preprocessor.

Data type casting in the style int(value) and float(value) are converted to the methods parseInt(value) and parseFloat(value). The parseXxxx() methods can be used with or without the preprocessor. One of the advantages of these methods is that they can also handle arrays. For instance, an entire String array can be converted to a float array with the following:

```
// With the Preprocessor
float[] f = float(stringValues);
// Without the preprocessor
float[] f = parseFloat(stringValues);
```

The color data type is simply an alias to int, and the two can be used interchangeably in Processing syntax. Processing offers the color type because beginning programmers often find it confusing that pixel data is stored as an integer value.

A web color such as #FFCC00 will be converted to 0xffFFCC00. The additional ff at the beginning is the alpha value for the color, with ff indicating fully opaque (255). The web color syntax is used as a convenience for web developers who are often familiar with web color format, but would find the 0x hex syntax needlessly cryptic.

No double values are used in the Processing API. Instances of 1.0 are converted to 1.0f by the preprocessor. For nearly all Processing projects, double values are overkill, wasting memory and slowing down calculations. In this context, trailing nearly every numerical value with an f is silly, if not annoying. The preprocessor automatically adds the f to all decimal values. If you need double values for functions such as cos(), you can always use Java's Math.cos() function instead of the built-in cos() method in PApplet.

Unless marked as protected or private, functions are automatically marked public. For this reason, void setup() is actually public void setup(), and using void setup() in a regular Java development environment will cause an error.

API Structure

Here we'll cover a few major components of the Processing Core API and show its structure.

Event Handling

You must have a draw() method to run an event loop. A program without a draw() method will be interpreted in Basic mode.

Because of their ubiquity in interactive applications, mouse coordinates and key presses are automatically tracked by the environment. That is a divergence from Java, which requires that the developer implement methods to handle even the most basic events. The following is the most basic use of mousePressed():

```
void mousePressed() {
  // The mouse was clicked; print its position to the console.
  println(mouseX + " " + mouseY);
}
```

The advantage of using the Processing event methods is that they are queued while the draw( ) method is running, and then the queue is emptied at the end of draw( ). That avoids synchronization problems with code that can arise in mouse*Xxxxx*( ) methods that draw to the screen. Because mouse and key events run on a separate thread from drawing, the two could be happening simultaneously, which can cause strange problems as they fight with one another for control of the drawing surface.

As a tip for Java programmers who are familiar with MouseEvent objects, the built-in mouseEvent field will always contain the most recent event:

```
void mousePressed() {
  int count = mouseEvent.getClickCount();
  // Do something based on the number of mouse clicks.
}
```

On the other hand, you can also override the event handling for mousePressed( ):

```
public void mousePressed(MouseEvent e) {
  // Do something with the event object here.
}
```

That is not recommended because you lose the queueing mechanism, and variables such as mouseButton, mouseX, and mouseY will no longer work properly. But it's available for those who enjoy the thrill of playing with matches.

The size( ) Method

With any Processing project, the size( ) method should always be the first line inside the setup( ) method. That is because changing from the default renderer to another requires all rendering to be restarted, and in the case of a renderer such as OpenGL, a different component must be added to the main window. To handle this situation smoothly, calling size( ) to change the renderer will first make the change, and then internally throw an exception that will force the setup( ) method to be run again. This complicated situation exists because it's also possible to draw inside setup( ). Although requiring size( ) to be at the beginning of setup( ) is not ideal, it's a minor trade-off for the ability to easily swap between renderers and draw inside the setup( ) method.

The main( ) Method

The main( ) method in PApplet launches a Processing applet inside a window. When a sketch is exported as an application, the following lines are inserted into the code:

```
static public void main(String[] args) {
  PApplet.main(new String[] { "YourSketchName" });
}
```

The `main( )` method takes a sketch name as a parameter. The method has several options that can be used to specify the location of the sketch or to enable Present mode (using full-screen exclusive mode to launch the sketch). See the `PApplet` documentation (*http://dev.processing.org/reference/core*) for more information.

The frame Object

The `PApplet` class has a variable named `frame`, of type `java.awt.Frame`, that specifies its parent frame. Calling `frame.setResizable(true)` is one way to make the sketch window resizable. Dragging the grow box of the sketch window will resize the sketch along with the window.

The `frame` field is set up by the `main( )` method, so if you are not using `PApplet.main( )`, `frame` will be `null`.

Embedding PApplet into Java Applications

Another option is to use the Processing API (specifically the `processing.core` package, and perhaps additional libraries) while working on a narrow piece of a larger project. A Processing sketch can be embedded into a Java program like any subclass of `java.awt.Component`. The base `PApplet` class subclasses `java.applet.Applet`, which itself subclasses `Component`. A larger project might consist of several `PApplet` components that interact with one another, or a `PApplet` component that's embedded into a larger project (for example, as part of a Swing-based interface).

The `size( )` method also sets the value returned by the Java `getPreferredSize( )` method so that it behaves like a regular Java `Component`. A `PApplet` will respond properly to resize events, so it can be placed using a standard layout manager.

Two Models for Updating the Screen

The Processing API supports two methods for updating the screen. The default is to run the `draw( )` method at up to 60 frames per second for continuous animation. The second is to update the screen only when necessary using the `redraw( )` method. Because the default animation thread runs at 60 frames per second, an embedded `PApplet` can make the parent application sluggish. You can use `frameRate( )` to make it update less often, or you can use `noLoop( )` and `loop( )` to disable and then re-enable looping. If you want to update just the sketch intermittently, use `noLoop( )` inside `setup( )`, and issue `redraw( )` whenever the screen needs to be updated once (or `loop( )` to re-enable the animation thread). The following example embeds a sketch and also uses the `noLoop( )` and `redraw( )` methods. You need not use `noLoop( )` and `redraw( )` when embedding if you want your application to animate continuously.

Code for the host application follows:

```java
import java.awt.*;
import processing.core.*;

public class ExampleFrame extends Frame {

    public ExampleFrame() {
        super("Embedded PApplet");

        setLayout(new BorderLayout());
        PApplet embed = new Embedded();
        add(embed, BorderLayout.CENTER);

        // important to call this whenever embedding a PApplet.
        // It ensures that the animation thread is started and
        // that other internal variables are properly set.
        embed.init();

        // Set the frame size based on the sketch size.
        pack();
        // Move the upper-left corner of the frame to 100, 100
        setLocation(100, 100);
        // And make the frame visible.
        setVisible(true);
    }
}
```

And here is the embedded sketch:

```java
import processing.core.*;

public class Embedded extends PApplet {

    public void setup() {
        // Original setup code here ...
        size(256, 256);

        // Prevent thread from starving everything else.
        noLoop();
    }

    public void draw() {
        // Drawing code goes here.
        background(mouseX);
    }

    public void mousePressed() {
        // Do something based on mouse movement.

        // Update the screen (run draw once).
        redraw();
    }
}
```

This program will open a 256×256 window to run the sketch. The draw( ) method will run each time the mouse is pressed, clearing the background to a gray value based on the horizontal location of the mouse.

Embedding in a Swing Application

It's also possible to use Processing with Swing, using the same structure as the previous example, only with a JFrame instead of a Frame. The Processing component need not be the only item on the screen. Additional interface elements, such as buttons, can be added and made to call functions inside the Processing component the same way you would with any custom component.

This example embeds a PApplet and a JSlider into a JFrame, showing how Swing components can be used to interact with a Processing sketch. The code for the host class follows:

```
import java.awt.*;
import javax.swing.*;
import javax.swing.border.*;


public class SwingExample extends JFrame {

    public SwingExample( ) {
        super("Swing Slider Example");

        setLayout(new BorderLayout( ));
        EmbeddedWithSlider embed = new EmbeddedWithSlider( );
        add(embed, BorderLayout.CENTER);
        embed.init( );

        Box box = Box.createHorizontalBox( );
        JLabel label = new JLabel("Hue:");
        box.add(label);
        JSlider slider = new JSlider(JSlider.HORIZONTAL, 0, 360, 0);
        slider.addChangeListener(embed);
        box.add(slider);
        box.setBorder(new EmptyBorder(5, 10, 5, 10));
        add(box, BorderLayout.SOUTH);

        pack( );
        setVisible(true);
        setLocation(100, 100);
    }

    static public void main(String[] args) {
        new SwingExample( );
    }
}
```

The embedded PApplet implements ChangeListener to recognize updates from the slider. As the slider moves, the hue value is updated and redraw( ) is called, which updates the background color based on the hue specified by the slider. The result is shown in Figure 11-1.

Figure 11-1. Using a JSlider to control a PApplet

```
import javax.swing.*;
import javax.swing.event.*;
import processing.core.PApplet;


public class EmbeddedWithSlider extends PApplet implements ChangeListener {

    float hue = 0;

    public void setup() {
        size(400, 400);
        noLoop();
    }

    public void draw() {
        colorMode(HSB, 360, 100, 100);
        background(hue, 80, 80);
    }
```

```
    public void stateChanged(ChangeEvent e) {
        JSlider source = (JSlider)e.getSource();
        hue = (int)source.getValue();
        redraw();
    }
}
```

If you use the default animation thread (rather than noLoop( ) and redraw( )) with an embedded PApplet, take care that the code is implemented in a thread-safe manner. The Processing animation thread can easily conflict with Swing's UI threads, leading to problems. If using Swing to drive the Processing sketch (as in the previous example), noLoop( ) and redraw( ) are the best bet. That means that Swing components will initiate updates in the Processing sketch, but this is better because they'll call redraw( ), which queues the draw( ) method to run when it's safe to do so. On the other hand, if you want to use the regular animation thread, query the Swing UI elements for updates inside the draw( ) method. To modify the previous example, for instance, simply call slider.getValue( ) inside draw( ), rather than use the ChangeListener interface and the stateChanged( ) method.

Using Java Code in a Processing Sketch

Some previous examples have included Java code inside a sketch. This section provides additional background on what's happening behind the scenes.

Using the Code Folder to Add .jar Files to a Sketch

The simplest way to use Java libraries inside a Processing sketch is to drag *.jar* files to the editor window or use Sketch → Add File. That will copy the file to a directory named *code* inside the sketch folder. This works for classes inside *.zip* and *.jar* files, and it will automatically add the files to the CLASSPATH of the sketch. The preprocessor will automatically import all packages found inside the files.

This method can be used to add native code found in *.dll*, *.jnilib*, and *.so* files. These files will also be automatically placed in the *code* folder and added to the Java library path so that the native code will load properly.

Packaging Code into Libraries

A Processing library can be any sort of Java code that's been given a package name and packed into a *.jar* file. It can also register itself with the parent applet to get notification of when events occur in the sketch—for instance, whenever draw( ) is called or a key is pressed.

To repackage your code as a library, consult the *howto.txt* file in the *libraries* folder of the Processing release.

Using Libraries

A common problem for users leaving the PDE for an IDE such as Eclipse or Net-beans is that libraries become a more complicated matter. To use a Processing library, add any *.jar* files from Processing → libraries → *libraryname* → library to your project. If no native code is used, that should be all that's necessary.

More complicated libraries include native code, which adds another layer of complexity. The OpenGL library, for instance, includes multiple files containing native code for different operating systems and architectures. To use the OpenGL library, you'll need to add libraries → *opengl* → library → *opengl.jar* and *jogl.jar* to your CLASSPATH (as described earlier), but you'll also need to set your java.library.path variable to include any folders that contain native libraries. This is usually done by adding a -D command-line option when running Java:

```
java -Djava.library.path=/path/to/Processing/libraries/opengl/library
```

Do this in addition to other options necessary to set the class path and the main class of your code.

Building with the Source for processing.core

If you're the type of person who prefers to work with the your libraries' sources whenever possible, you can always check out the code for the processing.core librar-ies from the source repository on *http://dev.processing.org*. And, of course, you're strongly encouraged to join the development community to help implement new features and fix bugs.

Depending on the development status, it might be a good idea to get a tagged version of the code that has already been released. The code is tagged whenever a Processing release occurs; for instance, processing-0126 is the tag for the Processing 0126 download. The current code is not guaranteed to be stable, so using the tag for the most recent release is safest.

Bibliography

This bibliography covers a handful of books on visualization that you may find helpful, as well as others that were mentioned in some fashion in the text.

Acquire and Parse

Not many books exist that cover acquiring and parsing data, which is part of the reason that we covered such a broad range of topics in Chapters 10 and 11. These chapters include more specific references for some topics.

Fisher, Maydene, Jon Ellis, and Jonathan Bruce. *JDBC API Tutorial and Reference*. 3rd ed. Upper Saddle River, NJ: Prentice Hall, 2003. This is the book for those who want to learn how to use databases with Java (and Processing).

Wilson, Greg. *Data Crunching: Solve Everyday Problems Using Java, Python, and More*. Raleigh, NC: The Pragmatic Bookshelf, 2005. This is one of the few books I've found that covers the sort of detective work described in Chapters 10 and 11. A useful (and indeed pragmatic) handbook that covers acquiring and parsing data in different languages, and the trade-offs for each.

Filter and Mine

Fayyad, Usama, Georges G. Grinstein, and Andreas Wierse, eds. *Information Visualization in Data Mining and Knowledge Discovery*. San Francisco: Morgan Kaufmann, 2002. From the editor: "This book is the result of two workshops whose goals were to open up the dialog between researchers in visualization and data mining, two key areas involved in data exploration." This book is an esoteric collection of papers with a few that I found extremely insightful.

Garfinkel, Simson. *Database Nation: The Death of Privacy in the 21st Century*. Cambridge, MA: O'Reilly Media, 2000. Garfinkel raises awareness about how data collection and analysis affect our daily lives.

Hand, David J., Heikki Manila, and Padhraic Smyth. *Principles of Data Mining (Adaptive Computation and Machine Learning)*. Cambridge, MA: MIT Press, 2001. This book covers the gap between data mining and statistics.

Gonick, Larry, and Woollcott Smith. *The Cartoon Guide to Statistics*. New York: HarperResource, 1994. This book illustrates the basics of statistics and probability. If you're disinclined to pick up a statistics text, it will provide a more entertaining introduction.

Shannon, Claude E., and Warren Weaver. *The Mathematical Theory of Communication*. Champaign, IL: University of Illinois Press, 1949. The classic text that introduced information theory.

Tukey, John Wilder. *Exploratory Data Analysis*. Boston: Addison-Wesley, 1977. Another classic book on the joy of figuring things out with numbers.

Represent

Bertin, Jacques. *Semiology of Graphics: Diagrams, Networks, Maps*. Madison, WI: University of Wisconsin Press, 1983. This is the English translation and later edition of the seminal text first published in 1967.

Harris, Robert L. *Information Graphics: A Comprehensive Illustrated Reference*. New York: Oxford University Press, 1999. An enormous catalog of visual representations. If you think you've invented a new way to represent data, chances are you'll find it in this book.

Huff, Darrell, and Irving Geis. *How to Lie with Statistics*. New York: W.W. Norton & Company, 1954. This is an older text that covers "lies" in statistical graphics; it is not a statistics book per se, but points out the pitfalls of misrepresentation.

Playfair, William. *Playfair's Commercial and Political Atlas and Statistical Breviary*. New York: Cambridge University Press, 2005. This is a lovely reprint of Playfair's original texts on graphics.

Ware, Colin. *Information Visualization: Perception for Design*. 2nd ed. San Francisco: Morgan Kaufmann, 2004. This is a text on visualization that also covers the psychology of design; it includes useful discussion on topics such as color and pre-attentive graphical features.

Refine

Bringhurst, Robert. *The Elements of Typographic Style*. Vancouver, BC: Hartley & Marks, 1992. The "bible" for typographers.

Garland, Ken. *Mr. Beck's Underground Map*. Middlesex, UK: Capitol Transport Publishing, 1994. Covers the history of Beck's map of the London Underground, discussed in Chapter 1.

Lupton, Ellen. *Thinking With Type: A Critical Guide*. New York: Princeton Architectural Press, 2004. A truly wonderful book that introduces typography in an engaging manner. Lupton is an outstanding writer, and the book is beautiful to look at and enjoyable to read.

Tufte, Edward R. *The Visual Display of Quantitative Information*. Cheshire, CT: Graphics Press, 1983. The first of Tufte's texts on information graphics, and still the best. His other books are interesting (and nice to look at), but if you purchase only one, this should be it.

Interact

Card, Stuart K., Jock D. Mackinlay, and Ben Shneiderman, eds. *Readings in Information Visualization: Using Vision to Think*. San Francisco: Morgan Kauffman, 1999. A woefully out-of-date text that collects several early papers from the field of information visualization.

The Office of Charles and Ray Eames. *Powers of ten: a film dealing with the relative size of things in the universe and the effect of adding another zero*. Pyramid Films, 1978. The film that definitvely shows us how scale works.

Wardrip-Fruin, Noah, and Nick Montfort, eds. *The New Media Reader*. Cambridge, MA: MIT Press, 2003. A truly definitive collection of papers from thinkers such as Vannevar Bush, Alan Turing, Norbert Wiener, Myron Krueger, and others on up to Tim Berners-Lee and Richard Stallman. A brilliant group of texts.

General

Kemp, Martin. *Visualizations: The Nature Book of Art and Science*. Berkeley, CA: The University of California Press, 2001. A collection of columns by Martin Kemp, who placed scientific visualization in context using art and science history.

Lewis, Michael. *Moneyball: The Art of Winning an Unfair Game*. New York: W.W. Norton & Company, 2003. First mentioned in Chapter 5, this book describes the statistical thinking sometimes used by baseball teams.

Maeda, John. *Design By Numbers*. Cambridge, MA: MIT Press, 1999. This book describes the predecessor to the Processing project.

Reas, Casey, and Ben Fry. *Processing: A Programming Handbook for Visual Designers and Artists*. Cambridge, MA: MIT Press, 2007. The definitive book on Processing, written by Casey and me. This is targeted toward people who have no background in programming.

Wurman, Richard Saul. *Information Anxiety*. New York: Doubleday, 1989. This book discusses early thinking about information overload by one of the statesmen of graphic design. Wurman was the person who later coined the term "Information Architect." A more recent second edition of this book exists; however, it's more of a second volume and covers different topics.

Index

Symbols

* (asterisk), zero or more matches in regular
expressions, 104

\ (backslash)
escaping characters in regular
expressions, 103
file paths on Windows, 186

: (colon) in regular expressions, 103

, (comma) in regular expressions, 104

{ (curly braces), data blocks in JSON, 101,
104

. (dot) files, 238

– (en dash), 126

(hash marks), 23

% (modulo) operator, 63

> and >> (output) operators, 298

( ) (parentheses), grouping in regular
expressions, 103

. (period)
matching anything in regular
expressions, 104
Unix system . (single dot) and .. (double
dot) directory entries, 183

| (pipe) command, 298

+ (plus sign), in regular expression
matching, 103

' (quotes, single), in regular expressions, 104

/ (slash)
// in comments, 74
URLs, 100

[ ] (square brackets), denoting regular
expression character class, 103

~ (tilde), Unix home directory, 186

A

absolute paths, 184, 269

access_log file (Apache server), 245

acquireStandings( ) method, 116
breaking date stamps into component
parts, 131

acquiring data, 5, 264–295
advanced web techniques, 284–288
forms, 284
pretending to be a web
browser, 286–288
asynchronous image downloads, 281–284
beverage consumption statistics
(USDA), 55
byte arrays, 284
changing data sources, 94
collecting data outpaces its use, 2
databases, 288–294
efficient retrieval of baseball standings for
the season, 133–144
ethics of, 266
files and folders, 276–280
large numbers of files, 295
listing files in a folder, 277–280
numbered file sequences, 280
files for use with Processing, 268
limiting amount of data, 17
loading data asynchronously using Thread
class, 178–180
loading text data, 270–276
parsing files during acquisition, 276
openStream( ) method as a bridge to
Java, 284

We'd like to hear your suggestions for improving our indexes. Send email to *index@oreilly.com*.

JavaScript, converting forms to use GET
    instead of POST, 285
joining multiple sets of data, 43
JRuby, 264
JSON (JavaScript Object Notation), 101
Jython, 264

K

keyPressed( ) method, 62, 131
    typing of digits in postal zip codes, 159
keywords (search), 265

L

labels
    axis labels on time series plot, 62–72
        titling both axes, 69–72
        volume labels on vertical axis, 65–68
        year labels on horizontal axis, 63–65
    text labels as tabbed panes, 83–87
Lambert, Johann Heinrich, 54
language syntax (Processing), 20
layout( ) method (treemaps), 197
leftX and rightX values (baseball
    project), 119
length of a file, 116
length of edges, 224
lerp( ) function, 37
lerpColor( ) function, 37
    changing color space used, 38
less command, 299
libraries, 27
    core.jar file, 243
    examples, 24
    HTML parsing, 311
    packaging code into, 342
    processing.core source code, 343
    time series or bar chart plotting, 93
    treemap, 190
    using, 343
    writing to different formats, 237
    XML, 314
line graph connecting points in time series
    plot, 73–76
line( ) method, scaling weights to baseball
    salaries, 121
LinkHandler class, 308
Links utility, 267
Linux systems, fonts, 123
list( ) method
    File class, 277
    PFont class, 61

live data, interaction with, 3
loadBytes( ) method, 266, 284
loadData( ) method
    reading a book, 229
loadFont( ) method, 42
loadImage( ) method, 26, 32, 266
loadStrings( ) method, 26, 112, 252, 266
    Java methods versus, 271
    loading text data, 270
locations on a map, 32–34
    displaying centers of U.S. states, 33
    plotting your own values to, 51
    taking data from the user, 52
logfile formats, 247
London Underground, map of, 3
longs
    converting to formatted dates, 128
    ranked array of, 207
loop( ) method, 133

M

Mac OS X
    command-line utilities, 266
    Georgia (default font), 123
    Graphviz, 238
    text editors and hex viewers, 298
    typefaces, built-in, 60
mag( ) function, 227
magnitude and positive/negative values, 40
    using transparency, 41
magnitude of a vector, 227
main( ) method, 337
Major League Baseball web site
    (MLB.com), 97
map( ) function, 36
    mapping zip code place coordinates to the
        screen, 157
    plotting time series data, 58
MapLayout algorithms, 197
mapping, 31–53
    baseball salaries to line stroke, 121
    data on a map, 34
    HashMap class, 112
    locations, specifying, 32–34
    mouse rollover interaction, 42–45
    plotting your own values to locations, 51
    Processing function calls, 32
    scatterplot maps, 145–181
        acquiring zip code data, 145
        parsing and filtering zip code
            data, 147

noLoop( ) method, 133, 192
non-lining numerals, 124
norm( ) function, 37
normalized range, 37
noStroke( ) function, 33
numbered sequences, saving program output
    as, 23
numeric data display, typeface, 123–125

O

OBJ (3D file format), 322
objects, 113
    Java and Processing, 249
old style figures, 124
Olympic Committee web site, 284
online community (Processing), 20
open source, 19
    databases, 289
    Graphviz tool, 238
    library for creating treemap
        structures, 190
    NanoXML project, 28
OpenGL library, 343
OpenGL renderer, 25
OpenOffice spreadsheet
    entering web data, 110
    opening a DBF file, 146
    unnecessary additions to TSV files, 147
openStream( ) method, 284
OpenType fonts, 61
operating systems
    built-in fonts, 60
    files associated with, modification
        times, 207
order variable, 195
ordering array elements, 112
output files, 269

P

P2D (Processing 2D) renderer, 25
P3D (Processing 3D) renderer, 25
packaged solutions, shortcomings of, 16
pagers, 299
PApplet class, 248, 334
    embedding into Java
        applications, 338–342
      Swing application, 340–342
    frame variable, 338
    main( ) method, 337

param( ) method, 129
parameterized objects, 251
parseInfo( ) method, 156
parsePlace( ) method, 156
parsing data, 5, 296–330
    beverage consumption statistics (time
        series example), 55
    binary data, 325–328
    command-line utilities, 298
    compressed data, 317–319
    directory structure, 194–198
    efficient parsing of baseball standing for
        the season, 133–144
    file formats, 328
    grammars in Backus Naur Form
        (BNF), 316
    JavaScript source file (baseball
        statistics), 100–107
        regular expressions, using, 102–107
    JSON (JavaScript Object Notation), 315
    levels of effort, 296
    network traffic, 328–330
    OBJ and AutoCAD DXF (3D), 322
    parsing large files as they are
        acquired, 276
    PostScript and PDF, 323
    reading a book, 229
    regular expressions (regexps), 316
    resources for further information, 345
    salary data (baseball project), 110
    Shapefile (SHP), 324
    SVG (Scalable Vector Graphics), 320–322
    text, 299–303
        CSV file, 299–302
        TSV file, 299
        with fixed column widths, 302
    text editors and hex viewers, 298
    text markup languages, 303–315
        HTML, 303–311
        XML, 311–315
    Well-known text (WKT), 324
    win-loss standings (baseball project), 115
    zip code database file, 147
    zip codes project (example), 8
pathnames for files, 116
    absolute path to local file, 269
Pattern object, 104
patterns (regular expression), 103
PDF files, 24, 323
    vector images, 236
PDF renderer, 25

typedChars array, 159
  creating new String object from, 160
typedCount array, 159
typedPartials array, 160
typedPartials variable, 159
typedString value, 160
typefaces, built into systems, 60
typography, 126, 346

U

U.S. Census Bureau TIGER/LINE site, 180
U.S. Census Bureau zip code data, 146
U.S. Postal Service ZIP system, 145
U.S. Postal Service zip system
  (see also zip code project)
understanding data, process of, 5
Unicode character escapes, 126
Unix epoch, 128
Unix systems
    . (single dot) and .. (double dot) directory
      entries, 183
    command-line utilities, 266
Unix-based systems, symbolic link files, 184
update( ) method, 255
    Integrator class, 48, 133
    Node class, 227
    SalaryList class, 115
updateAnimation( ) method, 166
updateColors( ) method, 202
    brightness values based on file
      modification times, 208
updateTable( ) function, 46–48
updateTyped( ) method, 160
    chosen variable, 164
updating the screen, 338
URL class, openStream( ) method, 26
URLs, 100
    files located at, 268
    length, 285
    loading files from, 270
    referer, 253
USA Today web site, 109
user agent (browser type and platform), 245

V

"value added" versions of zip code data, 145
variables
    baseball statistics project, 118
    places, number of, 155
    varying over time, 94

vectors, 227
    saving an image in vector format, 236
    SVG (Scalable Vector Graphics), 320–322
vertex( ) method, 73
vertices
    curve vertices, 77
    use in continually drawn time
      series, 73–76
Visitor class, 248, 260
    draw( ) method, 255
visual design, insight from diverse fields, 5
visual representation (see refining visual
      representation; representing data)
visualization versus information
      visualization, 6

W

\w (word) character in regular
      expressions, 103
W3C Extended logfile format, 247
web page for this book, xii
web server logfiles (Apache), 245–247
web services, data availability through, 96
web site (Processing), 20
Well-known text (WKT), 324
Wget utility, 267
whitespace characters, matching in regular
      expressions, 103
window size, 21
Windows systems
    Cygwin, 266
    file paths, 186
    Georgia (default font), 123
    text editors and hex viewers, 298
    typefaces, built-in, 60
Wireshark, 328–330
WKT (Well-known text), 324
WordItem class, 190
WordMap class, 191
writeData( ) method, 238
writing a program to convert data versus
      processing by hand, 111
Wurman, Richard Saul, 2, 348

X

Xerces project, 315
XML, 96, 311–315
    cleaning up with Tidy, 311
    other parsing methods, 314
    using Processing XML library to read
      geocoding data, 312–314

XML Import library, 28
XML Path Language (XPath), 314
XMLElement class, 28, 312–314

Z

ZIP (Zoning Improvement Plan), 145
zip code project, 6–15
    (see also mapping)
ZIP files, 317–319
zips.tsv file, 145
Zoning Improvement Plan (ZIP), 145
zooming
    changing drawing of points when
        zooming, 177
    treemap data display, 208–217
      updating FileItem, 210–213
      updating FolderItem, 213–217
    zooming in on zip code
        locations, 167–177

About the Author

Ben Fry received his doctorate from the Aesthetics + Computation Group at the MIT Media Laboratory. He was the 2006–2007 Nierenberg Chair of Design for the Carnegie Mellon School of Design. He worked with Casey Reas to develop Processing, which won a Golden Nica from the Prix Ars Electronica in 2005. Ben's work has received a New Media Fellowship from the Rockefeller Foundation and has been shown at the Museum of Modern Art, Ars Electronica, the 2002 Whitney Biennial, and the 2003 Cooper Hewitt Design Triennial.

Colophon

The animal on the cover of *Visualizing Data* is a Northern hawk owl (*Surnia ulula*). They are called Northern hawk owls because they are largely found in the boreal forests of North America and Eurasia, and because of their behavioral similarities to the hawk; they fly, hover, and soar low over open areas searching for prey. Also, more like hawks than owls, they predominantly use their sight, rather than their hearing, when hunting.

They are widely dispersed geographically, found from Eurasia to Norway, Sweden, and Finland; east through Siberia to Kamchatka; and in North China and Central Asia as far south as Tien Shan. In North America, they can be found from Alaska east to Labrador, Canada. They breed wherever food is plentiful; when food is scarce, they (mostly the young owls) may fly south of their normal distribution.

Medium-size owls, they are usually between 36–41cm long with a wingspan between 22–25cm wide. Typically, males weigh between 273–326g and females weigh more, between 306–392g. The sexes are very similar in appearance and can be most easily distinguished by their calls. The typical male call is a fast, melodious, purring trill; although the female call is similar, it has a higher pitch and is less clear.

Their heads are round and their faces whitish, bordered on each side with a thick black stripe. The upper half of their body is generally dark gray and black, with a densely spotted forehead and crown. Their tails are long with white stripes. Their bills are yellow and they have pale yellow eyes. (Young owls have golden yellow eyes that turn paler as they age.)

Northern hawk owls—unlike most other owls—are typically diurnal, meaning they hunt during the day. They feed on small mammals, such as lemmings, voles, and rabbits. Other prey includes birds, frogs, and even fish. Often, they sit on a perch—typically in a conspicuous spot—scoping out potential targets. Once prey is spotted, they quickly take flight and swoop down to attack. When food is plentiful, they catch an excess and hide it for later.

Their nesting period begins in April and lasts through the first half of May. Males scope out potential nesting sites, and females select the spot. (They are monogamous throughout the mating season.) Potential sites include empty woodpecker holes; abandoned squirrel, crow, and hawk nests; and rotting trees. They lay between 3–13 eggs at 1 to 2 day intervals, and incubate the eggs for approximately

25 to 30 days. The males feed the females during the incubation period. Chicks leave the nest after about 25 days and can fly well by the time they are 6 weeks old.

More research is necessary to better understand Northern hawk owls—one of the least researched bird species in North America—and their habitat needs and migration patterns. Habitat destruction is a major threat to them. The removal of dead trees and stumps deprives these owls of the nesting areas they need to procreate. Other concerns include poaching (even though they are protected under the Migratory Bird Treaty Act, which makes it illegal to harm or kill certain migratory bird species) and collisions with power lines and vehicles.

The cover image is from *Johnson's Natural History*. The cover font is Adobe ITC Garamond. The text font is Linotype Birka; the heading font is Adobe Myriad Condensed; and the code font is LucasFont's TheSans Mono Condensed.